BEGIN

BEGIN

A BIOGRAPHY

WITHDRAWN

Eric Silver

Weidenfeld and Nicolson
London

For my wife Bridget, with love and gratitude
for sustaining me through the summer of transitions
in which this book was written

Copyright © Eric Silver 1984

First published in Great Britain by
George Weidenfeld & Nicolson Limited
91 Clapham High Street, London SW4 7TA

ISBN 0 297 78399 8

Printed by Butler & Tanner Ltd, Frome and London

Contents

Illustrations

Begin and Yehuda Avner show Kurt Waldheim, Secretary-General of the
United Nations, a 'national security map'

BETWEEN PAGES 182 AND 183
With President Ceausescu of Romania, Bucharest, August 1977
An emotional moment in the Bucharest synagogue
Begin and President Ephraim Katzir greet President Sadat of Egypt on
his arrival in Israel, November 1977
Eyeball to eyeball: Sadat and Begin at the banquet at the King David
Hotel, 20 November 1977 (*photo: Ya'acov Sa'ar*)
Playing chess with Zbigniew Brzezinski, Camp David, September 1978
The Israeli delegation at Camp David, September 1978
Begin, Sadat and President Carter celebrate the agreement reached at
Camp David, 17 September 1978
Artur Rubinstein congratulates Begin on winning the Nobel Prize,
October 1978
Helping his granddaughter blow out the candles on her birthday cake,
1978
At the pyramids, Giza, April 1979
Entering 10 Downing Street with Margaret Thatcher, May 1979
Mixing with the Egyptian crowd during a visit to Alexandria, July 1979
With Aliza and their two daughters, Leah and Hassia, October 1979
Speaking at the press conference given after the bombing of the Iraqi
nuclear reactor, 1981 (© *Sally Soames, Sunday Times*)
With Defence Minister Ariel Sharon at Beaufort Castle, June 1982
(*Israel Defence Forces*)
'I can't go on' – Begin's meeting with coalition representatives after
announcing his resignation, 30 August 1983 (*photo: Nathan Harnik*)

*Unless otherwise indicated, all the photographs are reproduced by courtesy of
the Israel Government Press Office*

Acknowledgements

I am grateful to Menachem Begin's family, comrades-in-arms, colleagues, staff and adversaries for sharing their reminiscences and their understanding of this complex man. His sister, Rachel Halperin, was particularly helpful on the early years.

Susan Hattis-Rolef and Yisrael Medad gave inestimable assistance in researching the Hebrew sources, and were kind enough to read the manuscript and save me from aberrations. Norman Rose, of the Hebrew University, and David Landau, of the *Jerusalem Post*, also made valuable suggestions for improving the text.

Sharon Barnett and Ralph Mandel translated articles from the Hebrew press and other publications. Esther Valencia and Barbara Piperno transcribed tapes and typed the manuscript respectively.

I was received with patience and courtesy by the directors and staff of the Israel State Archive, the Jabotinsky Institute, the *Jerusalem Post* archive, the Kressel Collection of Hebrew press cuttings at the Oxford Centre for Postgraduate Hebrew Studies, and the Israel Government Press Office.

Finally my thanks are due to the editor of the *Guardian* for giving me leave to write this book, and to the Dean and fellows of St Catherine's College, Oxford, for their hospitality at an early stage of the project.

ERIC SILVER

1
Born unto Zion

Menachem Begin is the most consistent of men – in his beliefs, in his objectives and in his personal mythology. Although he has lived most of his adult life in Israel, the roots of his stubborn, assertive Jewish nationalism reach back to Brest-Litovsk, where he was born on 16 August 1913, the third and last child of Ze'ev Dov and Hassia Begin. The future Prime Minister paid frequent tribute to Vladimir Ze'ev Jabotinsky as his 'teacher and master', but most of his folk memories, the allusions of pride and martyrdom he was still invoking half a century later, can be traced to Ze'ev Dov Begin's teaching and example. Jabotinsky added an ideological and organizational frame, the excitement of a cosmopolitan intellect, a rhetorical model, a hero to be worshipped.

Brest-Litovsk, known also as Brisk, was one of those Eastern European border towns that was never quite sure to which country it belonged. In the Middle Ages it was firmly planted in the Grand Duchy of Lithuania. In the twentieth century it has been ruled by Russia, Poland and Germany. It is now capital of the Brest *oblast* (region) of the Belorussian Soviet Socialist Republic. The first Jews settled there in the fourteenth century, playing a leading part in its growth as a centre of commerce and communications. Although they alternated between privilege and persecution, the Jews flourished as importers and exporters, land-owners and customs contractors, scholars and rabbis.

Their faith was deep but worldly. Brest was a stronghold of the *Mitnagdim*, who rejected *Hassidic* mysticism. Characteristically, in 1495 when Lithuania expelled all Jews who refused to convert, only one Brest merchant embraced Christianity. The rest were allowed back eight years later, when the Grand Duke thought better of it. At the time of Menachem Begin's birth, the Jews comprised seventy per cent of the town's population. When the Second World War broke out in 1939, they numbered almost 30,000. After Brest was liberated from the Nazis in 1944, fewer than ten Jews were found there. 'The Jewish population was estimated at 2,000 in 1970,' the *Encyclopaedia Judaica* records. 'It has no synagogue, the last one having been converted into a movie house in 1959.'[1]

The Brest of Menachem Begin's youth, even allowing for the rosy spectacles of middle age, was a thriving Jewish metropolis. He recalled:

The town was full of synagogues and seminars. There were Jewish schools where the language of instruction was Hebrew. There were splendid Zionist youth movements with thousands of members. Every Lag Ba'omer festival we would go out on the streets, parades of thousands with blue and white flags, a demonstration of Jewish pride. The cultural life of the Jews was rich, with newspapers and theatres, for we conducted a life of our own.[2]

Menachem Begin was in the most literal sense a Zionist from birth. The midwife who delivered him was the grandmother of the future Israeli general and Defence Minister, Ariel Sharon. The local Zionists sent a cake in the form of a garland of roses to his circumcision feast eight days later. Ze'ev Dov Begin and Sharon's grandfather, Mordechai Sheinerman, were among the Zionist pioneers in Brest at a time when the movement was still fighting for recognition. After the death of Theodor Herzl, the founder of political Zionism, in 1904, Ze'ev Dov and Sheinerman broke down the door of the main synagogue with an axe, when the rabbi, Haimke Soloveichik, refused to let them hold a memorial service and took home the key. Herzl was too secular for the rabbi's taste, but the Zionists got their service, even if only three of them attended it.

Ze'ev Dov was an autodidact, whose formal education was limited to a traditional *heder*, which he entered at three and left fourteen years later with a rabbinical diploma. He remained an observant, but not a fanatical, Jew. His daughter, Rachel Halperin, remembers that he put on *tefillin* (ritual leather straps that pious Jews bind every morning on their arms and foreheads), but usually at home rather than in synagogue. He did not recite all of the morning, afternoon and evening prayers. Nor did he normally wear a hat indoors, except when blessing food. His beard was trimmed. Contrary to strict orthodox practice, he told his children to brush their teeth on the fast of Yom Kippur, but not to swallow the water. 'Today', he would explain, 'you are going to talk to God, so your mouth must be clean.' When Rachel, five years older than Menachem, had to sign some papers at Warsaw University on a Saturday, her father said she could do so without breaking the sabbath. 'Knowledge is like a matter of life and death,' he argued, 'so sign.'[3]

His first exposure to European culture came soon after he left the *heder* to work in his father's timber business. A German book-keeper spotted his potential and encouraged him to run away and study in Berlin, but he was soon hauled back by his parents, who arranged an unwanted marriage for him. Despite the birth of a daughter, Ze'ev Dov divorced his first wife after little more than a year. It was nearly twenty-five years before he married again. His bride, Hassia Korsovski, was the daughter of a Polish rabbinical dynasty. He was forty-three, she was twenty. She spoke only Yiddish, but that did not inhibit her thirst for ideas. 'She read all the world's great literature in Yiddish,' her daughter Rachel says. 'She had an intense curiosity, great intelligence and a strong character. She wanted to know, to know, to know.'[4]

The timber trade often took Ze'ev Dov abroad, above all to Berlin. 'He was a great Germanophile,' Mrs Halperin testifies. 'I remember when I was about six, at the beginning of the First World War, he would take me for walks and tell me: "You see, the Germans will come, that is a different culture, it is not Russia." '[5] He spoke Yiddish, Hebrew and Russian, as well as German. When his children learned Latin at high school, he picked it up from them. Like his younger son, Ze'ev Dov was not above tossing Latin tags at the uninitiated. '*Dura lex, sed lex*,' he once told some simple Jews who had asked him to mediate in a dispute – 'the law is hard, but it is the law.' The Jews were frightened out of their wits.

In his Judaism, Ze'ev Dov was an activist. For him, Jewish tradition and Jewish nationalism were as one. He taught his children to be proud of their identity. At the university when they had to specify their mother tongue, they always wrote: 'Hebrew'. The older Begin would not speak Polish, which he disdained as a language of anti-Semitism (to this day Menachem too will not use it, even though he studied at a Polish high school and Warsaw University).

Time and again, Ze'ev Dov drummed home the moral of the Beilis 'blood libel' trial, which took place in Kiev in the autumn of 1913, the year Menachem was born. Mendel Beilis, a thirty-seven-year-old Russian Jew, was accused of the ritual murder of a twelve-year-old Christian boy, Andrei Yushinsky. Beilis was acquitted after two years in prison and one month in court, but the libel continued to fuel anti-Semitism throughout Europe.

'Our father used to quote to us what Beilis's lawyer had said,' Mrs Halperin remembers. ' "If you, Beilis, have to go to jail for twenty-five years and do hard labour in Siberia, then go. The Jews of Spain went to the stake singing *Shema Yisrael*." So the jury said: "We have seen the Jewish God." Our father used to tell us this with great emphasis.'[6]

Another trial often cited by Ze'ev Dov was that of Captain Alfred Dreyfus, a French Jew who was falsely convicted of treason in 1894. Begin's father carried a cane topped by a silver knob fashioned like the head of Dreyfus's champion Emile Zola and inscribed with a text from Zola's *J'accuse*. One day, Ze'ev Dov was walking with a rabbi when a Polish sergeant tried to cut off the rabbi's beard, a popular sport among anti-Semites. Menachem Begin recounted:

> My father did not hesitate, and hit him with his cane on his hand. In those days,
> hitting a Polish sergeant had to be a signal for a pogrom. Both the rabbi and my
> father were arrested. They were taken to the river Bug, and their captors
> threatened to throw them in. They were beaten until they bled. My father came
> home in bad shape, but he was happy. He said he had defended the honour of
> the Jewish people and the honour of the rabbi. So I remember these two things
> from my childhood: Jews being persecuted and the courage of the Jews.[7]

Menachem Begin paid his father the ultimate filial tribute: 'I have never known a man braver than him. Perhaps it has been decreed by fate, but throughout my life I have worked with courageous people. Yet I shall never forget how my father fought to defend Jewish honour.'[8]

The Begins were often short of money. At one time Ze'ev Dov worked in a bank, but lost his job after exposing a financial scandal to a Yiddish newspaper. The family's hardest days were during and immediately after the First World War. Brest was a garrison town, and its Russian rulers feared a German invasion. Ze'ev Dov, who flaunted his pro–German sentiments, was banished, first to St Petersburg, then to Warsaw, leaving his wife and children without a breadwinner. As the Germans approached, the Russians evacuated the entire population and burned Brest to the ground. Hassia Begin took her daughter and two sons to stay with an uncle in the village of Drokitchin, near Pinsk in White Russia.

The house was small, barely a cottage. The Begins shared a room, which often had to provide bedspace for aunts and uncles arriving from town. Menachem was still a toddler, but his sister Rachel remembers it vividly. After a few months, as the German army came nearer and nearer, the village suffered the same scorched-earth fate as Brest. The local peasants were forced to leave, the Jews were threatened with a pogrom at the hands of the Russian cavalrymen.

> We heard the weeping of the villagers. The Russians expelled all the farmers so
> that they wouldn't work for the Germans, so that they wouldn't supply them
> with food. To this day I can hear the weeping of the farmers. Then suddenly, a
> Cossack appeared at our window, which was closed and curtained. The window
> was only as high as the legs of his horse, so we couldn't see him, but he banged
> on the door and shouted: 'Who lives here? *Zhidy* or Russians?' *Zhidy* is the ugly
> name for Jews in Russian. Our uncle had a Russian accent, and he went over to
> the window and answered: '*Russkie.*' I don't know where he found the inspira-
> tion, but otherwise the Cossack would have finished us off.
>
> One night, we were ordered to go into the fields because the Cossacks were
> setting fire to our village. With my own eyes I saw a Cossack pour oil and set it

alight. All of us went to a big field, the people were already beginning to dig trenches. Almost all the Jews were there. It was totally quiet, we were not allowed to say a word. The Germans were already close, we could hear their guns. In the morning we went back to uncle's house, which had been burned. We went into a different house. Early in the morning, the Germans came in. How the Jews rejoiced to see the Germans. We were all on the floor, a lot of people, and before the Germans arrived we had to keep giving the Cossacks money, otherwise they would have killed us. But the Germans treated the Jews marvellously.[9]

Soon afterwards, Ze'ev Dov found his way to his brother's village in the wake of the German advance, and the Begins were reunited. When times again became hard, the family moved to another village, then to the town of Kobrin. Ze'ev Dov made what living he could writing requests in German to the Kaiser's administration. Mrs Halperin recalls great hardship.

We were almost hungry for bread. We were all in one room, five people. Every month the Germans - we were very friendly with the Germans - would take mother and the little one [Menachem] by horse and carriage to the village, where she and uncle would cut trees to bring us wood for heating. Father stayed with the children. I was a big girl, I looked after them. After a few days, mother would return and there was great rejoicing. Everything was ready. There was wood, and we cooked potatoes. It was thanks to mother that we managed to survive the war. She was a romantic type, but at the same time very strong, a very strong character. . . .[10]

Brest stayed briefly under German rule after the war, but the population was not allowed back until 1919. Ze'ev Dov was one of the first Jews to return, leaving his family in Kobrin. Again, he made money writing requests in German. Rachel and the other children waited for his weekly Sabbath visits.

Father had a top hat, and once the little one went outside and saw one of our relatives sitting on the steps looking very sorry for herself. 'Auntie', he asked, 'why are you so sad? Don't you have any money? We didn't have any either, but now my father has a top hat full.' That was where mother kept the money. Before that, conditions were very difficult. Mother would take the two boys every Thursday afternoon and put them in bed while she washed their suits. On Friday she would iron them, and on Friday afternoon they went out saying they had new suits. Our mother was very strong, but once, she told me, she cried. A rich neighbour bought a cake in the bakery shop. We had no money for cakes. So our little brother went up to him and said: 'Let me just sniff it.' When mother heard that, she cried.[11]

Prospects improved when the Begins joined Ze'ev Dov in Brest. The father was appointed general secretary of the Jewish community, which guaranteed him a regular though by no means princely salary. As they grew older, all three children supplemented the family income by giving private lessons. It was a time of great reconstruction, of buildings and of institutions. At one point Ze'ev Dov was chairman of seven different organizations. When the Poles replaced the Germans as rulers of the town, they accused all the Jews of being dangerous Communists. Some were. Ze'ev Dov disguised seventeen party members as *yeshiva* students and packed them off to the relative safety of Vilna. For years afterwards, whenever the Communists of Brest saw him walking on the Sabbath, they put out their cigarettes as a mark of esteem.

At the Polish high school, the young Menachem excelled in the humanities. There too he insisted on his Jewishness. He refused to write on Saturdays. The Latin teacher retaliated by giving him an F grade. 'I said to my teacher,' he told a young Israeli interviewer four decades later, 'this is my belief, and I won't write on the sabbath under any circumstances. After a while he calmed down and gave me my normal good mark.'[12]

In later years, Menachem Begin remained an Orthodox, but not a strictly observant, Jew. During his travels as Prime Minister, he insisted on kosher food, and walked to Anwar Sadat's funeral, which took place on a Saturday. Yet he did not attend synagogue every day, or even every sabbath. He made no secret of the fact that he listened to the radio (the Voice of Israel and the BBC World Service) on the sabbath, which is how he learned about the Beirut massacre in September 1982. There was an element of show about his observance. He was conscious of representing his movement and Israel. As a prisoner of the Soviet secret police, he fasted on the Day of Atonement. As Leader of the Opposition in 1953, he arrived in Johannesburg late on a Friday afternoon after his airliner had been delayed by engine trouble. To the dismay of five thousand Zionist supporters who had come to greet him, he spurned the waiting limousine and stayed overnight at the airport hotel.

At Warsaw University, Menachem suffered the slings of anti-Semitism and relative poverty. After he became Prime Minister, the Polish Government sent him an album of personal documents from the university records. Since there were no diplomatic relations between Communist Poland and Zionist Israel, the gift arrived unannounced by way of the Polish embassy in London and the Board of Deputies of British Jews. Begin thanked the Poles graciously, but in English. Among the letters and photographs in twenty-three cellophane envelopes was an exchange in which the law student explained why he could not pay his fees on time. His family could not subsidize him and he had to work his way through college. The authorities agreed to let him pay in instalments.

Ze'ev Dov Begin was almost reckless in his refusal to kowtow to the ruling powers, whoever they might be. As an outspoken pro-German, he was lucky to escape prison or death at the hands of the Russians in 1914. His daughter thinks it was only because he played chess – another passion he bequeathed his son – with Russian officers that they spared him. As a Jewish functionary in 1921, he appealed to the Polish dictator, Jozef Pilsudsky, for emergency rations to feed the community. Pilsudsky replied that he would send the Jews food if Ze'ev Dov would give him the names and addresses of Jewish speculators. Begin flung the request back in his face, telling the Marshal that Jews were not informers. Let his secret police do the dirty work for him. When the Nazis reached Brest in 1939, he again insisted on his right to intercede for the Jews. Ze'ev Dov, by then well into his seventies, was soon to learn that this was a different breed of German from that he had admired in his youth.

Of the Begin family, only Menachem and his wife Aliza, his sister Rachel and her lawyer husband Yehoshua survived the war. Their parents and brother, Herzl, a gifted mathematician, perished. So did Rachel's baby son, left in the care of her mother. Herzl, three years older than Menachem, is known to have been the victim of a cruel trick played by the Germans in September 1939. He was one of a group of young Jews lined up in the market square with their faces to the wall. He described the episode to David Jutan, a colleague of Menachem's in the leadership of Betar, the Jabotinsky youth movement: soldiers surrounded them with machine-guns, but when the order was given to fire, they shot in the air. Asked what he had thought while he was waiting for death, Herzl answered that he had set himself a problem in algebra. He had not yet solved it.[13]

There are conflicting versions of Ze'ev Dov's end. Menachem favours the more operatic of them:

> We were told that he was drowned in the river Bug together with five hundred other Jews. They were taken to the river and machine-gun fire was opened on them from both sides. People who survived said that the river was actually red with their blood. As secretary of the Jewish community, my father went first. We were told that at his initiative the Jews started to sing *Hatikva* [the Zionist anthem], and also *Ani Ma'amin* ('I Believe'). And so he died.[14]

Rachel Halperin dismisses this account as so many '*maisses*' (folk tales):

> What I know, what my friends in Brisk told me, is that the Germans passed a

law forbidding Jews from burying their dead. My father went to bury a Jew in the cemetery. A German approached him and asked what he was doing. He told him in German, and the soldier killed him on the spot. About the rest of my family I know nothing. They died with all the other Jews. But I have all the details about my father. I know the name of the Jew who died and that there was a burial.[15]

Whichever is the truth, both versions are heroic enough and in character. Ze'ev Dov was not a man to go quietly to the gas chamber. For Menachem Begin, the lesson of the Holocaust was captured in Jabotinsky's warning to the Jews of Europe: 'If you do not put an end to the diaspora, the diaspora will put an end to you.' The Holocaust, Begin said as Prime Minister, was the mainspring of all he and his generation had done.

The defencelessness of the Jews was the real scourge of our life, for centuries, but mainly in our generation. That must never happen again. Therefore, we decided to take up arms and fight for liberation. In order to have a State, an army, a means of national defence. That was the prime mover. And to make sure that the Jewish State is secure, that the borders are unbreakable, that the land is unconquerable. That is the second prime mover of all our actions, when we were in opposition and now in the government.[16]

No post-war Zionist would dispute that thesis. Where some did differ was over Begin's application of it, the identification of all Israel's enemies with the Nazis, the invocation of the Holocaust to justify denying the national aspirations of the Palestinian Arabs, the hectoring of foreign statesmen. There were times when Begin risked devaluing the horror of the Jewish tragedy, and in the process gave Israel's critics a pretext for breaking the taboo and throwing the imagery of the Final Solution back in his face.

The slaughter of six million European Jews stamped Begin with an abiding hatred of all things German. As Leader of the Opposition in the 1950s and 1960s, he bitterly and sometimes violently resisted any contact between Israel and the Federal Republic, even under the anti-Nazi Konrad Adenauer. As Prime Minister, he maintained a minimum of correct relations with German politicians and diplomats, conducted a misplaced vendetta against Chancellor Helmut Schmidt, and declined to be interviewed by German journalists or speak their language. Such hostility is common to many Polish Jewish survivors, but one can only wonder whether Begin's emotion would have been quite so intense if Ze'ev Dov had not set such great store by Germany. Was the son perpetuating the pain of the father's disappointment?

His sister, who is old enough to remember German soldiers bringing relief to the Jews who had taken refuge in the countryside during the 1914–18 war, is more ambivalent. 'To this day', she confesses, 'I cannot hate the Germans the way a Jew should hate them. I remember the other Germans. They gave each child sweets and biscuits. They were different Germans, it was a different period.'[17]

2
At the Feet of the Master

Jabotinsky's Betar, with its aura of muscular Zionism, should have been the natural youth movement for the teenage Menachem Begin in Brest-Litovsk. After the Mizrahi Jewish primary school, he went on to a Polish high school and Warsaw University, where he took a degree in law, though he never practised in that profession. At both school and university, the diminutive Begin led the fight against the native, and often virulent, anti-Semitism of his classmates. On one occasion they tried to rub pork fat on his lips.

> When we were attacked, we would defend ourselves. We never consented to bow down and flee. We would return home bloody and beaten, but always with the awareness that we had not been humiliated. We soon learned that these brutal bullies would behave politely enough when they received blows in return.[1]

Yet surprisingly, the three Begin children – Menachem, his brother Herzl and sister Rachel – joined Hashomer Hatzair, which became the youth movement of the left-wing Mapam Party. Their father, Ze'ev Dov Begin, was one of its adult sponsors. But as Hashomer swung from scouting towards Marxism, the Begins took their leave. 'You must first of all fight for your own freedom,' Ze'ev Dov told his children, 'and when you are free, you will fight for the freedom of the world.'[2]

Menachem was a member of Hashomer for three years, from the age of ten to thirteen. When he was fifteen, he joined Betar. 'I was fascinated by the total Zionism of Betar,' he recalled, 'the ideal of *Eretz Yisrael* as a Jewish State in our time. All those elements which, from reading and listening to others, I accepted as true found expression in Betar, and I had no doubt whatsoever that this was the movement in which I would want to serve the Jewish people all my life.'[3]

Two years later, in 1930, Begin heard Jabotinsky speak for the first time. He was captivated. 'The greatest influence in my life I attribute to Jabotinsky. I was won over by his ideas, and I learned the doctrine of Zionism from him. My entire life has been influenced by him, both in the underground and in politics: the willingness to fight for the liberation of the homeland, and the logical analysis of facts in political matters.'[4]

Begin's conversion went further than that. Jabotinsky was revered almost like a god. He was a world figure, yet within touching distance of a budding Zionist orator from the provinces. Begin claimed:

> Ze'ev Jabotinsky had the kind of comprehensive mind that appears once in many generations, an Aristotle, a Leonardo da Vinci, our own Rambam [Maimonides]. In other words, they excel in many fields, not just in one field. Jabotinsky was a speaker, a writer, a philosopher, a statesman, a soldier, a linguist. He excelled in all these fields. But to those of us who were his pupils, he was not only their teacher, but also the bearer of their hope.[5]

Jabotinsky's charisma is acknowledged by his bitterest political foes, of whom he had many. So is his originality of mind and prolific pen. Whether he was a genius on the scale of Leonardo is another question. As a politician he had a talent for alienating even those in other Zionist parties open to his ideas, so that few of his aims were achieved in his lifetime. He lacked the patience to cultivate allies, the calculation to compromise. Gradualism was anathema. Jabotinsky wanted a Jewish State, and he wanted it now. Even tactically, he would not lobby for less.

His Revisionist movement, the precursor of Begin's Herut, likes to project Jabotinsky as a good, old-fashioned nineteenth-century European liberal, a cut above the roughnecks of the Irgun Zvai Leumi, an intellectual and a gentleman. This view won unexpected endorsement among British Arabists, who first locked him up then banished him from the Promised Land. Harold Beeley, who was Ernest Bevin's Middle East expert in the darkest days of the Zionist struggle, met Jabotinsky in London in 1940, a few months before the Revisionist leader's death.

> I called on him in the shabby offices of the New Zionist Organization, and remember finding his British disciples exceptionally unattractive. Jabotinsky himself, on the contrary, impressed me as a force to be reckoned with, and I invited him to come to Oxford and talk to members of the Chatham House organization there. They were certainly impressed by his eloquence, whatever they may have thought of his views. He seemed to me to belong in spirit to the revolutionary generation of 1848 - a sort of belated Mazzini.[6]

Jabotinsky, a devoted admirer of Italy and its national revival, would have relished the comparison. But the liberal label does not quite fit. There was a darker side to his philosophy: blood, fire and steel, the supremacy of the leader, discipline and ceremony, the manipulation of the masses, racial exclusivity as the heart of the nation.[7]

Jabotinsky wrote in an early essay *Man is a Wolf to Man:*

Sometimes we base too many rosy hopes on the fallacy that a certain people has itself suffered much and will therefore feel the agony of another people and understand it, and its conscience will not allow it to inflict on the weaker people what had earlier been inflicted on it.... But in reality it appears that these are pretty phrases. ... Only the Bible says 'thou shalt not oppress a stranger, for ye know the heart of a stranger, seeing ye were strangers in the land of Egypt'. Contemporary morality has no place for such childish humanism.[8]

Nor, one might say, has contemporary liberalism for such grown-up reality, even if Jabotinsky was extrapolating from the world as he saw it. And what are we to make of his assertions that 'there is no value in the world higher than the nation and the fatherland', or that 'it is the highest achievement of a multitude of free human beings to be able to act together with the absolute precision of a machine', or that 'without ceremony there is no liberty'?[9] Jabotinsky's pessimistic view of the human race may or may not have been justified (it enabled him to foresee the Holocaust), but it is hardly the stuff of liberalism. Nor is his attitude to the Palestinian Arabs, even though he did not seek to drive them out.

He wrote in 1923:

It is impossible to dream of a voluntary agreement between us and the Arabs of *Eretz Yisrael*.... Not now and not in the foreseeable future. ... Every nation, civilized or primitive, sees its land as its national home, where it wants to stay as the sole landlord forever. Such a nation will never willingly consent not only to new landlords, but even to partnership. ... Every nation of natives fights the settlers as long as there is a glimmer of hope of getting rid of the danger of foreign settlement. Thus they behave, and thus will the *Eretz Yisrael* Arabs behave, as long as there is a glimmer of hope in their hearts that they can prevent the changing of Palestine into *Eretz Yisrael*.[10]

Jabotinsky was more frank than most of his Zionist contemporaries. He made explicit what was implicit in their deeds and policies. But his answer to Arab resistance was an 'iron wall of Jewish bayonets' to force the Palestinians to recognize the inevitable. 'The only way to achieve an agreement in the future is the absolute abandonment of all attempts at an agreement in the present.' In an interview given when he was already Prime Minister, Menachem Begin put his own gloss on this concept: 'The iron wall meant that one could not realize Zionism unless force separates us from the Arabs. The Arabs would try to prevent it, even through bloodshed. There had to be a defensive force which would prevent this bloodshed. Jabotinsky professed a policy of justice, but we discovered that justice had to be defended.'[11] It was, however, the justice of minority status in a maximalist Jewish State, with no prospect of Arab sovereignty on either bank of the Jordan.

More than four decades after Jabotinsky's death at a Betar summer camp near New York, Begin remained his steadfast disciple, cherishing his doctrines, perpetuating his rhetorical style, the pathos and the cadences. He reproduced what Jabotinsky's in-house biographer called the 'cult of etiquette', the formal bow and the kiss on the lady's hand, the suit and tie and polished shoes in a land of open-necked pioneering and biblical sandals. He summoned up the ghost of Jabotinsky's hero Garibaldi, even lecturing a group of visiting Italian MPs on their own national liberator. When he abandoned opposition for the first time and joined the national unity government on the threshold of the 1967 war, Begin paid homage at Jabotinsky's tomb on Mount Herzl in Jerusalem. Like Jabotinsky, he was ready to accept the Palestinian Arabs, provided they knew their place, though he acknowledged that the east bank of the Jordan was not now a practical objective for the Zionist State (Betar only dropped the map showing Jabotinsky's 'both banks' from its emblem in 1980). Begin had little of Jabotinsky's sometimes gadfly originality and flare, but he was more skilled in the workaday arts of politics. The disciple steered Revisionist Zionism into the mainstream of modern Israel, turning it towards a society the master would have recognized as his own.

Jabotinsky was never an easy partner. Other Zionist luminaries often found him arrogant. On the platform and in print, he showed them no mercy. He could be opinionated and exasperating, but by 1920 his position in the pantheon of the movement was not disputed. His role as founder and one of the commanders of the Jewish Legion in the First World War established him as a man of action as well as ideas, a pioneer of Jewish self-defence as well as an exceptional evangelist. What led Jabotinsky into the Zionist wilderness was his single-minded demand for a Jewish State, the 'monism' which the young Begin found so attractive. Others were ready to compromise, if not in their long-term aims, at least in their diplomacy and in their short-term means. For Jabotinsky this was not only treacherous but misguided. The Jews' strength, as he saw it, was their moral case. They must never dilute it, especially since no one would be fooled anyway.

The first step was taken in January 1923, when Jabotinsky resigned from the Zionist executive in protest at what he regarded as Chaim Weizmann's acquiescence in the erosion of the British commitment embodied in the Balfour Declaration of 1917. 'Weizmann believes that mine is the way of a stubborn fantast,' he confided after a conversation with the Zionist leader, 'while I feel that his line is the line of renunciation, of subconscious Marranism.'[12]

The outcome was the creation of the Revisionist movement, openly dedicated to the establishment of a Jewish State, with a Jewish majority on the east and west banks of the Jordan, and a Jewish army to defend it. But the Revisionists remained an integral part of the Zionist movement until the seventeenth Zionist congress convened in Basle in July 1931. Weizmann went too far – not only for Jabotinsky – in contending that a state had never been an aim in itself, but only a means to an end. It cost Weizmann the leadership, but Jabotinsky was denied the opportunity to extract a clear-cut policy statement from the congress. When the Revisionist resolution was not even put to a vote, Jabotinsky climbed on a chair, shouted, 'This is no longer a Zionist congress,' and tore up his delegate's card.

The Revisionists were out, but they were not yet outcasts. They had to wait another three years for that trauma, which Menachem Begin was still trying to exorcize half a century later. On 16 June 1933, Haim Arlosoroff, head of the political department of the Jewish Agency, a rising star of the Labour Zionist movement, dined at a Tel Aviv hotel with his wife Sima. Afterwards, they strolled along the sea-front. Mrs Arlosoroff noticed two men following them. One, she testified later, was fair, tall, heavily built and waddled like a duck. The other was short, thin and oriental-looking. The two men, she said, accosted them. The big one shone a torch in Arlosoroff's face and asked him the time. Arlosoroff told them to stop bothering him. The smaller man drew a revolver and shot him in the stomach. Arlosoroff died in hospital five hours later. Sima claimed that the assailant had spoken Hebrew with no trace of an accent.

The British police circulated descriptions of the two men throughout mandatory Palestine. The trail led to Avraham Stavsky, a member of Brit Habirionim, an extremist group operating on the gory fringe of the Jabotinsky movement there. Brit Habirionim had condemned Arlosoroff as a collaborator for trying to open a channel through which German Jews, threatened by the rise of Nazism, could liquidate their property and emigrate to Palestine without sacrificing everything. The idea was that they would buy goods in Germany, export them, and pick up the money at the other end. Arlosoroff had come home to Tel Aviv on 14 June after shuttling in this cause between Berlin and London. At the same time, Jabotinsky and the Revisionists were campaigning for a worldwide Jewish boycott of German goods. On the day of the murder, Brit Habirionim's magazine had published an article accusing Arlosoroff of forming an alliance with Hitler and Stalin. He had, it said, sold the honour of his people.

Stavsky was arrested three days after the killing. Sima Arlosoroff identified him from a photograph as the man with the waddle who shone the light in Arlosoroff's face. Another Revisionist ultra, Zvi Rosenblatt, was charged with pulling the trigger. Abba Ahimeir, the theoretician of Brit

Habirionim, was charged with complicity. Mrs Arlosoroff's identification of Rosenblatt was more tentative than that of Stavsky. After committal proceedings before a magistrate, the case was tried by an assize court of four judges, two British, one Jewish and one Arab. Ahimeir was cleared in mid-trial. Rosenblatt was acquitted on the grounds that Sima's evidence was not corroborated by any other witness. Stavsky was found guilty and sentenced to hang. He appealed to a higher court, which quashed the conviction and set him free. Under Turkish law, which still applied in Palestine until 1937, the uncorroborated evidence of one witness was not enough to convict. Labour Zionists contended that Stavsky was convicted on the facts and acquitted on a technicality. The Revisionists rejoiced that justice had prevailed. An acquittal was an acquittal. For decades afterwards, the two parties produced further evidence and counter-evidence in a shouting match of the deaf – confessions by two Arabs, who then disappeared; opinions and retractions, from distinguished pulpits and equally distinguished death-beds. To the Labour movement the Revisionists had killed Arlosoroff. To the Revisionists Jew had spread blood libel against Jew.[13]

In Europe and in Palestine, the Arlosoroff case opened a wound which was running long after the details had faded into oblivion. Menachem Begin was scarred so deeply that he reacted to the publication of a new, unsympathetic account, by the Israeli journalist Shabtai Teveth, by appointing a commission of inquiry in March 1982. The Prime Minister told his Cabinet colleagues:

> To argue that forty-nine years have elapsed since then so how can we investigate now is to miss the point completely, to mislead the public, to blur the truth and to perpetuate a blood libel against a great Zionist movement and against innocent individuals, to perpetuate a wrong the like of which has never been perpetrated in Jewish history, save by the misdeeds of the Gentiles against the Jews.

Begin underlined his sense of a historic mission at last fulfilled by ordering that the entire transcript of the Cabinet debate be published.[14] He approached the subject 'with awe and trembling'. The commission's hearings were delayed for another year by the war in Lebanon. Of those directly involved in the murder trial, only Zvi Rosenblatt was still alive. Stavsky was killed on the Irgun Zvai Leumi arms ship *Altalena* when it was shelled by the Israeli army off the same Tel Aviv shore in June 1948.

As a Betar activist in Poland, the twenty-year-old Begin defended Jabotinsky with his body from stone-throwing Jewish assailants. In Brest-Litovsk, his mother was accosted in a grocer's shop: 'Your son's a good boy, but why does he mix with those murderers?' Stavsky was a childhood friend and neighbour of Begin's who took his innocence as axiomatic.

'Never mind,' he consoled the distressed Hassia Begin, 'you know that Abrasha murdered no one. The truth will come out.' Begin took Stavsky's mother to see Jabotinsky.

'To this day,' he wrote in 1982, 'her appeal and cry ring in my ears: "Mr Jabotinsky, save my child." Ze'ev Jabotinsky kissed her hand. Tears flowed from the mother's eyes. Those tears will never be forgotten.'[15]

The Revisionist minority was ostracized just as fiercely – and with more immediate effect on daily life – in Palestine. It cost Ya'acov Meridor his job and the roof over his head. Meridor, who served later as Begin's deputy in the Irgun high command, was then a labourer in the Tel Aviv area. In 1982, as Minister for Economic Co-ordination, he described the experience to the Cabinet:

> At ten o'clock the morning after the murder my landlord, who was active in the printing workers' union, came and told me in no uncertain terms that it was a political murder. Only a few hours after it happened there was already a political pogrom atmosphere. . . . A day later, my landlord ordered me to leave my room. Afterwards, I had trouble finding work.

On Kfar Malal, a smallholders' co-operative affiliated to the Labour movement, Ariel Sharon's family had an equally uncomfortable time after his parents protested against the branding of the Revisionists as murderers. He too told the Cabinet:

> The outcome was a struggle that went on for twenty years. As a boy, I was taken out of the local school. I couldn't learn there. For twenty years, till after the War of Independence, we couldn't get medical care at the local sick fund. . . . We weren't able to market our produce through the *moshav*'s channels. . . . I remember my parents taking turns standing guard by the path, protecting our produce from being spoiled by other *moshav* members. They raised, they produced, the children grew up and everything turned out fine. But all in a constant struggle with a hatred that never let up.

David Ben-Gurion and other Labour Zionist leaders compounded the injury by comparing Jabotinsky to Hitler and labelling the Revisionists as Jewish Nazis. Begin was convinced that the rift contributed to the scale of the Holocaust. But for the hatred generated by the Arlosoroff case, he maintained, the two wings of the movement might have pooled their efforts to smuggle illegal immigrants from Europe to Palestine, and tens of thousands of Jews might have been saved.

The young Begin made his first public speech at the age of thirteen standing on a table in a Brest-Litovsk park. It was one of the Lag Ba'omer Zionist festivals that his father organized every year. The speech was not one of

Begin's triumphs, but in no time he was a regular speaker at the annual Herzl memorial meetings. Aharon Zvi Propes, the head of Polish Betar, heard Begin, then eighteen, speak in 1931. 'He was magnificent,' Propes recalled. 'I knew that before us stood a young man blessed with rare talents.'[16] Propes's testimonial was particularly magnanimous. Eight years later he was shunted aside to make way for his protégé. While he was still at high school, Begin was Betar commander in the Brest district. When he left to study law at Warsaw University, Propes co-opted him to the Betar high commission. He was, Propes said, 'disciplined, liked by his comrades, ambitious'.

Betar, like its parent Revisionist movement, was dominated by the ideas, style and personality of Jabotinsky. Begin followed him around Poland, listening to his speeches, studying his technique, absorbing his doctrine. The youth movement was avowedly militaristic. Its members drilled and wore uniform. 'Jabotinsky taught us we had to learn to shoot,' says David Jutan, one of Begin's contemporaries.[17] As Betar's chief organizer in Poland, Begin toured the length and breadth of the land, speaking, cajoling, mobilizing recruits. By 1939 the movement numbered about 70,000 members in 700 branches.

'However they may sound in Israel today,' insists Yisrael Eldad, another Betar contemporary who became the ideologue of the Stern Gang and an enduring right-wing critic of Begin's,

> his phrases were not empty and demagogic for the Jews of Poland. They gave just the right expression of the feelings of the Jewish people. Nobody asked in those days how much a Jewish State would cost. It was for them a concrete problem of a republic of millions. When you talked about a Jewish soldier, it was an ideal. The Jew went to be a soldier for the Polish army, but he hated Poland. When Begin said 'Jewish soldier' it made people proud. People wanted it with all their heart. The Irgun was already active in Palestine. In Poland when you talked of retaliation, of no more pogroms, a Jewish boy became proud. Youth was ready to suffer, to sacrifice for an ideal. Youth had no patience. Betar and the Irgun offered them the revolutionary way. They offered a way to hundreds of thousands who had nothing to do.[18]

Begin's success in organizing Polish Betar prompted Jabotinsky to send him to Czechoslovakia, where the movement was small and languishing. Begin worked from the bottom up. According to Propes, he made do with one meal a day and sometimes slept on park benches. He was dedicated, tireless and uncomplaining. 'In Warsaw,' Propes recalled, 'he once went down with pneumonia. My wife, who was nursing him, took him to a boarding-house in Otwock to recuperate. When she went to see him two days later, she found he had slipped away and gone back to work, although he was very weak. With him, the job mattered more than any personal concern.'[19]

During one of his tours, Begin was invited by Dr Leon Arnold, a lawyer and a leading Revisionist in the small Polish town of Drohobycz, to dinner at the home of his father-in-law, Zvi Arnold. There he met Zvi Arnold's twin daughters, Aliza and Leah, who were then seventeen. Before returning to Warsaw to head Polish Betar, Begin served for a few months as an articled clerk to another local lawyer. He and Aliza met frequently, then continued their courtship by mail. They were married in the Drohobycz great synagogue on 29 May 1939. Both bride and groom wore the brown Betar uniform, though they reverted to civvies for their going away, Aliza in a well-cut knee-length coat and rakish hat, the lean bespectacled Menachem in a pale, shapeless mackintosh. The bride was nineteen, the bridegroom twenty-five. Jabotinsky came by train from Paris for the wedding. The marriage, which lasted until Aliza's death forty-three years later, weathered the stresses of separation, exile, danger and Israeli politics. Aliza shared her husband's conviction and tenacity, but was content to stay in his shadow. She seldom, if ever, forgave anyone who had crossed or betrayed him. They had three children, a son and two daughters, all born in Israel. Like most of Menachem's family, Aliza's twin sister died in the Holocaust.

Although Begin was proud to sit at Jabotinsky's feet, he was no mere sycophant. The disciple clashed with the master on two celebrated occasions. At the sixth Revisionist world congress in Cracow in January 1935, Begin remonstrated with Jabotinsky for his efforts to make peace with Ben-Gurion. Characteristically, Begin was more Jabotinskyite than Jabotinsky.

'You may have forgotten that Ben-Gurion once called you "Vladimir Hitler", but we have a better memory,' he said.

'I shall never forget that men like Ben-Gurion, Ben-Zvi, Eliahu Golomb once wore the uniform of the [Jewish] Legion,' Jabotinsky retorted, 'and I am confident that should the Zionist cause demand it, they would not hesitate to don this uniform again and fight. If there is a coalition, we will not rake up petty incidents. We have manifested strong Zionist patriotism.'[20]

The more serious challenge came at the third Betar world congress in Warsaw three years later. The movement faced a major split between the Irgun Zvai Leumi militants in Palestine, who were pressing for an active policy of retaliation for Arab attacks on Jews, and Jabotinsky, who took a strong stand against such counter-terrorism. The Irgun was impatient for a war against the British. Jabotinsky still believed that there was another Britain, which could be persuaded to see the Jewish cause as the true interest of the Empire. The Irgun was organizing its own cells inside Polish Betar and had opened a political office in Switzerland. It ran military training camps in co-operation with the Polish army, which was attracted by the prospect of shipping hundreds of thousands of Jews to fight in Palestine, thus solving Poland's Jewish problem (its 3,500,000 Jews represented eleven per cent of the population in the late 1930s). For once, Jabotinsky was concerned with tactics as well as principle. He wanted to keep the legal activity of Betar and the Revisionists separate from the underground operations of the Irgun, despite the fact that he was the nominal leader of both the political and military wings. Begin, who sided with the activists but wanted to avoid a fight, argued that the two had to be brought together under the same roof. The Irgun must work through Betar.

When the issues were debated at the Warsaw congress in September 1938, Begin waited until Jabotinsky was present before making his speech. Israel's national movement, he said, began with practical Zionism, then political Zionism. Now they were on the threshold of military Zionism, which would eventually merge with political Zionism. 'It can be compared to Cavour and Garibaldi,' he suggested. 'Cavour could not have achieved the emancipation of Italy without Garibaldi.' Begin was constantly interrupted by Jabotinsky, who reminded him that the Jews lacked the military manpower in their homeland. Begin replied that they had to make an immediate stand against the British plans for a predominantly Arab Palestine, regardless of numbers and regardless of the outcome. 'Even if we fall, we shall have fought.' Betar had to take up this cause 'in order to save Zionism'.

Begin proposed 'as a symbol of our work and our battle' (such gestures always were important to him) that they amend the fourth article of the Betar oath. Instead of, 'I will prepare my arms for the defence of my country, and I will not carry my arms except in defence,' Begin proposed: 'I will prepare my arms for the defence of my country, *and to capture my homeland.*' They had, he contended, always longed for force. The force had now been created. 'There are millions with nothing to lose. Our task is to use the strength that is in them.' The amendment was adopted with Jabotinsky's reluctant acquiescence, but not before the leader had unleashed an abrasive counter-attack on the young upstart:

> There are all kinds of noises. . . . We endure the creaking of machines, carriages and so forth. But the creaking of the door is not to be tolerated since it has no use. We have no need for it. Speeches and applause are also creaking doors, which have no use or reason. There is no room in Betar for such chatter.

Sometimes this creaking is pleasant, but we must beware of it. The things that have been said here by Mr Begin are such creaks, and we must cruelly suppress such creaks.[21]

Jabotinsky, less confident of his militancy than he had ever been, put his trust in the conscience of the world. He wanted the Western nations to provide a haven in Palestine for the threatened Jews of Europe. Begin scorned his old teacher. In the same month that Neville Chamberlain was negotiating an illusory 'peace for our time' with Hitler in Munich, the twenty-five-year-old Betari snapped back: 'The conscience of the world has ceased to react, the League of Nations has lost its value. Our British partner leads us to the gallows and imprisons the finest of our nation.' Jabotinsky answered that if that was how Begin felt, he might as well drown himself in the Vistula.

Yohanan Bader, a Revisionist lawyer who fell between the Jabotinsky and Begin generations, maintains that, despite his pique, the leader was 'charmed and delighted' that the youngsters stood up to him.[22] There are conflicting legends about what Jabotinsky thought of Begin. On one side, he is said to have singled him out as his heir. On the other, he is whispered to have despised Begin's provincial fanaticism and pietistic emotion (Jabotinsky was so removed from that side of Jewish tradition that he wrote in his will: 'I wish to be buried *or cremated* – it is the same to me – at the place in which death will find me.'). Begin himself claimed no great intimacy. He was conscious of their differences in age and status. It is clear that Jabotinsky valued Begin as an organizer and inspired subordinate, but there is no evidence that he was grooming him for the succession.

The Warsaw congress ended in victory for youth. The split between Betar and the Irgun was averted. In April 1939, Menachem Begin was appointed commissioner of Polish Betar, the powerhouse of the world movement, in place of Propes, who went like a gentleman. The Young Turks said uncharitably that Propes was good for culture and conferences, but not for fighting and politics (he later founded the Israel Festival, which he directed until his death in 1978). Begin celebrated his promotion by leading a demonstration against control of immigration to Palestine. The Polish police gave him his first taste of prison. He was released after three weeks with his head shaven. By then Warsaw and the world had other things to worry about.

3
Flight and Arrest

In the summer of 1939, the question facing the Jews of Europe was not so much whether there would be a war, as when. The priority for both wings of the Zionist movement was to rescue as many as possible from the Germany of the Nuremberg Decrees and *Kristallnacht*, if not yet of the Final Solution. Jabotinsky's prophecies of doom no longer sounded alarmist. His appeal to every Jew, 'in the name of God', to save his soul while he still could, no longer fell on deaf ears. But the barriers were dropping, the frontiers were closing in.

Two days before Hitler invaded Poland, Menachem Begin returned frustrated to Warsaw after escorting a convoy of 1,000 'illegal' Betar immigrants to the Romanian border. Until then, Romania had allowed Jews through on their way to Palestine, but the Molotov-Ribbentrop pact had been signed in Moscow on 23 August, and the Romanians could not afford to take other people's risks. The Betar members were dispersed to their home towns. Most of them perished in the death camps or the ranks of the Polish resistance.

When the German army entered Poland on 1 September, Begin's instinctive reaction was that of a Pole as well as a Jew. 'He called the Betar leadership together', Yisrael Eldad recounts, 'and told us to fortify Warsaw, to dig trenches. We must do our duty as Polish citizens, to be loyal to the law.'[1] The next day, the Revisionist poet Uri Zvi Greenberg came into the Betar office and was astonished by what he saw. 'What are you doing?' he shouted. 'The Russians will come. The Irgun has passports. Take them and go.' Begin and David Jutan went to see a Polish general and offered to form a Jewish battalion to fight with the Polish army against the Germans, but the response was discouraging. Only then did Begin and the other Betar leaders start to leave Warsaw in small groups. German bombs were already falling on the capital.

Begin and his wife Aliza travelled with Natan and Frieda Yellin-Mor, who had been married by the last Chief Rabbi of Warsaw, Shlomo David Kahana, on 5 September. The Begins had stood as witnesses. Yellin-Mor,

21

later one of the triumvirate that led the Stern Gang's campaign of terror
against the British mandate, was one of Begin's comrades in the Betar high
commission. As the trap closed, they trekked back and forth, by train,
farm-cart and on foot, sheltered by Betar loyalists, dodging the German
bombers and advancing Soviet tanks. Chaos and rumour reigned, refugee
families lined the roads and packed the trains. The bombing claimed its
first civilian casualties, broken and pathetic. 'We walked sleeping,' Begin
wrote later, 'we slept as we walked.' Begin was detained briefly by the
Russians when a Jewish woman accused him of owing her money she had
paid to escape through Romania. He settled the debt and bought his release.

The weary quartet rejected repeated advice to stay in one place, where
Betar members would look after them, though they were grateful for a
chance to celebrate the Jewish New Year among friends. After seven weeks
on the road, they made their way to Vilna, a famous centre of Jewish
learning and enterprise. The Russians had taken over the eastern part of
the Polish domain and proclaimed Vilna the capital of 'Free Lithuania'.
The leadership of Polish Betar gathered there in force, and was soon joined
by thousands of its members. Begin told them Lithuania would offer a way
out to Palestine. Betar rented a house, and sent its people to find boats to
ferry them through the Baltic. Looking back, some of them acknowledge
that they were naïve, that Lithuania's freedom could not last, but at the time
Vilna spelled hope.

The Betar leaders' confidence was tested by a letter from Shimshon
Juniczman, the head of the youth movement in Palestine. First, he informed
them that Avraham Stern, commander of the most aggressive wing of the
Irgun Zvai Leumi, had 'gone into business on his own'. Henceforth, there
were to be two underground forces on the Jewish Right: the Irgun Zvai
Leumi (the National Military Organization, known by its Hebrew acronym
as the Etzel) and the Stern Gang (Lohamei Herut Yisrael, in Hebrew,
Fighters for the Freedom of Israel, or Lehi). But nearer home for Begin
and his colleagues in Vilna, Juniczman added that 'many people here think
a captain shouldn't leave his ship so long as it is afloat'. Begin, with his
Jabotinskyite sense of honour, took this as a charge that they were deserting
the tens of thousands of Betarim still in Poland.

Yisrael Eldad remembers:

> Begin called us together and said maybe he is right, I want to go back to Warsaw.
> But in the end we decided we would not go back. The argument for not going
> back was that our front was now in Palestine. That was our homeland. We had
> no more to do in Poland. It was impossible to work there for more Betarim to go
> to Palestine. So we called them to Vilna to get them out through there.[2]

David Jutan is convinced that they were right to stay in Vilna, and that Juniczman was wrong:

First of all, we thought it was only a temporary move. We were convinced that the Polish army, with the British and the French, would win the war. Our argument was that Lithuania was a State from which you could go out. There was a connection with the free world. We sent cables to the United States – to Propes and other Jewish organizations – to make a pressure for visas and immigration permits for as many Betarim as possible. We needed a place where the British could send permits for legal immigrants.

Also, we had forged permits, which we made. To get an exit visa from the Lithuanians you needed at least a letter saying you had a permit for somewhere else. So we forged letters. Also the Dutch consulate in Vilna gave visas to Curaçao. After they closed the consulate, we forged the visas. The Japanese also gave visas.

The Russians tolerated all this activity because they wanted the foreign currency. The money was given by the Joint [the American Jewish Joint Distribution Committee]. We needed a base, and Vilna was a base we could operate from. Also, we made contact with Lithuanian fishermen in the port of Palanga. We gave them money because we thought they would take people to Sweden.[3]

In the event the war was not over quickly, and the decision to stay in Vilna proved momentous. Betar was the only mass movement of Polish Zionists left to face the Final Solution without its leaders. Yehuda Bauer, a foremost Israeli historian of the Holocaust, identifies this fact as the root cause of what he calls Menachem Begin's 'Holocaust complex', his survivor's sense of guilt. 'A large number of survivors who went through similar experiences suffer from deep guilt feelings,' Bauer wrote, adding: 'From a rational point of view, such guilt feelings are quite unjustified.'[4] The professor's thesis provides a plausible explanation of Begin's obsession with the Holocaust, which led him to write to President Ronald Reagan in August 1982, when the Israeli army was besieging Beirut: 'I feel these days as a Prime Minister empowered to instruct a valiant army facing Berlin where, amongst innocent civilians, Hitler and his henchmen hide in a bunker deep beneath the surface.'

As another Holocaust scholar, Ze'ev Mankowitz, wrote, the analogy was both delusive and dangerous:

The Nazi war against the Jews had no foundation in reality. It flowed from groundless hatred and fear of 'the Jews' as a satanic power bent on dominating the world. The horrible truth is that the Jewish people were the victims of an hallucination. The Palestinian people, however, are real. Their national aspirations are real, their symbolic significance for the Arab world is real and the political sympathy and recognition they have gained throughout the world is real.[5]

In 1939, as we have seen, Begin did argue a case for going back to Warsaw. Yisrael Eldad, for one, is still not sure that he meant it. Then, as later, Begin had the strength and prestige to impose his views on his colleagues – when he wanted to. 'I don't know until today', Eldad says, 'whether it was seriously meant or whether it was a gesture, whether it was a piece of theatre. We have seen that many times with him to this day. I don't know whether he ever really wanted to go back.'[6]

Despite their practical preoccupations, the Polish Betar leaders found time in the spring of 1940 to debate a wider dilemma racking the Revisionist movement: should they suspend the battle against British rule in Palestine for as long as Britain was waging war against the Nazis? Should they endorse Ben-Gurion's policy of fighting the war as if there were no White Paper restricting Jewish immigration, and fighting the White Paper as if there were no war? Jabotinsky ordered the Irgun to halt the struggle. In Palestine David Raziel, its commander, complied. According to Eldad, Begin condemned the suspension of hostilities as a betrayal. He was against stopping the fight. Eldad campaigned in the Betar magazine which he edited in Vilna for 'hostile neutrality', unless the British gave the Jews an army of their own under the Star of David flag. Begin's attitude was consistent with the stand he had taken at the Betar congress, but it suggests that his declaration of war on the mandate four years later was more than a response to the plight of European Jewry in 1944.

One day in the summer of 1940, the Betar commission organized a meeting at Vilna's Polish university – notorious as a hotbed of anti-Semitism – to commemorate three anniversaries: the deaths of Theodor Herzl, the father of political Zionism, and Chaim Nachman Bialik, the poet of the Hebrew revival, as well as the fifteenth birthday of the Hebrew University of Jerusalem. Begin was billed to speak in honour of Herzl, but in the middle of the meeting, attended by thousands of Jewish students, a note was handed to the platform. It read: 'Russian tanks have entered the city.' The professor speaking about the Hebrew University went pale and suggested that they all get out as quickly as possible. Begin stood up and announced; 'We shall finish the meeting, and we shall finish it with *Hatikva*.' The audience rose and sang the Zionist anthem. 'I shall never forget that *Hatikva*,' says Yisrael Eldad. 'We all thought this is the last time we shall be singing *Hatikva* in Europe.'[7]

The Betar leaders knew now that time was running out. The Kremlin was no friend of Zionism, which it despised as a 'national deviation' from the revolutionary path. Stalin was still Hitler's uneasy ally. But Begin and his colleagues had no answer other than to continue as before, seeking whatever escape routes they could find for their people. Betar kept a card index of its members who were in Vilna. When the Russians arrived, one young man, who was to attain a high position in the State of Israel, removed his card to evade detection. Begin expelled him from Betar on the spot.

The Revisionists suffered a double blow that summer. Barely a week after the entry of Soviet tanks and the end of Lithuania's fragile independence, Vladimir Ze'ev Jabotinsky died in the United States. Begin risked his freedom by going to Kovno to deliver a eulogy in the main synagogue. In Vilna, an eminent rabbi died a month after Jabotinsky. Among the thousands of *Hassidim* who attended the rabbi's funeral were fifteen Betar mourners. At the cemetery they peeled off and went to the grave of a young Betari who had died of cold and gangrene while trying to reach Palestine. Begin said *kaddish*, the prayer for the dead, and made a short speech. They all sang the Betar anthem, with its declaration of faith that Israel would rise from the decay and ashes. But Begin had been stricken more deeply than he cared to show by the death of his mentor.

His acts of defiance had not escaped the notice of the NKVD, the Soviet secret police. A Betar member was called to headquarters and asked whether he knew Begin. When he said yes, the officer replied: 'He made a fine speech at the cemetery, didn't he?' David Jutan was a native of Vilna and had studied at the university. One day an old acquaintance tipped him off that he and his friends were on the Russian wanted list. The NKVD called at his parents' flat, but Jutan had taken the precaution of sleeping elsewhere. The Betar leaders got the message, and moved out of Vilna to the nearby village of Pavilnius, where they rented rooms in peasants' houses.

Just before they left the city, Begin received a summons to Room 23 in the Vilna town hall 'in connection with your application'. Instead of being trapped, he was warned. He did not comply with the 'courteous invitation', not least because he had made no application. But he chose not to go into hiding and not to try and escape. In *White Nights*, a pioneering piece of Gulag literature, published in 1957, Begin wrote: 'The reason for the first part of my decision was simple. If the Soviet Government, I said to myself, wants to arrest me, let its agents put themselves out and come to my house. That is their job. Why should I disappear as if the earth had swallowed me up?'[8]

He added more archly: 'The reason for the second part of my decision was not simple, but I will not go into it.' It was another twenty years before he broke his silence:

After the death of Jabotinsky, the whole world blackened for me. Jabotinsky to us was more than a president, a leader, he was the bearer of hope, and so we looked up to him to bring us out of bondage.... The hope itself was lost, he passed away, there was nothing to hope for. So I was ready to get arrested by the Soviets because, as I said around the grave of a member of Betar, if we can't fight for our country, then we shall suffer for it. I will say frankly, it was an hour of hopelessness. We didn't see light. So I preferred to go to prison under these circumstances. I didn't even talk to my wife about it. My colleagues offered me a haven. I refused.[9]

Instead, the Betar leaders moved to Pavilnius. Begin and Aliza rented rooms in a widow's house, which they shared with Eldad (known then as Yisrael Sheib), his wife Batya and two others, one of them Mrs Begin's brother-in-law. The NKVD shadows went with them, following them everywhere. Begin even played a game with them. He invited Aliza to join him on the train to Vilna and appointed a Betar team to shadow the shadows. Wherever the Begins went, the spies followed – and their spies followed them. It was a game everyone knew could not last. In *White Nights*, Begin mocked the NKVD men for their lack of professionalism. They were so visible. But perhaps they simply did not care. If the Betar leaders left Lithuania, good riddance. If they stayed, the NKVD could pick them up at its convenience.

After ten days of cat and mouse, the secret police made its move on 20 September. The knock on the door came as a relief; at last Begin knew where he stood. Three men entered, interrupting a game of chess Begin was playing with Eldad. Their leader asked why Begin had ignored the summons to the town hall. Begin answered that he had no business with the municipality. If they wanted to talk to him, they knew where to find him. In his formal, lawyer's way, he asked the men to identify themselves. Their leader produced a card saying he was from Lithuanian intelligence. Begin asked if they had a warrant for his arrest. No, they replied, but we *have* come to arrest you. In the spirit of Jabotinsky, Begin was determined not to be rushed and not to go without dignity. He asked Aliza to offer their 'guests' tea, and made his preparations to leave.

Eldad says:

Begin performed what I call a concert. He polished his shoes, dressed in a suit and tie, he was very polite. At the last moment, they told him to leave. He said, 'I am in my home here, after you.' He said to me we shall continue the game of chess. Later, I got a message saying I was in a winning position and conceding the game. It was not true, there had only been five or six moves. He was allowed to take the Bible and one other book. My wife wept, his wife did not. She was very strong.[10]

As he left under escort, Begin saw David Jutan. They exchanged fatalistic glances as if to say: 'Well, this is it.' Despite promises that he would be back soon, the Betar leader's friends knew that he faced a long and uncertain incarceration. They had difficulty, however, persuading Aliza Begin to join them in going to Palestine on forged immigration papers. Jutan says she was almost hysterical.

I explained that the Soviets will not keep Menachem in Vilna. They'll send him to Siberia or somewhere. Before long the borders will be closed. The only way to make pressure for his release is to be in contact with the free world, especially the United States. We can only do that from Palestine or Istanbul.[11]

Eventually Aliza was persuaded to go. She travelled with Yisrael and Batya Eldad to Haifa by way of Odessa and Turkey. They were among 4,000 Jews the Russians allowed to leave Lithuania through Odessa and Vladivostok. The Joint paid $2,000 each for those going through Odessa and $4,000 for the Vladivostok contingent. The former made their way to Palestine, the latter to the United States.

In his fetid cell in the Lukishki prison, news of his wife's escape was conveyed to Begin by one of those brain-cracking word puzzles that is so obvious once you know the answer. Friends sent him a parcel of warm clothing. When Begin unwrapped it he found a handkerchief crudely embroidered with the letters OLA. At first he could not understand why Aliza's pet name, Ala, had been changed to Ola. A Jewish fellow prisoner finally worked it out. 'Ola' is the feminine form of the Hebrew word 'oleh', literally 'he who goes up', but also denoting an immigrant to Palestine. This solution was confirmed in May 1941, when the prisoners were allowed visits from their families. Begin asked to see his wife, thinking that perhaps she had not yet left. Paula Daiches, a Betar girl from Vilna, came in her place. 'Aunt Ala', she told him, 'is with Uncle Shimshon.' Begin understood immediately. 'Uncle Shimshon' was Shimshon Juniczman, the Betar leader in Palestine. Paula added that his parents were well and so were his brothers, who were with Aunt Ala. Since Begin had only one brother, he understood that his comrades had escaped too. Begin asked Paula to write and tell Aunt Ala that he was proud of her, that he was proud of them all. 'Write that I am strong and healthy, and I will come back.'

Long afterwards, Begin revived the Ala-ola pun when he dedicated a copy of *White Nights* to David Jutan with the inscription: 'To David, without whom Ala would not have been ola.' But two hard years that tested his strength and health were to pass before he kept his promise and came back.

4
Descent into the Gulag

Why, Menachem Begin asked himself after nine months' incarceration in the NKVD's Vilna headquarters and the chill Lukishki prison, do men held by the Soviet secret police so often end up confessing? The same puzzle was pondered by Arthur Koestler in his novel of the Kremlin purges, *Darkness at Noon*. Koestler's answer was that the old Bolsheviks remained loyal servants of the Revolution, whatever their misgivings about Stalin's excesses. They recognized that an individual who questioned the path of the Party endangered the Revolution. He *deserved* a bullet in the back of the neck. Koestler's Rubashov was a victim not only of the secret police but of his own Communist logic.

Begin took the question a step further. Why did political prisoners who were not Communists, who were dedicated to other ideals, follow the same road to oblivion? His conclusion lay in the 'double wall' erected by the NKVD around its prey, a wall which denied him not only his freedom but his audience.

> If the fighter knows that his service is rendered worthless, that no one will hear what he says, no one will learn of his stand, no one will receive his sacrifice from his hands, and no one will learn from him how to sacrifice, then the thread between him and the ideal is likely to be severed. It is then that his inner recognition of his mission is completely eradicated, and his tortured soul asks: Who will know? Who will follow after me? Who will come in my place? What point is there in my suffering, what purpose in the tortures I undergo?[1]

Begin added a second factor from his own experience: the inquisitors' trick of depriving the prisoner of sleep, an inseparable part of every Soviet interrogation. The NKVD worked mainly at night. Prisoners were returned to their cells just before reveille. As soon as they dozed off, it was time to wake up. By day sleeping was forbidden. The warders were instructed to watch for any prisoner taking even a light nap, and to threaten him with solitary confinement if they caught him at it again.

Night comes, bringing the darkness of the renewed interrogation. And again,

28

and again. . . . Night after night for weeks, for months, for time without end. In the head of the interrogated prisoner, a haze begins to form. His spirit is wearied to death, his legs are unsteady, and he has one sole desire: to sleep, to sleep just a little, not to get up, to lie, to rest, to forget. 'To sleep, to die, to sleep . . . no more.' Anyone who has experienced this desire knows that not even hunger or thirst are comparable with it. I came across prisoners who signed what they were ordered to sign, only to get what the interrogater promised them – uninterrupted sleep!

By his own testimony, Begin suffered from both forms of brainwashing. He was isolated from all but his immediate companions and the prison telegraph of dots and dashes tapped on walls and pipes. He scarcely slept. His eight-year sentence as 'an element dangerous to society' was delivered without trial. 'Trial,' fumed an NKVD major, 'give him a platform, give him a platform for his rhetoric!' Yet Begin did not crack. When he finally confessed he did so on his own terms. He refused to sign a statement reading: 'I admit I am guilty of having been the chairman of the Betar organization in Poland.' Through an interminable last night of disputation, he persuaded his interrogator to delete the acknowledgement of guilt. The definitive confession said as a simple fact: 'I admit that I was chairman of the Betar of Poland.' The interrogator, like others with whom Begin was to negotiate, was worn down by attrition. 'I never want to see you again,' he yelled as his tormentor was led back to his cell.

How then did Begin hold out? *White Nights* does not answer the question directly, but the answer is there if you read closely enough. First of all, Begin treated the interrogation, and indeed the whole prison experience, as an intellectual exploration, a deadly game of chess. How did the system work? What was the interrogator trying to achieve? Like the elaborate mathematical problems others might set themselves, it enabled him to keep his sanity, his sense of proportion, his self-respect. He did not become an animal.

With years of experience in Zionist politics behind him, he debated with his interrogator. Begin was stubborn, pedantic and proud. Even though he knew victory was worthless, he would not give the interrogator best. The disciple of Jabotinsky would not agree that Zionism was a bourgeois national deviation, that his leader, lately dead, had been a tool of British imperialism. Begin's resistance was instinctive. He argued and he instructed, though the interrogator was an unresponsive pupil and might make him pay for his presumption. It was an act of private heroism, of heroism for its own sake. Like the blow Ze'ev Dov Begin struck at the Polish sergeant snipping the rabbi's beard; like the concept of *Hadar*, dignity, Jabotinsky inculcated in his Betar boys and girls. There was something compulsive about the debate, perhaps on both sides. 'At times I had the impression', Begin wrote, 'that he had forgotten his function as interrogator, just as I forgot my role as the interrogated.'

But the nightly exercise in dialectics also kept him afloat. 'It was my faith against his faith,' he noted. 'I had something to fight for, even in the interrogation room.' As he wrote of a later act of defiance: 'I fight, therefore I am.' At the same time, Begin never quite abandoned hope of release – even at points of deep despair, when he considered sending Aliza a conditional divorce. This was partly because Begin succumbed, despite himself, to the interrogator's conditioning. He had been promised a period of re-education. 'Will I live to see the end of the period of re-education, will I live through it? Will I complete it and return?' Miron Sheskin, a fellow prisoner and former leader of the Revisionist Party in Poland, said that Begin never lost hope of getting out. 'We both knew that wherever we go, we shall eventually come to Israel. It was not a matter of religious faith, but a feeling which we had.'[2] Begin was aware of the uncertainties of the war that was being waged beyond the prison walls, and of the efforts being made on his behalf by friends in the West. It was common gossip among Begin's cellmates that Hitler would soon turn his guns against his Soviet ally of convenience. The Polish prisoners awaited the day with relish, the Jews with trepidation. But the future was far from sealed. It was worth staying alive, it was worth winning time.

Menachem Begin was no stranger to prison bars. He had seen the inside of a Polish jail two years earlier for demonstrating outside the British embassy in Warsaw. Neither the NKVD headquarters nor the Lukishki, to which he was soon transferred, shocked him. The gloom, the extremities of heat and cold, the stink of slops buckets in overcrowded cells, the hard bed, the meagre meals, the surly warders obeying their malign instructions, the separation from family and friends – all were familiar.

> I found all the usual items in the human cage – a straw mattress, a shelf, an ordinary table, a rickety stool, a small bowl, and, of course, the pail. Taken all in all, the prison of Vilna is like the one in Warsaw; and all the others built by man to cage his fellow men are no doubt just like it. There is nothing new. And it is just as well not to be a novice in prison.

The only difference he found between a Soviet prison and any other was that instead of asking, '*When* will I get out of here?' the prisoner of the NKVD asked, '*Will* I get out?' Begin's first taste of reality came when his guards confiscated the only book other than the Bible he had been allowed to bring from Pavilnius – André Maurois's life of Disraeli, which he had started to read in English. As punishment for treating the prison like a public library, he was forced to sit facing a blank wall for sixty hours, his knees pressed against its surface, eyes fixed on a single point. It was a subtle form of torture, which Begin endured by recalling the high peaks of his life. The relief when he was allowed to fling himself on his mattress was delirious.

For three months he shared a cell with two other men: a middle-aged reserve officer in the Polish army, a meticulous bachelor whose passion for order exasperated even Begin; and a young tailor turned corporal who became his pupil and surprised both older men by returning to the Church. The inherent anti-Semitism of his Polish cellmates was seldom far below the surface, but Begin was sad to leave them.

> There were barriers between us. We even quarrelled. But we managed to get to know each other, we learned to understand and to forgive. We had already become a small community, with its unwritten laws and its customs. Here I taught a little, and learned a lot. Here I had gone through the interrogation, here I had taken a heartbreaking decision.[3]

While awaiting verdict and sentence, Begin was housed in a communal cell which had sixteen beds for nearly sixty prisoners. They slept on the floor. His companions this time included a Jewish thief and a seventy-eight-year-old Polish colonel, a shaky pensioner punished retroactively for having fought in the army of the Czar. The prisoners who broke down under the strain of overcrowding and hunger tended to be the brawny, outdoor types. The intellectual 'weaklings', Begin wrote with a hint of self-satisfaction, did not fall sick and did not complain. 'Their spirit seemed to uphold them, and serve as an armour to their bodies.' The two groups united in staging a hunger strike in protest at the monotony of their diet, the constant ration of *kasha*, a thin, unappetising cereal soup. 'Verily, it came out of our nostrils,' Begin lamented, paraphrasing the Book of Numbers. 'And the *kasha* was loathsome to us. We could not bear it any more.' After a few days, the strikers were victorious. For the first time in two months, they were served a soup made of rotten cabbage leaves instead of the loathsome *kasha*.

It was at this time that Begin learned through the prison 'telegraph' that Miron Sheskin was in the next cell. The Revisionist leader, twelve years his senior, tapped a message asking how Jabotinsky was. Begin was distressed and embarrassed that Sheskin did not know, but after an interval informed him that Jabotinsky was dead. Sheskin was stunned, put on his hat and said *kaddish*. Although none of them was Jewish, his cellmates chorused 'Amen' at the end of the prayer.

For a while during Passover, Begin and Sheskin shared a cell. Sheskin recounted:

> We took our daily ration of bread, dipped it in coffee, then put it on the window to dry. This was our *matza*, our unleavened bread. We said the blessing, 'This is the bread of affliction', and recited, 'This year we are slaves, next year we will be free men; this year we are here, next year may we be in Jerusalem.' Then we sang *Hatikva*. We heard answers from different parts of the building. Jewish prisoners were singing *Hatikva*, even though demonstrations were forbidden.[4]

Somehow, the two Zionists escaped punishment, but Begin was less lucky when a Jewish warder overheard him telling a joke. Thinking it was at his expense, he complained to the prison superintendent, who promptly sentenced Begin to seven days' solitary confinement. He accepted the penalty philosophically, as another seminar in the ways of the NKVD and the lore and language of incarceration.

> The seven days and the seven nights went by. The solitary confinement weakened me considerably, but taught me much. I learned from the stifling heat by day and the freezing cold by night, from the filth and stench of the windowless cage, without any covering, from the chill, dirty cement floor which served as a bed for me and promenade for the rats – from all these things I learned that there is a worse place than a prison cell, just as I learned later that there is a worse place than the solitary confinement cell.

Begin survived his week of bread and water, but he did not forget the treachery of the Jewish warder in the service of the NKVD. This anonymous functionary joined Begin's gallery of household demons along with the smooth Jewish interrogator who urged him in Yiddish to write 'the truth', the lapsed-Zionist interpreter who worshipped at the shrine of Lenin and traded Herzl texts with Begin, and the Jewish prison barber who did his masters' dirty work by lulling the customers with an arcadian picture of life in the slave labour camps. There were to be other such renegades in Begin's history. Even when he was Prime Minister, he never spared them. 'That proud Jew,' he would say with rising scorn of any who flirted with the Palestinian enemy or tried to teach him his national duty. It was sometimes easier than debating the issues they raised.

Hard though they were, Begin's nine months in the Vilna prison proved to be no more than a prelude to his descent into Alexander Solzhenitzyn's Gulag archipelago, the Soviet underworld of forgotten, fossilized men and women branded for one capricious reason or another as enemies of the Revolution – the place worse 'than the solitary confinement cell'. Although his sojourn there lasted no more than three months, it left him with an enduring hostility to Russia and Communism, an enthusiasm for the cold war that survived the fashions of *détente*.

The odyssey began with a mutiny that in other circumstances might have passed for light relief – a refusal by prisoners awaiting transport to eat from spittoons. The Lukishki was so overpopulated that there were not enough plates to go round. But spittoons, even unused ones, were made for spitting in. The prisoners held out for two days. Like the hunger strikers before them, they won a Pyrrhic victory: a few bowls and cups which they had to pass from hand to hand, mouth to mouth, with the dregs of soup or coffee still in them. 'But we ate,' Begin rejoiced, 'and we did not eat out of spittoons.'

He was one of about 2,000 prisoners dispatched north from Vilna early in June 1941. Their destination, though they did not know it, was the *Pechor-Lag*, a work camp on the Pechora river, which flows through the northern tundra into the icy Barents Sea just south of the Arctic Circle. The 1,500-mile journey by rail and riverboat was a nightmare, with human beings packed tighter than cattle. Each truck of their prison train was designed for forty people or eight horses, a soldier confided. The Russians somehow jammed in nearer seventy prisoners. The truck had a single pipe opening onto the line which served as a lavatory, and two tiers of wooden bunks. If you chose a top bunk, you suffered from congestion. If you chose the bottom, you risked suffocation. The air entered through two tiny hatches. The doors were opened three times a day, twice for counting the prisoners and once for feeding them on a monotonous diet of bread and salted fish. Their only liquid was unboiled water, drunk from a bucket. On one occasion, Begin saw the guards scooping it up from a puddle covered in green slime. He drank it all the same.

The train ride lasted about six weeks, with unexplained halts for days on end. Along the way the prisoners heard that Germany had declared war on the Soviet Union. The Poles and Lithuanians among them were delighted. Their two enemies would be at each other's throats. Begin was not to know that the ominous new war in the east would soon bring his freedom. After the town of Kotlas the line deteriorated. 'The train rocked us about like a ship pitching and tossing in a stormy sea. Many of us became train-sick and vomited continuously. Our strength was exhausted. We dozed. No one spoke any longer.'

The prisoners left the train at a small station called Koshva, then marched for about five hours through muddy fields to a transit camp. They were guarded by soldiers with fixed bayonets and fierce bloodhounds. Anyone who stepped out of line, an officer bellowed, would be shot. On the march Begin fell into conversation with a soldier who assured him with grim conviction: 'People don't get out of here.' From the transit camp, the prisoners trudged through swamplands to the banks of the Pechora, where they were loaded onto a steam tug along with a consignment of iron rails. A conversation with a second guard gave Begin another hint of the miseries awaiting him. 'You'll see,' the guard said, jerking a thumb at Begin's modest bundle. 'They take it all.' He didn't say who 'they' were.

Miron Sheskin and another of Begin's Revisionist friends, David Kroll, were sent north on the same train, but in different trucks. At the *Pechor-Lag*, the resourceful Kroll bribed an officer to put the three of them in the camp hospital. It cost them three shirts each from their precious bundles. They were in the land of the 'white nights', where the Arctic sun barely set and winter lasted nine months a year. The patients had to run nearly a mile half-naked through sub-zero temperatures to the bath-house. 'You'll get used to it,' Begin was told. 'If you don't you'll die.' He feared he was going to perish on his first night in the hospital hut, when he was almost eaten alive by an army of red bugs.

> The terrible enemy, out for my blood, kept on increasing in number. I even tried evasive tactics and lay the other way round in my bed, but the manoeuvre did me no good. The enemy had me and held on. I did not close an eye that night. It was the same with all the other novices. But not so the veterans. They slept the sleep of the just. They had managed to get used to it.

After a week in the hospital, Begin was put to work, building the Kotlas-Varkuta railway, 'by order of the Party and the Government'. His work-mates were a motley crew: Russians, Poles, Lithuanians, Latvians, Estonians, Romanians and Jews. The latter included a disgraced assistant editor of *Pravda* with a heart complaint and a persistent temperature of about 100 degrees. But Begin soon learned that the only division that mattered was between the political prisoners and the criminals. The criminals ran the show, bragging of their physical toughness and terrorizing the despised intellectuals. Begin discovered what the friendly guard had meant when most of his belongings were stolen by one of the criminals while he slept. They did 'take it all', but in instalments.

To the accompaniment of a brass band playing hymns in praise of Soviet labour, the prisoners hauled iron rails a quarter of a mile from a ship on the Pechora, along a narrow plank then across country to a railway truck. The rails, one on each shoulder, burned off the skin. The pain was excruciating. The agony was augmented through a fourteen-hour day by swarms of mosquitoes. 'They sing and sting,' Begin complained, 'drink and buzz. There is no escaping them.' Although the prisoners worked in the open, conditions were worse than in jail. The cold was unbearable. Men fought for a place near a stove. Two young Jews in Sheskin's hut froze to death. The labour was back-breaking, the body cried out for sustenance, but the ration was even smaller. 'On the banks of the Pechor,' Begin recorded, 'I found animals walking on two legs.' For variety, the gangs were switched every ten days from day to night shift. The system vouchsafed them no sabbath.

'Are you a Pollak?' one of the guards asked Begin on his way to work one morning. With his usual fastidiousness, Begin explained that he was a Jew, but a Polish citizen. The guard was not concerned with such fine distinctions. He had news to impart. He had heard on the radio that all Polish prisoners were being amnestied. The Soviet and Polish Governments had agreed that they should be set free to join the battle against Germany. The rumour was confirmed. The camp superintendent had read the text in *Pravda*, but in the bureaucratic world of the Gulag that was no reason for releasing the Poles. The superintendent had yet to receive his instructions. Till then they must go on working in what was now the common cause of defeating the German foe. Begin and his fellows slaved for several more days in the *Pechor-Lag*, hauling, starving and scratching.

Instead of orders to release the Poles, the superintendent received orders to send a batch of men down-river to another camp where they could be put to more productive use. The Polish prisoners deputed Begin to intercede. If they were going free soon, what was the point of sending them north? But the superintendent had no powers of discretion. 'If the order to release you arrives, we'll even take you off the ship and send you where you have to go,' was the best he could offer.

Begin was one of 800 men crammed into a freighter that sailed for nearly three weeks along the Pechora. There was no room to stand, move or sit. The human cargo had to lie day and night on three tiers of bunks along the walls of the stinking hold. They drank cold river water, which gave most of them diarrhoea. The two rudimentary lavatories could not cope with the traffic. The prisoners were assailed by lice. The criminals taunted and bullied the politicals, collecting the vermin and dropping them in handfuls on their faces. The disgraced assistant editor of *Pravda*, convinced that the criminals were out to murder him, asked Begin to help him sing *Hatikva*, which he remembered from his youth in Odessa.

For Begin and the Poles, if not for the Russian Jew from *Pravda*, the ordeal was almost over. The superintendent kept his word. The order to release them finally arrived and was delivered to the freighter. They were to be set free before the worst of the northern winter. A guard shouted down the hold: 'Be-gin!' Then name after name in alphabetical order. Each acknowledged the summons, confirming his first name and father's name, Menachem Wolfovitch to the fore.[5] 'All those whose names I have called, collect your belongings,' the guard announced. 'An order has come to release the Poles. You are going free.' Envious to the last, one of the non-Polish criminals pointed at Begin and protested: 'He's a *Zhid* not a Pollak.' Menachem Wolfovitch ignored him. This was no time for being fastidious.

5
Eastwards to the Underground

The Polish prisoners were set free to fight the Germans, but they were left to find General Wladyslaw Anders' recruiting offices for themselves. The Russians took them by boat to a transit camp and signed them out of the Gulag without ceremony. Each Pole was given a sum of money and sent packing. Miron Sheskin received enough for a three-day train journey to Kuibishev, where he tried to persuade the Poles to establish a Jewish regiment patterned on Jabotinsky's First World War legion. Instead, they appointed him Jewish liaison officer to Anders' headquarters with the rank of major.

For some arcane reason, Begin's other Revisionist friend, David Kroll, who had been put in charge of a work gang, was not released, though he reported to the transit camp. Begin assumed for years afterwards that he had died a martyr's death in the far north, but in the early 1980s, a Russian Jew came to Israel from the Ural mountains with a message that Kroll was alive. He sent greetings to Begin and Sheskin and asked them to send him a *tallit*, a Jewish prayer shawl, but before they could comply, the visitor informed them that Kroll had died in a road accident.[1]

Begin's money did not last long. He tramped through the wastes of Soviet Central Asia, riding the railway without a ticket, sleeping rough, eating where and when he could amid the flotsam and jetsam of refugees and ex-prisoners drifting south in the last few months of 1941. He had learned the key to survival in the camps: *you can get used to anything*. The Polish army apparently was not interested in Jewish scarecrows, however hardy they had proved themselves. Begin was turned away. He journeyed on, hoping against hope that he might find his sister Rachel and her husband, who had been deported before Begin was arrested in Vilna.

One night, he was dozing on a railway platform when he overheard another vagabond talking about the copper mines in the Urals. The woman, who like Begin was waiting for a chance to snatch a free ride, mentioned the name Halperin. Without pitching his expectations too high, Begin asked her if this Halperin happened to be a lawyer from Warsaw and whether his

wife happened to be called Rachel. As luck would have it, the answers were
all yes. With the woman's help, Begin was reunited with his sister and
brother-in-law in what he described as 'a wretched mud hut in a little
Uzbeki town, at Dzhizak, between Tashkent and Samarkand'. The reunion
did not last long. Begin heard that the Russians had started rounding up
Jewish political leaders all over again. Since his past was well known, even
in Uzbekistan, he moved on to the town of Margilan, where the Polish
'Ninth' division was stationed. A few weeks later he heard from his sister
that some 'unknown person' had come to her shack asking where he could
be found.

At Margilan, Begin met Major Sheskin and two Betar members, who
gave him food and shelter. At Sheskin's suggestion, they sent for the
Revisionist lawyer, Yohanan Bader, who was living in exile in Russia. The
Betar grapevine was still working. Despite a typhoid epidemic that killed
tens of thousands, Bader trekked 1,200 miles to the meeting. Thanks to his
Betar hosts, Begin was in better shape than Bader had expected, wearing
boots and a leather jacket. Begin wanted to know how he could get to
Palestine and start a revolution against the British. 'Both of us agreed',
Bader recalls, 'that the task in *Eretz Yisrael* would be to fight against the
British Government.'[2] Again, it seems that Begin was not deflected by the
fact that the British were at war with the Nazis. But Bader explained that
there was no chance of getting a Soviet exit permit and that it would be
better to join the Polish army. 'I doubt whether, in all his judicial and
public career, he ever gave anyone a better piece of advice,' Begin reflected
a decade and a revolution later.[3]

Although he saw the logic of it, Begin was reluctant to present himself
for a medical examination. He had been rejected once, and his pride was
hurt. But the two older men – Bader and Sheskin – persuaded him to try
again. This time too, the doctor rejected him. His heart was weak, the
physician said, and his eyesight was poor. What kind of a soldier would he
make for Mother Poland? Sheskin was not prepared to leave it at that. He
lobbied the chief of staff to the divisional commander, Major Link. The
Polish officer interviewed Begin, then sent a note to the army doctor
instructing him to pass the recruit as fit for service. The doctor remembered
Begin's heart and his spectacles, but swallowed his scruples. 'Heart and
lungs, excellent,' he shouted. 'You are shortsighted, but in the army
you'll learn how to shoot properly.'[4] Begin's induction into the Polish
army was a turning-point. It brought him to Palestine and eventually to the
command of the Irgun Zvai Leumi. But in 1942, it was still a gamble. The
Revisionist leaders in Margilan had no guarantee that General Anders'
army would be sent to the Promised Land. 'It was a general belief,

no more,' Bader confides. 'There was still no decision.'[5] But the gamble paid off.

As before, Begin's experience with the Poles was anything but encouraging. His basic training was conducted in an atmosphere of anti-Semitism, of insults and humiliation. The consolation was that it did not last long. His unit was sent south, through the Caspian port of Krasnovodsk to Iran, Iraq and Transjordan. For Begin, the east bank of the Jordan was already *Eretz Yisrael*, the ancestral Land of Israel.

'The military convoy stopped,' he wrote later. 'We rested, I left the automobile, waded a little way into the grass, and drank in the odour of my homeland.'[6]

In May 1942, Begin was posted to Jerusalem, where he worked as a clerk in the town major's office. Not until he became Prime Minister of Israel was he promoted to anything higher than private. The Polish Government-in-Exile made him a brigadier-general retroactively. In Jerusalem, he was reunited with Aliza. He moved into her bed-sitting room on the ground floor of 25 Alfasi Street in Rehavia, a leafy middle-class suburb much favoured by Jewish university professors, lawyers and doctors, where you were as likely to hear German spoken as Hebrew or English. Their first child, Binyamin, was born in March 1943.

Begin plunged straight into Revisionist politics, but unlike many other Jewish soldiers, he refused to desert the Polish army. 'I gave my word,' he told his old chess partner, Yisrael Eldad, who was active in the Stern Gang. 'I have sworn on oath. I will not desert.'[7] While still in uniform he was, however, appointed head of Betar in Palestine, a position he quickly resigned when word reached the British CID, and they started asking questions. Nonetheless, he was consulted on Irgun Zvai Leumi problems and secretly visited its training camps. Despite his lack of military expertise, he was already being canvassed as commander of the underground fighters.

The Irgun was in an advanced state of disintegration when Begin arrived in Palestine. It had forfeited its sense of direction with the death of Jabotinsky, the split with Avraham Stern, and the loss of its inspiring young commander, David Raziel, killed on an undercover mission for the British in Iraq in May 1941.

'At the time of the split, the Irgun was very strong,' testifies Eitan Livni, who became the Irgun's chief of operations in 1943.

We got weapons officially from the Polish army, sent here by our people in Poland. The Irgun could bring out more than four battalions, nearly 4,000 members could be drafted to fight. We had thousands of rifles, many hundreds of pistols, many dozens of submachine-guns that we smuggled from Finland, a few dozen Polish heavy machine-guns, and grenades which we produced ourselves. These were up-to-date weapons.

When the split came, most of these arms disappeared. Of the 4,000 men, nearly 800 joined Stern. Less than 1,000 remained in the Irgun. The rest used the excuse – maybe they believed it sincerely – that now that there were two groups they couldn't make up their minds. They dropped out. The biggest tragedy was that nobody revealed where the arms were hidden. After the split, the Irgun had only about a dozen full-time organizers. The rest were working at their jobs and were called in for training and special tasks. About half of our 1,000 men joined the British army in 1942–3, as did many of the drop-outs.[8]

Raziel had been succeeded by Ya'acov Meridor, who rose from the second rank of Irgun commanders after the split with Stern. 'He was liked,' Livni says, 'he made an impression, he looked like a real *sabra*, rooted in the ground, far from the diaspora image. We looked on Meridor as the best of the possibilities at that time.' But both the native-born and the recent arrivals from Europe were disappointed. Livni found him too much of a dreamer:

Meridor was not a practical man, as the future was to prove. He picked commanders to work with him, but he did not always pick the best men. In the middle of 1943, there were intrigues in the high command. Meridor did not hold them all together. He was always a friendly type, he was one of the few of us who was already married. He tried to act as *primus inter pares*, the first among equals. Maybe he had come to his own conclusion that he didn't have the charisma of a commander-in-chief.[9]

Begin's comrade from Vilna, David Jutan, agrees: 'Meridor did not have a strong enough character for the situation. He was honest, he had a wide military knowledge, he was liked. But you needed then somebody with charisma. Meridor wasn't ambitious. He was brave in operations, but he was very modest.'[10]

Thoughts turned increasingly to Begin, but first he had to be winkled out of the Polish army. He could not be persuaded to desert, and there was no chance of getting him honourably discharged. The only practical option, his friends concluded, was for the Poles to grant him long-term leave, with the possibility of renewal. The task was assigned to Marek Kahan, a forty-year-old Revisionist lawyer from Warsaw, who arrived in Palestine a few months after Begin. In Poland in the late 1930s, he had served as the party's contact with the Polish establishment, many of whom he knew from school and university. Kahan was instrumental in obtaining passports and exit visas for Betarim, as well as military training and the right to wear uniform as a separate unit in the army cadet corps. He too had been sent north by the Russians, before being released to join the Polish army. Using his pre-war connections, he managed to get himself discharged on medical grounds while stationed in Iraq. He went to Palestine on a leave pass. The link that was to bring Begin out of the army and into the underground had been forged.

Kahan became a regular visitor to the Polish information department in Jerusalem, where he met Theresa Lipkowsky, a Polish aristocrat and relative of the Prime Minister, General Wladyslaw Sikorski. She was interested in the Jewish problem, and Kahan set about teaching her Zionism. Through her, he fostered the idea of a joint Polish–Jewish public relations campaign in the United States, pointing to the efforts of Hillel Kook and other Revisionists there. As part of this strategy, Kahan suggested that the Poles should discharge a few Jewish soldiers and send them to tour America. About this time, one of the Irgun's representatives in the United States, Arieh Ben-Eliezer, arrived back in Palestine. He brought with him an album of photographs, showing how the Revisionists had mobilized stage and film stars for their drive to rescue Jews from Nazi-occupied Europe. The presentation probably overestimated their influence, but the Poles were impressed. They asked for a list of Jewish soldiers who might be sent. Begin was one of them, but the plot seemed to have run into the sand when it was vetoed by the British.

What saved it was the transfer of the Polish general staff from Iraq to Rehovot, between Jerusalem and Tel Aviv. Kahan lobbied some of the senior officers he knew from Warsaw. There was no immediate answer, but one oppressively hot day in the autumn of 1943 Kahan was invited for lunch with a general (the same one who had arranged his own discharge). 'Today', the general said, 'I have signed long-term leave for all your boys.' Begin was among them. He was given one year's leave, on condition that the group started work in the United States. 'We never intended to send Begin,' Kahan confesses. In any case the British would not let the group leave the country, but the Poles conveniently neglected to call them back to the colours. 'There was', says Marek Kahan, 'sympathy among Polish officers for the Irgun.'[11]

Begin's path to command of the Irgun was still far from smooth. Even if Meridor was ready to serve as his deputy, other senior officers argued that the job should go to a military man. Begin was new in the country and had no experience as either an operational planner or field commander. Some regional commanders, disappointed in their own ambitions, left the Irgun after Begin's takeover. Begin's strength lay in his undisputed leadership of Polish Betar, which was the prime source of manpower for the Irgun, especially in the higher ranks. If Arieh Ben-Eliezer had not left Palestine for America in 1939, he would have been a powerful contender, a man who combined vision and action. But Ben-Eliezer felt he had been away too long and that his work abroad had made him too conspicuous. Instead, he threw his weight behind Begin's candidacy. He had come back primarily to find out why the Irgun was so inactive. He diagnosed a failure of leadership. 'He was the one who convinced Meridor that he had to leave,' says Eitan Livni. 'It was done with silken gloves.'[12] Ben-Eliezer was the only other figure Begin treated as a political equal and consulted on his evolving strategy of revolt.

The majority of the leadership agreed with Ben-Eliezer that they needed a commander who could rekindle the Irgun's old fire and self-confidence. 'At the end of 1943,' according to David Niv, an Irgun veteran and its official historian, 'it was not only a question of military operations, but a question of taking a stand. It was time for a man of politics rather than a professional military commander. All the decisions needed political sensitivity.'[13] Begin fitted the bill. He was admired, his radical reputation had gone before him, he had the political grasp. Others could supply the military know-how.

6
The End of the Truce

'Whatever you decide will be fulfilled,' Eitan Livni, the Irgun Zvai Leumi's chief of operations, informed Menachem Begin at the end of 1943. 'I and my boys are ready.' So by then was the Irgun's new commander. Undaunted by the knowledge that Livni could put barely 600 trained fighters into the field, Begin proclaimed his revolt against British rule on 1 February 1944. He had drafted his ringing appeal to the Jews of Palestine months before while still a private in the Polish army. Now it was ripe for the broadsheets and the billboards. Allied troops had not yet landed on the Normandy beaches, Britain was still locked in battle with the common enemy, Nazi Germany, but for Begin the truce between the Jews and the British was over: 'Every Jew in the homeland will fight.' Begin, as we have seen, had little patience for that truce anyway. What he learned of the slaughter of European Jewry and what he saw in Palestine - the stubborn implementation of the 1939 White Paper restrictions on Jewish immigration, the callous interception of boatloads of refugees - reinforced the instincts that had brought him into conflict with Jabotinsky six years earlier. The time had come to fight, 'to break through the gates from within'.

He announced:

Four years have passed since the war began, and all the hopes that beat in our hearts then have evaporated without a trace. We have not been accorded international status, no Jewish army has been set up, the gates of the country have not been opened. The British regime has sealed its shameful betrayal of the Jewish people and there is no moral basis whatsoever for its presence in *Eretz Yisrael*.

We shall fearlessly draw conclusions. There is no longer any armistice between the Jewish people and the British administration in *Eretz Yisrael* which hands our brothers over to Hitler. Our people is at war with this regime - war to the end.... This, then, is our demand: immediate transfer of power in *Eretz Yisrael* to a Provisional Hebrew Government.[1]

Begin tarred the British as accomplices of Hitler. Even without the benefit of historians' hindsight, enough was known to convince him that they shared the passive anti-Semite's indifference to the fate of the Jew. There was no alternative but to fight. Yet the Irgun's fight, Begin decreed, was to be a political struggle pursued by military means. Begin the politician imposed his own limits. Unlike the Stern Gang, the Irgun was not fighting the British Empire. Its war was directed against the Palestine administration, not the British Government and nation. During negotiations in 1944 for reunification of the two 'dissident' groups, Begin insisted that the Sternists stop using such terms as 'foreign rule' and 'British imperialism' in their propaganda. When the Stern Gang leaders, Natan Yellin-Mor and Yitzhak Shamir, asked what they should use instead, Begin suggested 'the rule of oppression'.

As so often with Begin's needling distinctions, there was more to his insistence than semantics. He argued that responsibility for Britain's anti-Zionist policy lay primarily with the Palestine administration. The fight had to be aimed at the administration in Jerusalem rather than the Government in London, which must be persuaded that the administration's policy was bankrupt. It would then be forced to change that policy for one more sympathetic to the Jewish cause. London would recognize the Jews as the decisive community and put its faith in them rather than the Arabs. The Sternists, needless to say, were not impressed.

Yellin-Mor wrote:

> I tried to explain to him that any separation between the local administration and the metropolis in London was an illusion. It had no foundation. In the course of the war of liberation we should have to strike at the nervous system of British rule in London. *Eretz Yisrael* was only important to the British Empire as a military base for its rule in the countries of the region, and as a way-station to the colonies and dominions further east.[2]

Begin stood firm, pointing the same distinction in a secret five-hour meeting with Moshe Sneh, then deputy commander of the mainstream Haganah defence force, whom he had known when they were students in Warsaw. As they sparred through a long October night in 1944, Sneh said: 'You declared war on England.' Begin corrected him: 'Not England, the rule of oppression, England is not our enemy. That is what the Sternists say, that they have declared war against England the enemy.'[3]

Since Britain as such was not the enemy, and British troops were fighting the Nazis, Begin placed his men under a self-denying ordinance. Until the end of the war in Europe, they would not attack military targets. Nor did the Irgun have any interest in assassinating individual British soldiers, officials or policemen. Instead, Begin trained his sights on British prestige.

Politically, he argued, every attack was an achievement, even if it did not succeed militarily:

> History and our observation persuaded us that if we could succeed in destroying the Government's prestige in *Eretz Yisrael*, the removal of its rule would follow automatically. Thenceforward we gave no peace to this weak spot. Throughout all the years of our uprising, we hit at the British Government's prestige, deliberately, tirelessly, unceasingly.
>
> The very existence of an underground which oppression, hangings, torture and deportations fail to crush or to weaken must in the end undermine the prestige of a colonial regime that lives by the legend of its omnipotence. Every attack which it fails to prevent is a blow at its standing. Even if the attack does not succeed, it makes a dent in that prestige, and that dent widens into a crack which is extended with every succeeding attack.[4]

In his conversation with Sneh, Begin emphasized that the objective was to force Britain to reassess its policies, to bring it to the negotiating table. Britain could not risk humiliation in the eyes of the Arab States.

> This is something which the British will not be able to swallow, they will not be able to ignore it. Today they swallow this, but when the tide of our activity will rise, they will not be able to swallow this. A moment will come when they will have to negotiate with us. This will influence political decisions.[5]

Begin was also playing to an American gallery. The United States, he contended, wanted to establish its influence in the Middle East. Any weakening of British power in the region would be a plus for the Americans. At the same time, continued turbulence in the Middle East would be a nuisance to the Americans while they were at war with the Japanese. They had a stake in a settlement. American public opinion, Begin predicted to Sneh, would be awakened. It would force Britain to change course.

In Palestine, Begin set out with a strong dash of wishful thinking to impress both the Arabs and his fellow Jews. He believed that for twenty-five years Zionism had made a fatal mistake in treating the Arabs as the enemy, leaving the British to adjudicate from the sidelines. In action and in leaflets distributed in the Arab towns and villages, the Irgun sought to demonstrate that the fight was between the Jews and the British. In the spirit of Jabotinsky, the Arabs were offered equality and autonomy, so long as they were content to live as a minority in a Jewish State. And if they were not, then they were shown that the Jews knew how to fight. This was a matter of tactics rather than philosophy. The Irgun under Raziel had not hesitated to retaliate brutally against Arab civilians for attacks on Jews in 1938, and would retaliate again under Begin from 1947.

As a relative newcomer from Europe, Begin was horrified by the complacency of the *Yishuv*, the Jewish community of Palestine. 'What did the *Yishuv* sacrifice?' he asked Sneh. 'It contributed a little to fund-raising, mobilization and rescue work, it closed its shops for a couple of hours on a day of mourning, but the cafés are open, the Jews are busy making profits.' The Irgun, he argued, was proving to them that the Jews must fight, that there were youngsters ready to sacrifice themselves. Despite the unpopularity of curfews and other collective punishments, Begin claimed that the Jews were with him. 'We are redeeming their feelings and preparing them for war. The *Yishuv* will not be activated on a given day without preparation. We are preparing it.'[6]

Begin suggested to Sneh, who had come to him as David Ben-Gurion's personal representative, that the rival military groups fulfilled a useful division of roles: the Sternists with their strategy of individual terror, the Irgun's sporadic military operations, and the Haganah which was preparing to throw in its weight for the final campaign. There were to be times when this thesis had its appeal, but 1944 was not one of them. Sneh retorted: 'If this division had resulted from a single political standpoint, it might have been fruitful, but when it emanates from three different standpoints, no good will come of it.'[7]

True to its strategy of pricking the bubble of British prestige, the Irgun struck first on the night of 12 February, bombing the immigration offices in Jerusalem, Tel Aviv and Haifa. It was a symbolic act, causing little damage and no casualties (apart from an Arab watchman, who went into shock after being decoyed from his post by a pair of ardent lovers in a neighbouring doorway). Begin's message was that the Irgun would not tolerate a department whose task was to keep Jews out of the Promised Land when they were being dragged to their deaths in Europe. These raids were followed two weeks later by the bombing of income tax offices in the three main cities and, on 23 March, by assaults on CID headquarters there. Whatever Begin's intentions, the Irgun had drawn and lost its first blood since he had taken command. Six CID men, including an inspector, were killed, as were two Irgun men. The British and the organized *Yishuv* sat up and took notice. A British intelligence officer reported on the danger of 'sudden attack by fanatical assassins, who can vanish back into the obscurity of a crowded city'. Another added that, despite the Irgun's belief that it had a divine mission to drive the British out of Palestine, 'this does not mean that they are careless in their methods, for they combine skill and cunning with reckless courage'.[8] Curfews were imposed, suspects rounded up, and the death penalty reactivated for possessing arms and laying explosives. The

Irgun learned, but did not heed, the lesson that sabotage operations always put lives at risk, however ingenious the saboteurs and however many warnings are given. The campaign grew in audacity and ambition. A radio station, the railways and police forts were the next targets.

With its 600 fighters, the Irgun at this time was more of a revolutionary conspiracy than an army on the march. Its active membership seldom rose above 2,000. It was compact and flexible, bound together by personal loyalties and the discipline of ideology. As a military novice, Begin learned quickly. From the start he set the objectives. For the first year he did not go into tactical details, but gradually he also became the military commander in the headquarters, though not in the field. He had great confidence in his successive operations chiefs, Livni and Amihai ('Gidi') Paglin. He asked the right questions. Livni had daily meetings with Begin:

> He was anxious to hear details, always pumping me. Begin wanted to know what was happening. For example, I had to recommend who was to be the commander of an action. I suggested whom to promote. We had a joke. I am an introverted type. I used to say it's easier to do it again instead of explaining it. He always believed in thinking aloud, developing ideas together. From action to action, he understood military matters more and more.
>
> I brought suggestions, but the targets were picked by Begin and the high command of five. Begin took notice of me on technical matters, but I wouldn't, for instance, have thought the third action should be attacking the CID. We started from little to big. We had to get experience, we hadn't acted for four years. In sessions of the high command, which met nearly every week, Begin wanted targets that would make a great impact in the world. Sometimes he wanted us to stop actions. What I admired about Begin was his analytical mind, his political analysis. It helped to convince me of the possibilities of our war, of the future.[9]

Like all backstreet revolutionaries, the Irgun had its problems of internal security and of resources, of traitors, finances and supplies. On his own testimony and that of his colleagues, Begin was reluctant to authorize the execution of informers. This was Begin the lawyer *manqué*, but also Begin the man of selective compassion for whom Jewish lives are sacred. According to Livni, only two suspects were shot under Begin, ten others were spared. 'I was in favour of eliminating a specific case. Begin told me: "My education is as a lawyer. The proofs that you bring would not be accepted as guilt by a civilian judge." We swallowed it.'

Begin's scruples allowed the most treacherous of the Irgun's informers to escape. The man was Ya'acov Chylewicz, a Revisionist fund-raiser from Vilna, with good Irgun connections. In March 1944, when Begin was still living with his family in Jerusalem, Chylewicz brought a present for Bin-

yamin Begin's first birthday. The next day the police came to arrest the
Irgun commander. As it happened he was out of the house. The visit served
as a warning. Begin went underground in Tel Aviv. He is convinced that
Chylewicz brought the gift in order to find out where Begin lived. Sub-
sequently, he gave a list of Irgun leaders – among them Begin, Meridor
and Ben-Eliezer – to the CID. As a result of this information, Ben-Eliezer
was arrested. The list fell into Irgun hands. They were not the only ones
with security problems.

When Irgun officers recommended revolutionary justice, Begin insisted
that Chylewicz be given a chance to defend himself against the charges. He
was summoned before a three-man court. When he refused to appear, he was
called again. This time he fled to Egypt. His flight was presented by Begin's
colleagues as proof enough, but the commander was not yet satisfied.

> I said that he might be frightened at being suspected of this terrible thing, and
> that might be why he fled to Egypt. I said we must send him an order to come
> back and face trial. In these days there were soldiers in the British army who
> were members of the Irgun. Two of these men went to see Chylewicz in a hotel
> in Cairo and asked him in my name to come back. Chylewicz handed them over
> to the military police. Then I agreed that this was proof enough. The British
> sent him over the ocean to the United States. We knew about it. They say
> Chylewicz is still in America, but we don't care about him.[10]

Because the Irgun was isolated by the official Zionist leadership from
access to funds and equipment, it had to find both where it could. At the
beginning of 1944, Eitan Livni had sixty functioning pistols, three sub-
machine-guns stolen from a British camp, a few rifles, a few hundred
grenades and two tons of explosives. That was hardly enough to make a
revolution. To get more, the Irgun stole, robbed and extorted from the
Jews it aspired to lead. In 1945 diamonds worth more than £38,000 were
seized during a raid on post office parcel dispatchers, and as much again in
cash was taken in a raid on a guarded train carrying railway workers' pay-
packets. Two passers-by who tried to intervene were killed when Irgun
gunmen held up the Eden cinema box-office in Tel Aviv. Livni claims that
wherever possible they stole from the British. 'We once confiscated from a
Jewish bank. I made the suggestion to Begin. He asked me with which
company this bank was insured. When I found out it was insured by
Lloyd's of London, he authorized the operation.'[11] Be that as it may,
Haganah intelligence obtained a list of Irgun 'contributors', which included
640 Jewish individuals, businesses and institutions in Tel Aviv alone,
including many who were Haganah members and had been intimidated
into paying up.[12]

*   *   *

Behind the ideological façade, Begin's early contacts with the Stern Gang and the Haganah led nowhere for the same basic reason: the Irgun commander's refusal to share authority, to yield to anyone else's judgement outside his own ranks. He was single-minded, determined and supremely self-confident. Nothing and no one must presume to stand in his way. Not even the local leadership of the Revisionist Party, from which Begin contemptuously divorced the Irgun for the duration of his revolt. The Revisionists were too respectable, they still adhered to the policy of wartime co-operation with Britain.

According to Yellin-Mor, Begin presented the Sternists with an ultimatum. As a condition for reunion, they had to recognize Jabotinsky as 'mentor of the generation'. Like Begin, Yellin-Mor had been reared at Jabotinsky's elbow, but unlike Begin he had moved on. Jabotinsky was no longer his first point of reference. Decades later, he was to display something of the same independence and imagination by preaching coexistence with the Palestinian Arabs while Begin was still quoting Jabotinsky's evidence to the 1937 Peel Commission. In 1944, Yellin-Mor and Shamir felt they could not kneel to the ghost of Jabotinsky without betraying the memory of their own leader, Avraham ('Yair') Stern, who had been shot dead by a British police inspector in February 1942. Stern had rebelled against Jabotinsky's call for a ceasefire with the British when war broke out in Europe. But, as Yellin-Mor explained, there was a more practical reason for the Sternists' rejection of Begin's terms:

> In differences of opinion that would certainly have arisen between us, we would always have had to turn to Jabotinsky's writings to draw from them solutions for situations which had not existed in his lifetime. And if there were differences of opinion as to the interpretation of the written word, who would decide? To clarify the matter, I asked Begin: 'What if differences of opinion will arise between the two organizations: who will decide between them?' Begin did not hesitate to suggest this too as a condition: in such a case, the decision would be left to him. Despite our long acquaintance and collaboration over many years, I was dumbfounded. Begin was so sure of his moral authority that he had no doubt that he deserved to be the single arbitrator without appeal.[13]

In his conversation with Moshe Sneh of the Haganah, Begin acknowledged Ben-Gurion as the political leader of the *Yishuv*. The Irgun, he said, had no desire to rule. It would rally to Ben-Gurion's banner as soon as he declared war on the British regime. But until then there could be no question of accepting a Haganah veto on Irgun activities, there could be no pause while the prospects for co-operation were examined. Sneh, Begin argued, was talking to him only because the Irgun was fighting. If it were not fighting, it would count for nothing. To bow to Ben-Gurion prematurely would spell voluntary liquidation. Begin was unmoved by the argument that the official leadership alone had a mandate from the *Yishuv*, or by Sneh's contention that Ben-Gurion knew more of what was happening in the wider diplomatic arena and was thus better qualified to take decisions in the Jewish interest.[14]

The two old acquaintances met in an atmosphere of incipient crisis. Rightly or wrongly, the official leadership detected signs of an improvement in the British attitude towards Zionist aspirations. Sneh told Begin of hints Winston Churchill had dropped to Chaim Weizmann of a 'good' partition once the world war was over. A Jewish Brigade, for which the Zionists had long been lobbying, was finally to be established in the British army. Ben-Gurion and his colleagues were worried that these hopes might be jeopardized by the terror campaign. At the same time, they feared that the revolt of the dissidents might not end with the British, though there is nothing in Begin's contemporary pronouncements to substantiate their scent of *putsch*. But Begin's answers did not dispel such suspicions. The Irgun commander had no faith in Churchill's half-promises. To Begin no partition, especially one restricted to 'Western *Eretz Yisrael*', could by definition be good. Perhaps more acutely than Begin, Sneh was conscious of growing demands for the Haganah to suppress the dissidents. His report of the meeting ended in despair: 'I said to him: "I do not know whether there is another Jew who wants to avoid war between Jews and Jews more than I do. ... As such, I say to you that I leave this conversation extremely depressed." The conclusion is clear: they want to impose their way on everyone.'[15]

As early as April 1944, Ben-Gurion had told the Jewish Agency executive: 'If there is no other alternative, we shall have to confront force with force. This will be a catastrophe, but a smaller catastrophe than the control of a small group over the *Yishuv*.'[16] By the end of the year, that nightmare of fraternal strife had become a reality. Begin had a final meeting with Moshe Sneh's chief, Eliahu Golomb, who had returned from an official mission to London more convinced than ever of the damage the dissidents were causing to Zionist diplomacy. 'If we are forced to go out and fight against those who perform these mad, harmful acts,' he told a press conference, 'we shall do so.' After his unproductive session with Begin, Golomb reiterated: 'The *Yishuv* must take all measures in order to stop the Irgun's activities.'[17]

The die was cast within a week. On 6 November 1944, two Sternist gunmen assassinated Lord Moyne, Churchill's Minister for Middle East affairs, in Cairo. Begin and the Irgun had received no advance warning of the operation, although this was a period of active liaison between the two groups. But it was the Irgun and not the Stern Gang which paid the price for Lord Moyne's murder. The Jewish Agency executive assembled immediately after the news broke and resolved that 'the *Yishuv* is required to spew up all members of this destructive and ruinous gang, to deny them shelter and refuge, not to give in to their threats and to grant the authorities all the aid required to prevent the acts of terror and liquidate its organization, for our lives depend on it'. Eliahu Golomb wrote that there was now 'no more room for debate on the means to uproot the plague of the terrorist crimes. The need to prevent without delay additional crimes supersedes any other consideration and necessitates taking all measures to grant the authorities active aid to do away with the murderers.'[18]

What became known as the *Saison* (the hunting season) left another scar on Menachem Begin's psyche. This was Cain and Abel in modern dress. If brother did not kill brother, he abducted, tortured and delivered him wholesale to the British enemy. He hounded him from his job and expelled his children from their schools. According to the official Haganah history, Jewish 'volunteers' detained about twenty men for interrogation and ninety-one others were investigated without being held. The names of about 700 persons and institutions, some of whom were involved in terrorist acts and extortion and some of whom were voluntary or involuntary contributors to Irgun funds, were handed over to the CID. About 300 of these are said to have been arrested on the basis of these lists. Other estimates put the tally of Irgun fighters and supporters delivered to the police as high as 1,000.[19] During the seven months of the *Saison*, almost all of the top leadership were caught. One of them, Eli Tavin, the chief of intelligence, was held by Haganah men from February to August 1945 in solitary confinement at Kibbutz Ein Harod. His captors wanted information. In order to get it they were ready to beat him, suspend him from a wall, knock out his teeth, keep him chained in his own filth, and stage mock executions. When the *Saison* finished in June, they were at first too embarrassed to set him free.

Begin himself eluded the pack. Shimon Avidan, who commanded the *Saison*, said: 'Several times attempts were made to catch Begin, but we were not successful. Whenever we reached the place where he had been, he was no longer there.'[20] One of those detailed to find him was Meir Pa'il, a young Haganah squad leader and future left-wing MP. Pa'il and his men were informed that Begin, heavily disguised, would be lunching at a restaurant in the Street of the Prophets in Jerusalem.

'I was ordered to collect him and bring him to Ein Harod, where the

Haganah had organized a small jail. We waited for two days, but he did not come. We ate in the restaurant in shifts. Four went inside while the fifth stayed outside with a taxi-driver.'

After Begin became Prime Minister in 1977, he asked his fellow MP if the story was true. Pa'il said yes, and if he had captured him he would have made a thorough job of it.

'What if I had resisted?'

'You would have been beaten.'

'And if there had been some people protecting me?'

'They would have been beaten too. If you had behaved yourself, we would have put you in the taxi with three people holding your arms. If we thought you were going to make trouble, we would have put some kind of a *shmatter* in your mouth and locked you in the trunk.'

As parting consolation, Pa'il added that in any case his mission was to deliver Begin alive – and not to the British. The Prime Minister embraced him.[21]

The mystery is not so much why Pa'il failed to catch Begin as why the Haganah thought he was due in Jerusalem. In fact the Irgun commander stayed in hiding under various aliases in the Tel Aviv area from the spring of 1944 until the end of the revolt. His first refuge was the modest Savoy Hotel, between Allenby Street and the sea shore, where he registered as Menachem Ben-Ze'ev. Thirty-one years later a boat-load of Palestinian terrorists seized the hotel, which had by then fallen on shabby times. The cement building was half demolished when an Israeli assault team stormed it and killed all but one of the terrorists. Begin chose the hotel because at short notice he could find nowhere else, but also on the principle that 'the darkest spot is right under the lamp'. He left the Savoy after a narrow squeak. The manager led a British search party discreetly past the door of room 17, which opened off a balcony instead of the corridor: 'That's all the rooms.' The man did not know Begin's true identity, but had a pretty good idea that he was not there on holiday.

From the Savoy, Begin moved with his wife and son to an isolated house in the Yemenite quarter of Petah Tikva. 'Conditions there were difficult,' he wrote. 'The house was neglected. The wind blew day and night through its broken shutters. At night it was cold and dark. There was no electricity and no central-heating.'[22] But to his great delight, he slept in sheets that had been bought for the British High Commissioner, Sir Harold Mac-Michael, whom the Irgun had once planned to kidnap. The little house was not only uncomfortable, it was risky. A Polish family stuck out like a sore thumb among the dark-skinned Yemenites. It was only a matter of time before somebody started asking questions about the stranger who never went out to work.

The Irgun transferred the Begins to the Hasidoff quarter, a working-class district on the edge of Petah Tikva, where Menachem adopted the name Yisrael Halperin. The house was often without water, and electricity had not yet been installed, but Begin, who was still in the 'open underground', found compensation in the neighbouring fields and orange groves, the greenery of gardens and woodland. The 'Halperins' introduced themselves as a Polish refugee family. To explain why her husband did not go to work, Aliza spread the story that he was studying for the Palestinian law examinations. Until he qualified, they were being helped by the Joint, an American Jewish charity. The Irgun high command used to meet in the kitchen by oil or candlelight. On Saturdays they would stroll in the orange groves. It was in the Hasidoff quarter that the Begins experienced their first massive search by the British army. On 5 September 1944, Petah Tikva, which had a reputation for being 'full of terrorists', was surrounded at dawn and a curfew was announced. Begin and one of his commanders, who had been staying for the night, decided that there was no point in fleeing into the woods. It would attract the attention of the neighbours, if not of the troops, and they would almost certainly be caught. They decided to play it cool and innocent. The two Irgun leaders sat on the doorstep watching the British tanks and armoured cars passing the end of the street. Mrs Seigel, the woman next door, was in great distress. 'It's all right for you, Mrs Halperin,' she confided in Aliza, 'you have nothing to worry about. But I've got an army blanket in my house.' By noon the danger had passed. For some reason the army ignored the Hasidoff quarter and the curfew was lifted. But with the approach of the *Saison*, the area felt less secure. People began to pry, and the time had come to move into Tel Aviv.

Yisrael Halperin vanished into history and Yisrael Sassover, a bearded Orthodox Jew in a black skull-cap, took up residence in Yehoshua Bin-Nun Street, between the municipal slaughterhouse and the municipal dogs' home. The beard added ten years to Begin's age. During his last month in Petah Tikva he explained away his five o'clock shadow by telling the neighbours that he was in mourning. As a good religious Jew in Tel Aviv, he prayed regularly at the local synagogue. The neighbours suspected that he was one of those perpetual *yeshiva* students who never take a job and live off their wives' dowries. The Begins' second child, named Hassia after his mother, was born while they were living in Yehoshua Bin-Nun Street. She was registered as Hassia Epstein, taking the name of one of Begin's closest friends, Yisrael Epstein, who had to act the happy father and visit Aliza and her daughter in hospital.

The British twice came close to discovering Begin's hiding-place between the abattoir and the dogs' home. On the first occasion they played searchlights over Yehoshua Bin-Nun Street, tramping back and forth looking for arms caches. Begin sat tight and waited, but there was no knock on his door and by dawn the alert was over. That was in late 1945. Nearly a year later, after the bombing of the King David Hotel in Jerusalem, the army seemed to know what it was looking for. Begin took cover in a secret cubbyhole under the roof that had been designed for such emergencies by Ya'acov Meridor. The search, he felt, was getting close. From the radio, which Aliza had left on conveniently loud, he learned that the curfew was to last several days. Every house would be searched, every resident examined. A party of soldiers pitched camp in the Begins' garden and Aliza was taken away with her two children for questioning. She pretended not to know English. Through a Hebrew-speaking interpreter, she said that her husband had gone to Jerusalem. A British policeman sent her home. But the army came back to make a search of the house, opening cupboards, checking under beds, tapping on the walls (they even tapped on Begin's hideaway). Begin was stuck in his cramped refuge for three excruciating days and nights of August heat. It reminded him of the solitary confinement cell in Vilna.

> There were certain comparisons between the two. In Lukishki it was hot by day and cold by night. Here it was cool at night – and purgatory by day. There the floor was of stone – here it was of wood. There your bones ached – and they ached no less here. There you could take three and a half steps. Here you dared not move. There you lacked food. Here you lacked water.
>
> That was the worst of it: no water. I had gone without food in Lukishki and elsewhere. Here for the first time, I learned what it meant to go without water. Hunger and thirst – it is best to know neither. But if I had to choose between them, I would unhesitatingly choose hunger. Prolonged thirst is terrifying. ... My head began to grow dizzy. My body began strangely to dry up.[23]

The soldiers camped in the garden increased his agony by repeatedly coming into the house and asking for a drink. But on the fourth day they drove away and Aliza sounded the all-clear with a broom handle. Begin celebrated his release by plunging his head over and over again into a bowl of cold water, and drinking. 'I had no patience, I was completely dry. Water, water, that was what I needed.'[24]

'The cordon and search method produced very modest results,' the British General Officer Commanding, General Sir Evelyn Barker, admitted later,

> but looking back, I can't see any other way of dealing with the problem. When we went into Tel Aviv, Begin was there hiding in a cupboard. There was a

lance-corporal and three men camping in his garden, but they did not search the house properly. This is one of the problems of search operations. You have to rely on very junior people, and if they make a mistake, the whole operation can be damaged.[25]

The Begins lived in Yehoshua Bin-Nun Street for nearly two years, but again the house lost its anonymity. The British were paying too much attention to the neighbourhood, the Haganah knew of Begin's beard. The Irgun security men recommended another move. Yisrael Sassover shaved his beard, Dr Jona Koenigshoffer took up residence on the corner of Rosenbaum Street and Yosef Eliahu Street, near the Habima Theatre in the heart of Tel Aviv. The name, with its reassuring whiff of German–Jewish respectability, was taken from an identity card which had been found in a public library. Begin's photograph, complete with moustache, was grafted on to it. This move in early 1947 proved the last in the Begins' underground travels. A second daughter, Leah, was born while they were living in Rosenbaum Street. She too was registered as Epstein. The British never let up in their search for the 'arch-terrorist'. A reward of £2,000 was placed on his head (Natan Yellin-Mor of the Stern Gang merited only £1,000), but no one betrayed him.[26]

The *Saison* of 1944–5 put a severe strain on Begin's judgement and on his control of his young fighters. The abductions and betrayal by Jews hurt and humiliated them. Their instinct was to hit back. Begin's own bitter emotions echo through a scathing proclamation he wrote in February 1945, under the heading '*We shall repay you, Cain ...*':

You have used your might, Cain, but you did not use it when millions of our brothers perished as they turned their eyes to Zion – a Zion of closed doors, a Zion enslaved by an evil Government; you did not display it when the survivors of the sword were deported; you did not unsheath it to break down the gates locked by the White Paper. ...

You mobilized the money of the nation, Cain, but you did not spend it for rescue, to help the families of soldiers, nor to organize free immigration from the countries of extermination. You embezzle the nation's monies, tens of thousands of pounds, to finance detectives, kidnappers, gangs of informers. You chose yourself an ally, Cain: the oppressive regime in the homeland, and the Nazi-British CID are your allies. To them you give brothers – into hands stained with the blood of millions thrown back from the doors of the homeland into the ovens of Maidanek. ...

You abduct, Cain. In the depths of night you break into Hebrew homes. Ten against one – you thrash till the blood pours. ... By trickery and deceit, in the name of the police, and always with brutality, you weed out your 'suspects', taking them off in unknown directions, torturing them with Gestapo methods in the shadows of orange groves, and finally handing them over to your ally, the Nazi–British CID, for further tortures, for exile in Eritrea. . . .[27]

Nonetheless, Begin opted for restraint. He was convinced that the time would soon come when the Irgun and the Haganah would have to fight together. A full-scale civil war would destroy the possibility of such co-operation, and even the prospects of achieving a Jewish State. In the heat of the *Saison*, it was an unpopular policy to impose. Ya'acov ('Yoel') Amrami, who succeeded Eli Tavin as chief of intelligence, estimates that half the leadership was against it.[28] But Begin's logic prevailed. As early as November 1944, he drafted strong and explicit instructions for his men:

Do not raise a hand and do not use arms against Hebrew youths. They are not responsible. They are our brothers. They are being misdirected and incited. But the day will come when they will realize their error and fight side by side with us against the foreign oppression. In your behaviour, the behaviour of patriots who do not deviate from their course, you will hasten the process of their disintegration and their rebellion against those who sent them, and the inciters will achieve the exact opposite of what they seek. There will be no fraternal war, but the great day will approach in which the people will rise – despite the wishes of those who place obstacles – as a single fighting camp, and that is what matters. . . . This is the only way to save the *Yishuv* from a fraternal war, to save the country from destruction, to preserve the true purity of our flag and weapons, to lift Israel in the eyes of the gentiles. And this is also the way – believe me – to victory.[29]

Reluctantly, the Irgun high command agreed. Begin's colleagues may also have been swayed by the knowledge that open war between the Irgun and the more numerous, better-equipped Haganah would almost certainly have ended in the destruction of the Irgun. The decisive factor, however, was the commander's unique authority. Despite the provocation, discipline held and the Irgun did not retaliate. Ya'acov Amrami, who had argued against restraint, acknowledges that 'in the end, Begin was right. After eight months, the Haganah joined us in the fight against the British.'

The *Saison* dealt a grievous blow to the Irgun, but it did not wipe it out. Eliahu Golomb's claim that 'their power is terminated' was discounted on reflection by the Haganah's official historian. Both the Irgun and the Stern Gang were paralysed for the last seven months of the world war. The Sternists avoided the rigours of the *Saison* by voluntarily suspending operations after the murder of Lord Moyne. Ya'acov Meridor, who was arrested in the spring of 1945 and deported to East Africa, admitted that 'except for distributing broadsheets, we were not engaged in any serious action'. But Begin himself evaded the hunters, and the Irgun quickly found new young commanders to replace those who had been detained.

At the same time, the Irgun won public sympathy within the *Yishuv* for not retaliating. There was little appetite for the chase among members of the Haganah, so much so that officially the *Saison* was said to have been carried out by volunteers at the behest of the national leadership. Moshe Sneh maintained afterwards that it was in no way a Haganah campaign:

> No institution of the Haganah ever decided about the *Saison*, and no institution of the Haganah was ordered to implement the *Saison*. The matter was brought before the Zionist Actions Committee by the Zionist Executive, and the decision was taken. Later on, the matter was brought before the Histadrut Council, and there a decision was taken. The Haganah did not undertake this thing. There were people who were mobilized on a personal basis for the *Saison*. The Haganah Council never discussed this matter, never received an order and never gave an order.[30]

Sneh regretted the co-operation with the British, which he described as 'a grave mistake'. Nonetheless, he accepted it at the time. His deputy, Yisrael Galili, claims that he himself opposed handing over dissidents to the CID. The Haganah's dilemma was that it did not have the necessary judicial or penal system to handle them on its own. According to Galili, the reason the Haganah as such was not mobilized was its doctrine of universality. The Haganah was not the 'red army' of the Labour movement, it was the defence force of the *Yishuv*. In principle at least, there was parity in the Haganah's controlling institutions between the Labour movement and the Zionist parties of the Right and Centre. The attitude of Labour's partners towards the Irgun and the Stern Gang was at best ambivalent. Ben-Gurion did not want to strain the allegiance of these partners.[31]

In practice, however, the *Saison* was pursued by the Haganah and its strike force, the Palmah. A rank-and-file member protested at the same 1966 symposium at which Sneh spoke that he and his platoon in Rishon le Zion 'were ordered by our immediate commander to perform a *Saison* operation, to beat up a man who belonged to the underground'. It was doubtless the same elsewhere, despite the niceties of Zionist coalition politics.

The *Saison* petered out with the end of the European war and the approach of a British general election. The official leadership was disappointed that Churchill showed no disposition to reward the Jews for their assistance. 'The action against the dissidents', the Haganah history comments unequivocally, 'was for the members of the Haganah a bitter and tragic necessity. For many days to come the fraternal hatred which accumulated in those tragic days still permeated the body of the *Yishuv*.' Menachem Begin never forgave and never forgot.

7
A Tragedy of Errors

To Menachem Begin, 1945 was a year of vindication. The British – under Conservative and Labour Governments – dismayed those like Weizmann and Ben-Gurion who still hoped for a political solution by turning a deaf ear to the clamour for a Jewish State in Palestine. Begin's scepticism had proved well founded. As a result, the Haganah lived up to another of his predictions, one that had provoked the only crisis of confidence he experienced as commander of the Irgun Zvai Leumi. The Haganah proposed a common front with the Irgun and the Stern Gang, a united and active resistance campaign against British rule.

With the end of the war in Europe, Britain began coming to terms with the fact that it was no longer a dominant power. Its economy had been sapped by six years of hostilities. Once the euphoria of victory had subsided, the world of 1945 was seen to be different from, but no less dangerous than, that of 1939. Whatever Britain decided about the conflicting Jewish and Arab claims to Palestine, its leaders could not discount the effect on Britain's relations with the United States, the Soviet Union, the Arab and Moslem States, or with its traditional oil suppliers in Iraq and the Persian Gulf. Even before the July general election, the wind was blowing against a simple, pro-Zionist solution. Winston Churchill's sympathy for the Jewish cause was inconsistent at the best of times. It was neutralized by the assassination of Lord Moyne. He did not demur when his Foreign Secretary, Anthony Eden, advised the Cabinet: 'If we lose Arab goodwill, the Americans and the Russians will be on hand to profit from our mistakes.'

The mainstream Zionist leaders remained confident, however, that the prospects would be more rosy if Labour came to power. At its Blackpool conference in December 1944, the Party had undertaken to abolish the 1939 White Paper restrictions on Jewish immigration to Palestine and to support the establishment of a Jewish national home there. Yet within weeks of taking office, Labour began its disorderly retreat from the Blackpool commitment. On 25 August, the Colonial Office informed Chaim Weizmann that the immigration quota of 1,500 Jews a month would not be increased. It was a blow to Weizmann's personal authority as the champion of dialogue with the British and to the Labour Zionist establishment in Palestine, which had invested so many hopes in its special relationship with British Labour. The immediate turning-point was Clement Attlee's choice of Ernest Bevin, trade union leader and wartime Minister of Labour, as Foreign Secretary instead of the pro-Zionist Hugh Dalton. In the end, British policy might not have been much different, but the Foreign Office would have had to work harder to convince Dalton to abandon the Party platform.

Dalton, who became Chancellor of the Exchequer, was an enthusiastic advocate of the Zionist case. Bevin was not, as is commonly supposed, a novice in foreign affairs or a man of instinct rather than reflection. He knew the world and had pondered Britain's position in it. In the 1930s the Zionists considered him an ally. But in Churchill's coalition Cabinet his energies had been concentrated on mobilizing manpower for the war effort. Harold Beeley, his chief Foreign Office adviser on Middle East affairs, doubts whether he was familiar with the Blackpool resolution: 'Party policy was brushed aside at the outset. I sometimes wondered if Bevin knew what it was. As for the opinion of those colleagues who were interested, such as Dalton and Cripps, this was heavily discounted by Bevin because he knew they were being assiduously lobbied by the Zionists.'[1]

Bevin went through a process of 'absorption' by the Foreign Office, which briefed him and persuaded him that Zionism was unjust to the Arabs and bad for Britain. To establish a Jewish State would seriously undermine the British position in the Middle East, the 'nodal point' in Britain's communications system with India, Australia and the Far East, and the Empire's main source of oil. The Foreign Secretary tried to steer a middle course between keeping the Arabs sweet and not alienating the Americans. Menachem Begin was hardly surprised that Bevin proved insensitive to the plight of the European Jewish survivors or to the arguments of Zionist lobbyists. He had expected nothing different. If the Jews wanted a State, they had to take it for themselves.

Nonetheless, if Beeley and other witnesses are to be believed and Bevin was not inherently anti-Semitic, it is hard to understand the degree of British blindness to Jewish suffering. Bevin and Attlee were irritated by American pressure, which they regarded as a product of unfair domestic agitation on President Harry Truman. This was compounded by Truman's reluctance to share the financial and military burden of imposing any solution on Palestine. The British were also worried about the impact of a pro-Zionist decision on the ninety million Moslems of India, whose future was still undetermined, and on Soviet designs on Turkey, Greece and Iran.

In Palestine itself, the military was warning its masters of a new Arab rising. Bevin's policy, it has been argued, was pro-British rather than pro-Arab. Yet none of this explains away the Labour leaders' blinkered perception of the Zionist argument that the Jews of Europe had a special claim on their compassion, if not their consciences, and that Palestine was the refugees' natural haven.

'Bevin felt he was being coerced by the Americans on the one hand, and by attempts to influence his colleagues in the Cabinet through the Zionist organization in Great Britain on the other,' Beeley maintains. 'All this he greatly resented.'

Whatever the virtues of his policy, this resentment led the Foreign Secretary into pronouncements that were good neither for Britain nor for his own reputation. He saw the world through the eyes of a British democratic Socialist. The war had been fought to make Europe safe for democracy. Now that Hitler had been routed, the Jews could settle back to their old lives just like everyone else. He had no conception of the Jews' unique trauma. They had been the victims of an extermination programme which had almost succeeded. Six million Jews had died for no crime other than being Jewish.

'They have gone through, it is true, the most terrible massacres and persecutions,' Bevin said, 'but on the other hand they have got through it and a number have survived. Now succour and help should be brought to assist them to resettle in Germany and to help them to get over the fears and nerves that arise from such treatment.'

Later, the Foreign Secretary picked up a line of Attlee's that had somehow gone unnoticed. The Jewish refugees in Europe must not 'try to push to the head of the queue'. Britain had not promised them a Jewish State in Palestine, but only a national home. This, Bevin suggested, might still be achieved 'so long as it was recognized that the tragic task of saving the Jewish people was not one to be borne by Palestine alone.' The Foreign Secretary gave final offence at the Labour Party conference in Bournemouth the following June, when he attacked an American demand for Palestine to be opened to 100,000 immigrants. 'I hope I will not be misunderstood in America if I say that this was proposed with the purest motives. They did not want too many Jews in New York.' He was understood all too well.

Britain's task was impossible. The Foreign Office talked Attlee and Bevin into a policy of holding the line in Palestine. Yet the dynamics on the ground made that a hopeless cause. The Jews, shocked by the revelations of Belsen and Auschwitz, were desperate. In the face of British indifference, moderation was a dwindling option, for the *Yishuv* and for world Jewry. At the same time the Palestinian Arabs were making themselves heard after

five years of slumber. The Whitehall mandarins were getting out of their
depth and out of their element.

David Ben-Gurion, the elected leader of the *Yishuv*, had always been more
wary of British intentions than Chaim Weizmann, the ageing president of
the world Zionist movement. After walking through the blitzed but ecstatic
streets of London on VE Day, 8 May 1945, Ben-Gurion wrote one line in
his diary: 'Victory day – sad, very sad.' The Jews had not won the war. Six
million of them had been slaughtered, and the battle for statehood still lay
ahead. By the end of September, Ben-Gurion was convinced that diplomacy
had run its course. He flew from London to Paris and on 1 October sent a
coded telegram to Moshe Sneh instructing the Haganah commander to
institute an armed rising against Britain. The order was given on his own
initiative and without informing Weizmann. Ben-Gurion's opposition to
violence had long been more tactical than moral. The telegram, his biographer wrote, went far beyond anything he had outlined to his colleagues
in London.

> He did not delude himself that the armed struggle could drive the British out of
> Palestine, but he hoped that it would provoke such deep sympathetic response
> in world public opinion that Britain would be forced to alter its policy. With
> that end in mind, he told a press conference held in Paris that 'the acts of the
> British Government are a continuation of Hitler's policy of hostility'.[2]

In Tel Aviv, Sneh's first problem was how to approach Begin. The
Saison was barely over, there had been no contact between them for a year.
Sneh's answer was to make his overture through the Stern Gang. Natan
Yellin-Mor, whose mixture of compliance and threats had kept the Sternists
immune from the *Saison*, delivered the invitation. The Irgun commander,
delighted that Ben-Gurion was at last talking and acting like Begin, was
ready to co-operate – but, as ever, on his terms. At a clandestine meeting
with Sneh and Yisrael Galili of the Haganah and Yellin-Mor of the Stern
Gang, Begin rejected out of hand a proposal that the two dissident groups
disband and join the Haganah.

'We want a common front against the British. So long as the Haganah
continues to fight, the common front will exist. But on the day that the
Haganah abandons the military campaign against the British, we shall
continue.'[3]

Begin was conscious of the ambiguity of the Haganah's position. It was
the defence force of the Jewish Agency, which operated within the law as
the elected representative of the *Yishuv*. If the Haganah performed illegal
activities, it would endanger the legal status of its political parent. The

Jewish Agency would have to choose at some time between being dragged into the underground and reasserting its legality by calling the Haganah to heel. For Begin, the strength of the Irgun's position was that it had never pretended to be anything other than illegal. The Irgun, he made clear from the start, would 'continue to fight until the British depart from *Eretz Yisrael*, no matter how long the war lasts'.

Sneh and Galili bowed to Begin's logic, but insisted that the Haganah must be the senior partner in what became known as *T'nuat Hameri Haivri*, the Hebrew Resistance Movement. According to Galili, an understanding was reached without offending the honour of the two junior partners.

> It was not the case that they said, 'We salute the Haganah's authority', but it was clear that we had a veto. In other words, one could only do things where there was agreement. The goal was to prevent their doing things which we considered harmful, whether from the point of view of the political timing or from the point of view of the operational plan. It was exceptionally important to prevent dangerous operations, which could lead to one organization tripping up another.[4]

The Haganah's veto power is acknowledged by both Begin and the Irgun's chief propagandist, Shmuel Katz, though the dissidents reserved the right to act independently to steal arms from the British and to 'confiscate' funds elsewhere.[5] The assault on the King David Hotel in July 1946 was to demonstrate how brittle an instrument the senior partner's control was. Unless Begin was satisfied with the reasoning behind a Haganah decision, he still felt free to exercise his own judgement. The trouble was that despite the impact made by the united resistance, there was little mutual confidence between the component groups. Old suspicions lingered, there was no sense of permanent cohabitation, let alone marriage. The Haganah and the Stern Gang remembered the early 1940s when the pre-Begin Irgun, then co-operating with the British, informed on Sternists. The Irgun and Sternists remembered the *Saison*.

Galili says:

> We had no reason to rely on the Irgun. . . . Not Begin personally, Heaven forbid. Begin was a man one could depend on, but a man strongly influenced by the people he worked with, especially if they tried to explain things to him with operational or technical arguments. But we didn't know who was in his entourage, also one didn't know who was in my entourage. You know a *provocateur* only after you know that he is a *provocateur*. Before that you do not know. You may think, these Jews, they feared each other, they didn't trust each other. It is a fact.[6]

Ideological and tactical differences persisted too, though the inhibitions about attacking the British while they were fighting Hitler no longer applied. The Haganah was more scrupulous about taking lives than the Irgun, which in turn did not endorse the Stern Gang's use of assassination as a legitimate weapon. The Haganah was constantly looking over its shoulder at the visible political leadership. It was anxious to justify operations either as a proportionate response to British provocation or as a contribution to the other half of its resistance campaign, illegal immigration. As a trial run, for instance, a Haganah force, commanded by Yitzhak Rabin, released 208 Jews from a British detention camp at Atlit, south of Haifa, on 10 October, although the Hebrew Resistance pact had not yet been sealed. Its favourite targets were communications links, especially the railways, and coastguard stations.

Nevertheless, the Hebrew Resistance Movement functioned with a tolerable degree of co-ordination from October 1945 to July 1946. It was destroyed, along with many other things, by the King David disaster. The days of unity were, according to Begin, the happiest of his life. Not only had his dream of a common front been realized, but he and his men were no longer outcasts. Begin was not a compulsive rebel. Legitimacy mattered to him. Forty years on, he still split hairs between 'terrorists' and 'freedom fighters'. He would not sacrifice principle for respectability, but he was more comfortable when he could reconcile the two:

> In the days of the Resistance Movement, we were not publicly recognized, but we were recognized nevertheless. Part of the responsibility - though, indeed only part - was taken off our shoulders. The whole people were behind us.[7]

The Hebrew Resistance struck its inaugural blow on the night of 31 October-1 November 1945. The Palmah sank three police patrol-boats in Haifa and Jaffa; the Haganah blew up railway lines at 153 points throughout Palestine and damaged other railway installations in Jerusalem and Tel Aviv; the Irgun destroyed one locomotive and damaged six others in a daring raid on Lydda goods yard and station. The Sternists alone failed in their objective, the most ambitious of them all. An explosive charge went off prematurely before it could be set under storage tanks at the Haifa oil refinery. Within the terms of the tripartite agreement, the Irgun and Stern Gang raided British police, army and air force installations through the winter in search of weapons. On one night, 27 December, the British lost ten dead and twelve wounded. The joint offensive was resumed on 25 February, when the Irgun destroyed some twenty RAF planes on the ground at Lydda, Qastina and Kfar Sirkin, causing damage variously estimated at anything from £750,000 to £2,000,000. The war against the railways and the police continued through March. On the night of 26 April, the Stern

Gang raised British anger and frustration to a climax when it murdered six paratroopers in their beds in a Tel Aviv encampment. Four others were wounded. The GOC, Lieutenant-General John D'Arcy, reported to the chiefs of staff in London that if similar attacks occurred, he would not be able to restrain his men, some of whom had already gone on the rampage in the streets of Netanya. The Hebrew Resistance mounted its last concerted operations in June. The Irgun caused £100,000 worth of damage to railway rolling stock. Palmah sappers demolished ten of the eleven road and rail bridges linking Palestine to its neighbours. But the Sternists suffered another calamity when eleven of their fighters were killed and twenty captured on the way back from attacking the railway workshops in Haifa.

By 1946, the British had 80,000 troops and 20,000 policemen stationed in Palestine, where the Jewish population was barely 600,000. Yet they had no answer to the campaign of sabotage and terror conducted by the 5,000 or so fighters available to the Hebrew Resistance Movement. 'The Mandate became a garrison State under internal siege,' J. Bowyer Bell wrote in his study of the Irgun and Stern Gang, 'and the garrison, despite its size, equipment and determination, proved ineffectual and self-defeating.' The Sixth Airborne Division, veterans of Normandy and Arnhem, provided the main British muscle, but the Red Berets were not trained to deal with urban guerrillas who melted into an increasingly sympathetic landscape. The army was hamstrung. All-out war on the *Yishuv* was unthinkable in the shadow of the Holocaust. In any case the Americans would not tolerate it. The argument went round in circles. The administration in Jerusalem contended that the only answer was a political settlement. The army agreed, but was not prepared to have its nose tweaked until one came along. After the 'night of the bridges' and the Irgun's abduction of five British officers from a Tel Aviv club as hostages for two Irgun men sentenced to death, Field Marshal Bernard Montgomery, the Chief of the Imperial General Staff, persuaded the Cabinet to act. The army, he said after visiting Palestine, was fully prepared for 'a war against a fanatical and cunning enemy'. The Cabinet agreed that it could 'no longer tolerate a position in which the authority of government was set at nought'. By now the British appreciated that their enemy was not just the fringe fighters of the Irgun and the Stern Gang. The High Commissioner, Sir Alan Cunningham, was authorized to crush the 'more extreme elements' in the Jewish Agency, who were thought to be controlling terrorism through the Haganah.

What the British called 'Operation Agatha' and the Jews 'Black Saturday' began at dawn on 29 June 1946. Every available soldier and policeman was mobilized for a concerted swoop on the Jewish Agency headquarters and other offices in Jerusalem, and twenty-five settlements elsewhere in the land; 2,718 Jews were detained, among them such leading lights as Moshe Sharett, Dov Yosef and Rabbi Yehuda Leib Fishman; and a Haganah arsenal was unearthed at Kibbutz Yagur, south-east of Haifa. A curfew was declared throughout Jewish Palestine. Yet the operation was not the un-qualified success Montgomery had sought. Ben-Gurion, the biggest fish of them all, was in Paris beyond the reach of his net. The Haganah comman-der, Moshe Sneh, profited from a last-minute intelligence warning and went into hiding. His two deputies, Yisrael Galili and Yitzhak Sadeh, the founder of the Palmah, evaded detection. And the Irgun and Stern Gang were left untouched. This was one time when Begin did not regret the dissidents' lack of rural bases in *kibbutzim* and *moshavim*, the Labour movement's collective and co-operative villages. The British did not know where to find them. The failure of Black Saturday was that it did not in itself induce Weizmann and other moderates to form an alternative leader-ship, and that it did not undermine the unity of the Resistance Movement. Most of the *Yishuv* felt that something had to be done in reply. The question was what. Golda Meir, one of the handful of political leaders left at liberty, proposed a campaign of civil disobedience. Moshe Sneh and Menachem Begin had more spectacular ambitions.

Begin was concerned about the psychological rather than the strategic effect Black Saturday would have on the *Yishuv*. Despite their losses in manpower and weapons, the Haganah and Palmah had not been neutralized. There was more reason than ever for an active common front with the Irgun and the Sternists. But Black Saturday was a stunning display of British might. Begin was worried that it would sow defeatism among the Jews, and defeatism was fatal to any war of liberation. 'We realized that Jewish self-confidence could be restored only by a successful counter-attack.'

The Irgun commander had just the plan up his sleeve. Earlier in the year, Gidi Paglin, his inventive operational expert, had proposed sabotaging the King David Hotel, whose southern wing housed the headquarters of the British administration, with the military police and special investiga-tions branch in an annexe. The rest of the six-storey King David, opened in 1932 by Egyptian Jewish investors as the first modern luxury hotel in Jerusalem, remained the social magnet of the mandate, a place for cocktails and intrigue, celebrated by Chips Channon, who stayed there as a British MP in 1941, as 'next to the Ritz in Paris, surely the world's best hotel'. In the spring of 1946 the Haganah had vetoed Paglin's plan as too provocative. When Begin resubmitted it two days after Black Saturday, Sneh gave his blessing. 'Operation Malonchik' (from the Hebrew word for hotel – *malon* – with a Yiddish diminutive, later shortened for greater security to 'Operation Chick') was adopted as one of the three prongs of the *Yishuv*'s retaliation. The Stern Gang would bomb the nearby David Brothers building, which housed the government information office, and the Haganah would raid the British arsenal at Bat Galim, in Haifa, and take back the arms captured at Yagur. The Sternist operation was codenamed 'Your Slave and Redeemer' and the Haganah raid 'Return the Lost Property'. Sneh justified each as an eye for an eye, an assault on the British Government in return for an attack on the Jewish Government. The three plans were endorsed by the top-secret X Committee, which supervised the Hebrew Resistance on behalf of the Jewish Agency, though its five members were simply told that 'an important government building' would be hit, not which building.

Both Begin and Yisrael Galili agree that the objective at the King David was to humiliate the British, not to kill them. 'The aim', says Galili, who was Sneh's deputy and flatmate at the time, 'was to sabotage a building which was the secretariat building and army headquarters, in reaction to Black Saturday. This was daring, audacious, a great danger, a blow at the nerve centre. It was not intended to destroy the King David Hotel, and certainly not to cause victims.'[8] From the start, Paglin was ordered to allow enough time for people in the secretariat and the hotel to get out.

There is, however, an unbridgeable gap between the Irgun and Haganah accounts of the technical consultations that followed between Paglin and Yitzhak Sadeh. According to Begin, Paglin proposed giving the British forty-five minutes' notice, while Sadeh suggested only fifteen minutes. They compromised on thirty minutes. The Irgun maintains that Sadeh pressed Paglin to increase the explosive charge he intended placing in the hotel basement. The Haganah, it is said, wanted to ensure that the British did not have time to cart away hundreds of incriminating documents they had seized from the Jewish Agency.

This version is roundly rejected by Galili (he and Begin were the only material witnesses to survive into the 1980s, and in the nature of such conspiracies no details were put in writing). The Haganah, he insists, had no interest in a bigger bang. It saw the operation as essentially symbolic. Sadeh was so concerned with minimizing casualties that he proposed detonating the bombs in the afternoon, when most of the staff would have gone home (this is not disputed). As for the documents, Galili dismisses as nonsense the idea that they were a factor in Haganah calculations.[9] After the event, both the Irgun and the Haganah had powerful motives for reducing their own share of the blame. It would not be surprising if they engaged in black propaganda, or at least put the best possible gloss on their respective roles. The Haganah case draws some reinforcement from British statements that they learned little they did not know already from the Jewish Agency papers, not least because they were desperately short of trustworthy (i.e. non-Jewish) Hebrew translators. A Jewish policeman, quoted in *The Palestine Triangle*, said: 'They had nobody else, so they had to use people like me, whose loyalty was to the Haganah, to work against the Haganah. We went through all the papers, but anything we found that was incriminating or might have harmed the Jewish Agency, we flushed down the lavatory. After two days all the drains at CID headquarters were totally blocked.'[10]

On 1 July, Begin received authorization for 'Operation Chick' and Paglin went on perfecting his elaborate scheme for infiltrating the Régence restaurant through a service entrance and a basement corridor running the whole length of the hotel. But on 17 July, for reasons that were never explained to Begin, the Haganah requested a postponement. Sneh had been visited in Tel Aviv by Meyer Weisgal, Chaim Weizmann's bustling, intensely loyal personal assistant. Weizmann evidently knew that something was afoot, though he had not been informed specifically what was planned. In a fading, heroic effort to control the direction of Zionist strategy, Weizmann drew on the last ounce of his authority.

Weisgal read from a prepared text:

We are standing on the edge of a precipice ... If you continue your operations this will be the equivalent of a declaration of war on Great Britain. I am certain Britain will fight back and everything we have worked for may be destroyed. I am still the president of the Zionist movement, and in democracies it is generally accepted that the president is the commander of all the armed forces. ... I am now using this authority. I demand that you stop all operations by all three underground groups.[11]

Weizmann threatened to resign immediately and publish the reasons why, if Sneh did not comply with this ultimatum. At the very least, he insisted that all operations be halted until the Jewish Agency executive, due to meet in Paris in August, could debate the best way to carry on the struggle. Although Sneh did not share Weizmann's misgivings and was eager to act, he had no choice. This was the first time that the old leader had intervened directly in a Haganah matter. Galili advised Sneh to go straight back to the X Committee. 'This was outside proper channels,' he explains. 'We could have played along, we could have said that Weizmann should turn to Ben-Gurion. But this was too serious a matter to play with formalities. It had to be brought to the X Committeee, the committee had to decide.' Although Sneh still did not tell the committee precisely which government building was to be hit, he spelled out Weizmann's objections.

One committee member, the future Prime Minister Levi Eshkol, changed sides and authorization for the three operations was rescinded.

Begin knew nothing of these exchanges. Sneh simply asked for a delay. The Stern Gang was content to wait. Its planning was in any case behind schedule. Begin was restive. The longer the hiatus, the less chance there was of keeping the King David operation secret. He agreed twice to give Sneh more time, but his patience was running out. The Haganah commander was playing a devious and dangerous game, navigating between his own political masters and the Irgun. His loyalty was to one, but his fighting instincts were with the other. Evidently Sneh still hoped to change the official policy once he could talk to Ben-Gurion before the Paris executive meeting, but he did not trust Begin sufficiently to take him into his confidence. According to Galili, he did not want to alarm the Irgun commander.

> He did not tell the whole story. First of all, he didn't have to. He didn't have to tell Begin Zionist movement secrets, secrets of the organized *Yishuv*. But there was a more serious reason. He didn't want to discourage Begin. If Begin were discouraged by the fact that the Zionist movement was withdrawing from the struggle, he would draw far-reaching conclusions.[12]

Sneh's prevarication had precisely the effect he was trying to avoid. On 20 July, the Haganah commander advised Begin that the Jewish Agency was planning to announce its policy of non-co-operation with the British on 25 July. This was 'another reason' why no operations should be carried out before then. Begin did not respond, and on the morning of 22 July, Sneh sent a final one-sentence appeal: 'You should hold up for the time being the Jerusalem operation.'[13] But the Irgun was no longer taking orders.

The bombs, concealed in four milk churns, were already in Jerusalem. Too many people - in the Irgun, the Haganah and the Stern Gang - knew of the King David plan to keep it on ice much longer. As far as Begin was concerned, 'Operation Chick' had been approved by the Haganah. No one had told him it had been cancelled. Ya'acov Amrami, who had succeeded Eli Tavin as chief of intelligence, says the Irgun was 'fed up' with Sneh's postponements.

> We didn't know about Weizmann's ultimatum, but we knew that Weizmann was against the struggle with the British and was trying to minimize that struggle. We thought that they just wanted a postponement. We counted more on the fact that they asked us originally to do it. We didn't see any reason to postpone it. Sneh didn't explain why.[14]

Begin himself declined to go beyond what he wrote in *The Revolt*, where he offered no explanation for his rejection of the Haganah commander's request.

At 12.37 p.m. on Monday, 22 July 1946, six minutes ahead of schedule, 350 kilograms of TNT exploded in the empty Régence restaurant, blowing the central piles from under the southern wing of the King David Hotel. Fifty offices of the British civil and military administration collapsed in a roar of smoke and cement dust, masonry was hurled into the main road outside, killing and maiming passers-by. One British official was flung against the wall of the YMCA opposite the hotel, leaving a silhouette of blood and a severed head behind him. Rescue workers were still finding bodies a week later. The final casualty figures were announced on 31 July. Of the ninety-one dead, twenty-eight were British, forty-one Arabs, seventeen Jews, two Armenians, one Russian, one Greek and one Egyptian. There were forty-six wounded. More than half the dead were clerks, typists, messengers and other junior staff of the secretariat and the hotel. Menachem Begin was shocked by the casualties, but sprang to the defence of his men. Four decades later he still held the British responsible. They did not heed the warning given by telephone to the hotel switchboard. The Irgun's clandestine radio announced with typical Begin selectivity that it mourned the Jewish victims. It would not mourn the British dead, since Britain had not mourned the six million Jews who died in the Nazi Holocaust. 'And with this mourning and with this anger over the deep Jewish tragedy, we shall continue going our way, the way of suffering, the way of struggle.' The Irgun seemed not to have noticed that most of the dead were neither Jewish nor British, but Arab. In the words of Thurston Clarke, 'For the Irgun, the Arabs were invisible.'

There is now no doubt that the Irgun did transmit a warning, but it did not reach the British authorities in a form that they took seriously or at a time that would have allowed the staff to evacuate the hotel before the TNT went off. What happened that grim lunchtime was a tragedy of errors, but the Irgun and its commander cannot escape all responsibility. Whatever had been their experience in the past, any sabotage operation on such a scale may go wrong. Bombs detonate prematurely, messages are misdirected. Jerusalem had been plagued by false alarms. There could be no guarantee that this would not be treated as one more in the series. Monday was known to be the busiest day in the secretariat's week, coming as it did after the Moslem, Jewish and Christian sabbaths, and most staff did not leave for lunch before one o'clock. That is why the Haganah had suggested carrying out the operation later in the day, even though it would have increased the risks for Gidi Paglin's team.

The warning was telephoned to the King David by Adina Hai, a sixteen-year-old Jerusalem schoolgirl and Irgun courier. As soon as the sabotage squad withdrew from the hotel basement, she began her round. The commander of the operation, she says, gave a prearranged signal.

I went into a shop near the King David – it was either a perfumery or an optician, or perhaps both at once – and telephoned the King David. I said in Hebrew and English: 'This is the Jewish resistance. We have planted bombs, please vacate the place immediately. See, we warned you.' Then I ran across the road to King George Street. There was a telephone booth where there is a park now. I called the French consulate, which is opposite the side of the hotel. I told them in French that there was a bomb in the King David and asked them to open their windows so that it would cause no damage. Then I went to Jaffa Road, near the old bus station. I used the telephone in a paint shop and called the *Palestine Post*. I told them in Hebrew that we had planted bombs in the King David and had warned them. I asked the paper to warn them again. After that, I walked up Jaffa Road towards Mahaneh Yehuda. By the time I reached the police station there, there was an enormous blast. That was the King David explosion.[15]

Even for a teenage girl in a hurry, this odyssey would take the best part of half an hour, allowing for the three telephone calls. There is independent evidence that all three were received. Naim Nisan, the King David's *maître d'hotel*, testifies that he was summoned to the hotel telephone exchange.

The operator was very pale, white and shaking. He said this woman had phoned and said there is a bomb in the King David. I told him to calm down and not to create panic. I rushed to the manager, Mr (Max) Hamburger. He said it was very easy to say there's a bomb, there had been lots of calls. I said why take a chance, why not report it to the authorities. He picked up the phone and dialled directly to the British headquarters. Then he told me: 'Don't tell anyone. No one is going to evacuate the hotel.' He had asked the British: 'Shall I evacuate?' I don't know what they told him, but I presume they said no. That's why he told me not to tell anyone and no one is going to leave the hotel. After that, I went to resume my duties at the far end of the building, away from the Régence. I was there when the explosion took place.[16]

Nisan never asked Hamburger afterwards to whom he had spoken in the secretariat. 'He never talked about it, and I didn't open the subject again. He was very strict.' Nisan was an Iraqi Jew, who had worked for the royal family in Baghdad. Four years after the King David disaster, he married Adina Hai, but he was in no way involved with the Irgun. He knew Adina's uncle, but did not meet her till long afterwards. The essence of his story is confirmed by the assistant manager of the hotel, Emile Soutter, who at first dismissed the warning as a bomb hoax. Soutter, a Swiss Christian with a

British wife, has acknowledged being notified of the warnings on three occasions by the hotel operators.[17]

The other warnings are also confirmed by the *Palestine* (now the *Jerusalem*) *Post* and the French consulate, and a message passed on by the newspaper switchboard to the police is logged in CID records. A French soldier serving with the United Nations peacekeeping force in Southern Lebanon when Thurston Clarke's reconstruction was published in 1981 wrote to Adina Nisan. He said his father had been French consul in Jerusalem in 1946, and that he remembered the whole episode from his childhood.

With hindsight, it is clear that the British would have been warned more expeditiously if Adina Hai had telephoned directly to the secretariat and not only to the hotel switchboard. The secretariat number was not a secret. But the Irgun believed that a single call was the most efficient way of alerting both the hotel and the secretariat. Its Jerusalem commander, Yitzhak Avinoam, the man who gave Adina her orders, thought that an alarm had been installed at the hotel switchboard which, at the touch of a button, would deliver his message to the management and the British.[18] But unknown to the Irgun, the switchboard operators evidently did not have the authority to sound the alarm on their own initiative.

The question remains: when the British did hear of the warning, from Hamburger and from the police, why did they not evacuate the secretariat? The simplest answer is that by then it was too late. But there is more to it than that. As recently as 1976, Menachem Begin was still telling interviewers that the Chief Secretary, Sir John Shaw, had received the warning and responded with characteristic *hauteur*: 'I am here to give orders to the Jews, not to take orders from them.' The story was told to Begin within days of the disaster by Yisrael Galili of the Haganah. He in turn says that he heard it from a Haganah intelligence officer, who heard it from an American reporter, now dead. Shaw sued a small London Jewish newspaper for libel as early as 1948 when it published the story. He and his secretary, Marjorie King, swore on oath that they had received no warning. The paper withdrew the allegation rather than defend the action. It could produce no witness to the story. Shaw's wife, Josephine, contends that it was a lie to discredit Sir John and shift some of the blame from the Irgun,[19] but there is no evidence to prove that either. Shmuel Katz, Begin's propaganda chief, concedes in his history of the Irgun struggle that the story of Shaw's retort 'may be dismissed'.[20]

Nonetheless, someone in the administration did receive the warnings, and there was plenty of other information that something was amiss. That, perhaps, was the trouble. Paglin and his men had entered the hotel basement disguised as Arab workers. While they were setting the fuses in the Régence, a British major spotted them and raised the alarm. In the hue and cry, one of the Irgun men shot him. This incident was reported to British security, but it was assumed that he had tangled with Arab pilferers. Later, the Irgun detonated two small charges in Julian's Way, the main road outside the King David, to force the police to close the carriageway and thus reduce the risk of casualties. The bombs went off at half-cock, and simply added to the general confusion. In his fourth-floor office at the back of the hotel, Sir John Shaw heard these explosions, walked across the corridor to investigate, and concluded that it was business as usual, 1946 style. The police could look after it, he had better things to do. Adina Hai's warning, filtered as it was through the hotel and security networks, was not assessed in isolation. It was part of the prevailing chaos of Jerusalem, where bangs and shots, alarums and excursions had become routine. If there was a British security failure, it was a very human one. The British, their staff and visitors paid a heavy price for it.

They forfeited much of the initial sympathy, however, when a letter the new GOC, General Sir Evelyn Barker, issued to his troops, reached the press and the Zionists. It was written in anger, and Barker regreted circulating it, but it was seen as confirming the worst suspicions about British motives:

> No British soldier is to have any social intercourse with any Jew and any intercourse in the way of duty should be as brief as possible and kept strictly to business in hand. I appreciate that these measures will inflict some hardship on the troops, but I am certain that if my reasons are fully explained to them they will understand their propriety and will be punishing the Jews in a way the race dislikes as much as any by striking at their pockets and showing our contempt for them.

The King David attack intensified the British public's hostility to 'Jewish terrorism' but at the same time it reinforced the Government's conviction that a political solution had to be found. British prestige did suffer, and with it the will to go on ruling Palestine. In the Jewish camp, it signed the death warrant of united resistance. Moshe Sneh, the most activist of the Haganah commanders, was forced to resign. In Paris, Ben-Gurion acquiesced in a return to diplomacy, which included a formal acceptance of the principle of partition. Virtually all sabotage operations by the Haganah came to a halt for seventeen months. As Menachem Begin had foreseen, the Irgun and the Stern Gang were left to go it alone. That was one vindication he did not relish.

8
A Rope for a Rope

'May the Lord avenge their blood!' The jaded Jerusalem press corps was shaken out of its Sunday afternoon torpor by this imprecation echoing at the end of the weekly Cabinet communiqué on 14 February 1982. It could only have had one author: the man who had been Israel's Prime Minister for five years past, Menachem Begin. Although the handout began with the leave-taking of a veteran ambassador and an enigmatic survey of diplomatic and security affairs, this was no ordinary Cabinet. Clause three announced what in other circumstances might have been equally prosaic: the issue of a new set of stamps. But it was an exercise in piety as much as philately. The twenty stamps were dedicated 'to the memory of the martyrs of the generation of the establishment of the State of Israel'. For form's sake they included such national heroes as Hanna Senesh, the *kibbutz* poet who was executed by the Nazis after parachuting into occupied Europe, and Eli Cohen, the Damascus spy. But to no one's surprise, ten of the twenty portraits were of Irgun and Stern Gang fighters hanged by the British, and two of men who blew themselves up in the condemned cell.

Their old commander was settling a debt of honour. For Menachem Begin, these were the ultimate martyrs, the stars of his personal mythology. Far and above the Irgun and other soldiers who fell in battle, Begin holds them in awe. These were the men, he rhapsodized in *The Revolt*, who passed the test:

There is no glorious battle, no storming assault. There are only thoughts – thoughts of the time that is running out with every tick of the clock. And thoughts beyond time. The days are long, the nights longer. There is too much time to think. There is something and somebody that crops up. The voice of an old mother, the voice of a young betrothed, distant yet clearly heard. The crimson clothes in which the hangmen have dressed him are an ever-present reminder that the number of his days has been set, that the sun rising beyond the dim cell is not driving away the night but is bringing it closer, the infinite night. Here there can be no swift subjugation of the instinct of self-preservation. The sickening struggle with it is continuous; it begins all over again every

74

morning, every hour and every minute when he lies down and when he gets up, and as he paces the lonely and locked cell.[1]

The test was not just one of courage, but of discipline and commitment. 'They went to the gallows', Ya'acov Amrami, the Irgun intelligence chief, explains, 'because they didn't recognize British rule. At least some could have saved themselves if they had accepted the jurisdiction of the British courts. They were not forced to reject it, they were free to choose.'[2] Dov Gruner, the most dedicated of them, tore up a power of attorney he had signed to permit a last-minute appeal. These were martyrs in the most literal sense, men who chose to die for a cause. Their sacrifice appealed to the romantic and the ideologue in Begin, the commander and the spectator. They behaved like characters in a Jabotinsky novel, instructing their judges and singing *Hatikva* on the scaffold. When Aliza Begin died in November 1982, she was buried on the Mount of Olives near the graves of Meir Feinstein and Moshe Barazani, who cheated the hangman with a smuggled grenade in the Jerusalem central prison. After he was elected Prime Minister in 1977, Begin directed in his will that he and his wife be buried beside them.

As commander of the Irgun, Begin valued the lives of his fighters. Before approving any operation, he insisted that the plan must include a viable escape route. Yet he appreciated that sometimes they would be challenged, some would die or be maimed, others would be captured and even exiled. That was the price of the revolt. If the struggle was worthwhile, so was the sacrifice. But Begin would not tolerate the calculated humiliation of the rope or the whip. In the diaspora, Jews had suffered such indignities in silence, but they would not do so in their ancient homeland. Begin remembered as a child being forced to witness the public flogging of Jewish leaders in Brest-Litovsk at the order of a Polish general. 'I was seven years old at the time, but the horror of that degrading scene has never faded from my mind.'

To the British, hanging and whipping were routine, if extreme, methods for suppressing colonial rebellion. They hanged infinitely more Arabs than Jews in Palestine. But alone among subject troublemakers, the Irgun Zvai Leumi retaliated in kind. It stopped the hanging and the whipping, by hanging and whipping British officers and sergeants. It returned humiliation for humiliation, not just on individual soldiers, but on the entire regime. The effrontery still rankles. Three decades later, Margaret Thatcher was reported to have told another Commonwealth premier that she could never shake the hand of a man responsible for hanging two British sergeants (yet she did receive Menachem Begin at 10 Downing Street).

The Irgun's first threat of reprisal paid off. Two of its men, Michael Ashbel and Yosef Simhon, were captured on their way to hospital after being wounded in an arms raid on the Sarafand army camp on 7 March 1946. The Irgun squad had penetrated the base disguised as British paratroopers, but was spotted when one man was too greedy and tried to wrest a Vickers machine-gun from the top of a tank. The party retreated in disorder. Ashbel, the poet of the Irgun, and Simhon were sentenced to death. The Irgun responded by kidnapping six British officers, five in a Tel Aviv club, one in Jerusalem. The latter, to Begin's lasting shame, escaped. The authorities clamped a curfew on Tel Aviv and began searching from house to house. Begin announced that the Irgun would 'answer gallows with gallows'. Negotiations were conducted through Jewish intermediaries. As a gesture of goodwill, the Irgun released two of the officers, giving them each a pound note as compensation for any damage they had suffered. The officers reported that they had been well treated. When the two Irgun men were reprieved, the remaining British hostages were dumped in the middle of Tel Aviv in a packing-case. They emerged, smartly turned out with their uniforms freshly pressed, to derision from the passers-by. A bargain had been struck and kept.

The next such confrontation ended less happily, but again in victory for the Irgun. Binyamin Kimche, a seventeen-year-old Irgun fighter, was sentenced to fifteen years' prison and eighteen lashes for carrying arms. The Irgun retorted: 'If you whip us, we shall whip you.' Nonetheless, Kimche was beaten. Begin was true to his word. A British major and three non-commissioned officers were abducted in Tel Aviv, Netanya and Rishon le Zion. Each received eighteen lashes before being set free. The Irgun communiqué, published under the emblem of the two banks of the Jordan and a rifle with the slogan 'Only Thus', underlined the message: 'If the oppressors dare in the future to abuse the bodies and the human and national honour of Jewish youths, we shall no longer reply with the whip. We shall reply with fire.' The British swallowed their pride. A second Irgun youth who had been sentenced with Kimche was spared the whip, and the British flogged no more Jews or Arabs for the rest of their unhappy sojourn in the Promised Land. At least one British tommy was disappointed. He had scrawled on an Irgun notice warning every officer in the British army that he was liable to be whipped, 'Don't forget my sergeant-major.'

The rope took more stopping. Seven of Begin's men were to be hanged before its rule was brought to a halt. Two British sergeants whose only crime was their nationality and their presence in Palestine had first to join their company on a makeshift gallows. In an atmosphere of increasingly audacious terrorism, Attlee's Government and the administration in Jerusalem were under intense public pressure to demonstrate their authority. Dov Gruner, a twenty-eight-year-old Hungarian Jewish immigrant who had been wounded twice while serving in the British army, became a symbol of Irgun defiance and of British resolve.

Gruner was captured at the end of an arms raid on the Ramat Gan police station on 23 April 1946. An Irgun team had entered the building disguised as British soldiers bringing in a batch of Arab prisoners. When nobody could find a key, they blew open the armoury, thus alerting a Bren-gunner on the roof and a policeman who telephoned for reinforcements. In the unsought battle, the Irgun lost three dead. Gruner's jaw was shattered by a bullet, and he was more dead than alive when the army picked him up. After a series of operations, he was fit enough to be brought for trial in Jerusalem in January 1947. Explaining why he refused to accept the court's right to try him, he accused Britain of transforming *Eretz Yisrael* into a military base and stealing it from the Jewish people:

> Nothing has therefore remained of the legal basis of your rule, which now rests on one principle only: brute force. The bayonet and a reign of terror disguised ·as so-called laws. These laws are drafted by the bearers of the bayonets. They promulgate them, and they enforce them contrary to the fundamental rights of man, contrary to the wishes of the locai population and contrary to international law.

When the three military judges sentenced him to hang, he sang the Zionist anthem from the dock. Gruner preferred life to death, but on his terms, not those of his prosecutors. The Irgun prisoners drew a distinction between martyrdom and suicide. They wanted to be rescued or reprieved, but not at the price of appealing for mercy. The Irgun posted a warning, less explicit than before: 'Execution of prisoners of war is premeditated murder. We warn the British regime of blood against the commission of this crime.' Again, Begin's first response was to kidnap British hostages. Major H. A. Collins, identified as an intelligence officer, but in fact a retired soldier who had gone into business, was picked up from his Jerusalem tea-table. Judge Ralph Windham was abducted in his Tel Aviv court. The second kidnapping seems to have disturbed the British more than the first, though Begin's contention that this was because of Windham's link with the aristocracy is open to doubt. After first deciding to hang Gruner regardless, the Government played for time, announcing an indefinite postponement to allow him to appeal to the Privy Council. This was the turning-point in the case. The Irgun was outmanoeuvred. Begin saw no value in continuing to hold the hostages, especially when Judge Windham's hiding-place was far from secure. But when it became clear that the British were still determined to hang Gruner and three others – Yehiel Drezner, Mordehai Alkoshi and Eliezer Kashani – the Irgun was too slow in putting together a rescue operation. With the whole country placed under martial law, the four condemned men were transferred from Jerusalem to Acre fortress, where they were hanged behind a legal smoke-screen on 16 April 1947. A week later, Feinstein and Barazani, of the Irgun and Stern Gang respectively, pulled the pin on a grenade which had been smuggled to them inside an orange. They had planned to take the hangman with them to the grave, but changed their minds when the prison rabbi insisted on accompanying them to the scaffold.

That summer saw the Irgun's greatest triumph – the storming of the Acre fortress, an apparently impregnable Crusader keep – but also the anguish of more executions and the reluctant decision to hang the sergeants. The fortress, in the middle of an Arab town, was breached by an elaborate combined operation from the inside and the out. In all, 251 prisoners – 131 Arabs and 120 Jews – escaped through the hole blown in the thick stone wall. But the losses were heavy; fifteen Jews died in the chase and fifteen others were captured. One of the dead was Michael Ashbel, who had been saved from the gallows a year earlier. Three of the new prisoners – Avshalom Haviv, Meir Nakar and Ya'acov Weiss – were put on trial for their lives. One of them told the judges:

> We know there will be one outcome of this fight. Our people will attain its freedom and its enslaver will disappear from the land. That is why we are calm. More, we are happy. For there can be no greater happiness than to give our lives for a great ideal and to know, to know absolutely, that we are among those who are directly bringing about its fulfilment.

Begin knew that if they were to be saved, the Irgun would have to take hostages of rank. But the British had been on the alert since the previous executions, and the quest was hard. Eventually, the hunters had to settle for two sergeants of the intelligence corps, walking home in civilian clothes from an unauthorized night out in the seaside resort of Netanya. Sergeants Clifford Martin and Mervyn Paice were clubbed, chloroformed and whisked away to a specially-prepared hideout under a Netanya diamond-polishing factory. Their jailor was the Irgun's operation chief, Gidi Paglin. The British put the entire population of the Jewish town under house arrest, 1,427 of them were interrogated, but the sergeants remained undetected in their stifling bunker with its canvas latrine and bottled oxygen. On 29 July 1947, the three Irgun prisoners, Haviv, Nakar and Weiss, were led to the gallows in Acre. Within hours, Sergeants Martin and Paice followed them. After consulting Begin and assuring him that it could be done, Paglin hanged them from a rafter in the deserted diamond factory. Their bodies were taken to a eucalyptus grove, where they were left suspended from two trees. Paglin laid a mine nearby, hoping to kill a third soldier to level the score. When the British were slow in finding the bodies, the Irgun told the police where to look, adding a warning that there were mines. Paglin did not want to kill any Jewish policemen who might be sent to the spot. Thus warned, the British dragged the bodies clear with hooks and ropes, assuming that the bodies themselves were booby-trapped. To add to the horror of the recovery party of soldiers, police, reporters and photographers, the first body triggered Paglin's mine as it fell and was blown to pieces. The tree holding the second body was uprooted by the blast and a Royal Engineers captain directing the operation was wounded in the face and shoulder.[3]

Like the King David bombing and the Acre break-out, the hanging of the sergeants reverberated around the world. Yet Menachem Begin, who gave the go-ahead, was strangely reticent about the decision. 'The next day,' he wrote in *The Revolt*, 'the two Britons were hanged. We repaid our enemy in kind. We had warned him again and again and again. He had callously disregarded our warnings. He forced us to answer gallows with gallows. But the days were black as starless nights.' Beyond that, in less than a page devoted to the hanging, there is only recrimination against the British for carrying out their 'senseless executions'.

But the decision to kill the sergeants was not taken lightly. Begin went to extraordinary lengths to consult his colleagues in the Irgun high command, though there is no evidence that he was against the hangings. Ya'acov Amrami suspects that he was not sure what to do:

> He asked everyone their views. He didn't want to influence others by committing himself. I was for it. Six or seven of us were consulted – separately, or two at a time. There was no one who was against. I wouldn't say there were people who had misgivings. It was a nuance of degree. Some had no doubt at all, some had doubts but said yes. Begin wanted to make it easier for anybody to say no, or express reservations.
>
> Consulting all the leadership like this was exceptional. Usually it was enough for a majority of those who were available to decide. Afterwards, I never heard Begin say he had doubts. If he had been against it, he would have fought for his opinion. There was nothing to indicate at the time that he was against it. Paglin was the strongest for the hanging – they were his fighters the British hanged.[4]

Thirty-five years later, an Israeli researcher discovered that Sergeant Martin had an Egyptian Jewish mother. His father had married her while posted as a colonial civil servant in Sudan. According to rabbinic law, this would make the sergeant a Jew. An aide to Menachem Begin, by then Israel's Prime Minister, was asked whether it would have made any difference if Martin had revealed this at the time. His answer was 'Probably not.' The underground had, after all, killed other Jews it considered traitors.

The hanging of the sergeants achieved its aim. No more Jewish terrorists were executed, though five innocent Jews died when bands of British soldiers and policemen ran riot in Tel Aviv in reaction to the hanging. Begin rested his case on the assumption that the execution of the sergeants saved the lives of dozens of his men and those of the Stern Gang in the last year of the British mandate. Yet it is perhaps no coincidence that, as Prime Minister, Begin steadily resisted demands from his own right wing to execute Arab terrorists. He had had enough of hangings, and he knew the value of martyrdom.

9
Out of the Wasps' Nest

The hanging of Sergeants Martin and Paice proved the last straw for British public and parliamentary opinion. The first reaction was one of anger. Anti-Jewish riots broke out in London, Liverpool, Manchester, Glasgow and other cities. But revulsion soon gave way to questioning. Was Palestine worth the cost in British lives, prestige and interests? In the summer of 1947, the answer hardened into an emphatic no.

The Colonial Secretary, Arthur Creech-Jones, acknowledged in the House of Commons on 12 August that 'among the British public there is a fierce questioning as to the burden and cost to Britain, and the tragedy involved by Britain continuing to shoulder this international liability'.[1] MPs, recalled from their summer recess to debate the sergeants' hanging, were almost unanimous in demanding an early withdrawal of British forces. In a speech to an Opposition Conservative Party gathering at Blenheim Palace, Winston Churchill said:

Nearly one hundred thousand British soldiers have been kept in Palestine, and £30 million or £40 million a year of our hard-earned money has been cast away there.... No British interest is involved in our retention of the Palestine Mandate. For nearly thirty years we have done our best to carry out an honourable and self-imposed task. A year ago, I urged the Government to give notice to the United Nations that we could and would bear the burden of insults and injuries no longer. But the Ministers only gaped in shameful indecision, and they are only gaping still.

Within the Labour Cabinet, Hugh Dalton wrote to the Prime Minister, Clement Attlee:

I am quite sure that the time has almost come when we might bring our troops out of Palestine altogether. The present state of affairs is not only costly to us in manpower and money, but is, as you and I agree, of no real value from the strategic point of view - you cannot in any case have a secure base on top of a wasps' nest - and it is exposing our young men, for no good purpose, to most abominable experience, and is breeding anti-Semites at a most shocking speed.

81

The British Middle East expert, Elizabeth Monroe, gave first place in her list of reasons for the 'enormous change' in Britain's position to the force of public opinion at home after the hanging of the sergeants:

> The British public had taken Palestine in its stride for years, and had looked on 'disturbances' and 'violence' there much as it had viewed 'the trouble' in Ireland – as an unpleasant experience that was part of the white man's burden. But on 1 August 1947, its attitude changed, and the cause of the change was the hanging of the two young sergeants whom Jewish terrorists executed as a reprisal. All home comment on that deed is different in tone from that on earlier terrorist acts, many of which caused greater loss of life – for instance, the blowing up of the King David Hotel. Picture papers frontpaged photographs of the hanged men; disgust was expressed at the placing of booby-traps on their bodies; liberal opinion was exercised over small outbursts of anti-Semitism in several British towns. At a most unsuitable moment, the event quickened anti-American feeling.[2]

On 2 August, the Foreign Secretary warned the American ambassador, Lewis Douglas, that Britain was 'disillusioned and disappointed by our thankless task as mandatory and might be forced to give up the charge'. The situation was poisoning relations between the US and Britain.[3]

Despite Churchill's charge of ministerial inertia, the Government had taken a first step towards abandoning the mandate five months before the sergeants were hanged. Ernest Bevin indicated to the Commons on 18 February that 'the only course now open to us is to submit the problem to the judgement of the United Nations'. The Foreign Secretary recognized that Britain could satisfy neither the Jews nor the Arabs – and that it could not impose a solution of its own. Bevin was still reluctant to admit the bankruptcy of his policy and return the mandate, but at the beginning of April Britain asked the UN to appoint a special committee to examine the options in Palestine and report to the General Assembly in the autumn. Harold Beeley, Bevin's Middle East expert, suspects that the initiative was Attlee's rather than the Foreign Secretary's.[4] On 31 August 1947, the UN Special Committee on Palestine recommended the end of the British mandate and the establishment of separate Jewish and Arab States. On 29 November, the General Assembly approved the partition by a two-thirds majority.

This was not the solution sought by Menachem Begin and the Irgun Zvai Leumi. On 26 June 1947, Begin had a cloak-and-dagger meeting with the UNSCOP chairman, Emil Sandström. The encounter, which conferred a measure of international recognition on the Irgun, was arranged through the good offices of an American journalist, Carter Davidson of the Associated Press, who was rewarded with the only eyewitness report of their three-hour discussion.

Sandström and Begin 'conversed quietly and amiably about Palestine's history, religion and politics', Davidson wrote in a dispatch delayed for a month until the UN team had left the Middle East. 'So affable was the conversation that it was Sandström who at last cautioned Begin: "The street is near. Should we not better lower our voices?" Begin chuckled: "It doesn't matter. Our men are there. They will tell us if we attract attention."

While sipping wine and nibbling fruit in the Tel Aviv home of the poet Ya'acov Cohen, the Irgun commander set out his aims. His programme called for Jewish sovereignty on both sides of the Jordan to be attained by the following means:

1 The abolition of British occupation in *Eretz Yisrael*.
2 The transfer of power to a democratic representative body of our people.
3 The repatriation to Palestine, with aid by an international body, of all Jews wishing to transfer.
4 The holding of democratic general elections after the repatriation is completed.
5 The obtaining of an international loan for the development of the soil for the use of both repatriate Hebrews and Arab peasants, who suffer from chronic want under the double yoke of serfdom and exploitation.

As Sandström got up to leave, Begin shook his hand and said: 'I wish you luck in your deliberations, but none of us have any illusions that your decision will cause us to give up the fight.'[5]

Partition was accepted grudgingly by David Ben-Gurion on behalf of the organized *Yishuv* and in his private capacity by Chaim Weizmann, the most persistent of the Zionist diplomats. But it was anathema to Begin, who proved true to his valedictory words to the UN committee. He fought the partition on the ground until the declaration of the State of Israel on 14 May 1948; in the Knesset for twenty-six years from the Opposition benches; and in government after 1977 by trying to make sure that the occupied West Bank could never be returned to Jordan.

Israeli opinion has long been divided over the contribution of the Irgun and Stern Gang to the establishment of the State. Under the Mapai interpretation of history, the 'dissidents' were dismissed as a minor irritant. The real work of nation-building was done by the Labour movement (led by the Mapai Party) and its middle-class and religious allies, the General Zionists and Mizrahi. The heirs of Jabotinsky were written out of the story. After the election of a Likud Government under Begin in 1977, the Revisionists (in both senses) came into their own, the pendulum swung the other way. Menachem Begin was the man who 'drove the British out of the land'. Ben Gurion and company were a lot of effete compromisers, men without vision and without the guts to fight the alien oppressor.

The new orthodoxy is as much a distortion as the old. It is clear from the British documents and debates that 'Jewish terror' played a significant part in undermining the will to stay in Palestine. Britain had other preoccupations, at home and abroad. Sterling was under pressure, fuel was in short supply after an exceptionally hard winter. India was on the brink of independence. Britain's strategic perspectives were changing with the beginning of the end of empire. The Government could not jeopardize the American alliance and financial assistance in the face of growing Soviet threats in Europe. Palestine became a liability especially since it did not, in Elizabeth Monroe's words, 'contribute a matter of life and death for the United Kingdom balance of payments or standard of living, or for Britain's military security or Commonwealth relations'. By 1947, the cost of maintaining law and order in Palestine was prohibitive. How long could Britain continue to keep 100,000 men tied up there? In any case, 100,000 was not enough to do the job. There seemed less and less profit in it. Neither the generals nor the politicians could find an acceptable answer to the sustained urban guerrilla campaign of the Irgun and the Stern Gang. There were no precedents to consult. They could not subdue the dissidents without crushing the *Yishuv* as a whole.

Meanwhile, young men were being killed far from home for no convincing reason. Britain was being mocked and humiliated. In the three years from 1945 to 1948, from the end of the world war to the departure of the last High Commissioner, 338 British subjects met violent deaths at the hands of Jewish groups. After the Haganah withdrew from the Hebrew Resistance Movement in July 1946, some ninety-nine Britons were killed in the six weeks from 1 October to 18 November. In January 1947, some 2,000 men, women and children were evacuated to Britain, and the remaining civilians were housed behind barbed-wire in 'security compounds'. In March, more than twenty Britons, including twelve officers hit when their Jerusalem club was blown up by the Irgun, were killed and thirty wounded in a single night. The Sternists set the Haifa oil refinery blazing for three weeks. In London, the Chiefs of Staff recommended selective imposition of martial law, but they acknowledged that 'to enforce restrictions throughout the whole country simultaneously, would be beyond the capabilities of the forces now available, and imposition of martial law would add a further burden without compensating advantages'. As Nicholas Bethell put it:

Since each of the 338 was killed in a personal way, either singly with bullets or in a small group with a bomb, their deaths made as much impact on British public opinion, perhaps more impact, than the heavier British casualties of the Second World War, which were endured with fortitude and resolution. The 338, it seemed, had died quite unnecessarily. Political pressure to bring the killings to a halt was therefore all the stronger.[6]

In May 1947, the American consul in Jerusalem reported to Washington that

with its officials attempting to administrate from behind masses of barbed-wire, in heavily-defended buildings, and with those same officials (minus wives and children) living in pathetic seclusion in security zones, one cannot escape the conclusion that the Government of Palestine is a hunted organization with little hope of ever being able to cope with conditions in this country as they exist today.

Michael J. Cohen, an Israeli historian with roots on the Left of Zionist politics, concluded after an exhaustive study of British and American documents: 'History would seem to indicate that the IZL's draconian methods, morally reprehensible as they were, were decisive in transforming the evacuation option of February 1947 into a determined resolve to give up the burdens of the mandate by August that year.'[7]

But the contribution of the Irgun and the Stern Gang cannot be assessed in a vacuum. The Haganah was waging a different kind of campaign which was no less damaging to Britain's reputation and self-esteem, and which incidentally projected the Jewish cause in a much more sympathetic light. Between 1945 and May 1948, it brought some 70,000 Jews illegally to Palestine. Of these, 51,500 were intercepted by the Royal Navy and interned in Cyprus. The most celebrated of the illegal immigrant boats, *Exodus 1947*, set sail from the small French port of Port-de-Bouc in July that year with a cargo of 4,500 Jews. It was shadowed across the Mediterranean by the RAF and the navy. With the Cyprus camps already overflowing, Bevin adopted a punitive policy of sending the blockade-runners back where they came from. The *Exodus* was boarded by marines on 18 July off the coast near Gaza. The Haganah pursued a dual strategy of resistance and public relations. The fight with the marine boarding-party was relayed to the shore by powerful transmitters. Rather than attempt to land at least some of the passengers, the Haganah decided to play to an international gallery. Ike Aranne, the ship's captain, was ordered to use it 'as a big demonstration with banners to show how poor and weak and helpless we were, and how cruel the British were'. The British acted out the Haganah script with an exuberance beyond the Haganah's dreams. Having brought the *Exodus* under control, they sailed it into Haifa port, where it was a sitting duck for the world's cameramen and reporters. Emil Sandström, the UNSCOP chairman, and two colleagues, watched its arrival at the invitation of Abba Eban, a future Israeli Foreign Minister then working for the Jewish Agency. Eban wrote in his memoirs that the immigrants had decided not to accept banishment with docility. Winston Churchill had accused Bevin of waging 'a squalid war' against the Jews.

Eban commented:

> If anyone had wanted to know what Churchill meant, he would have found out by watching British soldiers using rifle-butts, hosepipes and tear-gas against the survivors of the death camps. Men, women and children were forcibly taken off to prison ships, locked in cages below-decks and sent out of Palestine waters. . . . While Sandström, Brilej and Granados watched this gruesome operation, I awaited their return to Jerusalem with great tension. When they came back, they were pale with shock. I could see that they were preoccupied with one point alone: if this was the only way that the British mandate could continue, it would be better not to continue it at all.[8]

The British compounded their folly by shipping the displaced persons back to Port-de-Bouc, where, despite a French offer of asylum, most of the 4,500 refused to go ashore. The international press had another field day reporting and photographing the deteriorating sanitary conditions. The French Communist daily, *Humanité*, called the three British vessels 'a floating Auschwitz'. Bevin then made his biggest blunder of all, sending the Jews back to Germany. His new policy proved a public relations disaster for Britain, especially in the United States, and a triumph for the Zionists. 'The Zionists had made pawns of the passengers,' Elizabeth Monroe wrote. 'The British Government, immensely provoked, committed the same wrong, and its act of sending Jews back to a former charnel house horrified millions, as no other destination would have done.'

At this period, illegal immigration was a monopoly of the Haganah and the Jewish Agency. According to their own highest estimates, the Revisionists brought 40,000 Jews to Palestine from Europe between 1937 and 1944, but their activity then ceased. They concentrated instead on the armed struggle of the Irgun and the Sternists.[9]

Despite a strident propaganda campaign by the Revisionists in America, the mainstream Zionists also had a monopoly of diplomatic activity, in London and New York as well as in Palestine itself. If it is true that Britain would not have surrendered the mandate at the time it did without the spur of the dissidents, it is equally true that there would have been no majority for the United Nations resolution of 29 November 1947 without the superhuman lobbying in Washington and New York of the despised diplomats. Similarly, without the long, patient pioneering of the Labour Zionists and their allies, there would have been no Jewish State in the making, no infrastructure of sovereignty. Without *kibbutzim* and *moshavim* in the Negev and Galilee, the borders of Israel would not have been delineated as they were. There would have been no industry and no agriculture.

Jabotinsky's biographer and collaborator, Joseph B. Schechtman, wrote:

> Of all the Palestinian Zionist formations, the Revisionist Party and its affiliates were the only one who (with few minor exceptions) possessed no settlements, economic enterprises, or institutions of their own. This enabled them to preserve the integrity of their Zionist ideal and their freedom of action, making them the militant vanguard of the *Yishuv*. The price they paid for it was, however, very high: they were the have-nots of the Jewish community, and their economic poverty more than once affected their political chances.[10]

Again, it was the Haganah which provided the nucleus of a Jewish army capable of blocking and turning the invasion of five Arab armies. The Irgun and the Stern Gang were trained for guerrilla strikes, for sabotage and reprisal raids, but not for conventional warfare. In mid-1947, the Haganah had a nominal strength of 43,000 men and women, but 32,000 belonged to the static 'Home Guard', ill-trained and poorly armed. The Haganah had a 'Field Corps' of 8,000 part-time volunteers, who trained regularly, and the full-time Palmah, with 3,100 men and women, which provided most of the senior commanders for the infant Israeli army. With the approach of war, Haganah forces were organized into field battalions and underwent combat training. Four regional headquarters were set up, but by the end of 1947 the Haganah was still desperately under-equipped. It could muster only 17,600 assorted rifles, 3,700 sub-machine-guns, and fewer than 1,000 machine-guns. The Irgun is estimated to have had about 2,000 members at this time, but only half of them had any military training. The Stern Gang numbered a few hundred.[11] Ben-Gurion's fighters had prepared for a war of independence, Begin's conducted a revolt against the British. Neither can, or should, be written off.

10
As in Deir Yassin...

Accept my congratulations on this splendid act of conquest. Convey my regards to all the commanders and soldiers. We shake your hands. We are all proud of the excellent leadership and the fighting spirit in this great attack. We stand to attention in memory of the slain. We lovingly shake the hands of the wounded. Tell the soldiers: you have made history in Israel with your attack and your conquest. Continue thus until victory. As in Deir Yassin, so everywhere, we will attack and smite the enemy. God, God, Thou hast chosen us for conquest.[1]

Menachem Begin, who dispatched this exultant order of the day to his Jerusalem command, knew little at the time of what had happened before, during or after the massacre in Deir Yassin, an Arab village on the north-western rim of Jerusalem, on 9 April 1948. But in a broadcast two days later over the Irgun Zvai Leumi's *Voice of Fighting Zion*, he celebrated it as 'a mighty battle in which, for the first time, soldiers of the IZL, Lehi and Palmah took part'. For more than three decades, the Irgun commander remained firm in his conviction that Deir Yassin was a conventional military operation in which his men fought bravely and honourably, tried to keep civilian casualties to a minimum, and lived up to the ethics in which they had been raised. His latest interviews, like his earliest proclamations, denounced Ben-Gurion and anyone else who suggested otherwise as 'narrow-minded hypocrites', if not downright liars. This consistency is impressive evidence of Begin's loyalty to his fighters, and perhaps also of his abiding paranoia. It is increasingly remote from what actually took place on that Judean hilltop one Friday morning a month before Britain washed its hands of the Palestine mandate.

Deir Yassin, a village of 800-1,000 inhabitants who made their living from quarrying and stone-crushing, continues to haunt Menachem Begin and the State he helped to create. By accident or design, Jewish or Arab, Deir Yassin sounded an alarm, speeding the flight of 700,000 Arabs from what soon became Israel. The name has never lost its resonance. Among Zionists, the story is still taboo, documents and photographs remain classified long after they can do harm to Israel's security. Politicians and writers of both Zionist camps find it prudent to close ranks. There are skeletons in everyone's cupboard. Even though Ben-Gurion was quick to condemn the massacre and send a telegram of condolences to the Emir Abdullah in Amman, the Haganah was already busy covering up the more horrendous evidence. A newsreel cameraman shot 400 feet of the later stages of the slaughter, but made the mistake of bragging about it to a colleague who worked undercover for Palmah intelligence. The colleague drove to Lydda airport and switched the film before it could be flown to London. Movietone News received 400 feet of Jerusalem cloud formations.

The Arabs of Deir Yassin believed they were safe. Despite the undeclared war that broke out after the United Nations voted to partition Palestine, they put their faith in the non-belligerency pact their *muhtar* (village headman) had struck with the neighbouring Jewish suburb of Givat Shaul. 'There was an agreement that there would be no problems between them,' explains Muhammad Arif Sammour, a retired schools inspector who was a twenty-six-year-old teacher at the time of the massacre. 'If any of their young people attacked Deir Yassin, the Jews would catch them and stop them. If anyone from Deir Yassin attacked Givat Shaul, the Arabs would stop him. There were no problems between Jews and Arabs there at the time.'[2] To the Haganah, Deir Yassin was a passive Arab village that would have to be brought under Jewish control sooner or later, but not necessarily by conquest. It had strategic value for two reasons. In the hands of an enemy, its hilltop position would make it a danger to the Jewish suburbs of Givat Shaul, Beit Hakerem, Yafeh Nof and Bayit V'gan. And the Haganah was planning to lay an airstrip along the ridge between Givat Shaul and Deir Yassin, which would keep communications between Jerusalem and the coast open in an emergency. In the case of Abu Ghosh, another 'neutral' village four miles down the road towards Tel Aviv, the Arabs agreed to keep out of the way for the duration of the war and were allowed to come back afterwards. Something comparable might have been arranged for Deir Yassin.

The Irgun and the Stern Gang had other ideas. As they emerged from the underground, they were eager to prove their mettle, to show the Haganah and the Arabs that they were not just street-fighters. They were worried too that Ben-Gurion might acquiesce in the internationalization of Jerusalem, as proposed by the UN, or at least do a deal with Abdullah. Yet the dissidents were aware of how few men and arms they could deploy and of their lack of battle-training. Yehuda Lapidot, a senior Irgun officer, now a Hebrew University science professor, estimates that his group had no more than 300 fighters in Jerusalem and the Sternists barely 100.[3] In testimony deposited in the Jabotinsky archives in the mid-1950s, Lapidot said that the original idea to attack Deir Yassin came from the Irgun operations officer in Jerusalem, Yehoshua Goldshmidt: 'The reason was mainly economic. That is to capture booty in order to maintain the bases which we had then established with very poor resources. The main idea, despite this, remained the conquest of the village by force of arms, something which was then unknown in the country, and became a turning-point in Jewish military operations.'

The Sternists, who were looking for a reconciliation with the Irgun, jumped at the proposal, which was referred to a joint meeting of senior combat officers, four from each group. According to Lapidot, who was one of them, the Stern Gang suggested turning the operation into a punitive raid:

> Apart from the military discussion, the Lehi put forward a proposal to liquidate the residents of the village after the conquest, in order to show the Arabs what happens when the IZL and the Lehi set out together on an operation, and for another main reason – it would cause a great uproar throughout the land and would be an important turning-point in the course of the battles. The clear aim was to break the Arab morale and to raise somewhat the morale of the Jewish community in Jerusalem, which had been hit hard time after time, especially recently by the desecration of Jewish bodies which fell into Arab hands.[4]

Benzion Cohen, the Irgun commander of the operation who was wounded in the early exchanges, added: 'When it comes to prisoners, women, old people and children, there were differences of opinion, but the majority was for liquidation of all the men in the village and any other force that opposed us, whether it be old people, women or children.' The wish for revenge, he said, was strong after Arab blows to Gush Etzion and Atarot, two Jewish settlements near Jerusalem that were lost until 1967.[5]

The Irgun officers declined to take a decision on the Stern Gang proposal, but referred it to headquarters. Lapidot says it was vetoed by Begin, who insisted that they use a loudspeaker to warn the villagers and give them a chance to surrender without bloodshed.[6] This is confirmed by Haganah sources, who knew of both the debate and the order.[7] The Irgun field commanders agreed against their better judgement to take along a loud-speaker van. They hesitated to sacrifice the advantage of surprise. Lapidot maintains that every soldier was instructed to avoid casualties:

> The intention was that the Arabs would surrender. The message from the loudspeaker was to have been: 'You are surrounded by Irgun and Lehi people. If you don't fight, nothing will happen to you.' There were two possibilities – either to control the village, but leave the people there, or transfer them to the

Arab part of Jerusalem. We didn't make a hard-and-fast decision in advance. We decided to wait and see what developed. The only decision was to have as few casualties as possible.[8]

The Haganah commander in Jerusalem, David Shaltiel, learned of the dissidents' plan to attack Deir Yassin. At first he tried to discourage them. The village was low on his list of priorities. It did not overlook the Jerusalem-Tel Aviv road and had not given shelter to roving bands of Arab irregulars. The Haganah was engaged in a desperate battle for the Kastel, a strategic peak which controlled the highway. Shaltiel suggested that the Irgun and Sternists add their men and weapons to the struggle for the Kastel, but they refused. They also turned down a proposal to take another Arab village closer to the road such as Colonia, near the Jewish village of Motza. 'We wanted to concentrate on the fight in Jerusalem,' Lapidot explains, 'and leave the fight on the road to the Palmah and Haganah. We didn't have a big enough force in Jerusalem. We couldn't split it.'[9] Deir Yassin, it seems, was a more manageable target.

Contrary to the Haganah disclaimer issued straight after the massacre, Shaltiel reluctantly approved the Deir Yassin raid, but he set stringent conditions in a letter to the local Irgun and Stern Gang commanders:

> I have heard that you are planning to carry out an operation against Deir Yassin. I should like to draw your attention to the fact that the capture of Deir Yassin and holding it is a stage in our overall plan. I have nothing against your carrying out the operation, on condition that you have the forces to hold it. If you are unable to do so, I warn you against blowing up the village, which will lead to the departure of the inhabitants and occupation of the ruined houses by outside forces. This situation will make the general campaign more difficult rather than easier, and a renewed occupation of the place will involve heavy losses to our men. An additional argument which I should like to present to you [is that] if outside forces are drawn to the place, this will disrupt our plan to construct an airfield.[10]

Shaltiel hoped that would be enough to put the dissidents with their meagre resources off Deir Yassin, but when they insisted on going ahead, the Haganah commander gave them his blessing rather than risk an armed confrontation between rival Jewish forces. This was a breach of standing orders from the Haganah's national commander, Yisrael Galili, not to co-operate with the Irgun and Sternists, but Shaltiel felt he had to exercise his discretion.[11]

The combined force of about eighty Irgun fighters and forty from the Stern Gang crept up on Deir Yassin in a two-pronged attack at dawn on Friday

9 April 1948. Before any warning could be sounded, the loudspeaker van overturned in a ditch. Although Begin continued to claim for years afterwards that the villagers had disregarded the message, witnesses are unanimous that it was never transmitted – or at least not from a distance where the Arabs could hear it. In any case, Yehuda Lapidot argues, it would have made no difference. The Arabs preferred to fight, and were better prepared than their assailants had bargained for. Like most villages in troubled Palestine, Deir Yassin posted watchmen through the night. One of them spotted the raiding-party – who regretted later that they had not attacked under cover of darkness – and raised the alarm. Almost every household had a rifle, however antiquated. The menfolk seized their guns and started to defend themselves and their families. The commander, Benzion Cohen, was one of the first of the thirty-five Jewish wounded. In all, four Irgun men and one Sternist died. There is no evidence of machine-guns or other heavy weapons, nor of the Iraqi or Syrian soldiers who became part of the Irgun alibi. The Jewish witnesses speak of sniper fire, but it was persistent and accurate. According to Lapidot, who took over command, the Irgun and Sternists had about twenty rifles, three Bren guns (their most effective weapons), thirty to forty Sten light machine-guns, most of which did not work, having been made by amateurs in the Irgun's Tel Aviv workshops, a few revolvers and grenades.

> The tragic trouble about Deir Yassin was that the Arabs were stronger than us. They had more rifles, more ammunition, and they fought from house to house. It is true that the resistance was concentrated on one hill to the west, but this was the centre of the village, ninety per cent of the village.[12]

A runner was dispatched to the Haganah's Jerusalem headquarters in the Schneller barracks, and Shaltiel sent a Palmah platoon with a two-inch mortar and a machine-gun. The Palmah unit circled the western hill from the right and silenced the resistance without loss, then it withdrew. Whatever Begin back in Tel Aviv may have thought about the dissidents and the Palmah fighting shoulder-to-shoulder, that was the limit of the Haganah's active involvement in the battle. With the backbone of Arab defence broken, the Irgun and the Sternists resumed the fight, shooting at everything that moved, blowing up houses, with or without their inhabitants inside, and running more and more out of control. It is not disputed that Begin ordered restraint, but the longer the operation lasted, the more chaotic it became, and the more the raiders seem to have reverted to their original rapacious instincts. After suffering casualties, Yehoshua Gorodentchik, an Irgun officer, recalled, they thought of retreating.

We had prisoners, and before the retreat we decided to liquidate them. We also liquidated the wounded, as anyway we could not give them first aid. In one place, about eighty Arab prisoners were killed after some of them had opened fire and killed one of the people who came to give them first aid. Arabs who dressed up as Arab women were also found, and so they started to shoot the women also who did not hurry to the area where the prisoners were concentrated.[13]

The story of Arab men disguised as women is confirmed by Yair Tsaban, now a left-wing Mapam member of Knesset, who, as a seventeen-year-old Jerusalem high-school boy, was drafted by the Haganah to bury the dead after the perpetrators had left the field. But he puts a different interpretation on it:

What we saw were women, young children and old men. What shocked us was at least two or three cases of old men dressed in women's clothes. I remember entering the living-room of a certain house. In the far corner was a small woman with her back towards the door, sitting dead. When we reached the body we saw an old man with a beard. My conclusion was that what happened in the village so terrorized these old men that they knew being old men would not save them. They hoped that if they were seen as old women that would save them.[14]

Unknown to the Irgun and Stern Gang, the entire operation – attack, resistance and massacre – was witnessed by another future left-wing politician. Meir Pa'il, then a Haganah intelligence officer in Jerusalem, knew of the planned assault and decided, without informing his superiors, to go and see how the dissidents performed. He took a photographer with him. His objective was to report to headquarters on their combat capability. The British would soon be leaving. The Haganah would become the national army and would have to absorb the dissidents, either as self-contained units or dispersed among other fighters. At worst, if they refused to give up their independent status, the Haganah would have to suppress them by force. Either way, it would be useful to assess their performance in their first conventional operation. Pa'il's report to Yisrael Galili began with the opening lines of a celebrated Hebrew poem, written by Chaim Nachman Bialik after the 1903 Kishinev pogrom in which a Russian mob killed forty-nine Jews and wounded five hundred:

Arise and go to the city of the killing and you will come to the courtyards,
and with your eyes you will see and with your hands you will feel on the fences
and on the trees and on the stones and on the plaster
the congealed blood and the battered brains of the slain.

The Pa'il report is still classified, but what he remembers is 'a disorganized massacre' after most of the Arab resistance had ended:

It was a massacre in hot blood, it was not pre-planned. It was an outburst from below with no one to control it. Groups of men went from house to house looting and shooting, shooting and looting. You could hear the cries from within the houses of Arab women, Arab elders, Arab kids. I tried to find the commanders, but I did not succeed. I tried to shout and to hold them, but they took no notice. Their eyes were glazed. It was as if they were drugged, mentally poisoned, in ecstasy.[15]

To Muhammad Arif Sammour, the victims were not just anonymous Arabs. They were cousins, neighbours, friends. The young teacher watched the slaughter from his house high up on the far side of Deir Yassin until about four p.m. when he managed to escape to Ein Karem, John the Baptist's birth-place a couple of miles to the west. Most of the people, he says, were killed inside their houses:

In one case – the Zahran family – only one out of twenty-five survived. In another house they caught the sixteen-year-old son, Fuad. His mother was holding him. They killed him with a knife. The mother spent twenty years after that in a mental hospital. A young woman and her two-year-old baby were shot in the street. Their bodies were left there. They moved to the centre of the village and started to kill everybody they saw or heard, as soon as anybody opened his door. They were using bombs [grenades], machine-guns, sub-machine-guns. My cousin escaped with bullet-holes in his clothes. One of the officers put his machine-gun through a window and started shooting outwards, killing everybody who moved. They killed my uncle, Ali Hassan Zeidan, and my aunt Fatima. She heard him call, 'Help me'. She ran to him and they killed her. Another neighbour, Haj Yarah, heard some voices and came out. They killed him too. His son Muhammad, who was about seventeen, heard his father call him and went to the same place. They killed him. His mother heard her son cry for help. She ran out and they killed her. That was near my house. I saw this.[16]

Both Sammour and Pa'il speak of twenty to twenty-five men being executed by firing-squad in a quarry between Deir Yassin and Givat Shaul. Sammour admits that he did not see the shooting, but says he heard of it from a woman witness. Pa'il, however, has no doubts: 'They put them in a quarry with their backs to the wall and shot them. I saw the shooting, then later I photographed the bodies.' Yehoshua Arieli, a veteran of the British army who commanded the Haganah cadets sent to bury the dead, saw 'several men' lying dead in the quarry.[17] Yehuda Lapidot maintains that he never heard of such executions, and that as acting commander, he would have done so. But the balance of evidence is against him.

More lurid accounts of Irgun and Sternist atrocities were published in *O Jerusalem!*, whose authors, Larry Collins and Dominique Lapierre, relay tales of rape and the alleged slitting of a pregnant woman's belly.[18] Their main sources are the International Red Cross representative in Jerusalem, Jacques de Reynier, and British CID interviews with survivors. In his own published account,[19] de Reynier acknowledges that he arrived at Deir Yassin on the Sunday, two days after the fighting, but while the Irgun and Sternists were still there. Collins and Lapierre recognize an 'Arab tendency to magnify the events in retrospect'. Other available evidence points to a verdict of 'not proven'. Yair Tsaban, who watched their evacuation, saw no blood on the Irgun and Sternists' clothes. 'When we buried the victims,' he adds, 'I saw no evidence of killing by knives.'[20] Muhammad Arif Sammour, who has no reason to minimize the atrocities, is convinced that there were no sexual assaults: 'I didn't hear or see anything of rape or attacks on pregnant women. None of the other survivors ever talked to me about that kind of thing. If anybody told you that, I don't believe it.'[21] Two Jerusalem doctors, sent by the Jewish Agency to examine the bodies, reported no sign of maltreatment or mutilation.[22]

What is not disputed is that the dissidents paraded prisoners in triumph through Jewish Jerusalem before releasing them on the Arab side of town, and that they refused to hold Deir Yassin, as Shaltiel had ordered, or to bury their victims. Lapidot agrees in retrospect that the refusal to bury the dead was a great mistake: 'You don't leave dead bodies on the field, even if they are bodies of the enemy. We weren't organized to do it, we didn't know what to do. This was the first time we had had such a battle with so many casualties. We were exhausted. We were also afraid the British would bomb us from the air.'[23]

This last fear was well-founded and decisive. The British authorities had identified the culprits and were eager to settle scores with them, but they did not have the aircraft or other forces available in time. After a tense confrontation, the Hanagah allowed the Irgun and Stern fighters to leave. Young Yair Tsaban and up to 100 fellow cadets were mobilized for burial duty because the mainstream Zionist leadership did not want the British, the Red Cross or the international press to see the full horror of Deir Yassin. They buried so quickly that no one stopped to count the corpses. The generally accepted Arab death toll is 240–50, though Begin wrote in *The Revolt* of something more like half that figure. Surprisingly, Muhammad Arif Sammour agrees with him. He says that ninety-three people were killed in the village and twenty-three were executed in the neighbouring quarry, making a total of 116. 'About three days after the massacre, representatives of each of the five *hamulas* [clans] in Deir Yassin met in Jerusalem in the Moslem offices near the Al Aqsa mosque and made a list of the people who had not been found. We went through the names.

It came to 116. Nothing has happened since 1948 to make me think this figure was wrong.'[24]

Again, Sammour has every reason for exaggerating rather than playing down the casualties. His case is reinforced by Yehoshua Arieli, now a professor of history and Israeli peace campaigner. 'The 116 figure', he says, 'makes sense. I don't think we could have buried more than 120-40.'[25] Since the graves were not marked and the Arabs have not been allowed to return to Deir Yassin, the true figure will never be known. In any case, the legend has outgrown the statistics.

11
Mutiny on the *Altalena*

The active life of the Irgun Zvai Leumi ended on Tuesday, 22 June 1948, with the Technicolor melodrama of a Hollywood spectacular, a Jewish *Gone with the Wind*: a cast of thousands milling on the Tel Aviv beach, brother killing brother, a brave ship laden with arms, ammunition and high explosives burning off the shore, rumours of war, treason and treachery, high passions and low rhetoric. The epic of the Irgun arms ship *Altalena*, sunk by the Israeli army on the orders of the Prime Minister, was another trauma, like the 'blood libel' of the Arlosoroff murder and the betrayal of the *Saison*, for which Menachem Begin never forgave David Ben-Gurion and the Labour Zionist movement which he led. Yet the Irgun commander must take his share of responsibility for the crossed wires and miscalculation that brought the infant Jewish State to the threshold of civil war.

As the Irgun emerged from the underground, Begin's control weakened. The Jerusalem command, isolated at the end of a vulnerable road from headquarters in Tel Aviv, acted with increasing independence. Irgun units were being integrated into the national army, whose structure and commanders were drawn from the Haganah. Offices abroad took their own unco-ordinated initiatives. As senior colleagues returned home from exile and from prison, Begin was no longer acknowledged to have a monopoly of political wisdom. Men like Ya'acov Meridor and Eliahu Lankin, Arieh Ben-Eliezer and Hillel Kook, with their accumulated experience in Africa, Europe and the United States, did not take Begin's judgements on trust. Nor did younger fighters like Amihai Paglin, who had matured under fire. All of them felt a greater freedom to question, and sometimes to disregard, his decisions. Times and the State itself were fluid. The Irgun was far from unanimous in acknowledging the sovereignty of Ben-Gurion's Provisional Government, or in renouncing the spirit of the underground. As the *Altalena*, named after Jabotinsky's *nom de plume*, sailed east across the Mediterranean, the line between strategy and tactics, the political and the operational, on which Begin had thrived, became blurred. The commander

97

came out of his bunker and into the field. It was an unfamiliar element in which other Irgun men thought they knew better.

Because of this diffusion of authority, Begin's dialogue with Yisrael Galili, by then Ben-Gurion's deputy at the Defence Ministry, was faltering and ambiguous, blighted by the long legacy of mutual distrust and ideological competition. The historical record suggests that both sides were mistaken in their suspicions.[1] Begin was not planning a *putsch*, just as Ben-Gurion did not lure the Irgun chieftain into a trap designed to destroy him and his residual power-base. But both behaved as if they might be so conspiring. Begin misread Ben-Gurion's motives and determination. He did not appreciate how far the Prime Minister would go to establish the primacy of the State, its Government and its army. The Irgun's hesitation fuelled Ben-Gurion's doubts, as well as the pathological hatred he nourished for everything the Irgun and Menachem Begin stood for – violence, indiscipline, an impudent challenge to the divine right of his Mapai Party.

The *Altalena* tragedy should never have happened. The State of Israel, born a month earlier on 14 May 1948, was fighting for its survival. Jewish Jerusalem was menaced from the east, Tel Aviv from the south. The army, still evolving out of the Haganah, the Irgun, the Stern Gang and the motley ranks of overseas Jewish volunteers, was desperately short of arms and ammunition. The *Altalena* was bringing about 5,000 British Lee-Enfield rifles, more than 3,000,000 rifle and machine-gun bullets, 250 Bren guns, 250 Stens, 150 German Spandau machine-guns, 50 mortars, 5,000 shells and tons of TNT, as well as some 940 volunteers, not all of them Irgun sympathizers. It should have been a godsend. The ship was a war-surplus American tank-landing craft, launched in 1944 and bought three years later for $75,000 by Hillel Kook's Hebrew Committee for National Liberation, the Irgun's American supporters' club. It was registered under a Panamanian flag by Avraham Stavsky. After a frustrating search for arms, the Irgun's European office received the *Altalena*'s cargo as a gift from the French Government, which was apparently paying back the British for patronizing Charles de Gaulle before and after the liberation.

Three days before the end of the Palestine mandate, Galili informed Begin that Ben-Gurion was going to proclaim a Jewish State. The Irgun commander, who had been planning a declaration of his own if Ben-Gurion defaulted, agreed to recognize the Provisional Government, and soon afterwards offered to sell the *Altalena* to the authorities for $250,000. Galili turned him down on the grounds that the ship was too well known to run arms without being spotted. On 1 June, Begin undertook to merge the Irgun into the national army. He and Galili signed a six-point accord:

1 Irgun members would enlist in the army;
2 Special units, made up of Irgun fighters, would be established in army brigades;
3 Arms, equipment and installations for their manufacture would be handed over to the authority of the army;
4 A provisional staff, comprising Irgun officers, would function on behalf of the army until all Irgun members had enlisted (no time limit was specified, but Ben-Gurion assumed this would take about a month and then the Irgun staff would be disbanded);
5 Separate purchasing activities would be terminated and contacts transferred to the army;
6 The Irgun and its command would cease to operate as a military unit in the State of Israel and within the sphere of the Israeli Government.

In deference to Begin's self-respect, Galili added a sentence stating that the Irgun was dissolving itself of its own free will. Nothing was said in so many words about Irgun units in Jerusalem, but Begin assumed that the disputed city was temporarily outside the Government's sphere.

There is no reason to doubt Begin's sincerity in signing this compact. His revolt was directed against the British, its objective was the establishment of a Jewish State in the ancient homeland. He recognized that Ben-Gurion, who enjoyed the support of the majority, was its natural leader. In principle, he was ready to abandon the barricades for democratic politics, but on one critical point – the boundaries of the State – he differed so radically from the mainstream Zionist leadership that his loyalty could not be taken for granted. Begin repudiated partition and continued to talk and act as if he might deploy the Irgun to undermine it, whatever the Government decided. That was the rational basis for Ben-Gurion's suspicion. Begin did nothing to dispel it.

In an independence day broadcast on 15 May, Begin announced that the Irgun was leaving the underground '*within the boundaries of the Hebrew independent State*'. He added in a carefully-worded explanation: 'We went down into the underground under the rule of oppression. Now we have Hebrew rule in part of our homeland. In this part there is no need for a Hebrew underground. In the State of Israel we shall be soldiers and builders.'

While the Irgun was negotiating with Ben-Gurion's aides, Begin wrote to his colleagues abroad that the Irgun would be the only Jewish fighting force 'to put the nation in command of the whole country'. Since the official Zionist leadership and the Haganah would not be ready for that, the Irgun would need arms and equipment for 10,000 men (far more than it could deploy at the time). He urged his representatives 'to accumulate iron'.

When the authorities complained after the June agreement had been signed that Irgun agents were still buying arms abroad and raising funds at home, Begin replied that there had been a technical hitch. The Government was not convinced. Its purchasing mission in France waited in vain for the Irgun to get in touch. In Israel, Begin reiterated at an Irgun parade in Netanya that the role of the underground abroad was to collect arms until the time was ripe for an assault to conquer the whole country. Levi Eshkol, Galili's partner in negotiations with the Irgun, was disturbed by signs of a division of roles, with Begin playing the politician, while his colleagues preserved a military option. The Israeli journalist Shlomo Nakdimon wrote in his broadly pro-Irgun account of the *Altalena* affair: 'The idea was not dropped that it might be necessary for the IZL to exist outside the borders of the country and in international Jerusalem.' This was confirmed by Shmuel Katz, a member of the Irgun's team in Europe:

> We would not disband entirely. We never forgot Jerusalem, where the Israeli Government refused to claim sovereignty, where the Old City had fallen and the New was in danger. There the Irgun would have to continue its independent existence to struggle for the inclusion of the whole city in the Jewish State. Until then, a remnant of the Irgun abroad had to be kept in being.[2]

Outside the borders, it seemed, meant outside the partition frontiers. Government misgivings grew on 16 June, after the *Altalena* set sail from Port-de-Bouc, near Marseilles, when an Irgun unit forced its way through an army road-block. Similar acts of mutiny were to proliferate in the week of the *Altalena* crisis. Stamping out such threats to the unity of the State and its army was an article of faith for Ben-Gurion. On 26 May, he banned the maintenance of any armed force outside the army. This was no routine decree, he contended:

> It conditioned the fate of the new State and its existence and that of those living in it. Its significance was to prevent the undermining of the State and the destruction of the army, for only a single army, subject to the State and only the State, which acts on its behalf, can stand for ever, and not private, partisan armies.[3]

To his credit, Ben-Gurion applied the same logic just as remorselessly to the Palmah, the private army of the Left, but he waited until the end of the War of Independence.

The five million dollars' worth of arms were delivered to the Irgun by order of the French Foreign Minister, Georges Bidault, on Wednesday, 9 June. Two days later, despite a stevedores' strike, the 1,820-ton *Altalena* put to

sea with a full load. The sailing coincided with the start of a month-long
ceasefire between Israeli and Arab forces monitored by United Nations
observers. The truce froze the dispositions on the ground and forbade the
introduction of additional arms. In the Irgun's Paris office, Shmuel Katz
resented these terms as a grotesque weighting of the scale against the Jews.
The truce did not prevent Britain from shipping arms to Iraq, Jordan or
Egypt, whose ports were remote from the fighting zone. The only effective
check was on shipments to Israel.

Katz wrote:

> The truce complicated our calculations about the *Altalena*, which would now be
> open to attack by the Egyptians, or by the British, as a breach of the truce. . . .
> We decided that in the light of the gravity of the arms situation, we must take
> the risk that might ensue from a formal breach of the truce; that the ship should
> therefore sail, taking whatever action its commander thought necessary to evade
> or resist enemy action; that the commander should do whatever possible to evade
> United Nations truce surveillance.[4]

This was a unilateral decision by the Paris staff, which kept the sailing
date secret from Irgun headquarters in Tel Aviv. Paris knew Begin had
reservations about violating the truce, even though he opposed it in principle. 'No matter what our attitude to the truce,' he had told his colleagues,
'we may not take upon ourselves responsibility for the possible consequences of its breach.' But the Paris staff was confident that the Government
would acquiesce in a *fait accompli*. It had no intention of allowing Tel Aviv
to rule when and whether the *Altalena* would leave. Fears that a cable or
telephone call might be intercepted furnished a thin excuse after the event.
In any case, the craft's departure was noted almost immediately. As in
another and later crisis, Begin learned of the sailing from the BBC World
Service. He cabled Katz, who confirmed – three days later – that the cargo
was on its way. Preferring to let the Government decide whether to hazard
the truce by bringing the *Altalena* into an Israeli port, Begin radioed the
ship's captain, Monroe Fein, and the commander of the Irgun contingent
on board, Eliahu Lankin, ordering them to keep away and await further
instructions. Although the message was received, Lankin chose to disregard
it. The *Altalena* sailed on.

Begin and Arieh Ben-Eliezer, lately arrived from France, told Galili
about the landing craft and its precious cargo at a meeting on 15 June. For
once, Begin overrode his colleagues' objections and informed the Government of what was on board. Until then, he had kept Bidault's gift a secret.
After consulting Ben-Gurion, Galili telephoned the Government's approval
for bringing the *Altalena* into shore, but ordered the Irgun to beach it at

Kfar Vitkin, a *moshav* between Netanya and Caesaria, rather than the more conspicuous Tel Aviv foreshore. Begin later pointed to the landing at Kfar Vitkin, a Mapai stronghold, as evidence that he was not planning an insurrection. Galili assumed that Begin was handing over the vessel and its contents to the Government unconditionally. The Irgun negotiators, stung by the sharpness of some of Galili's questions, experienced their first uneasiness about his motives.

Mutual suspicions came to a head during further talks on 17 and 18 June. Galili agreed that twenty per cent of the arms should be sent to Jerusalem. Begin took this to mean that the Defence Ministry was conceding his demand that they go to Irgun fighters still operating independently in the city, whereas Galili says he meant they should be sent to the regular army (the Government did not make the Irgun's distinction between Jerusalem and the rest of the country, and counted the former Haganah troops there as part of the Israel Defence Forces). Galili rejected out of hand a second demand that the remaining eighty per cent of the arms should be distributed first to Irgun units now serving in the national army. He saw this as the thin end of the wedge. If the Government gave way on the arms, the Irgun would soon try to force it to abandon its commitment to partition. The Irgun units, Galili retorted, would get arms on the same terms as the other units. In a celebrated broadcast on 22 June, the night after the *Altalena* was destroyed, Begin argued that his men would not have listened to him if he had yielded on their claim to priority. In the process he revealed how far he was from reconciling himself to the integration of the Irgun battalions:

> For years they had dreamed of these arms. What didn't they do, what didn't they sacrifice for every gun, for every machine-gun? And now these liberating arms arrived, this large quantity of modern weapons. How could we not give it to our fighters in the army? How could we refrain from making sure that our men would get it first? We had brought it, so how could we refrain from arming them with it?[5]

But Begin's insistence was vigorously opposed by Hillel Kook, whose American committee had bought the *Altalena*. Kook, visiting Tel Aviv before winding up the Irgun's affairs in the United States, was furious:

> I blew up. I said look, this is our first and last ship, the Haganah has several ships on the way. We have to do everything we possibly can so that there shall be no discrimination against the Irgun people in the army. If you start with discriminating in favour of Irgun people, you will give them a licence to discriminate against us two or three months from now.[6]

After consulting two senior colleagues, Ya'acov Meridor and Haim Landau, Begin took the point and telephoned back to Galili. According to

Kook, Begin now agreed that the eighty per cent would go to the army as a whole, but no sooner had he removed the main bone of contention than he replaced it with another. Begin insisted that an Irgun representative, presumably himself, would attend a parade of the units receiving the arms and hand them over in the name of the Irgun. 'I chuckled inside myself,' Kook says, 'thinking he wants to deliver a speech.' Galili checked, then reported back that there could be no conditions. Kook believes that Begin's vanity needlessly perpetuated the dispute. 'It was typical of Begin, ceremony before substance.' For want of a speech, the ship was lost.

The two sides also disagreed over who should unload the *Altalena*, and where the arms should be stored. The Irgun maintained that it should be in charge, and that the arms should be stored in Irgun depots under joint IZL-IDF guard. The Defence Ministry insisted that the army must have sole responsibility for unloading and storage. Gidi Paglin, the Irgun's operations chief, adopted a more combative stance than Begin intended. According to Meridor, the Irgun commander had not meant to pose any conditions, but Paglin dragged him into an extreme position.[7] Pinhas Vazeh, head of the IDF purchasing staff, and David Hacohen, an IDF liaison officer, who were conducting this part of the negotiations, reported a stalemate. Galili concluded that the Irgun was preparing to go it alone. On Saturday, 19 June, he advised Ben-Gurion that 'a new and dangerous situation has arisen, a demand for a kind of private army, with private weapons, for certain units in the army'.[8] The *Altalena* tragedy was nearing the point of no return.

Amid reports that the ship was approaching the Israeli coast and that hundreds of Irgun soldiers were deserting their units and streaming towards Kfar Vitkin, Ben-Gurion called the Cabinet into emergency session on Sunday, 20 June. Old anxieties were fanned by news that Begin and the rest of the Irgun command were waiting on the beach.

'There are not going to be two States,' Ben-Gurion thundered, 'and there are not going to be two armies. And Mr Begin will not do whatever he feels like. We must decide whether to hand over power to Begin or to tell him to cease his separatist activities. If he does not give in, we shall open fire.'[9]

The Cabinet unanimously adopted a one-sentence motion: 'The Government charges the Defence Minister with taking action in accordance with the laws of the land.' In case any of those present harboured illusions about what they were deciding, Ben-Gurion (who was both Prime Minister and Defence Minister) added: 'Taking action means shooting.' Galili and the acting Chief of Staff, General Yigael Yadin, who had been summoned to the meeting, reported that the *Altalena* would arrive at nine o'clock that

evening, that 600 IDF men were already in the vicinity, and that two more
battalions could be brought up. They were ordered to assemble a force to
take counteraction. 'The officer in charge should endeavour to avoid the
use of force,' the Cabinet decreed, 'but if his orders are not obeyed, force
will be employed.' Ben-Gurion, who was surprised at the Cabinet's unan-
imity, urged Yadin privately to 'act quickly'. Galili interpreted the Cabinet
vote as a unanimous decision to relieve the Irgun of all the arms. General
Dan Even, the local army commander, explained to his men that the goal
of the impending operation was 'to force the IZL to hand the ship and arms
over and to disarm the weapons which they have placed against us'.

Galili was reluctant to strike without making one more effort to reach
agreement. He sent Vazeh to Kfar Vitkin to invite Begin to talk. Meridor
stopped Begin from going because, as he explained later, he was convinced
that it was a trick to 'finish off' Begin along the way.[10] According to Vazeh,
Paglin refused to talk to him and said that if Galili wanted to see Begin,
he should come to Kfar Vitkin.[11] When Vazeh reported back, Galili
drafted an ultimatum which was delivered to Begin over General Even's
signature:

> By special order of the Chief of Staff of the IDF, I order the confiscation of all
> weapons and war materials that have arrived on the shores of Israel in the area
> of my jurisdiction, and their immediate placing at the disposal of the State of
> Israel. I have been instructed to demand of you all the weapons that have come
> ashore, to place them in my safekeeping, and to inform you that you must
> contact the High Command. You are required to carry out this order imme-
> diately. If you do not agree to do so, I will immediately use all the means at my
> disposal to implement the order. I hereby inform you that the entire area is
> surrounded by army units and the roads are blocked. The complete responsi-
> bility for the results, in the event of a refusal to comply with this order, is yours.
> You have ten minutes in which to reply.

Galili claims that the ultimatum offered Begin 'an honourable way out',
though that is hardly how it reads. Ten minutes was long enough, he says,
since the Irgun had only two alternatives: yes or no. But Begin did not take
'such a foolish ultimatum' seriously. He said afterwards that he thought
Even was acting on his own initiative without knowing the background. In
any case, Galili did not enforce the ten-minute deadline. While Irgun men
continued unloading the arms, the Government sent Oved Ben-Ami, the
mayor of Netanya, to mediate. Ben-Ami was convinced that the Irgun was
not planning a coup, but failed to bring the two sides together.

Begin was still having trouble with his subordinates. In an atmosphere
of gathering paranoia, Paglin concluded that the army was preparing a trap

and started reloading some of the arms that had already been taken off the *Altalena*. He wanted to take the ship back to sea until the truce was over, then unload it at Gaza or El Arish further south. Begin still thought he could call the army's bluff. 'Leave it,' he told Paglin, 'we must unload the arms here before the United Nations arrive. I do not believe the army have bad intentions towards us. The problem is only the UN.'[12] Begin summarily relieved Paglin of his post, appointing Meridor in his place, but he was soon to learn that the army's intentions were far from benign. After Galili had reported the rejection of Even's ultimatum, Ben-Gurion barred any more negotiations: 'This time it is impossible to compromise. Either they accept orders and carry them out, or [we] shoot. I am opposed to any negotiations with them and to any agreement. The time for agreements has passed. . . . If force is available, force must be employed without hesitation.'[13]

Ben-Gurion added in his own handwriting: '*Immediately!*' At Kfar Vitkin, at 5 p.m. on Monday, 21 June, unloading stopped while Meridor, Monroe Fein and Avraham Stavsky, who had sailed on the *Altalena* from France, tried to persuade a reluctant Begin to take the ship to Tel Aviv, where the population would be more friendly and they thought the Government would be less disposed to start a battle. While Begin was reviewing his troops, shooting broke out. In his broadcast, the Irgun commander blamed the army for attacking 'from all directions with all types of weapons'. Nakdimon suggested that IDF soldiers opened fire against orders. In the general confusion, he wrote, the Irgun shot back. But Hillel Kook, who was on the beach at Kfar Vitkin, maintains that the Irgun fired first – not at the army, but towards the sea as if to show that they meant business and were ready for anything.[14] Whatever the truth, the Irgun lost six killed and eighteen wounded, and the IDF two dead and six wounded in fighting that went on through the night. Begin, lying flat on the sand as bullets winged overhead, still refused to leave; it would be construed as a dishonourable retreat. But as two naval corvettes closed in on the launch that had brought Fein and Stavsky ashore, Begin was bundled aboard, cursing and protesting in Hebrew and Yiddish, and manoeuvred out to the *Altalena*. Only Fein's navigational skill, learned with the United States navy in the Pacific, prevented them from being hit.

Pursued by a flotilla of hostile Israeli warships, the *Altalena* left Kfar Vitkin at about 9.35 p.m., reaching Tel Aviv around midnight. Early on Tuesday, 22 June, a loudspeaker broadcast a final Government offer: 'Listen, listen, a representative of the Government and the army will board the ship and arrange to have the people taken off, help for the wounded and unloading of cargo.'[15] Begin and his colleagues again ignored a chance to settle matters without bloodshed. On board the *Altalena* it was suggested that Begin should go ashore and negotiate. Eliahu Lankin stopped him, fearing that he might be harmed. Lankin acknowledged afterwards that it might have been wiser to have let Begin go. What followed might have been averted, but, on the other hand, Begin might have been killed.[16]

The Government was worried not only by the Irgun's refusal to comply with its orders, but by the concentration of Begin's supporters on the Tel Aviv beach and by the wholesale desertion of Irgun battalions from Sarafand and other army camps. As Ben-Gurion saw it, the sovereignty of the State was in the balance. The Prime Minister strode back and forth at a meeting of the high command, furiously muttering to himself. One witness described him as 'like a lion in a cage'. The chief of naval operations, Shmuel Yanai, was asked for his expert opinion on what to do about the *Altalena*.

> I put forward all kinds of ideas: lobbing smoke-bombs to force her to pull out, seizing the ship from boats, unloading the cargo. . . . Ben-Gurion dismissed all my proposals with a wave of the hand. I was off-target. Only later on did I understand what he wanted to hear from me – what his true aim was. He wanted to destroy the ship. The vessel had become the pretext for fraternal strife. He wanted to destroy it to remove the issue over which people were prepared to fight. Later on there would be arguments, mutual recriminations – but there would no longer be a pretext for fighting.[17]

In the same spirit, Ben-Gurion ordered Yadin: 'You are to take all steps: concentrating army [units], firepower, flame-throwers, and all the other means we possess in order to bring about the ship's unconditional surrender. All these forces will be employed if instructions are issued by the Government.' At an emergency Cabinet meeting, the Prime Minister beat down any reservations. To those among his ministers who favoured concessions rather than war, Ben-Gurion retorted: 'What has happened . . . endangers the State. . . . This is an attempt to destroy the army, and this is an attempt to murder the State. On these two points there cannot, in my view, be any compromise. And if, to our great misfortune, it becomes necessary to fight over this, we shall have to fight.' The doubters had no answer, and the Cabinet voted seven to two to demand that the Irgun hand over the *Altalena* to the Government. Force was to be used if necessary. Ben-Gurion immediately ordered Yadin to act.

The *Altalena*, moored off the busiest stretch of Tel Aviv foreshore, in full view of guests, reporters and United Nations observers on their hotel balconies, became a focus for pilgrimage and counter-pilgrimage. Pro-Government and pro-Begin soldiers, in uniform and bearing arms, con-

verged on the rebel ship. Civilians swarmed to the beach like spectators to
a cup final. Irgun men at Begin's side shouted anti-Government slogans.
The army struggled against the odds to keep back the Irgun reinforcements.
A boatload of armed men was lowered from the *Altalena*. In the swirling
chaos, shooting broke out. Yigal Allon, the young commander of the
Palmah, was put in charge of the operation. His orders from Ben-Gurion
were sharp and to the point: 'Catch Begin! Catch Begin!'

As the skirmishing spread, with the Irgun appealing by loudspeaker for
the people of Tel Aviv to rally to their side, Allon sent for a cannon. The
streets within range of the *Altalena*'s floating powder-keg were evacuated.
Allon and his deputy, Yitzhak Rabin, surveyed the battlefield from Palmah
headquarters in the Ritz Hotel. In the afternoon a ceasefire was agreed to
evacuate the wounded. According to one account, the Palmah commanders
spotted the Irgun setting up a heavy machine-gun on the deck, aimed at
the Ritz. Allon sought permission to use the cannon. At about four p.m.,
Ben-Gurion agreed, and the shelling began. Begin was convinced that Allon
had every intention of hitting the *Altalena*. 'Suddenly something whistled
over our heads,' he wrote in *The Revolt*. 'We called to the Palmah commander, reminding him that he had promised a complete cessation of fire. He
did not reply. A second shell, a third, a fourth. They had bracketed the
ship and were creeping up to their target. ...'

Allon, a future Foreign Minister and Deputy Premier, claimed that he
was firing 'warning shots' in a final hope of persuading the *Altalena* to
surrender. According to the Palmah version, only five or six shells were
fired all told. Allon said he was 'surprised' that the ship had been hit and
immediately ordered his men to stop the artillery fire. True or false, the
direct hit fulfilled Ben-Gurion's instructions and his imperatives. It set the
Altalena ablaze, nipped the unplanned and unwanted civil war in the bud,
and facilitated the rapid dissolution of the Irgun Zvai Leumi as a separate
military force. The only target Allon did not hit was Menachem Begin, but
if the Irgun commander is right it was not for want of trying. 'Each time I
went up to the captain's bridge, it was subjected to particularly intense fire.
When I left the bridge, the shooting was directed elsewhere.'

The shell pierced the middle of the deck and exploded in the hold below.
Smoke surged out and the ammunition began to pop. Monroe Fein managed to turn on the sprinkler system and flood the hold, but as the shooting
continued it seemed only a matter of time before the smoking ship would
blow up. Despite vociferous objections from Begin, the captain raised a
makeshift white flag and called out to the Palmah to stop firing. Begin was
pinned to the deck, stomach down, with a sailor's knee in his back. He
refused to abandon ship until the last of his men had left. In his broadcast

that night he said his subordinates had threatened to remove him by force, but he would not agree to go.

> If I continued to stand on the burning ship, it was not out of heroism, but because of a sense of duty. How could I leave the ship which was about to blow up? And there were wounded on board! And the catastrophe could happen at any moment! The commander said to me: 'I promise you that we shall all get off. Get off! Most of the wounded have been taken off already.' So I jumped into the water.

Others say that he was tossed into the sea by a pair of Monroe Fein's burly crew.[18] Fein and Lankin, the captain of the ship and the commander of its Irgun fighters, were the last to leave. The battle of the Tel Aviv foreshore cost the Irgun fourteen dead and sixty-nine wounded to two IDF soldiers dead and six wounded. Among those who lost their lives were Avraham Stavsky, Begin's boyhood friend, who had been convicted and then acquitted of murdering Haim Arlosoroff on that same humid beach fifteen years earlier. Some of the arms were salvaged later from the broken-backed *Altalena*. The wreck remained within sight of Tel Aviv as a monument to the folly of politicians – Ben-Gurion or Begin according to prejudice.

It was hardly the Irgun commander's finest hour, and the broadcast he delivered for two hours that night over the Irgun's underground radio was hardly one of his more elevating orations. Begin lost control of himself, breaking into bitter tears. He cursed Ben-Gurion as 'that fool, that idiot', who had plotted to murder him. He boasted that with a wave of his finger he could have eliminated the Prime Minister, and he threatened 'doom' to anyone who raised a hand against the Irgun prisoners. Later the same night, the Irgun published a statement labelling Ben-Gurion a 'crazy dictator', and his Cabinet 'a government of criminal tyrants, traitors and fratricides'. The statement cancelled the previous order to Irgun troops to join the army, but Begin warned his men not to open fire on the IDF. 'There will be no fraternal strife while the foe is at the gate.'

Some of Begin's worst strictures were reserved for Yisrael Galili, 'a petty trader who trades in Hebrew blood and Hebrew property'. The Irgun chief was in the habit long afterwards of citing an anonymous 'man high up in the State, one of the people closest to Ben-Gurion', who was said to have told him: 'In the *Altalena* affair, Ben-Gurion was deceived.'[19] Although he did not name the culprit, it was assumed that he believed Galili was the deceiver. Not surprisingly, Galili hotly denied anything of the kind: 'The argument is either malice or folly, or both. It has no basis in fact. There was no detail concerning the contacts with the IZL, at any level, which was not brought to the full and immediate knowledge of the Minister of Defence.'[20]

Ben-Gurion too denied the charge. Galili claims that Ben-Gurion was 'much more aggressive' than he was. 'When I was at the headquarters in Kfar Vitkin, I received a letter from him saying that he didn't understand why we weren't acting.'[21] There was no significant difference of purpose or perception between the two Labour leaders. The evidence indicates that Galili more than once hesitated to act, wanting to give Begin a chance to obey the Government's orders. It was, as we have seen, Ben-Gurion who forced the pace, and it was Ben-Gurion, on the night of the *Altalena* disaster, who told a meeting of the People's Council: 'Blessed be the cannon that shelled that ship!' It was a benediction to which few Israelis, even among Ben-Gurion's admirers, could breathe an untroubled: 'Amen!'

12
Chosen to Oppose

Menachem Begin must be the only party leader in the democratic world to have lost eight consecutive elections and lived to win a ninth and a tenth. It was not that he was immune to criticism from his own ultra-nationalist ranks. He was constantly challenged, but never by anyone with the prestige, the popular appeal and the political skill to supplant him. *T'nuat Haherut*, the 'Freedom Movement', which he founded in August 1948, at a conclave of old underground comrades, projected itself as the party of the Irgun Zvai Leumi. Its central core was, and remained for more than three decades, what he called 'the Fighting Family', among whom his personal authority was unassailable. Begin was still the commander, they were still his boys, calling each other by their codenames, sharing and perpetuating legends of glory, sacrifice and persecution.

In the first Knesset elections in January 1949, Herut was not the sole claimant to the legacy of Vladimir Jabotinsky. Three other parties – the old-school Revisionists, spurned by the Irgun during the years of revolt, the Fighters' Party launched by the Stern Gang, and the State Party of Meir Grossman, who had broken with Jabotinsky in 1931 – competed with it for the nationalist vote. But Begin's only serious rivals were the Revisionists, still represented in the Zionist institutions, whom he soon outflanked by persuading the executive of the World Union of Revisionists to recognize Herut as the Israeli branch of the movement. In a pattern that was to repeat itself whenever Begin's leadership was questioned, many of the veteran Revisionists dropped out of active politics. He conquered from the inside, isolating his challengers and freezing them out of the party. Over the years such critics were left bitter, but impotent – an Eri Jabotinsky, the son of the prophet; a Hillel Kook refighting obscure constitutional battles; a Shmuel Tamir pursuing a prosperous legal career, but beholden to Begin for any influence he might hope to exercise from the political fringe; an Ezer Weizman, waiting like an Israeli de Gaulle to be called to save the nation.

From its inception Herut was an alliance of Jabotinskyite ideologues and disaffected oriental Jewish voters. What bound them together was Menachem Begin. He planted and nurtured the Party, which grew from the top downwards. There was no network of local branches active between elections, and Betar was more of a sports federation than a youth movement. Begin's dominance was established with the elections to the first Knesset, when he drew up the list of candidates, a fertile field for patronage in the Israeli system of proportional representation. Particularly on overseas speaking tours, Begin fostered his image as a national hero, a Jewish Garibaldi. In the street and in parliament, he spread his rhetorical wings, confirming his gifts (unique in Herut) as a populist leader, reaching out to people who had no appetite for doctrinal intricacy. The personality cult, bequeathed to the Revisionists by Jabotinsky, descended on Begin. The leader insulated himself in the inner circle of Irgun veterans, holding aloof from domestic party quarrels, deploying his friends to fight on his behalf. At no time did he groom a successor. He preferred to divide and rule. The ambitious were left to eye each other, the faithful to cleave to the old commander. At moments of incipient rebellion he confronted them with the consequences by offering to resign. On one occasion he rented a room in Jerusalem and resumed his studies for the bar. After the débâcle of the 1951 elections to the second Knesset, when Herut's strength plunged from fourteen seats to eight and its total vote fell by 4,000 despite a 418,000 growth in the electorate, Begin and his wife Aliza sailed for a holiday in Italy. He left behind a resignation letter with his deputy, Arieh Ben-Eliezer, but the Party's grey eminence, Yohanan Bader, stopped anyone opening it.[1]

After Begin won the 1977 election, his political secretary, Yehiel Kadishai, was asked how the leader had survived twenty-nine years of defeat. 'I don't think we ever expected to win,' Kadishai answered. In the 1950s Herut platforms were festooned with the slogan: 'God chose us to rule.' Begin often warned the Prime Minister, David Ben-Gurion, what vengeance he would wreak when he won office. But both the slogan and the polemic reflected messianic dreams rather than any expectation of power. Herut was conceived as a party of opposition. Its mission was to keep the banner of 'true' Zionism flying, to fight on for a proud and undivided *Eretz Yisrael*, and to give the lie to the pragmatism of the Mapai majority.

Although Begin abandoned the underground for the hustings as soon as Ben-Gurion proclaimed the Jewish State, his commitment to parliamentary democracy remained ambivalent. He admired the Westminster model, despite his hatred of British rule in Palestine. He argued for constitutional propriety and safeguards for the individual when the Knesset was debating various 'basic laws'. But there was a lingering nostalgia for revolution, if not for dictatorship. The Government was often wrong, the Knesset was not the final repository of wisdom or legitimacy. In one of his first press conferences as leader of Herut, for instance, Begin dissociated the party from the Stern Gang's assassination of the United Nations mediator, the Swedish Count Folke Bernadotte, but he could not resist laying indirect responsibility at the door of 'the British sowers of intrigue', together with their 'latent and patent partners in the American State Department', as well as 'the mistaken policy' of the Provisional Government of Israel.

> We warned this Provisional Government that it must not erect, by a tyrannical regime on the internal front and by appeasement on the external front, a new underground. This warning was sounded on 15 May, but the Provisional Government, which talks high and mighty of sovereignty, while exercising tyranny and shameful surrender, paid no heed to our warning. It cannot, therefore, be entirely exempt from indirect responsibility for the Jerusalem tragedy because of its own policy.[2]

For all his bravado, Begin waged his guerrilla campaign against the 'appeasement' of partition by words rather than by force of arms. Even if he had wanted to, he lacked the means to do otherwise. Many of the Irgun deserters were arrested after the *Altalena* affair. In Jerusalem the last independent Irgun units yielded to a Government ultimatum on 20 September 1948. 'Mr Begin', said Ben-Gurion, never the most charitable of men, 'only knew the authority of force, and he surrendered only to it.'[3] The Herut leader took up the struggle for *Eretz Yisrael* three weeks after the first Knesset assembled and two weeks after an armistice agreement had been signed between Israel and Egypt. It was a grave illusion, Begin said, to think that Israel was entering an era of peace.

> There exists now in the eastern part of Western *Eretz Yisrael*, as in Transjordan, an indirect British occupation.... There will be no peace for our State, and there will be no peace for our people, if we do not liberate that part of the homeland from the invading troops. ... Our official foreign policy is leading in the direction of freezing the artificial borders, the borders of dismemberment.[4]

He returned to the attack in April 1949, after Israeli diplomats and officers had negotiated an armistice with King Abdullah in Rhodes. In an attempt to divide Ben-Gurion's coalition, his case was pitched in theological as well as political terms.

> This Government has signed an agreement of servitude with Britain's servant, with the ruler of the State which calls itself – and to our great disgrace this name was approved in an official document which was signed by the Government of Israel – the Hashemite Kingdom of Jordan, which spreads with the *de facto* approval of the Government of Israel along both banks of the Jordan.... The

significance of this agreement is that the British can return to Western *Eretz Yisrael* at will and establish their military bases there. . . .

I should like to direct a few words to the members of Knesset from the Religious Front. Gentlemen, I should like to ask your conscience – and I am one of the believers in Israel – how is it that your hand did not shake in giving your consent to a plan which involves recognition of the Transjordanian Hashemite Kingdom, in other words the abandonment of the Jordan – the whole Jordan – to the hands of the enemy? How is it that your hand did not shake in officially recognizing the control of Abdullah in the Old City of Jerusalem?[5]

Despite the presence of Jordanian sentries on the walls of the Old City, despite the ordeal of the War of Independence, in which the *Yishuv* lost 6,500 dead from a community of 650,000, despite the problems besetting an infant State which doubled its population in four years through immigration, Begin insisted on keeping the flame of *Eretz Yisrael* alive. It was an article of faith on which he would countenance no compromise. 'Don't tell us that there is no value to declarations,' he said in proposing that the Knesset proclaim 'united Jerusalem', and not just the western half of the city, its capital. 'The foreign nations must know that Jerusalem is ours, it is all ours – the Temple Mount, the Western Wall – and Jerusalem on both sides of the wall is ours, and Jerusalem is our capital, not only in theory but in practice.'[6]

The whole of Jerusalem was the capital, and the whole of *Eretz Yisrael*, Jabotinsky's both banks of the Jordan, was the Jewish homeland, whether or not Israel was in any position to redeem them. 'Rabat Amon [Amman] like Shechem [Nablus], Gilead like Samaria, the Bashan like the Sharon', Begin preached, 'are our homeland.'[7] However much President Jimmy Carter may have chafed at Camp David in 1978, he could not accuse the Israeli leader of inconsistency. Yet Begin's attachment was always to the concept of place, to names and historical echoes. There was none of Moshe Dayan's love of the land for its own sake, nor indeed of the *sabra* familiarity with it.

In May 1950, after Jordan had formally annexed the West Bank, Begin blamed the Foreign Minister, Moshe Sharett, for giving a green light to 'Abdullah and the Bevin Government which stands behind him to turn the act of plunder and conquest into a legal and recognized political act'. For Begin the Hashemite Kingdom remained 'the British occupied territory of Eastern *Eretz Yisrael*'. If words could conquer . . .

Who gave the Government the authority, he demanded of Ben-Gurion, to recognize the 'surrender' of Jerusalem and the Temple Mount, the Tomb of the Patriarchs and the grave of Rachel, Hebron and Bethlehem, Shechem, Gilead and Bashan?

You were elected to run the affairs of the State. Possibly the people will replace you; perhaps the people will elect you anew. But who gave you the right, in what election were you given the authority, to give up in the name of the people of Israel the legacy of our forefathers, the testament of generations, the command of history given at the cost of the blood of millions in the course of 120 generations? ... No election gave this authority, and it was certainly not given to you in the last election. Let us have a contest of power over this question. If you want the authority, let us go out to the people and ask them if they are willing to announce that Abdullah and not we should have Jerusalem, Hebron and Bethlehem.[8]

Begin gave notice in the same debate that the Government's recognition of the Jordanian annexation would not bind Herut. 'When another government will come – and it will come – it will announce that this signature is invalid. The whole of *Eretz Yisrael* belongs to the people of Israel, and we shall not recognize Abdullah's right, nor that of the British, to rule over a single inch of our homeland.'

The struggle for *Eretz Yisrael*, however utopian in the reality of the 1950s, respected the limits of parliamentary democracy. Begin was putting down markers rather than mounting the barricades. He displayed no such scruples in his second historic quarrel with Ben-Gurion's Government in this period – the battle against Israeli acceptance of German reparations. The Herut leader reverted to the politics of the street, incited a mob to march on the Knesset, and consciously put his constitutional future at risk. The issue, coming so soon after the Nazi Holocaust, excited turbulent emotions throughout Israeli society. The left-wing Mapam, which had stayed out of the ruling coalition, opposed any deal with Bonn as bitterly as Herut. The two movements shared common roots in Polish Zionism, and Polish Jewry had come nearer than any other to annihilation under the Final Solution. But Begin alone raised the flag of insurrection.

Ben-Gurion's overture to the German Chancellor, Konrad Adenauer, was a hard-headed last resort. Its purpose was not a quick reconciliation between bereaved and murderers, but a desperate attempt to keep the strained Israeli economy afloat, and to shore up the State against its Arab enemies. The Prime Minister recognized that Israel could not stand in isolation. It needed a powerful ally. He turned first to Britain, even hinting that Israel was ready to join the Commonwealth, and then to the United States, but both prospective patrons disappointed him. British Labour and Conservative Governments opened exploratory talks, but interest soon faded. The Foreign Office, Ben-Gurion's advisers concluded, was against the idea from the start and made sure it had no chance. In Washington the

Secretary of State, John Foster Dulles, was more concerned with restoring American links with the Arabs. 'Our basic problem', he told a Senate committee, 'is to improve the Moslem states' attitude towards the Western democracies, because our prestige in that area has been in constant decline ever since the war.' Ben-Gurion's proposal for making Israel the West's 'base, granary and workshop' in the Middle East fell on deaf ears. An appeal to American Jews was received more sympathetically. The Prime Minister inaugurated the Israel Bonds campaign at a mass rally in Madison Square Garden in May 1951. But despite its success, his biographer wrote, 'the money it brought in was not enough for a long-term stabilization of the State's feeble economy. Israel needed prolonged and massive financial help.'[9]

Israel made its first tentative approach for reparations in March 1951, but tried to avoid dealing directly with the Germans. It submitted a $1.5 billion claim to the occupying Powers – the United States, the Soviet Union, Britain and France – for the Jewish property pillaged by the Nazis, but the Big Four refused to have anything to do with it. Reparation was a matter for the Germans. It was at this stage that Adenauer, the new Federal Republic's anti-Nazi leader, indicated his readiness to pay compensation to Israel. There was, wrote the British author Terence Prittie in his biography of Adenauer, no question of settling the German account with the Jews. 'What was possible was to make the maximum material restitution, within Germany's available means. Adenauer seems always to have understood this, and to have regarded this task as his duty.'[10] Nonetheless many Israelis, including members of Ben-Gurion's Cabinet and leaders of his Mapai Party, were horrified at the prospect. The Prime Minister had no trouble, however, squaring his conscience. He knew that the only way to make reparations acceptable to the country was to put the full weight of his authority behind them. 'In a single sentence,' he said, 'the reason lay in the final injunction of the inarticulate six millions, the victims of Nazism, whose very murder was a ringing cry for Israel to rise, to be strong and prosperous, to safeguard her peace and security, and so prevent such a disaster from ever again overwhelming the Jewish people.' Ben-Gurion defended his ground no less ingeniously in the Knesset:

> Over six million Jews were put to death by torture, starvation, massacre and mass suffocation. . . . Before, during and after this systematic mass murder, came the pillage – this too on an unprecedented scale. . . . A crime of such enormous proportions can have no material compensation. Any compensation, of whatever size, is no restitution for the loss of human life or expiation for the sufferings and agonies of men and women, children, old people and infants. However, even after the defeat of the Hitler regime, the German people continues to enjoy the

fruits of that massacre and pillage, of the plunder and robbery of the Jews who were murdered. The Government of Israel considers itself bound to demand of the German people restitution for this stolen Jewish property. Let not the murderers of our people also be the beneficiaries of its property![11]

Menachem Begin, whose own parents and brother were numbered among the six million, was outraged. There is no reason to question his sincerity in taking up the cudgels for Jewish self-respect. But others in the Herut machine seized on the reparations issue as a means of revitalizing the movement and bringing Begin back into active politics after the 1951 election setback. Begin revelled in the part for which they cast him. Yehoshua Ophir, who was at that time a reporter on the party newspaper *Herut*, described a visit he paid to the movement's general secretary, Ya'acov Rubin.

> He read the *Yediot Aharonot* newspaper I had with me and noticed a small item. Dr Nahum Goldmann was to visit Germany to complete the reparations agreement. Suddenly he called to Arieh Ben-Eliezer: 'Arieh, Arieh, this will return him. Menachem will come back for this campaign. This is a campaign for the nation's honour, and he is the only one who can lead it.' Two weeks later Begin returned from Europe and the Herut movement came out of its deep freeze.[12]

On the afternoon of 7 January 1952, Begin addressed a crowd estimated at anything from 2,000 (the police) to 15,000 (Begin) Jerusalemites from the balcony of the Tel Aviv Hotel in Zion Square. A thin drizzle was falling, but there was nothing damp about his oratory.

The *Jerusalem Post* recorded:

> Mr Begin spoke with emotion, frequently shouting, interspersing his words with many biblical quotations. He referred to the Government statement in support of German reparations discussions as the culmination of the policies of 'that maniac who is now the Prime Minister'.
>
> Midway through his harangue, Mr Begin pulled a note from his pocket, held it aloft dramatically and said: 'I have not come here to inflame you, but this note which has just been handed to me states that the police have grenades which contain gas made in Germany – the same gas which was used to kill your fathers and mothers. We are prepared to suffer anything, torture chambers, concentration camps and subterranean prisons, so that any decision to deal with Germany will not come to pass.'

The reference to German gas seems to have been a classic case of Begin's carelessness with facts. Whatever its national origin, tear-gas is not the same as Zyklon-B, but the allusion served its purpose. Speaking a few hundred yards from the old Knesset building, where Ben-Gurion was defending Government policy, Begin warned the Prime Minister:

When you fired at us with a cannon, I gave an order: No! Today I shall give the order: Yes! This will be a battle of life and death. . . . Today the Jewish Premier is about to announce that he will go to Germany to receive money, that he will sell the honour of the Jewish people for monetary gain, casting eternal shame upon it. . . . There is not one German who did not murder our parents. Every German is a Nazi. Every German is a murderer. Adenauer is a murderer. All his aides are murderers. But their reckoning is money, money, money. This abomination will be perpetrated for a few million dollars.

With a cry of 'Freedom or death, there is no way back!' Begin strode up Ben-Yehuda Street to beard Ben-Gurion in the Knesset, a block that now houses the Ministry of Tourism. The mob followed. 'Violence surged in the streets of Jerusalem for two hours,' the *Jerusalem Post* reported.

Police barbed-wire barricades were broken through, parked cars overturned and rocks thrown into the Knesset chamber and at police protecting the building. Injuries had reached ninety-two policemen and thirty-six civilians by 7 p.m. when an army detachment arrived on the scene and drew up in formation alongside the Knesset. By 7.30 order had been restored and the littered streets before the Knesset building were virtually abandoned.

Inside the Knesset another reporter chronicled a debate taking place in 'an atmosphere of violence unprecedented in Israeli parliamentary life':

The shouting of a mob not far off, the intermittent wail of police cars and ambulance sirens, sporadic explosions of gas grenades and the glow of flames from a burning car came through the windows of the Knesset building, and later the window-panes were splintered by rocks, and fumes of tear-gas bombs from the battle-scarred street outside permeated the chamber. One member was hit on the head by a stone.

Through all this disturbance, the meeting went on. The section of the hall where stones and glass splinters fell, the Mapam, General Zionist and Hapoel Hamizrahi benches, were vacated and members stood around elsewhere. But later the proceedings were interrupted by obstruction within the Knesset itself when Mr Menachem Begin (Herut) called the Prime Minister a hooligan and refused to recant. He also declined to leave the platform when ordered to do so by the Deputy Speaker, saying 'If I don't speak, no one will speak.' The meeting was closed by the Deputy Speaker amidst an uproar.

In other circumstances Begin's speech against German reparation might have gone down as one of his greatest parliamentary performances. Read cold thirty years later, it is passionate, eloquent, reasoned, an appeal to Jewish pride, a scourge for those who were preparing to compromise it, a piece of theatre, pathetic and brave, if a little overblown. But inevitably it is remembered under the shadow of the riots that accompanied the debate,

the stones and tear-gas and broken glass, and of Begin's lurch into unparliamentary language and anti-democratic braggadocio. He was aware of the
risks and took them with his eyes open. After eventually withdrawing his
description of Ben-Gurion as a hooligan and his insistence that 'if I don't
speak, no one will speak', he confirmed the Speaker's announcement of the
retraction 'not as a result of threats that I shall be expelled from the Knesset
– I take my expulsion from the Knesset lightly, when we are speaking of
the present campaign. I confirm it because I still have a task to perform
here, *perhaps the last*, and I shall fulfil it to the end.'

The main thrust of his case was that the German people as a whole was
guilty of the Final Solution – the millions who voted for the Nazis, who
served in Hitler's army, the Gestapo, the SS and the SA, Adenauer's
diplomats who had once been Ribbentrop's diplomats. 'From a Jewish
point of view there is not a single German who is not a Nazi, and there is
not a single German who is not a murderer. And you are going to them to
receive money.' Begin was worried about the way the world would interpret
acceptance of reparations.

> The *goyim* will see only one fact: you sat at one table with the murderers of your
> people, you admitted that they are capable of signing an agreement, that they
> are capable of keeping an agreement, that they are a nation in the family of
> nations. The *goyim* not only hated us, not only murdered us, not only burnt us,
> were not only jealous of us – it was especially contempt that they felt for us. And
> in this generation, which we call the last of servitude and the first of redemption
> – in the generation when we gained a position of honour, in which we came out
> from slavery to liberty – you come, and because of a few million defiled dollars,
> because of foul goods, and throw away the little bit of dignity which we have
> earned for ourselves. . . . You cut the ground from under our feet, you endanger
> our honour and independence. How we shall be scorned.

After appealing again to Ben-Gurion to hold a referendum rather than
override what he believed was the will of the majority of Israelis, Begin
made his final defiant gesture. There were things in life which were more
terrible than death itself, he said.

> This is one of those things over which we shall give our lives, for which we shall
> be willing to die. We shall leave our families, we shall part from our children,
> and there will be no negotiation with Germany. . . . I know that you have power.
> You have prisons, concentration camps, an army, a police force, spies, cannons,
> machine-guns. No matter. Over this issue all this power will shatter like glass on
> a rock. On a question of justice we shall fight to the end. Physical force in such
> cases has no value. It is nonsense and vanity.
>
> I warn, but I do not threaten. Whom should I threaten? I know that you will
> drag us to concentration camps. You imprisoned hundreds today, perhaps you

TOP Menachem Begin (centre) with his parents, brother and sister, 1932
ABOVE Begin stands on Ze'ev Jabotinsky's left as he reviews members of Betar, Pinsk, 1933

TOP LEFT Begin in his Betar uniform, 1938
TOP RIGHT Aliza and Begin after their wedding, 1939
ABOVE Begin, wearing a Polish army uniform, with Aliza and
friends, 1942

TOP LEFT 'Rabbi Sassover', with Aliza and Benny, Tel Aviv, 1946

TOP RIGHT Begin's first public appearance after leaving the undergound, Zion Square, Jerusalem, August 1948

ABOVE Reviewing a parade of Irgun exiles back from East Africa, Jerusalem, August 1948. Shmuel Katz (with glasses) is walking behind Begin.

TOP The burning of the *Altalena* off the beach at
Tel Aviv, 1948

ABOVE Herut demonstrations outside the Knesset
protesting against German reparations, January 1952

TOP Begin touring an Oriental immigrants camp, Talpiot,
Jerusalem, July 1955
ABOVE Addressing the Knesset, 1961. David Ben-Gurion,
Golda Meir and Yosef Burg are on the front bench.

ABOVE Election night, May 1977. Ezer
Weizman is extreme right; Simha Erlich, the
Liberal leader and later deputy Prime
Minister, is third from right.

RIGHT Praying at the Western Wall after
being asked to form a government, May 1977

OPPOSITE: above, with Prime Minister Levi
Eshkol and General Yeshayahu Gavish, Chief
of Southern Command, in the Sinai during the
Six Day War, June 1967; below, lunching with
David Ben-Gurion at the Régence Restaurant,
King David Hotel, December 1967

TOP Demonstrations during Begin's first and second visits to the United States, 1977 and 1978

ABOVE Begin and Yehuda Avner (left) show Kurt Waldheim, Secretary-General of the United Nations, a 'national security map'

will imprison thousands. No matter, they will go, they will sit. We shall sit together with them. If need be, we shall be killed with them. And there will be no reparations with Germany. And God will help us, that we shall prevent a catastrophe for our people, for our future and for our honour.

Whatever Begin's intentions on the night of 7 January 1952, his peroration dissolved into empty rhetoric. The Knesset endorsed Ben-Gurion's German policy by sixty-one votes to fifty (including one Herut member who had suffered a heart attack and was brought to the chamber on a stretcher). Two weeks later the house voted fifty-six to forty-seven to suspend Begin for the remaining three months of the session as punishment for his unparliamentary conduct during the debate. In March, Begin harangued a Tel Aviv rally of 70,000 angry opponents of a reparations deal, but begged his listeners not to indulge in violence (according to his critics, he had been advised that thousands of brawny *kibbutzniks* had come into town to guard public buildings and put down any riots). 'Mr Ben-Gurion,' he proclaimed, 'the God of Israel will decide who is right.'

An agreement with Germany was signed soon afterwards. Bonn undertook to provide Israel with $715 million worth of goods and services over twelve years, and to pay a further $107 million to a committee representing world Jewish organizations. Among the capital equipment which Israel received were forty-one merchant ships, four tankers, a floating dock, a steelworks and a copper-smelting plant. Adenauer, who despite Begin's scepticism had served time in a Nazi prison camp, repelled Arab threats to the West German economy. 'There are higher things to think about than good business deals,' he told them. 'We want a different sort of Germany from the Germany of Hitler.'[13]

Menachem Begin was never reconciled to this 'new' Germany. For the rest of the 1950s and 1960s, the long, frustrating opposition years, he seldom missed an opportunity to tilt at the Government for coming to terms with the 'murderers of the Jewish people'. He condemned exchange visits between Israeli and German schools, inveighed against the sale of Uzi sub-machine-guns to Bonn, delivered one of his ringing 'I accuse' speeches against the establishment of diplomatic relations (in 1965), and called for a national day of mourning when the first German ambassador presented his credentials. But there was no martyrdom, no dungeons and concentration camps for those who resisted reparations and their consequences. Neither Begin nor his followers died in the last ditch.

It was another bitter-sweet victory for Ben-Gurion in a spirited gladiatorial contest, sometimes noble, often petty, that became an Israeli spectator sport. It was intensely personal, with Ben-Gurion generally taking the initiative or provoking Begin into doing so. The Prime Minister at one stage declined to recognize the Herut leader's existence, referring to him in the Knesset as 'the member sitting next to Dr Bader', and leaving the chamber whenever Begin went to the rostrum. Begin got his own back by reciting the '*Shehehiyanu*' prayer (thanking the Lord for 'keeping us alive, sustaining us, and bringing us to this time') on a rare occasion when Ben-Gurion stayed in his place. The duel of insults reached its peak, or perhaps its nadir, with a rancid, belated debate on the *Altalena* affair in January 1959. Ben-Gurion accused Begin of sitting out the War of Independence, Begin taunted Ben-Gurion with fighting the British amid the fleshpots of Paris. 'Do not interrupt me,' rapped Ben-Gurion, 'you still do not have a Cheka and a Gestapo.' When Begin invited the Prime Minister to take *Altalena* out of the Knesset to a commission of inquiry, Ben-Gurion answered: 'No sir, I shall not go anywhere with you outside the Knesset. Here I am subject to the law, and I respect the law, and I must pay heed to you and to every other member of the Knesset. Here everyone has equal rights and duties. Outside this place I have no intention of being in the same room with you.' Three years earlier Begin had informed his party that he would not attend the Knesset foreign affairs committee if Ben-Gurion were present. He could not bear to sit at the same table with the Prime Minister, who had 'offended him several times during the past year'.

During the *Altalena* debate, Ben-Gurion accused Begin of lying. 'This single lie which he has told here is sufficient for me to know the truth which he is capable of. I do not think that he lies on purpose; he is simply incapable of distinguishing between truth and imagination.' But the Prime Minister's hostility went deeper than personal antipathy. At the root of the quarrel was his conviction that Herut, like the Irgun at the time of the *Altalena* crisis, posed a challenge to Israel's still frail democracy. 'It is the same movement,' he said, 'and its nature was noted by Mr Abba Ahimeir under a sincere heading: "From the Notebook of a Fascist".' Ben-Gurion did not hesitate to compare Begin with Hitler.[14] It was an impression Begin had enhanced by fighting the 1955 general election from an open-topped Cadillac with an escort of young, leather-clad motorcycle outriders. The picture was imprinted on the voters' minds long after Ben-Gurion's jibe was forgotten.

If Ben-Gurion made the running in their exchange of invective, Begin had the last word. In May 1962, with the old warrior increasingly at odds with his own party, Begin turned the knife:

> This State will feel relief and the nation will feel better; hatred and animosity will fall and mutual respect will rise; vindictiveness will disappear and in its stead rivalry, even bitter rivalry, will arise – but it will be honest and dignified;

distortion will be removed and truth will thrive; the distance of hearts will lessen and the consciousness of unity will deepen, hypocrisy will be vanquished and candour will arise; and an end will be put to Byzantine flattery, and civil courage and freedom of thought will come in its place; and the people will advance in all areas: moral, political, security and economic – on the day that the leader of Mapai, who serves as Prime Minister, will retire. The sooner the better![15]

13
Out of the Wilderness

Despite their long-running feud, it was Ben-Gurion who gave Menachem Begin his first taste of respectability, the accolade due to a loyal opposition leader. On Sunday, 28 October 1956, the Prime Minister summoned Begin to his Tel Aviv bedside, where he was nursing a high fever, and informed him that Israel was about to attack Egypt. Ben-Gurion had briefed his Cabinet earlier that day on the Anglo–French–Israeli stratagem which the world was to know as the Suez War and Israelis as the Sinai Campaign. Now he wanted to be sure of maximum support in the Knesset and the country. One by one he received the leaders of every opposition party except the Communists in his Keren Kayemet Street flat. Begin was not the only one taken into his confidence, but the significance of the meeting was not lost on either of them. After every election Ben-Gurion let it be known that he was ready to form a coalition with 'all parties except Herut and the Communists'. Herut members were still ostracized in the public services, Irgun veterans had to struggle for promotion in the regular army, doors were closed in the trade unions and the multiplicity of enterprises controlled by the Labour movement. Begin's party was mocked and distrusted. The Revisionists were still the outcasts of Zionism. However limited, Ben-Gurion's summons was a gesture of acceptance.

Begin, who had been campaigning for a 'preventive war' since the beginning of the year and for a strategy of 'positive activism' in response to Arab guerrilla infiltration before that, seized the Prime Minister's hand. 'I applaud your courageous decision,' he assured him, 'you can depend on our support.' When the war was debated in the Knesset, the Herut leader was true to his word, but the *rapprochement* did not last. Begin turned all his old anger on Ben-Gurion the following January when the Prime Minister bowed to American pressure and withdrew the army from Sinai. Israel, he charged, had won a military victory and suffered a political defeat. 'After this withdrawal remember, supporters of the Government, that the majority is not always right.' Begin was even more scathing two months later when Ben-Gurion pulled his troops out of the Gaza Strip, a 'liberated part of the homeland'. The Prime Minister, he argued, had ridden roughshod over the elected representatives of the people. 'Woe unto the eyes that read and unto the ears that hear these words.'

Begin's trek out of the political wilderness remained slow and faltering. In the decade between the Suez and Six Day wars, Herut established itself as the second biggest party after Mapai, but did not break through to a point where it threatened the Labour hegemony. It won fifteen out of 120 Knesset seats in 1955, rising to a plateau of seventeen in 1959 and 1961, but Mapai's share never fell below forty, with the other Labour parties – Mapam and Ahdut Ha'avoda – adding to the weight of the democratic Left.

Rumbles against the style and aspiration of Begin's leadership went back to the early 1950s. After almost every election he went to ground. It was a pattern that was to become familiar when he was Prime Minister. Begin loved a triumph and relished a fight. They brought out the best and the worst in him, the showman, the orator, the compulsive scrapper. He was happy in his paranoia. The merest mention of the *Altalena*, the slightest sneer at the Irgun, was stimulus enough. But he never liked having to explain away a disaster. He was bored by the prosaic. It went against the romantic grain. By the end of the 1950s some of his followers were becoming tired of eternal opposition.

One of them, a member of the Fighting Family of Irgun veterans, wrote privately to Begin in November 1959 complaining that the Party's propaganda was directed exclusively at those already committed rather than at the floating voter. Herut was *anti-*Mapai, but not *for* anything that could command his confidence. Many voters, the letter said, were repelled by the adulation of one man, not to mention the motorcycle escort. There was too much 'Begin to power' and not enough 'Herut to power'. A sense of opportunism had taken root, a chase after cheap victories, a simplistic appeal to the masses rather than an information campaign aimed at the thinking public. Too many decisions were taken on the whim of the leader. The movement had stopped educating the young and was generating no new ideas.[1] The critics were uneasy too at Begin's wooing of the religious voter, especially when it entailed sacrificing individual liberty. After the disappointment of the 1959 election, when Herut won only two more seats, one of the younger activists, Shmuel Tamir, publicly condemned Begin's leadership as 'bankrupt'.

This taunt proved a rallying cry to the most serious challenge Begin had faced since 1948, an open revolt that for once looked like calling his bluff and allowing him to resign. A showdown was delayed by an agreement between Herut and the Liberals, the middle-class heirs of the General Zionists, to form the Gahal alliance (an acronym from *Gush Herut-*

Liberalim, the Herut-Liberal Block). This was not a full merger. Each partner retained its identity, its separate policy and organization. But it was an
important step towards the creation of a broad, centre-right alternative to
Labour, and it brought Herut into the mainstream of Israeli politics. The
first overtures had been made as early as 1950, when the Mayor of Tel Aviv,
Yisrael Rokach, suggested to Begin that Herut and his General Zionists
join forces for the impending municipal elections. Begin spurned the offer,
but in 1955 after Herut had overtaken the General Zionists in the Knesset
it was Begin's turn to take the initiative. This time the General Zionists
said no because Herut was too extreme for their allies in the small Progres-
sive faction, who eventually broke away to form the Independent Liberal
Party of Moshe Kol and Gideon Hausner. But the General Zionists kept
the door ajar by offering to co-operate in the Knesset. Secret negotiations
failed again after the Suez war, but were more successful before the 1965
elections. The agreement, which soon opened a way into the all-pervasive
Histadrut trade union federation for Herut, was sealed on 26 April 1965.
Begin assured his new partners, led by the veteran Liberals Yosef Sapir
and Elimelech Rimalt, that they would not be in opposition much longer.
The union was a marriage of convenience rather than a meeting of minds.
It worked because the Liberals were ready to defer to Herut on defence
and foreign policy, while Begin yielded to them on the economy. But
Begin's hopes were dashed at the polls on 2 November 1965. Gahal won
twenty-six seats, one fewer than the previous combined Herut-Liberal
tally, while the Labour Alignment won forty-five, four more than the pre-
election strength of its constituent parties, despite the defection of Ben-
Gurion, whose Rafi won ten seats. After eighteen years Herut's Young
Turks had had enough.

Shmuel Tamir, an ambitious Tel Aviv lawyer and former Irgun intelligence
officer, was joined in revolt against Begin's leadership by Eliezer Shostak
and Avraham Tayer of the National Labour Federation, the Histadrut's
small but well-organized right-wing competitor. Yohanan Bader had
warned Begin against promoting Tamir too quickly, but Begin replied that
he had 'unlimited confidence' in him.[2] Shostak threw down the gauntlet at
a meeting of the Herut central committee two weeks after the elections. The
argument between them, he said, went back to the creation of the State in
1948.

> Begin came to the conclusion that the path of the [Revisionist] movement up to
> the establishment of the State had not led to government, but that his way would
> bring the Herut movement to power. He demanded credit: 'Give me the chance
> and I will prove to you that the movement will succeed my way.' Thus the

relationship between the movement and Begin was mystical. Many things that the members did not understand, or did not agree to, were accepted with the hope that he might prove right.[3]

Begin met the challenge head-on. 'Ever since the second and fourth Knessets,' he said, 'there have been rumours and whisperings. This time I myself will raise the issue.' The central committee gave the leader an overwhelming vote of confidence, twenty-eight to five with eleven abstaining, but the stage had been set for Herut's raucous eighth national convention at the Maccabiah village outside Tel Aviv at the end of June 1966.

The pro-Begin and anti-Begin camps had organized their forces with the stealth of old underground conspirators. The opening speeches gave no hint of a concerted opposition, which emerged only with the voting for the presidium. Rival lists were presented to the 600 delegates, and the opposition won by a ratio of more than two-to-one of those present and voting (253-131). It was left to a Herut student leader from the Hebrew University, Ehud Olmert, to blurt out that the emperor had no clothes. 'Up to now,' he said, 'Begin has led the movement as an opposition to the ruling regime, but he has not succeeded in leading it to rule. He must accept the consequences and resign together with the entire leadership.' Pandemonium broke out in the hall with loyalist delegates waving their fists and shouting down the young upstart. Begin, still perhaps not appreciating the gravity of the challenge, sprang to Olmert's defence. If they would not let him go on, Begin would leave the convention. He was, he said, proud that there were delegates ready to express such opinions and make such proposals. Olmert, the son of a former Herut MP and himself a future Likud member of the Knesset, went on to assail the moral image of the movement, its lack of internal democracy and the wholesale distribution of membership cards. When the leadership took to the offensive, it trained its guns on the more substantial target of Shmuel Tamir and his National Labour Federation allies.

On the third day of the convention, Begin turned the tide by resigning the party leadership and offering to give up his parliamentary seat. 'It was immediately rejected by the stunned delegates,' the *Jerusalem Post* reported, 'but Mr Begin declined to change his decision.' Earlier in the day he had told the central committee: 'When we win at elections, we are all victorious; when we lose, I am to blame.' The old loyalists took the hint. Bader pressed the delegates to re-elect Begin immediately. The convention chairman, Avraham Shechterman, urged Begin to retract his resignation. 'He is not a private person, but belongs to the movement and is part of the nation's history.' Begin returned to the rostrum to 'qualify' his earlier statement, and 'consented' to remain a member of the Party executive. The leadership was regaining control. Its official list for the key steering committee emerged victorious by four votes (253-249) from a secret ballot that ended at three a.m. But the revolt was not over. Tamir drew blood with a distinction between the men of the past and the men of the future, the diaspora politicians and the *sabras* eager for office. 'As a free man, born in this country, as your subordinate in the IZL, I herewith come out and oppose you, in the open, and declare that I am in the opposition not over ideology but over methods.' To the astonishment of Begin and the assembled delegates, the opposition pulled a rabbit out of the hat. Amihai Paglin, the former Irgun operations chief who had played no part in politics since 1948, mounted the rostrum and poured scorn on the leadership.

The convention dispersed with the issue unresolved after a highly emotional three-hour speech by Menachem Begin:

> There is a limit to what a public figure can bear. There is a limit to public cruelty towards a man. They call on me to retire from public life. I did not retire, neither because I was hated nor because I was loved. But what wrong did I do to this people all my life? What wrong did I do to Mr Ben-Gurion that he hated me so? Was it because I and my friends fought for the State, of which Ben-Gurion became the first Prime Minister with our consent?

Begin settled a few scores with the press, then lambasted the internal opposition. 'Shostak, Tamir and Tayer worked behind my back. They set up a coalition. They did not inform me. Mr Tamir knew I intended resigning. They left me like a blind man groping in the dark. Did they think I was the Prime Minister of Monaco to have a Cabinet thrust upon me without my knowledge?' Mark Segal, an Israeli political correspondent not noted for his sympathy towards the Herut leader, commented:

> The speech was a painful experience because of the confession of deep personal hurt. Some of the journalists at the press table to whom I spoke afterwards confessed to a considerable measure of embarrassment, as they sat in the midst of this intimate confession from the distraught man on the rostrum, while around us sat crying women. We felt that we were witnessing the disintegration of a public figure.[4]

But the press table was not the gallery Begin was playing to. As Segal had reported on the night: 'The hall reverberated to thunderous applause as pale-faced and red-eyed he stepped slowly off the platform.' Begin had been careful to restrict his resignation to the duration of the eighth Herut convention. No successor was elected at the Maccabiah village, the permanent home of the world Jewish sports championships. Bader temporarily replaced Begin as head of the Knesset faction. Ya'acov Meridor filled in for him as party chairman. The devious Bader managed to placate the opposition but keep a majority for the old guard on the central committee. As chairman of the steering committee, he accepted a proposal to give the opposition parity on the central committee, on condition that all the Herut MPs served on it too. Each side appointed forty-six members to the committee, but the loyalists had a majority of twelve to three among the MPs. 'I would rather stay in the political wilderness with Menachem Begin than sit in the Cabinet with Shmuel Tamir,' Bader said. The following November, after running Herut from the wings, Begin quietly resumed the leadership. Tamir, Shostak and young Ehud Olmert went their own way after a scandal over a forged anti-Begin letter to *Ha'aretz*, returning to the fold under a ragged assortment of banners in time to sit on the Government benches a decade later.

Despite Liberal misgivings after the 1965 election and during the turbulence of the Herut leadership struggle, Gahal remained intact. The Liberals marked time and looked the other way. Events conspired to bring them and Menachem Begin into government far sooner than any of them imagined. On 15 May 1967, as Israel was celebrating its nineteenth independence day, President Gamal Abdel Nasser of Egypt sent his tanks across the Suez Canal into Sinai, provoking a crisis of confidence that in retrospect seems absurdly misplaced. The Arabs were girding for war, the Israelis felt themselves vulnerable. For the first time in the short history of the Jewish State, they lacked faith in their leaders' capacity to meet such a challenge. Ben-Gurion had retired to Sdeh Boker, his *kibbutz* in the Negev desert. His successor, Levi Eshkol, was notoriously indecisive. For all his wiles as a party politician, the new Prime Minister had no military background. Like Ben-Gurion, he served as his own Defence Minister. Unlike Ben-Gurion, he was not up to the task.

As leader of the main opposition block, Begin was consulted and informed as the crisis unrolled. He was acutely aware of the vacuum of authority at the top and of the growing anxiety in the country. His first thought was to bring back Ben-Gurion. Despite their long-standing mutual hostility, Begin grudgingly respected him as the man who led the Jews to independence after 2,000 years of exile. He would have preferred a different relationship. Ben-Gurion, as Begin saw him, was above all an activist, a statesman who did not shirk hard decisions. What he did not know in the spring of 1967 was that Ben-Gurion, who had turned eighty, was no longer the confident old lion. The Chief of Staff, General Yitzhak Rabin, who complained that he was being asked to bear too much of the political as well as the military burden, turned to Ben-Gurion for moral support. He went away disappointed. Rabin wrote years later:

It was painful to see him in his present state, totally cut off from any sources of information and, worse, clinging staunchly to outmoded concepts. He erred in his assessment of the IDF's strength. He was convinced that Israel was in an intolerable political situation and doubted that she could extricate herself by starting a war with Egypt.[5]

Begin sounded out the leaders of the other opposition parties, including Shimon Peres, secretary-general of Ben-Gurion's own Rafi, which had broken away from Labour in 1965. He was satisfied that they shared his diagnosis and endorsed his prescription. On 24 May, the day after Nasser made war inevitable by closing the Straits of Tiran, the lifeline of Israel's Red Sea port of Eilat, Begin suggested discreetly to Eshkol that Ben-Gurion should be invited to lead a government of national unity. Eshkol, whose quarrel with Ben-Gurion had been no less acrid than Begin's, replied: 'Two such horses cannot pull the same cart.' Although he was impressed by the finality of Eshkol's answer, Begin accepted an invitation to join other opposition leaders at a private meeting in Ben-Gurion's Tel Aviv home. He left as dismayed as Yitzhak Rabin. The old man was still fighting his personal war with the Labour establishment. He dismissed an Israeli pre-emptive strike as dangerous adventurism, and urged the Government to seek Great Power assistance. Begin dropped the idea of mobilizing Ben-Gurion, and told the Prime Minister that Gahal was ready to join a wall-to-wall coalition provided Moshe Dayan, another Rafi MP, replaced Eshkol as Minister of Defence. He was, he said, 'the right man in the right place'. The tide was already flowing for Dayan, who had been Chief of Staff in the Suez war, but Golda Meir, Labour's secretary-general, was reluctant to let bygones be bygones. Begin insisted, however, that Gahal would not join the Government without Rafi. According to his political secretary, Yehiel Kadishai, he was less concerned with Dayan's activist reputation than with ensuring as wide a span of unity as possible. In the end Eshkol yielded to the clamour of public opinion, and to Begin.

On 1 June 1967, Menachem Begin came in from the cold. The heirs of Jabotinsky, the despised terrorists of the Irgun Zvai Leumi, joined the Government of Israel. Begin honoured his historic debts. He invited his three most faithful comrades, Ya'acov Meridor, Arieh Ben-Eliezer and Yohanan Bader, to drive with him to the Prime Minister's office, where he embraced them and took his leave. The next morning, on his way to the Knesset in Jerusalem, Begin stood for a moment beside the grave of his master. Appropriately, Jabotinsky's bones had been brought to Israel three years earlier by Eshkol's Government and reinterred on Mount Herzl alongside the leaders of Zion. Moshe Dayan recorded that after Eshkol had welcomed the new ministers to their first Cabinet meeting, 'Menachem Begin replied in a brief speech, passionately sincere and studded with biblical epigrams, which a good-humoured Eshkol punctuated with "Amen, Amen".'[6]

14
Apprenticeship of Power

In this war Menachem Begin did not have to wait for an invitation. As a Cabinet Minister, albeit one who had still to be sworn in, he joined an inquisitive throng of politicians and retired generals at the Prime Minister's Tel Aviv office on the morning of 5 June 1967. He was one of the first to hear of the co-ordinated air strike that caught the pride of the Egyptian air force at breakfast and won Israel the decisive command of the skies. From 7.45 that Monday morning waves of French-built Mirage fighter-bombers, flying low under the radar horizon, destroyed nearly 300 Egyptian warplanes and disrupted every major Egyptian air base from Sinai to the Upper Nile. By lunchtime the Jordanian and Syrian air forces had gone the same way. Begin's joy in this triumph and his excitement at being one of the inner circle let into the secret was almost boyish. He was bursting with the news, which was held back from the press and the enemy. He embraced the former Chief of Staff, Haim Laskov, a dour veteran of the British army and of the 1948 and 1956 wars, and told him what had happened. On the drive to Jerusalem later in the day he flagged down Golda Meir's car and brought her up to date. The future Labour Prime Minister was at that time secretary-general of the party and not a member of the Cabinet. In the Knesset, Begin sought out David Ben-Gurion in case they had forgotten to tell the old man.

While still in the ante-room of Levi Eshkol's office Begin struck an informal alliance with his old Palmah adversary, Yigal Allon, who was now Minister of Labour. Both of them recognized the possibilities opened up by Israel's initial success. Eshkol had sent a message to King Hussein through the United Nations urging him to keep Jordan out of the war. If he complied, Israel undertook not to attack the Hashemite Kingdom. In order to avoid a war on three fronts the Cabinet was ready to forgo the chance of conquering the West Bank and Arab East Jerusalem. Neither Begin nor Allon opposed the decision to send the signal to Amman, but as soon as it became clear on the Monday morning that Hussein was disregarding it, they started pressing the Prime Minister to give priority to reuniting the divided capital. 'Begin and I want Jerusalem,' Allon told him. With an ironic twinkle, Eshkol replied in Yiddish: 'That's not a bad idea.'

By the time Begin reached Jerusalem for a special parliamentary session the new Knesset, a squat pagoda of a building opened a year earlier on the exposed crest of Givat Ram, was being shelled from the direction of Bethlehem. Begin realized that his dream was becoming a practical option even quicker than he had expected. Learning that Eshkol had not yet arrived, he posted his political secretary, Yehiel Kadishai, at the members' entrance with instructions to let him know as soon as the Prime Minister's car came into view. Begin waylaid Eshkol as he was entering the building and asked for an emergency Cabinet meeting before the Knesset sitting. Eshkol agreed and the ministers assembled in the Cabinet room on the second floor. The Sergeant-at-Arms soon bustled them into a narrow cluttered underground shelter. Mortar bombs were falling dangerously close. One exploded on the lawn outside. The meeting voted unanimously to take the Old City, the site of the holiest of Jewish shrines, the Western Wall of the vast, square platform on which Herod had rebuilt Solomon's Temple. Begin's contribution was to keep Jerusalem in the forefront of Government concerns and to emphasize the need to move quickly before the United Nations could interfere. At the end of the meeting the Religious Affairs Minister, Zerah Warhaftig of the National Religious Party, raised his glass and proposed a toast: 'Next week at the Western Wall.' But the Cabinet was sensitive to the risks of damaging the holy places – Christian and Moslem as well as Jewish – if the walled city were taken by frontal assault. The army was ordered to encircle it in the hope that the Jordanian garrison would see the hopelessness of its cause and surrender.

That evening Begin and his Gahal colleague, Yosef Sapir of the Liberal Party, were confirmed in office by the Knesset and sworn in as ministers without portfolio. After calling on President Zalman Shazar, Begin and Kadishai went to the King David Hotel. The building, with the ravages of the Irgun Zvai Leumi now made good, was within sight of the Old City. 'The hotel was empty,' Begin's aide recalls. 'There were a few journalists, no switchboard, no reception. The door was open, neighbours brought mattresses to sleep in the Régence. The King David was free for all. Shooting was going on, you could see the firing from east and west behind the hotel. I remember a member of Knesset who was afraid to sleep in a room, so he came to the cellar.'[1] Begin was too exhilarated to sleep. He and Kadishai wandered the streets, talking to any other insomniacs they chanced to encounter.

The next night, too, the Herut leader stayed awake in Tel Aviv, listening to the BBC World Service and waiting for the early editions of the morning papers. By then East Jerusalem was encircled, with Israeli tanks and infantrymen controlling Mount Scopus and the Mount of Olives, the key heights above the Old City. After midnight Begin heard on the radio that the United Nations was preparing to order a ceasefire in place on all fronts. He was haunted by the memory of 1948 when the Haganah, the Irgun and the Stern Gang were frustrated by a ceasefire from making another attempt to recapture the ancient Jewish Quarter from King Abdullah's Arab Legion. The first newspaper to arrive on his doorstep, the left-wing Mapam's *Al Hamishmar*, took the story a step further. A ceasefire resolution was imminent. At 4 a.m. Begin woke Eshkol and proposed that they order the army to enter the Old City before it was too late. The Prime Minister asked Begin to telephone Moshe Dayan. 'Although we agreed yesterday to continue surrounding the Old City,' Begin told the Defence Minister, 'the Security Council resolution changes everything. We cannot wait any longer.' Dayan, until then the leading advocate of the more cautious strategy, agreed. At his suggestion, Begin talked again to the Prime Minister and demanded immediate action. Eshkol concurred, consulted his Cabinet colleagues, and ordered Colonel Mordechai Gur and his paratroop brigade to penetrate the walls – the first time they had been stormed since the Turkish Sultan Suleiman the Magnificent built them in 1540. At 10.15 a.m. on Wednesday, 7 June, after fierce combat in the narrow lanes leading from St Stephen's Gate, the Star of David was flying over the Temple Mount and a handful of grimy, sweat-stained paratroops were giving thanks at the Western Wall. The ceasefire did not come into force for another twenty-four hours, by which time Israel had completed its conquest of the West Bank of the Jordan and of the Sinai peninsula. Despite the risk of provoking Syria's Soviet ally, Israel stretched hostilities long enough to seize the Golan Heights on a fifth and sixth day.

Barely three weeks later, on 27 June, Israel extended its laws to East Jerusalem. To all but the most finicky of constitutional lawyers, that was tantamount to annexation. Begin's utopian vision of a united Jerusalem under Jewish sovereignty had come true and the crucial step had been taken to ensure that it would never be redivided short of defeat in war. Even the secular majority of Israelis was touched by a sense that something miraculous had occurred. It was a mixture of deliverance from what had been perceived as a grave danger and wonder at the demolition of the concrete and psychological barriers that had mutilated the holy city. Scores of Israelis streamed in a disorganized pilgrimage day and night to the Western Wall. Whether or not the Old City would have been taken without his dawn initiative, Begin was satisfied that he had played his part.

*   *   *

On Jerusalem Herut shared in a national consensus. No organized body of Israeli opinion advocated returning the eastern half of the city to Arab rule. But on Judea and Samaria, the newly-occupied West Bank, Begin still spoke for a minority. Few imagined that two decades later Israel would be ruling over the whole of Palestine west of the river. Labour leaders talked of 'awaiting a telephone call' from Amman. The Mapam Housing Minister, Mordechai Bentov, said the territories were being 'kept in safe-keeping for King Hussein until he is ready to take them back'. The National Religious Party had not yet been radicalized. Its leader, Haim Moshe Shapiro, told the NRP's 1968 convention that territorial compromise was essential. But from the start Begin was determined to do everything possible to block 'the repartition of *Eretz Yisrael*'. He did not object when the Cabinet decided to put out feelers to the Jordanians, but Abba Eban, who was then Foreign Minister, suspected that if Hussein had responded positively Begin would have resigned. 'I remember how Begin chuckled when he heard the phrase "total rejection" in Hussein's reply.'[2] In July 1967, Begin helped Eban and Warhaftig to draft a letter opening the way to a compromise between Israel's national rights in Jerusalem and the interests of the world community. Israel, it stated, 'does not claim unilateral control or exclusive jurisdiction in the holy places of Christianity and Islam'. In a peace settlement it would be 'prepared to give appropriate expression to this principle'. But this declaration offered no compromise over sovereignty. Eban hoped it would create the possibility of an enclave solution for Al Aqsa mosque and the Dome of the Rock, the Moslem shrines on the Temple Mount, if and when a political settlement with Jordan was being negotiated. Begin was prepared to take that risk.

From the end of the year, he bent all his semantic skill to ensuring that Israel accepted Resolution 242 of the United Nations Security Council in the most non-committal of terms. This resolution, drafted by Britain in November 1967 as a minimum agreed basis for comprehensive peace negotiations between Israel and the Arabs, emphasized the 'inadmissibility of the acquisition of territory by war', and called among other things for 'withdrawal of Israeli armed forces from territories of recent conflict'. Begin's first objective was to prevent the use of the word 'withdrawal' by the Israeli Government. He boasted later that Herut had managed to achieve this for two and a half years.

Three times it was proposed to the Cabinet to use the word 'withdrawal' and the Cabinet refused. In one of the sessions Levi Eshkol determined this. The use of the word 'withdrawal' was suggested to us, and I was against it. We proposed the word 'deployment' of forces. The Prime Minister was asked by one of my colleagues in the Cabinet what the difference was between withdrawal and deployment of forces. He answered very characteristically: 'If we say withdrawal, then we're committed to it. If we say deployment of forces, then Eban will interpret it as he thinks right and Begin will interpret it as he thinks right.'[3]

After further niggling by Begin – 'deployment' was not suitable for a peace treaty, he argued, because deployment usually meant activating forces for attack – the Cabinet eventually settled for: 'The disposition of forces will be in full accordance with the permanent borders to be determined in the peace treaties.' For Begin the difference between 'withdrawal' and 'disposition' was decisive. He was careful not to employ the prefix 're'. The Government of Israel spoke neither of 're-deployment' nor of 're-disposition'. It was not pledging itself to pull back. 'Withdrawal means moving backwards,' Begin explained. 'In disposition there is no movement. It will be decided by the borders, as determined in the peace treaty.'

Eban, one of the most flexible ministers, complained in his memoirs that 'it was not easy for me to draft moderate proposals in a Cabinet composed of all parties, including Gahal, whose representatives professed to believe that peace treaties could be obtained without any territorial sacrifice at all'.[4] Begin did not, however, exercise a veto over Israeli diplomacy. 'Eshkol discreetly and quietly gave me his backing for formulations that were not always pleasing to Begin and his colleagues,' Eban claimed. Nonetheless, Gahal applied a brake at a critical stage before the occupation had set in its mould.

Gahal's participation in the National Unity Government – under Eshkol until his death of a heart attack in February 1969, and under Golda Meir until August 1970 – completed Menachem Begin's transition to respectability. He was fastidious in his attendance at Knesset and Cabinet meetings. Relations with his former foes were cordial and businesslike. He even made peace with the ageing Ben-Gurion. They chanced to meet one day in the Régence restaurant at the King David, and Ben-Gurion invited Begin to join him for lunch. The old warrior wrote to him afterwards:

Paula, my wife, was for some reason an admirer of yours. I opposed your road sometimes strongly – both before the State and after it arose – exactly as I would have opposed the road of Jabotinsky. I strongly objected to a number of your actions and opinions after statehood, and I do not regret my opposition. For in my opinion I was in the right. But personally I never harboured any grudge against you, and as I got to know you better over recent years my esteem for you grew and my Paula rejoiced in it.

Begin was delighted by the compliment, however backhanded it might be. He was equally pleased to discover that Eshkol was a far stronger Prime Minister than he had expected or than his reputation gave him credit for. Eshkol, he testified later, proved to be a man who could take decisions.

> I saw him at work in difficult times and I repeat that he was either an initiator, or a partner, or a decisive factor in critical decisions which are the ones closest to my heart – concerning Jerusalem, concerning the Golan Heights, concerning the unification of Jerusalem – and I know how much he influenced these decisions. [5]

The Herut leader was one minister among others. He enjoyed no privileged relationship with Eshkol, but he was accepted on the same terms. 'It was Eshkol's style to treat his ministers as equals,' said Ya'acov Shimshon Shapiro, the veteran Mapai Justice Minister. 'He tended to accept the existence of another side to the coin, unlike Ben-Gurion and especially Sharett, who regarded himself as the fount of all wisdom.' [6]

The advent of Golda Meir seemed at first to threaten the honeymoon. The new Prime Minister had resisted the establishment of a wall-to-wall coalition on the eve of the June war. She was more interesting in keeping out Dayan, whom she could not forgive for deserting the party with Ben-Gurion, than with blackballing Begin. But she was a woman of forthright views who personified the historic loyalty and prejudices of Mapai. Mrs Meir was a great hater, and Menachem Begin had long been among her targets. But she knew how to charm and to adapt. Like Eshkol, she valued the National Unity Government once it was functioning. She was determined to make it work. If that meant co-existing with Begin, so be it. To the surprise of the political community, they collaborated smoothly and even amicably while the coalition lasted. Although Mrs Meir did not share his absolute commitment to Greater Israel, she was just as sceptical about Palestinian intentions, just as proud in her Jewishness.

Begin, who always had a civilian's soft spot for military heroes, developed a partnership at this time with Dayan, a mutual regard which led to the eventual recruitment of the Labour maverick to serve in a Herut government. The two had little apparent affinity. Dayan was of a native-born generation that knew Arabs as people and not just as faceless enemies. He knew the land in its length and its breadth with all his senses. Begin was at home in Jerusalem, in Tel Aviv and in his biblical dreams. But within the Cabinet they became the nucleus of what one Israeli commentator called 'a hawk coalition that crossed party boundaries'. [7] They joined in dissenting from the de facto endorsement of the Allon Plan, which drew a distinction between sovereignty and security and envisaged an Israeli withdrawal from the main centres of Arab population in a deal with Jordan. Begin and Dayan came to a common position from different starting-points. The one was as mystical as the other. Begin believed in a God-given Jewish right to the whole land. Dayan remembered boyhood wanderings, nights under the stars, and rejected any solution that would deny other Jews the same intimacy. Annexation was an unnecessary provocation, but there must be no impassable border.

The three apprentice years of office from 1967 to 1970 were fruitful, but often frustrating for Begin. As Minister Without Portfolio, he had no area of responsibility. Departmental ministers are by nature jealous of their turf, zealous in leaving no empty spaces. To his colleagues, Begin often seemed to be making work for himself, inventing new sub-committees, monitoring the press, answering the Government's critics. To the chagrin of one of the great *prima donnas* of the Knesset, his parliamentary opportunities were circumscribed too. Backbenchers seldom challenge ministers in a vacuum, party managers do not give old enemies a chance to shine, especially when they might be back in opposition at any moment. When the split finally came, Abba Eban for one felt that Begin 'exchanged the Cabinet table for the Knesset rostrum with a measure of relief'.

When Mrs Meir succeeded Eshkol as Prime Minister, Gahal's continued membership of the coalition was by no means automatic. Begin and his colleagues were uneasy about the drift towards territorial compromise among the Cabinet majority and increasingly sensitive to the danger of being outflanked from the right by the Greater Israel lobby. But they forced the issue on domestic rather than foreign policy. At a time of growing militancy among Israel's workers, Begin demanded legislation making arbitration compulsory in essential industries and services. When the Labour Party, with its roots in the trade union movement and its commitment to the right to strike, refused, Begin declared himself ready to return to the opposition benches. It was the gut issue of *Eretz Yisrael* which persuaded him to change his mind, and the same issue which eventually took Gahal out of office.

By December 1969, Gunnar Jarring's United Nations peace mission, launched after the Security Council had adopted Resolution 242, had run into the sand. Heavy fighting had broken out between Israeli and Egyptian forces astride the Suez Canal. The Palestinian guerrilla campaign from Jordan and Syria was escalating. The world began to fear another conflagration. In Washington the Nixon administration estimated that the time was ripe for a new international initiative to bring the Middle East to its senses. On 9 December the Secretary of State, William Rogers, announced that the Big Four members of the Security Council would co-operate with

Jarring in working out a settlement in accordance with Resolution 242. The Americans had also decided 'to consult directly with the Soviet Union, hoping to achieve as wide an area of agreement as possible between us'. Israel was alarmed by both points – the search for a settlement in the framework of Resolution 242 and the involvement of the Soviet Union, its enemies' friend which had broken off diplomatic relations during the 1967 war. Resistance to the American proposal was hardened by Rogers's clarification of the administration's policy on borders. The United States, he explained, endorsed the principle of the non-acquisition of territory by war and the withdrawal of Israeli armed forces from territories occupied in 1967.

The boundaries from which the 1967 war began were established in the 1949 armistice agreements and have defined the areas of national jurisdiction in the Middle East for twenty years. Those boundaries were armistice lines, not final political borders. The rights, claims and positions of the parties in an ultimate peaceful settlement were reserved by the armistice agreements. The Security Council resolution neither endorses nor precludes these armistice lines as the definitive political boundaries. However, it calls for withdrawal from occupied territories, the non-acquisition of territory by war, and for the establishment of secure and recognized boundaries.

We believe that while recognized political boundaries must be established, and agreed upon by the parties, any change in the pre-existing lines should not reflect the weight of conquest and should be confined to insubstantial alterations required for mutual security. We do not support expansionism. We believe troops must be withdrawn as the resolution provides. We support Israel's security and the security of the Arab States as well. We are for a lasting peace that requires security for both.[8]

Such, in its first formulaton, was the Rogers Plan. It was more balanced than the Israelis acknowledged, but what stuck in their throats was the idea of withdrawal from virtually all the territories, and the whiff of an imposed solution. That was enough to keep Menachem Begin in the Government. Labour relations suddenly seemed trivial. Gahal signed a new coalition agreement. Its ministerial team rose from two to six, including Ezer Weizman, who went straight from the number two spot in the Israel Defence Forces into Herut and the Cabinet room as Minister of Transport. On 22 December, the Government rejected the Rogers Plan root and branch. The American proposals, it said,

prejudice the chances of establishing peace; disregard the essential need to determine secure and agreed borders through the signing of peace treaties by direct negotiation; affect Israel's sovereign rights and security in the drafting of resolutions concerning refugees and the status of Jerusalem; and contain no actual obligation of the Arab States to put a stop to the hostile activities of the sabotage and terror organizations.

Begin was content but wary. The Cabinet, stiffened by Gahal, had held the line. But no one expected the Israeli rejection to kill the American initiative, especially since the Suez war of attrition was intensifying daily and so were Israeli casualties. The Herut leader was alerted by a carefully worded foreign policy statement at the end of May 1970, in which Mrs Meir came closer than ever to accepting Resolution 242 without the semantic qualifications. Begin complained that Gahal had not been consulted, but was temporarily mollified by the Prime Minister's assurance that nothing had changed. In the Knesset vote on her statement, the twenty-six Gahal MPs returned at the 1969 election abstained, but the Herut-Liberal block stayed in the coalition to fight any further concessions to the Americans. Begin did not have to wait long for the challenge.

On 19 June 1970, Rogers made his second move. The United States proposed to Israel, Egypt and Jordan that they start negotiations under Jarring's auspices to reach a peace agreement based on mutual acknowledgement by Israel and Jordan of each other's sovereignty, territorial integrity and political independence; and on Israeli withdrawal from territories occupied in 1967. At the same time, the parties would observe a strict ceasefire for at least three months. To sweeten the pill President Richard Nixon was more specific than before in underwriting Israel's security. At the White House in May he had hinted to Eban that Israel could depend on him for the Phantom fighter-bombers it needed for the war of attrition. According to the Foreign Minister, Nixon now deepened his commitment.

> He let us understand that his undertaking to me about the Phantoms should be taken seriously, and he gave assurance that Israel would not be expected to withdraw a single soldier from any of the ceasefire lines except in the context of a contractual peace agreement which Israel would regard as satisfactory for its security. There was also an undertaking to use the American veto power in the Security Council to resist resolutions calling for a complete withdrawal to the pre-1967 lines.[9]

Eban and Mrs Meir concluded that the risk of accepting the American proposal was less than the danger of rejecting it. To turn down the ceasefire package would bring a continuation of the war with Egypt, the prospect of tangling with the Soviet Union, and a decline in American support for Israel. As Begin saw it, however, they were selling the pass. 'I will cut off my right hand rather than sign such a document,' he told the Gahal Knesset caucus. He warned an anti-Rogers rally against 'a Middle Eastern Munich'.

To preserve the historical homeland, Israel would rely on 'ourselves, our soldiers and our God'. Gahal wanted the ceasefire, but refused to agree to any negotiations on withdrawal until there was peace. Mrs Meir tried to convince Begin that Israel couldn't have one half of the package without the other. Nor could it expect any arms from the United States. Begin's answer was that the Americans didn't give Israel arms out of the kindness of their hearts. Israel had done more for America than America for Israel. Mrs Meir's exasperation is reflected in her memoirs:

> I couldn't get it through to him that although the American commitment to Israel's survival was certainly great, we needed Mr Nixon and Mr Rogers much more than they needed us, and Israel's policies couldn't be based entirely on the assumption that American Jewry either would or could force Mr Nixon to adopt a position against his will or better judgement. But Gahal, intoxicated by its own rhetoric, had convinced itself that all we had to do was to go on telling the United States that we wouldn't give in to any pressure whatsoever, and if we did this long enough and loud enough, one day that pressure would just vanish.[10]

Gahal was less monolithic than the Prime Minister thought. The Liberals sympathized with Begin's stand against withdrawal, but did not want to leave the coalition over what was still a hypothetical question. Arieh Dulzin, one of the Gahal ministers and chairman of the Liberal central committee, was their main spokesman against returning to the opposition. 'We were not impressed by statements,' he says. 'Our major argument was that only if the Government takes a *decision* to withdraw should we leave. Let's stay in the Government to see to it that there will be no withdrawal.'[11] A minority in Herut, including Ezer Weizman, took the same view. 'I was convinced that for Israel to accede to the Rogers Plan would be a disaster,' he wrote. 'But precisely for that reason, I contended that we must remain and not leave the decision on that plan to a Cabinet without Herut ministers.'[12] But Begin was not to be deflected. For him words were as solid as deeds. Once Israel agreed to 'withdrawal', it was on the slippery slope to abandoning the 'domain of our forefathers'. To surrender the Jewish right to the land was but a short step from surrendering the land itself. He exploited all his powers to whip Herut into line, but he had less leverage over the Liberals.

The issue was decided at a joint meeting in the national lottery building of the Herut and Liberal central committees. Each party sent 117 delegates. Mrs Meir tried to influence the outcome by allowing Gahal MPs to vote against Rogers in the Knesset without having to leave the coalition. 'Begin tried very hard to convince us,' Dulzin remembers. 'With us he never threatened, he never got angry. He always tried to convince. He tried very,

very hard, but he did not succeed.' Voting was by secret ballot. As the slips
were counted, the lead swung back and forth. The tension rose to a
crescendo as the last box was emptied after three a.m. Begin won by one of
the smallest majorities of his life, three votes out of 234. About eight
dissident Liberals voted with Herut. Dulzin believes they were voting
against their own leadership rather than for Begin. A smaller number of
Herut defectors voted to stay in the coalition. The Liberals accepted the
verdict rather than dismember Gahal. Dulzin insisted that they had to keep
faith. 'We had walked into the Government together, and we should walk
out together. We had given our word that whatever the vote, we would
respect it.' But the Liberal acquiescence was political as well as moral,
long-term as well as short. 'There was only one possibility to create an
alternative to Labour,' Dulzin maintains, 'and that was together. That is
why we had created Gahal. Historically it was wrong that we left the
Government, but it was good that we didn't part from Herut.'

Menachem Begin and his five Gahal colleagues resigned from the Cabinet
on 4 August 1970, the day that Golda Meir informed the Americans and
the Knesset that Israel accepted Resolution 242 'in all its parts', with the
object of achieving among other things 'withdrawal of Israeli forces from
territories occupied in the 1967 conflict'. The wall Begin believed he had
built around the people of Israel had collapsed, but he would not be a party
to the demolition. He told a gathering of Herut colleagues that he had never
been more at peace with his conscience than he was now. The Government
decision was a victory for the Labour doves, but their relief at the departure
of Gahal was tinged by a passing regret. Abba Eban, the most doveish of
them all, wrote with unusual generosity: 'The departure of Begin and his
able colleagues left the Cabinet table more compact and tranquil. But the
spice and zest of intellectual combat were reduced.'

The split was inevitable, sooner or later. In Israeli politics, national unity
governments are better at making war than peace. The consequences of this
episode remain a matter of conjecture and contention. Mrs Meir claimed
that the 1973 Yom Kippur War vindicated her decision. Without it Israel
would not have been equipped to meet the test of the Egyptian and Syrian
surprise attacks. President Nixon kept his promise. The Phantoms and
other American weapons systems did arrive between 1970 and 1973. Arieh
Dulzin believes that if Gahal had stayed in the Government, the war might
never have happened. 'After we left, the Cabinet security committee ceased
to exist. Mr Begin was one of the major factors in this committee. Security
was his major interest. The Government would have been more conscious
of the security situation, and would not have relied on the legendary figure
of Dayan as the guarantee for everything.' The Liberals also argue that if

they had broken the Gahal alliance by remaining in office, Begin would not have won the 1977 election. But that assumes that a parting of the ways would have been irreversible. One thing is indisputable. Begin's forebodings were not fulfilled. Israel endorsed Resolution 242, including the principle of withdrawal. But, for good or ill, it was not forced to give up an inch of *Eretz Yisrael* west of the Jordan.

15
Unity or Bust

Gahal's defection from Golda Meir's National Unity Government in August 1970 restored the issue of power versus principle to Herut's agenda. Menachem Begin was proud that his party had kept faith with its voters and with its commitment to an undivided *Eretz Yisrael*. He was happy to have frustrated all those smart columnists and cartoonists who were only too ready to sneer that 'you couldn't get Gahal out of the Government, even with a bulldozer, that those people only had to get a taste of ministerial status (with an office and a car) and they couldn't give it (or them) up'. But other, younger Herut members were less complacent, less resigned to a life of pious abstinence. Ezer Weizman became their standard-bearer. The former general was a doer, a man of action. He shared Begin's right-wing nationalism. He too believed that abandoning Israel's claim to the East Bank of the Jordan was compromise enough. But he lacked his leader's ideological underpinning. Weizman had entered politics to get things done, to end the Mapai monopoly, not to worship at the shrine of Jabotinsky. He was a *sabra*, a nephew of the first President, Chaim Weizmann. His Zionism had its roots in Haifa rather than Brest-Litovsk, in the IDF rather than the IZL. As the architect of the modern Israeli air force, he had known the satisfaction of command and achievement. Once he recognized that he would never make Chief of Staff, he was eager to transfer his energies to civilian life. Nothing could have been more flattering than the *fiesta* with which Begin welcomed him to Herut, or the swift transition from general staff to Cabinet table, but the euphoria could not last. Begin wanted Weizman as a star, a war hero, a vote-catcher, as a courtier but not a rival. Herut was still his party, and he alone would determine its policies and its goals.

The conflict came to a head at the party convention in Tel Aviv in December 1972. Begin assumed the offensive from the start, warning the rebels and their potential supporters that a successful challenge to his authority might force his retirement. 'I will find it more than difficult', he said, 'to work with a central committee unacceptable to me.' It was a familiar ploy, but it worked again. Delegates took the hint and gave the loyalists a two-thirds majority on the central committee. After a withering personal assault from Begin, Weizman had little choice but to resign the chairmanship of the party executive, to which Begin had appointed him. 'I have learned some very serious lessons about the democratic process,' he reflected. In a private exchange, he questioned whether Begin wished ever to move from opposition to government. The party leader retorted: 'We cleave to principles, not to Cabinet seats.' That, as far as Begin was concerned, was the end of the debate. He was back in his element. All attempts at reconciliation failed. Begin was as confident as an Old Testament prophet of his own wisdom. There was no room for doubt. 'We have never been mistaken,' he wrote in *Ma'ariv*, 'we have always judged things correctly, so we have never changed, for we have never needed to change.' In the same spirit, Begin dismissed the very fostering of dissent within Herut as anti-democratic. Weizman could only fulminate from the minority benches: 'This is a movement of passive people fearful of change. It does not project, to put it mildly, an image of a vital political movement.' With victory now complete, Begin left it to his old Irgun henchman, Haim Landau, to deliver the *coup de grâce*: 'Don't tell me tales about seeking to renew the movement, when all you were after was power.' Weizman wrote in his book *On Eagles' Wings*: 'Within the structure of the party, with its hierarchy and the nature of the relationships at the top level, it became quite clear that there was no room for a creature like me.' Herut, he concluded in a later volume of memoirs, was 'a tiny preserve for an endangered species'.

It was at this period that the old Irgun chieftain paid a first, unhappy visit to Britain, a visit that brought out all his combative instincts. Time had passed and he was ready to let bygones be bygones. The British, or rather their press and pro-Arab MPs, were not. In an editorial headed, 'A killer calls', the *Sunday Express* reminded its readers of the hanging of the two British sergeants.[1] Begin, it said, had never been punished for the atrocity.

> It is extraordinary that Begin should wish to come to a country for which he nourished such hatred. Even more incredible are his reported remarks that he feels a sufficient interval has passed and that he expects traditional British hospitality. What kind of people does he think we are?
> No one can live for ever with anger and a thirst for revenge. And in Britain there is, rightly, an enormous goodwill for Israel. But there is not goodwill for murderers. Does Begin really imagine that even after a quarter of a century the British people should be eager to put their arms round an unpunished killer?

The Times published a diatribe comparing Deir Yassin to the My Lai massacre in Vietnam. The *Guardian* brought the attack up to date. 'His aim', it commented, 'is to draw support away from his government, which is prepared to negotiate withdrawal. Mr Begin's contribution makes the Middle East problem more intractable and increases the likelihood of war. He is no help or credit to Israel.'

Begin seized every opportunity to reply in the press, on radio and on television. When a reporter asked how it felt being guarded by British policemen instead of being hunted by them, he answered: 'This is one of the most interesting episodes of my life. I think it is very touching. Your policemen are very devoted.' Told that certain Arab ambassadors had asked Whitehall to extradite him to face war crimes charges in an Arab country, he smiled: 'I would be the first Knesset member to visit an Arab country. Maybe this will be the beginning of direct negotiations for a just and lasting peace.' Despite bomb threats, hostile demonstrations and questions in the House, Begin refused to cut short his three-day trip. But menacing telephone calls prompted the managers of the Royal Garden Hotel and the Central Hall, Westminster, to cancel the main public meetings planned by British Herut. On his return to Israel, Begin blithely described the visit as 'the most wonderful three days in my life'. But the old enemy's long, selective memory left a bitter taste. After all, other national leaders who had been branded terrorists in the dying days of empire – Jomo Kenyatta and Archbishop Makarios – were now received with honour in London. So was Emperor Hirohito of Japan. Begin did not need to be paranoid to sniff anti-Semitism.

Like Ezer Weizman, General Ariel Sharon was too right-wing, and perhaps too egotistical, to achieve his highest military ambition, certainly under a Labour Government. In early July 1973, Sharon retired from the army and plunged into Gahal politics. Instead of Herut, he chose the staid Liberal Party for no better reason than that it seemed more ripe for seduction. Within two months, he had changed the face of the Israeli democratic Right – and launched Menachem Begin a decisive step nearer the premiership. His target was not just to transform Gahal into a party of government, but to broaden its base so that it presented a plausible alternative to Labour hegemony. Sharon approached the task with the same exuberance that had won the adulation of his paratroops and the trepidation of his superiors. He was a political novice without modesty. He pushed, exhorted and cajoled. He would not take no for an answer. Within a fortnight, Herut gave its blessing to a new 'Likud' (unity) block encompassing the two Gahal partners plus Shmuel Tamir's Free Centre and the State List, a splinter of a splinter of Ben-Gurion dissidents who had not gone back to Labour. Despite his reservations about the mutinous Tamir, whom he had driven out of Herut in 1966, Begin was among Sharon's most enthusiastic backers. The senior partner would still be Herut, and Herut would still be Begin. Sharon posed no challenge to the leader's prestige.

Despite his drive, however, the negotiations turned sour and dragged on into September. The two smaller parties wrangled about who should have thirty-fifth or thirty-sixth place on the joint list for the Knesset elections due on 30 October. Elimelech Rimalt, the patient, scholarly Liberal leader, snapped at Tamir: 'Anyone who quibbles over the thirty-fifth place at this stage of the talks does not really want the Likud.' For tactical reasons, Begin switched Herut negotiators, replacing the outspokenly pro-Likud Binyamin Halevy with the old loyalist Yohanan Bader, who could not forgive Tamir his revolt at the Maccabiah village. Tamir played even harder to get, demanding fifth rather than eighth place for himself. Ezer Weizman, who had been encouraged by the prospect of a broader alliance to patch up a reconciliation with Begin, was so disgusted that he withdrew again. In a letter to the Herut leader, Weizman wrote:

> I have never taken part in such an ugly and disgraceful process in a body that should set an example in honesty and leadership. Not that I am without blame. All of us created this negative spectacle. We all took part in bickering over Knesset seats in which slander was slung around and terrible untruths uttered. What has happened in the past few weeks has undermined our chances of providing leadership. For the sake of public hygiene, I feel it necessary to step down from the bandwaggon that I have been sitting on and return to political inactivity, to soul-searching and the quest for a political path.[2]

Begin was in no mood for another confrontation with the former air force commander. 'I think everyone should act in keeping with his conscience and understanding,' he replied. Rather than appealing to Weizman to stay, Begin allowed his aides to leak the exchange to the press. Ariel Sharon was made of sterner stuff. He mollified and he nudged, shaming the party professionals into unity. 'It must be all together, or nothing at all,' he urged, with elections creeping perilously close. On 16 September 1973, the Likud agreement was sealed. 'He raped four parties', one of Sharon's Liberal colleagues reported, half admiring, half shell-shocked.

Some Israel commentators predicted that the creation of the new bloc would mark the beginning of the end of Begin's career. It was possible, Begin wrote in a teasing *Ma'ariv* column, that their wish would come true, but it was equally possible that they would be disappointed. Meanwhile he defined the Likud's three main targets as: a Knesset majority which would reject any proposal to redivide *Eretz Yisrael*; a practical initiative to abolish poverty; and the consolidation of an alternative to Labour. 'But for now,' Begin added on the eve of the Jewish New Year, 'no one among us is going to the beginning of his political end. We are all at the start of a new year, and perhaps – who knows? – at the start of a new era.'[3] He proved both less and more of a prophet than he, or his readers, imagined.

On the eve of the new year, 26 September, the Defence Minister, Moshe Dayan, toured the Israeli front line on the Golan Heights. There had been disturbing reports of a build-up of Syrian armour. Having seen for himself, Dayan ordered a limited reinforcement of the Israeli garrison. He was taking no chances. 'On the Jordanian border we have civilian settlements but no enemy,' he told the general staff. 'On the Egyptian border we have an enemy but no settlements. On the Syrian border we have both. If the Syrians get to our settlements, it will be calamitous.' Eleven days later, on Yom Kippur, the holiest day in the Jewish calendar, the Syrian and Egyptian armies struck simultaneously on the Golan and the Suez Canal. Despite ominous signs, Israel was inadequately prepared. For the first time since 1948, it was fighting a desperate war of national survival. Politics went on hold. Ariel Sharon returned to the colours and commanded one of the three divisions that blocked the Egyptian offensive, then led the assault force that took the battle back across the canal. As Leader of the Opposition, Begin was briefed by Golda Meir when Israeli intelligence reported that the invasions were imminent. Like everyone else, however, he was surprised when the Arab armies opened fire at two p.m. on 6 October, four hours earlier than predicted. The Herut leader was praying in the synagogue of his party's Tel Aviv headquarters, known affectionately as Fortress Jabotinsky, when his daughter Leah brought the news. For the three weeks of the war, Begin refrained from criticizing either the Government or the high command for the mistakes that had brought the country so close to disaster. This was no time for a responsible opposition to be scoring party points. But he was only waiting for a suitable opportunity.

With elections now rescheduled for the end of the year, and the nation demanding the heads of the 'guilty men', Begin took up the cudgels. In a Knesset debate on 14 November, he demanded Mrs Meir's resignation. 'Why did you not mobilize the reserves before Yom Kippur? Why did you not move reinforcements to the fronts?' he repeated again and again in a rhyming Hebrew refrain. 'You may well say, blessed is the nation which has such soldiers to fight for it. But you cannot say, blessed is the nation which has such a government to lead it!' The Prime Minister was shocked by the easy flow of Begin's rhetoric. 'If only he had stammered or hesitated occasionally,' she wrote. The Opposition speakers were 'talking about a near catastrophe, about men who had been killed or crippled, about terrible things, but they spoke smoothly, without as much as a pause and I was disgusted'.[4]

The national mood was nearer to Begin than to Mrs Meir. Bereaved families abused Dayan at the graveside. The bubble of the 1967 war, Israel's inflated assurance of military supremacy, had been pricked. The Government and the army had lumbered into a trap of their own making. They had assumed that since the Arabs could not win a war, they would not start a war. Middle Eastern logic proved more dense than that. Although the army eventually turned the tables on the Egyptian and Syrian invaders, Israeli self-confidence was badly shaken. Most people blamed the Government, especially Dayan, whose military expertise ought to have alerted him to the dangers.

Begin had never fought a campaign in more propitious circumstances, but the result of the 31 December poll was disappointing. The electorate punished Labour, but they did not turn it out. The ruling party and its associates won fifty-four seats to the Likud's thirty-nine. This was a decline of six seats for Labour and a gain of seven for the Likud parties, their best performance so far. But the protest vote was divided. Shulamit Aloni's Citizens' Rights Movement, a left-of-centre list thrown together at the last minute, won three seats. Israelis were not quite ready for a Begin Government, but a trend had been established. The Likud fared particularly well among young, army-age voters. The oriental Jews in development towns, immigrant *moshavim* and city slums were shedding their deference to the Mapai machine, which had once spelled housing, jobs and welfare services. The 1973 election was the first tremor of an earthquake.

16
A Summer Earthquake

Menachem Begin started the eighth Knesset with the bit between his teeth. The Labour Party, which had ruled continuously at the head of assorted coalitions since independence, was in disarray. The Yom Kippur War had demonstrated that it was neither omnipotent nor omnicompetent. It had come to take power too much for granted. The triumph of 1967 had eroded the Government's vigilance. Patronage, which had been widely tolerated during the pioneering phase, had begun to degenerate into corruption. Labour's command of the electorate was shaken, if not yet loosened. Dissatisfaction with its performance was spreading beyond the ranks of the traditional opposition voters. Begin had everything to fight for when the session opened in January 1974. Although few were predicting a Likud victory at the next time of asking, the new alliance looked more like a plausible alternative. Begin led a block of thirty-nine MPs, representing 30.1 per cent of the electorate. It was harder to dismiss him as a mere firebrand on the fringe of Israeli politics. The old underground fighter had mellowed, in his manner if not in his ideas. He was more stocky, the moustache had gone, his hair was thinning, he had stopped smoking his habitual cigarettes. In the Knesset he was recognized as an able and assiduous parliamentarian, not only on the rostrum but in the committee room and the members' dining-room. He was at ease with fellow MPs of all parties, accessible to the press, always ready with a courtly 'Welcome to our country' for foreign visitors. His three years in the National Unity Government had established that he could be constructive as well as critical. Despite his hostile reception in London in 1972, the Leader of the Opposition became a welcome guest at the British ambassador's annual Queen's Birthday party.

With Israel still paying for its October complacency, Begin had no shortage of targets. He was at his best, as orator and showman, when he was attacking. In the despondent aftermath of a war that Israel had lost politically if not on the battlefield, his strictures seemed more legitimate than before, his misgivings were more widely shared. History was, however, to prove him wrong in his suspicion of Anwar Sadat's protestations of peace, and in his distrust of Henry Kissinger's Middle Eastern diplomacy. Egypt's 'glorious crossing' of the Suez Canal did make it possible for the biggest Arab State to come to terms with Israel; the Sinai agreements of 1974 and 1975 did not furnish a springboard for another invasion. But the wildest prophet would not have suggested that within five years Begin and Sadat would be sharing the Nobel Peace Prize.

In a cold wind and driving rain on the evening after Israel's first pullback, Begin told 4,000 umbrella-toting protesters in a Tel Aviv square: 'This is a demonstration against the Chamberlain umbrella policy.' The echoes of appeasement were picked up by the star of the evening, Ariel Sharon, who had reverted from the army to politics. The Government, he charged, was throwing away Israel's best card. 'Our victorious army is pulling back under the leadership of a defeated and defeatist Government from an area for which we paid thousands of lives and for which we got nothing.' The Likud was speaking with a single voice, although it had still not merged into a single party. The Liberal leader, Elimelech Rimalt, feared that Golda Meir 'could léad Israel to retreat to the borders of 1948'. Shmuel Tamir added a warning against a Middle Eastern Munich. In the Knesset, Begin started calling the Government 'the transitional administration'. With a show of reluctance (remembering their 'harmonious work' in the National Unity Government), he repeatedly challenged Dayan's contention that Sadat sincerely sought peace. 'Who told you that,' he asked, 'that you so mislead this nation?' The Government was not thinning out forces, it was thinning out Israel's security. Begin's scepticism about Kissinger was heightened by the Secretary of State's origins. Kissinger should be reminded, he said, that he was not the first Jew in history who had risen to high rank. Other Jews too had suffered from a complex that they might be accused of partiality to their brother Jews, and so had gone to the opposite extreme. 'This is bondage', he said, 'in the midst of freedom.' When a Government back-bencher asked whether he would say as much to Kissinger's face, Begin replied: 'I certainly would.'[1]

For all that, Begin was not immune to the contagion of peace. At Herut's 1975 convention, which opened with a symbolic flourish at Kiryat Arba, the Jewish settler suburb of Hebron, he presented an eight-point peace plan to the Arab world. It included a three-year truce on land, sea and air; negotiations for peace treaties between Israel and its neighbouring states, which would define the borders once and for all; and an attempt to find a humane solution to the Arab refugee problem and to the property claims of Jews who had left Arab lands for Israel. But the leopard had not changed his spots. In the same speech, Begin stood by 'the doctrine to which we have dedicated our lives', the Jewish right to the whole land of Israel.

Failing peace, he added, Israel should make no further withdrawals, which merely brought the enemy closer to Israel's population centres and endangered the security of the nation. 'Withdrawals without peace are the ruin of the very chance of peace.'

Golda Meir's Government proved indeed to be a transitional administration. Although the Agranat Commission, which investigated the failings that produced the October war, blamed the soldiers rather than the politicians, public confidence in the old guard was waning. Once a separation of forces agreement had been signed with Syria at the end of May 1974, the ailing Prime Minister was content to retire with honour. Moshe Dayan, her Minister of Defence, stepped down at the same time. But the public's taste for new faces was met by the elevation of another Labour generation rather than the change of party, or at least the creation of a second National Unity Government, for which Begin had been clamouring. Yitzhak Rabin, a native Israeli who had served as ambassador to Washington after retiring as Chief of Staff, shot to the premiership after barely six months in parliament. He was identified with success, the Six Day War and a fruitful period in Israel–American relations. More to the point, he was untainted by the '*mehdal*', the mess of October 1973. The Likud would have to wait for another election before it could hope for office.

Begin was not unduly perturbed. He had, after all, been marking time for twenty-six years on the opposition benches. Ariel Sharon was less patient. The parliamentary life, with its polite conventions and hours of meaningless chatter, had no appeal. In uniform he had earned the reputation of a maverick, a fighter who personified the aggressive spirit of the IDF, an individualist who fired first and argued afterwards. In the Suez War, Sharon disobeyed orders and dropped with his paratroops in the Mitla Pass. It was a costly and unnecessary operation in which thirty-eight Israelis died and 120 were wounded. Four of his junior officers (two of whom later became Chiefs of Staff and one a head of the Mossad secret service) accused him of sending men to their deaths for his own glory. The Chief of Staff, Moshe Dayan, wrote in his 1956 diary that Sharon had escaped court-martial because the Israeli army did not punish a commander for doing too much, but only for doing too little. Sharon entered politics in 1973 because his military career had reached its limit. He was not looking for a quiet retirement, but for a new way of imprinting his ego on the nation. When that seemed to have failed, he resigned his Knesset seat and accepted command of a reserve division. In June 1975, he became adviser on security affairs to his old comrade-in-arms, Yitzhak Rabin. When that too turned out to be an empty shell of a job, and when he recognized that it was not going to give him a second stab at Chief of Staff, Sharon went home to his farm in the Negev desert. The Likud, or so it appeared, would have to manage without the man who had whipped it into unity.

Israel's first *sabra* Prime Minister disappointed many of those who had invested their hopes in him. Rabin proved a stubborn negotiator when Kissinger was pressing for a second Sinai agreement. The deal he signed in September 1975 gave Israel a better basis for defending itself than the one the Secretary of State tried to foist on him in March. The Egyptian army did not enter the strategic Gidi and Mitla passes. Troop movements east of the Suez Canal were to be monitored by Israeli and American early-warning stations. But Begin's charge that Rabin had reversed his previous stand found ready echoes among the unsophisticated, who saw only that Israel was giving up the passes and the lucrative Abu Rodeis oilfields without an Egyptian promise to end the state of war, and that the Prime Minister had needlessly alienated the Americans in the process. The doves, meanwhile, were distressed by Rabin's rigid approch to the future of the West Bank. He was as obsessed as Begin with the dangers of a Palestinian State. By rejecting an overture from King Hussein to negotiate a Jericho disengagement comparable to those in Sinai and on the Golan Heights, he left Jordan with no defence against the radical Arabs, who persuaded the Rabat summit of Arab states to crown the Palestine Liberation Organization as the 'sole legitimate representative of the Palestine people'.

Rabin's abiding triumph was the Entebbe rescue in July 1976, an unprecedented feat of audacity and skill, of political nerve as much as military planning. But the Labour leaders were reluctant to steal the paratroops' thunder by making political capital out of the operation. Begin, who played no part in it except to respect the Prime Minister's confidence in briefing him, had no such inhibitions. He went to Ben-Gurion airport with a quart bottle of whisky to greet the returning hostages. Many of them, Moroccan-born Israelis who had been flying to Paris on the hijacked plane, were Likud voters. They and their jubilant families hoisted him shoulder-high and broke into chants of 'Be-gin, Be-gin' as if he were the hero of the hour.

On the domestic front, Rabin made few friends. Israelis respected his analytical mind, his soldier's caution, but they found him too introverted in relations with his colleagues and the public, sepulchral to the point of caricature in his speeches and television interviews. He lacked the politician's antennae, the patience to cultivate useful borcs. In his self-imposed isolation, he did not always spot trouble early enough. Shimon Peres, whom he had defeated for the Labour leadership, conspired against him from the Defence Ministry, but Rabin did not know how to counter him. Despite his family roots in the Labour movement, Rabin spent his formative years in the army. In the last resort, even in the IDF, a commander can assert rank and expect to be obeyed. Politics, he found the hard way, did not work like that.

The sense that Labour was losing its grip increased. Scandal followed scandal, most of them other men's chickens dating back to the heyday of Pinhas Sapir, the earthy Finance Minister and machine politician extra-ordinary, who was reputed to control the Israeli economy from a small, black notebook. One of his protégés, Michael Tsur, managing director of the Israel Corporation, was sentenced to fifteen years in prison after pleading guilty to fourteen charges of bribe-taking, theft, breach of trust, illegal transfer of funds, unauthorized foreign currency transactions and falsifying documents. Millions of dollars, earmarked by foreign investors for building up Israeli industry, were involved. Asher Yadlin, director of the Kupat Holim trade union sick fund and (as ill luck, and perhaps ill judgement, would have it) Rabin's nominee for Governor of the Bank of Israel, was sent to prison for five years for taking bribes and making false tax declara-tions. The judge rejected his claim that he had channelled some of the money to Labour Party funds, but the mud stuck. The Housing Minister, Avraham Ofer, committed suicide amid unsubstantiated rumours of feath-ering his own nest while managing the Histadrut's development company. All this was grist to the mill for the cynics and the opposition. Labour, they said, had been corrupted by power. Counter-rumours of obscure misde-meanours by Herut's Tel-Hai Fund made little or no impact.

In this atmosphere of moral disintegration, the National Religious Party, Labour's most adhesive partner through three decades, inflated a technical breach of the Sabbath to bring down the coalition. Late on Friday after-noon, 10 December 1976, Israel celebrated the delivery of its first three F-15 air-superiority fighters from McDonnell Douglas. As the three Eagles performed elaborate aerobatics for the assembled dignitaries, the Prime Minister exulted: 'This day is a holiday that inspires us with faith and trust, which we so need – trust in our might and faith in a better future.' The Chief of Staff, General Mordechai Gur, added, 'Today the State of Israel is a different State and the IDF is a different IDF.' Unfortunately for Rabin, the F-15s, the most advanced aircraft Israel had ever received, arrived perilously close to the Sabbath and the guests risked violating religious law by driving home after nightfall. Poalei Agudat Yisrael, a small ultra-Orthodox party which was outside the coalition, introduced a motion of no-confidence. When it came to a vote on 14 December, nine of the ten National Religious Party MPs abstained, despite an apology from Rabin. The Government scraped home, but the Prime Minister dismissed his three NRP ministers. 'A Government which cannot stick to the principle of collective responsibility', Rabin contended, 'has no business functioning as a Government.' A week later, since he could no longer be sure of a majority, he resigned and called for early elections.

In the Israeli system, that is easier said than done. The Knesset has to pass legislation setting the date. Every party endures a festival of horse-trading before publishing its list of candidates. Public servants and army officers must be allowed 100 days to resign and offer themselves at the hustings. Ballot papers inexplicably take weeks to print. In the event, polling day was set for 17 May – long enough for another scandal to drive one more nail in Labour's coffin, and in that of the first *sabra* Prime Minister.

Two months before the election, on 15 March, the Washington corres-pondent of *Ha'aretz* reported that Rabin's wife, Leah, had retained a dollar account in an American bank after her husband ended his ambassadorial tour in 1973. This was in breach of Israeli exchange control regulations. Since at least $10,000 was involved, the Attorney-General, Aharon Barak, insisted on prosecuting Mrs Rabin. No one was above the law. Just before midnight on Thursday, 7 April, having waited for Maccabi Tel Aviv to win the European basketball championship by a single point, the Prime Minister announced on television and radio that he was standing down. He accepted equal responsibility for the bank account. Although the constitution pre-vented his resigning the premiership in a caretaker administration, he handed over his duties and the number one spot on the Labour slate to the Defence Minister, Shimon Peres. Leah Rabin was fined the equivalent of $27,000.

The Likud fought the 1977 election on Menachem Begin's name, but with minimal campaigning by the party leader. It was partly choice and partly necessity. In the last week of March, with nearly two months still to go, Begin suffered his first, most serious heart attack and was admitted to a Tel Aviv hospital. But Likud strategy had been set long before. This was Israel's first ad-man's election. Ezer Weizman, who had returned to the fold, was appointed to run the Likud campaign. He insisted on doing so on his own terms, with the help of Eliezer Zhurabin, a leading advertising agent. 'Read between the lines,' Weizman urged reporters after unveiling his opening shot. 'Look for what is not there.' What wasn't there, wrote Yosef Goell in the *Jerusalem Post*, was 'that part of the Likud's and Herut's political image which is suspected of having turned off enough voters in the past to keep electoral victory out of their reach. There is no unnecessary sabre-rattling, no reference to the divisive issue of the territories.'

Begin remained the Likud's most marketable asset, but a more benign

Begin, one who would not frighten the floating voter. 'He is an honest man,' Weizman explained, 'no small thing in these days. He lives modestly, and not just for public relations purposes, and he has never shilly-shallied about what he is for and what he is against.'² Begin was promoted as a democrat, a fighter ('from the age of sixteen, Menachem Begin has devoted all his energy, talent and ability to one cause, the establishment of the Jewish people in its land'), the incorruptible ('modest and pure of deed'), and the family man. The contrast with his Labour opponents was implicit. The Likud had no need to spell it out. The voters were well aware of recent scandals, and of Peres's reputation for deviousness and inconsistency. Begin was shown playing with his grandchildren, orating, visiting the army, and finally holding his baby grandson during the circumcision ceremony. 'The Likud', Labour quipped in return, 'has made the startling discovery that Begin is actually a human being.' Briefing party workers, Eliahu Ben-Elissar, joint chairman of the Likud's publicity committee, said:

> Gentlemen, I want to present to you, and then through you, the face of the country under Likud rule, under the rule of Menachem Begin. It will be a beautiful country, a country where it will be a pleasure and an honour to live. A country where there will be no desire to go on strike, where a person will be ashamed to steal. There will be respect between Jew and Jew. A country whose sons will not have to feel ashamed of being Jews or Zionists. We shall educate the youth so that service on behalf of the State, in the army or any other national service, will be an honour and a privilege.³

No mention of the occupied territories, of biblical rights, of old betrayals or martyrs mounting the scaffold. But Begin still controlled the policy behind the façade. He had yielded the campaign to Ezer Weizman and his new men, but not the party. 'The platform', Ben-Elissar testifies, 'was always his work, in 1977 as in previous years. He defined the political line, especially as far as foreign policy was concerned, the Palestinian issue, peace and war, Judea and Samaria.'⁴ Begin emerged from hospital and the shadows for an eve-of-poll television debate with Shimon Peres, another innovation in Israeli elections. The pundits were reluctant to pick an outright winner. The Labour contender held his own, though Begin made most of the running. What mattered for the Likud was that the debate stilled any immediate doubts about Begin's health. He was combative, relaxed, jocular, clearly in control of himself and his material, surprising Peres by quoting the Defence Minister's own statements at him.

The final opinion polls showed Labour still slightly ahead, but with the Likud gaining rapidly in the home straight. At least one pollster suggested that Begin might yet make it, if the late rally were sustained, but few

commentators took him seriously. Old assumptions die hard. Despite everything, Labour was seen to the last as the party of government. Menachem
Begin was still convalescing. He toured the polling stations during the day,
but returned to his Tel Aviv home at 1 Rosenbaum Street for a restful
evening with his wife Aliza, daughters Hassia and Leah, and two of the
family's oldest friends, Max and Yehudit Ferber. They ate a simple supper
and watched television in the cramped room that served Menachem and
Aliza as living-room, bedroom and study. The flat, where they had lived
since 1946, had one other bedroom, shared through their teens by the three
Begin children, a small entrance-hall, bathroom and kitchen. The Begins'
son, Binyamin, was in the United States working for a doctorate in geology.
He was the most political of the children, but the least conspicuous, a young
man who valued his privacy.

At 11 p.m. soon after the polls had closed, Israel television's chief
anchorman, Haim Yavin, startled viewers by predicting a Likud victory on
the strength of the TV's own unofficial sample ballot. In Rosenbaum Street,
the Begin daughters could hardly suppress their excitement, but their father
took the news quietly, even sceptically. The result was neither final nor
official. 'Our parents were the most calm,' Hassia recalls, 'especially our
mother. Father sat in his favourite armchair with a dressing-gown over his
shirt and trousers. We went on chatting as if it was nothing special.'[5] A
crowd gathered outside; police guards, the harbingers of change, were
posted to protect the new Prime Minister. But Begin was still waiting. It
was too early to celebrate. When his political secretary, Yehiel Kadishai,
arrived at 1.30 a.m. to invite him to party headquarters, five minutes' walk
away, Begin replied: 'We have time. This is only a guess by the boys at the
television.' Kadishai found him surprisingly relaxed, a cool contrast to the
jubilation he had left behind at Fortress Jabotinsky. 'He was dressed, but
with no tie and no jacket. He went to have a shave, then he came back and
went on watching television. It was only at about 2.15, when the results
were clear, that he decided it was time to go.'[6]

Hundreds of Likud loyalists gathered in the second-floor Independence
Hall on King George Street. Ezer Weizman tried to clear some of the more
obscure party members, but this was a night that had been too long coming
and none of them was going to miss the climax. As the news of victory broke
on the television monitors, they swirled in a mixture of shock and ecstasy.
Could it really be true? Ze'ev Chafets, a young American immigrant re-
cruited by the Liberals to work in the Likud press office, enthusiastically
joined the pandemonium. 'We were all cheering,' he says, 'we had worked
hard and we had won an election.' Suddenly a gnarled Irgun veteran
grabbed him by the shirt. 'He was very angry. He said: "Who are you?

You've been here a couple of months, I've been waiting thirty years for this!" '[7]

Rumour crowded upon rumour. Begin was coming, no he wasn't. Finally at about 2.30 the leader and his family arrived. Begin looked thin and drawn from his recent heart attack. His aides tried to protect him from the crush, but he joyously embraced the Liberal leader, Simha Erlich, and the Likud campaign manager, Ezer Weizman. A guard stopped Aliza and the two daughters at the door. There were enough people inside already. 'But he's my father,' Hassia beseeched him. 'This is my mother, Mrs Aliza Begin. We came with my father, with Begin.' The guard was unimpressed until Yitzhak Shamir, a future Foreign Minister and Begin's eventual successor, came to their rescue. On the stage, Begin joined the crowd in singing *Am Yisrael Hai*, 'The People of Israel Lives', clapping his hands to the patriotic beat. Everyone was pushing to get as near as possible, the politicians and the campaign staff, all hoping to squeeze into the historic photographs and film-clips. A space was cleared at last and Begin stood alone under giant portraits of Jabotinsky and Herzl. He drew a black skull-cap from the pocket of a suit that had seen better days, then a little black-bound book from which he recited Psalms. The speech that followed was unexpectedly conciliatory, no crowing and no threats. Begin quoted from Abraham Lincoln's second inaugural address: 'With malice towards none; with charity for all; with firmness in the right, as God gives us to see the right, let us strive on to finish the work we are in; to bind up the nation's wounds. . . .' Adapting the Prophet Jeremiah, he thanked Aliza for her years of devotion at his side: 'I remember thee, the kindness of thy youth, the love of thine espousals, when thou wentest after me in the wilderness, in a land that was not sown.' After invoking the memory of Jabotinsky, he invited all the Zionist parties, including Labour, to join a National Unity Government. By now the exultant Likudniks were submerged in the bustle of police, reporters and cameramen. Begin left as expeditiously as he arrived, still shielded by anxious assistants. The summer earthquake had come and gone. The Israeli voter had turned out the heirs of Ben-Gurion and elected the heirs of Jabotinsky. The outcasts became the establishment.

The Likud won the 1977 election with a modest advance, Labour lost it with a devastating decline. Begin's share of the total poll rose by only 3.2 per cent. His party won forty-three seats compared with thirty-nine in 1973. Labour's share of the vote fell by fifteen per cent, following a similar drop between 1969 and 1973. It lost more than half of its supporters in the two elections of the 1970s. Labour's Knesset representation crashed from fifty-one plus three affiliated Arab MPs in 1973 to thirty-two plus one Arab in 1977. The biggest gains in 1977 were registered by the Democratic Movement for Change, a new crusading party of the Centre led by Yigael Yadin, the archaeologist of Masada and former general. Yadin's list won fifteen seats (11.6 per cent of the vote) in its first campaign. Despite the presence on the DMC slate of the right-wing Likud defector Shmuel Tamir, its biggest block of support came from disillusioned Labour voters allowing themselves the luxury of an anti-party demonstration. They were punishing Labour without, or so they imagined, rewarding the Likud. Yadin also drew votes from the Likud Liberals and smaller centre parties. But the 1977 results confirmed a far more radical shift than that of the disaffected middle class, a transfer of allegiance that threatened to change the face of Israeli politics for a generation. The oriental Jews voted with their hearts instead of their pockets, and the oriental Jews were already half the total population and would soon be half the electorate.

In development towns, villages and big-city neighbourhoods where the population is overwhelmingly oriental (Jews who originated in Arabic-speaking countries), the Likud won twice as many votes as Labour, with the religious parties registering smaller gains. In towns which are almost exclusively oriental, such as Ofakim and Netivot in the south and Kiryat Shmona and Beit Shean in the north, the Likud increased its vote by eleven per cent, while Labour's share dropped by seventeen per cent (the religious parties picked up the other six per cent). The trend was similar in towns of mixed eastern and western Jewish population, but with the swing to the Likud in inverse proportion to the number of westerners. The more Jews of American or European origin, the smaller the swing. Jerusalem, with an oriental majority and a large religious community, gave Begin a huge lead. Tel Aviv, with a western majority, increased Begin's share by only two per cent, giving Yadin thirteen per cent. In overwhelmingly western Haifa, the Likud share actually fell by two per cent, even though Labour dropped seventeen per cent. Yadin captured twenty per cent of the vote in the port city.[8]

The appeal to oriental and Sephardi Jews (those whose ancestors were expelled from Spain in 1492) reaches back to the dawn of Revisionist Zionism. Jabotinsky visited and cultivated them, even adding Ladino (Judeo-Spanish) to his quiver of ten languages. He urged the Zionist movement to give them parity in settlement of the land, and championed the Sephardi pronunciation of Hebrew. The Irgun Zvai Leumi followed suit, recruiting among the orientals while the Haganah and Palmah concentrated on the *kibbutzim* and predominantly western high-school graduates. After the creation of the State, Begin projected himself as the tribune of the underdog, the scourge of Jews who looked down on their brethren. Herut

identified itself as the party of 'the poor, the suffering and the oppressed'.
Begin recalled that one of the Haganah commanders had once asked him
how the Irgun 'solved the problem of the oriental communities'. He had
replied that the Irgun had no such problem.

> But since he insisted that I explain it to him, and I understood what was
> troubling him, I explained that in the fighting underground, top positions were
> distributed without distinction of origin. Then he understood. This is how one
> solves the problem, this is how one overcomes it, this is how one produces a
> situation in which the problem stops being a problem.[9]

In fact both the Irgun and Herut were slower than Begin claimed in
giving authority, as distinct from an active role, to the orientals. The high
command of the Irgun was exclusively European. Even in 1977, the Likud
returned fewer oriental MPs than Labour, though Begin was more generous
in promoting oriental ministers to his Cabinet.

From the earliest days of mass immigration after 1948, Begin sought out
his constituency. He toured *ma'abarot* (transit camps) without appearing to
patronize. He never ceased to be a Polish Jew, but he appealed to the
orientals in their own broad, emotional terms, invoking the Almighty
without affectation. He did not teach them Jabotinsky, but he preached
Jewish strength and scorned the Labour Zionist establishment. It amounted
to the same thing. Begin was one of them, no matter what he ate or how he
dressed.

Labour had no one to blame but itself. Its Zionist ideology was an
offshoot of the nationalist and Socialist revolutions of nineteenth-century
Europe. Its aim was to create a new type of Jew, a farmer, a worker, a
builder. Its essence was secular, a deliberate repudiation of the ghetto
values. The orientals lived at a slower tempo, they were at ease with their
traditions. Their young people had not been educated for change. They
came to Israel out of piety or necessity. The Labour leaders were alarmed
by the oriental influx, which they feared would 'Levantinize' the Jewish
State. Without asking the newcomers where they would like to go, they sent
them to populate the borders and fill the empty spaces. The pioneers went
there too, but of their own free will. Labour Governments housed the
immigrants and found them jobs – no mean achievement – but in a way
that often smacked of condescension. They absorbed them into the politics
of Mapai, the network of patronage and bossism, but as objects rather than
subjects. The first generation, most of whom arrived destitute, conformed
to type. They deferred to the ruling power, as they had done in North
Africa or Iraq. But within their own four walls they resented it, and their
children listened.

'My parents came from North Africa,' a young man shouted at the *kibbutz* novelist Amos Oz when he took his notebook to a development town. 'All right, from Morocco. So what? Didn't they have their self-respect? No? Their values? Their faith? I am not a religious person. I travel on Saturday. But my parents, why did they make fun of their faith? Why were they scrubbed with Lysol in Haifa port? Why?'[10]

The second generation identified as Israelis. They owed Labour no greenhorn's debts, and they knew how to assert themselves. Begin taught them that they had nothing to be ashamed of. But while restoring their dignity, he also legitimized their hatred of the western Ashkenazim and all they represented, the positive as well as the negative, the creative energy as well as the cultural insensitivity, the democratic institutions as well as the assumption of superiority. He was sowing the wind.

17
A Terrifying Credibility

'These are not *occupied* territories. You've used this expression for ten years, but from May 1977, I hope you'll start using the word *liberated* territories. A Jew has every right to settle these liberated territories of the Jewish land.' Within forty-eight hours of his election victory, Menachem Begin served notice on a still bemused international community that Begin the Prime Minister would be the same man as Begin the perennial leader of the Opposition. He was giving an improvised press conference while visiting a band of militant settlers at Kaddum, near Nablus, the biggest Arab town on the West Bank. The group had been transferred to Kaddum, within the perimeter of an army camp, after establishing a token settlement called Eilon Moreh in defiance of the Labour Government among the ruins of biblical Sebastia. Begin's visit had been arranged in advance to mark the installation of a scroll of the Law in the Kaddum synagogue, but the election turned it into a media event and the beginning of the absorption of the Gush Emunim settlement rebels in the fabric of the West Bank administration. 'In a few weeks or months there will be many Eilon Morehs,' Begin promised the settlers. 'There will be no need for Kaddum.' When a reporter asked the Prime Minister-designate whether his Government would annex the territories, he replied: 'We don't use the word annexation. You annex foreign land, not your own country.' Would Israeli law be extended to the West Bank, asked another, a little wiser in the language of the new Zionism. 'You used the words West Bank,' Begin chided. 'Say Judea and Samaria. Use them always.' The semantics were clear enough, but Begin hedged on the substance of the question: 'It is a matter for consideration. When the Government is formed, we shall come to the Knesset and ask for a vote of confidence, and then we shall consider what steps to take.' The Likud manifesto had been less mealy-mouthed about annexation. The reason for his caution emerged a week later. It surprised his own party as much as the Opposition and the nation.

Begin invited Moshe Dayan, who had been re-elected to the Knesset on the Labour ticket, to serve as his Foreign Minister. Despite being readmitted to hospital with recurrent heart trouble, Begin resisted strident demands from the Liberals to allocate the post to them. The Liberal choice, Arieh Dulzin, claims that while he had no personal pledge, there was an agreement between the Herut and Liberal leaders, Begin and Simha Erlich, that the top four jobs would be divided between their parties. Herut would get the premiership and defence, the Liberals would get finance and foreign affairs.[1] The Liberals expected Begin to keep the bargain, but his ideas were now running ahead of coalition politics. Begin was equally unmoved by the outraged reaction of the Labour Party and the press, and by renewed anti-Dayan demonstrations by bereaved families of the Yom Kippur War, who stoned Begin's flat in Rosenbaum Street. He was convinced that Dayan's reputation abroad remained high, even if he had not been forgiven at home. The man in the eye-patch was still Mr Israel. He said from his hospital bed:

> I decided to recommend Mr Dayan as Foreign Minister, beyond all party considerations, because we need in the coming years a foreign minister who enjoys international prestige and standing. I have no doubt Mr Dayan will enjoy a very high prestige among ambassadors, foreign ministers and other leaders, and this is of supreme importance as regards Israel's relations with peoples near and far.

Begin's olive branch to the Arabs was no public relations gimmick. He wanted to explore the prospects, particularly with Egypt. In opposition, he had been sceptical of Sadat's intentions, but now he was eager to test them for himself. If Sadat proved sincere, it would be easier to make peace with Egypt than with the other 'peoples near'. Sinai was not *Eretz Yisrael*. Choosing Dayan was an acknowledgement that the Likud had no candidate of comparable calibre or experience. Of potential Likud ministers, only Ezer Weizman had presided over a department in Golda Meir's National Unity coalition. Dayan's appointment also underlined continuity, as did Begin's retention of senior men in the Prime Minister's office who were identified with his Labour predecessor: the spokesman, Dan Pattir; the diaspora relations adviser and English speech-writer, Yehuda Avner; the military secretary, Brigadier-General Ephraim Poran; and the head of bureau, Eli Mizrahi. The world was being shown that this was a democratic transition, not a *coup d'état* by a bunch of superannuated terrorists.

Dayan had left office with Mrs Meir in 1974, but had retained his Knesset seat and was a member of the panel that drafted Labour's 1977 election platform. He told inquirers that having served the State under such giants as Ben-Gurion and Golda Meir, he would not play second fiddle to younger (and, by implication, lesser) leaders like Yitzhak Rabin and Shimon Peres.

Begin, it seems, rated as one of the heroic generation, even if he was only two years older than Dayan. The former Defence Minister's roots were deep in the Labour movement. He was born on Degania, the first *kibbutz*, and grew up on Nahalal, the first *moshav*. But he had always been a lone wolf, a man of shifting loyalties, recognizing neither personal nor intellectual debts. He had unshakeable confidence in his own judgement, but never let it harden into dogma. Retirement proved more difficult than he had expected. If there were to be action, he wanted part of it, but not unconditionally. 'I judged that Israel would soon have to take critical decisions which would shape her future, and that if I were to participate in determining policy, I could exert considerable influence on those Government decisions,' he wrote.[2] The sticking-point for Dayan was the fate of the West Bank and Gaza Strip. He was against their annexation, as much as he opposed their return to Arab sovereignty. He dreamed of a *modus vivendi* that would somehow satisfy both Israel and Jordan without resorting to such European innovations as national boundaries. At Dayan's behest, Begin agreed that the territories would not be annexed 'while peace negotiations are in progress', and that the Arab residents could continue to send their representatives to the Jordanian parliament and to receive financial help from the Arab states through Amman. Dayan had fathered the 'open-bridges' policy in 1967; he did not want to witness its demise a decade later. Begin's undertakings, confirmed in the hospital ward, satisfied Dayan. He wrote to a *kibbutz* critic:

> The alternative to a peace arrangement with the Arabs could well be war. Would a Begin Government without me be better for Israel? And if I joined it, would there be a chance of gaining our aims – as I see them? Do I, in fact, have a solution to the problem of our conflict with the Arabs, and would I be able to act according to my perceptions in such a government? If the answer to this last question is positive, should I, despite that, reject Begin's proposal?

The dice were loaded. It is hard to believe that Dayan lost much sleep over his decision. 'The question which I had to face', he told a fellow Labour MP, Gad Yacobi, 'was whether my acceptance of Begin's proposal and working with him could materially change the situation for the good of Israel.' Dayan was vain enough to answer with an unequivocal yes, and to prove himself right.

Begin's offer had come as no bolt from the blue. The first, secret soundings had been taken early in the election campaign, when the Herut leader called at Dayan's Tel Aviv villa in the retired officers' suburb of Zahala. According to Dayan's version, what they were discussing was an offer to run on the Likud list. He refused because Begin could not at that

stage give him the assurances he sought on the West Bank and Gaza. Begin
suggested they left the door open. In a Knesset debate five years later, the
Prime Minister put a different gloss on these talks. The initiative, he said,
had come from Dayan, who had volunteered his readiness to serve under
Begin if he formed the next government.[3] Yehiel Kadishai adds that the
explorations continued after Begin was admitted to the Ichilov Hospital in
March. According to Kadishai, Begin had gone there for a check-up, and
it was during Dayan's visit that he suffered his first heart attack.[4]

Despite their collaboration in the National Unity Government, the
Begin-Dayan flirtation was an affair of the head. Naphtali Lavie, who
served Dayan as spokesman in both the Meir and Begin administrations,
says that Dayan had no love for the Herut leader.

> He appreciated his determination, his authority, and the way he knew how to
> exercise it. Dayan appreciated more than anything else Begin's faithfulness to
> Judea and Samaria, even though his motives for wanting them connected to
> *Eretz Yisrael* were not the same as Dayan's. But he disliked Begin's style, his
> bombastic language, his use of superlatives, what he considered cheap acting.
> He thought Begin does not understand Arabs, doesn't know how to deal with
> them, how to accommodate them with a reasonable agreement that would not
> hurt their pride, that would give them the utmost Israel could offer them without
> taking too great a risk with our own security.
>   Dayan could live with a political solution where the West Bank would not be
> part of Israel. His attachment to places there did not mean we had to take over.
> Dayan was ready for others to live there according to their own style of life, but
> he was scared that Arab rule might turn into something we could not control.
> He was very much against annexation. Jews must be sensitive not to take people
> who are foreigners and hostile, and force them to be Israelis. The West Bank
> Palestinians must not have their own army, or the right to invite in other Arab
> armies. Short of that, Dayan was willing to give them a lot. He favoured giving
> Jordan a significant role in establishing a self-governing community.[5]

As for Begin's attitude towards Dayan, one of his staff puts it this way:
'He appointed Dayan first of all because of the man's international reputation. He also had a respect for Dayan that accrues to everybody who has
been an outstanding general in the IDF. He would tolerate the maverick in
Dayan.'

It takes Israel nearly as long to form a government as it does to tee up to a
general election. Menachem Begin had to wait three weeks after his victory
at the polls before President Ephraim Katzir completed the ritual consultations with all thirteen parties which won seats in the ninth Knesset, then
offered him the premiership. In that time Begin had reversed Labour's

policy of keeping Jewish settlements away from the hill country of Judea
and Samaria, where most of the West Bank Arabs are concentrated; plucked
Moshe Dayan from the Labour benches; and emerged from a second spell
in hospital with nothing worse than inflammation of the membrane around
his heart. At the President's Jerusalem residence, he was photographed
shaking hands with the head of State and kissing Mrs Nina Katzir's
knuckles with the gallantry of a mediaeval knight. From the President's
house, he drove to the Western Wall, where he again donned his black,
election-night skull-cap. Begin was the first Prime Minister who identified
himself as a Jew rather than as an Israeli. The State was the land of the
Jews, not just that minority of the race that happened to live there, and for
him Judaism could not be divorced from the Jewish religion. The visit to
the Wall was an act of dedication by a man who considered himself a ruler
among the Jews, not simply Prime Minister of Israel. When he went there
again after the 1981 election he wore the knitted skull-cap that had become
the badge of the Gush Emunim settlers.

Two more weeks were to pass before Begin was ready to present his
Cabinet to the Knesset and take the oath of office. He was sixty-three and
had been in the land thirty-five years. The main question at issue in
protracted coalition negotiations was whether the ruling team would include
Yigael Yadin's new Democratic Movement for Change, which came out of
its first elections as the third biggest party after Likud and Labour. The
Democrats were eager for government. They were a reforming movement,
pledged to regenerate the nation after the corruption and cynicism of
Labour's last years. The thrust of their programme was domestic rather
than foreign, although they had come out in favour of territorial compromise on the West Bank. Their leaders included defectors from the Right as
well as from the Left. To keep faith with their voters, they needed a share
in power, a chance to achieve results. Opposition was not enough. Nor
would it satisfy the ambitions of men like Yadin and Shmuel Tamir. The
trouble was that Begin could form a viable coalition without the Democrats'
fifteen seats. An agreement with the National Religious Party and the
ultra-Orthodox Agudat Yisrael would give the Likud – reinforced by Ariel
Sharon, who had won two seats on a private list but soon merged with
Herut – sixty-two votes in the 120-member chamber. If Dayan resigned
the Labour whip but kept his Knesset mandate, the tally would rise to
sixty-three, giving Begin a majority of at least six (another lone MP, Shmuel
Flatto Sharon, wanted on charges of financial misdemeanour in France,
promised to support the Government, but the Likud was careful to keep
him at arm's length).

With the experience of thirty years of party intrigue behind him, Begin easily outmanœuvred Yadin. He wanted the Democrats in the coalition. They would broaden its base so that no one could accuse him of heading an alliance of right-wing ideologues and theocratic bigots, and they would give him the security of numbers. But he wanted them on his terms. Yadin objected to the nomination of Dayan and to Begin's agreement with his Foreign Minister-designate on a West Bank formula. The Likud leader was pre-empting the negotiations. Yadin was being forced to focus on foreign and security affairs. He demanded that the Dayan offer be withdrawn and that the coalition leave open the possibility of territorial compromise. But he was no match for Begin; the Likud executive authorized its leader to continue negotiating for the widest possible coalition, specifying that a decision on the allocation of portfolios would await the final stage of the bargaining process. At the same time the executive 'took note' of Begin's suggestion that Dayan should go to the Foreign Ministry. 'There is a suggestion,' the Liberals' Simha Erlich soothed the doubters. 'We shall talk about it when the posts are assigned.' In practice, nothing had changed. Begin wanted Dayan, and in the end nobody would gainsay him. But it gave the Democrats a pretext for returning to the table. Similarly Begin agreed that the West Bank and Gaza would not be annexed, and asserted his Government's 'readiness to participate in the Geneva peace conference if and when it shall be convened by the United States and the Soviet Union on the basis of Security Council resolutions 242 and 338'. Seven years earlier, he had pulled his party out of the National Unity Government over Golda Meir's endorsement of Resolution 242. The undertaking not to rescind that endorsement was inadequate for the DMC doves, but again encouraged those who wanted to be encouraged. Begin duly presented his Cabinet to parliament, but left three seats temporarily vacant for the Democrats. Four months later, Begin's brew of patience, menace and enticement did the trick, as he had calculated it would. Yadin joined the coalition as Deputy Premier, with little to show beyond a right of delay (but not veto) on new West Bank settlements and a titular role as co-ordinator of social policy. Begin's majority rose overnight from six to thirty-six, while the DMC set out, however innocently, on the road of compromise and disintegration that left the movement no more than a memory and a warning by the time the next elections were called in 1981.

Begin willingly paid a higher price for the votes of the religious parties, especially those of Agudat Yisrael, which was controlled from outside parliament by a council of venerable sages. The National Religious Party, the standard-bearer of religious Zionism, had always fought to preserve the *status quo* in the balance between the secular and the holy in the Jewish State. It had prevented the introduction of civil marriage and civil divorce, maintained an institutional monopoly for the Orthodox stream of Judaism, and resisted a drift away from Sabbath observance in the public services. Agudat Yisrael strove to go further and change the balance in favour of theocracy. It drove a hard bargain because that – and access to public funds for its private educational system – was its sole motive for entering the political arena. Foreign and security policies were outside its ken. Begin had fewer inhibitions than Labour prime ministers in coming to terms. He was, as he rejoiced in proclaiming, 'one of the believers in Israel'. For him there was only one kind of Judaism, and Israel owed it to generations of pious Jews to honour its values and practices. All but ten of the forty-three clauses in the coalition agreement signed on 19 June 1977, dealt with religious enforcement and privileges. Under the first Begin Government, girls from 'traditional' families found it easier to escape military service; it became harder to have an abortion within the law; doctors were restricted in carrying out autopsies, which led to a shortage of kidneys and other 'spare parts' for transplant surgery; and Christian missionary activity was curbed.

Four years after the Yom Kippur War, Begin was satisfied that he had constructed a ruling coalition that was not only securely based at home, but was credible enough to deter any enemy state contemplating a re-run of the October invasions. At one time his Cabinet included five retired generals: Yadin, Dayan, Weizman (rewarded with the Defence Ministry for his management of the election campaign), Sharon (agriculture and settlement), and Meir Amit (a former intelligence chief elected on the DMC slate, who served briefly as Transport Minister).

Begin's accession to power provoked an orgy of apprehension and hostility in the West, particularly in Britain, where memories of the Irgun Zvai Leumi were stirred as if nothing had happened since 1948. 'Israel's founding father reaps the rewards of terrorism,' wrote Louis Heren in the London *Times*. 'Terrorism does pay. Arafat should be encouraged.' A veteran of the Sixth Airborne Division, who lost a leg in an Irgun attack in Netanya, wrote to the Israeli embassy: 'If Begin comes here, I will kill him. Pity Eichmann never got him and the others. . . .' Across the Atlantic, the *New York Times* worried that politics in the Middle East was now dangerously 'out of sync'. *Time* magazine fed Begin's paranoia by advising its readers that 'Begin rhymes with Fagin'. Begin was stung by the world's selective memory and perverse refusal to see the Irgun through the eyes of its commander. He demanded and received an apology from the American CBS network for branding him an ex-terrorist. He told an Israeli interviewer:

If someone presents me as a terrorist and Yasser Arafat as a guerrilla fighter, I
have only contempt for him. We fought for the liberation of our people when it
was being annihilated in Europe. I believe these foolish reactions will pass after
I form the Government and am invited to meet President Carter. If it doesn't
stop even then, I shall know how to react.[6]

Israelis of all political persuasions appreciated more clearly than the
foreigners that they had elected their first ideological prime minister, a man
who had been singing the same song for forty years and meant every bar of
it. 'He will be ready to back every word to the last dollar or the last shell,'
Meir Merhav wrote in the *Jerusalem Post*. 'His is a terrifying credibility.'
Arguably, Begin came to office better-read than any of his predecessors,
but he freely admitted that he looked to his favourite historians and biog-
raphers to furnish him with quotations for his speeches. His world remained
the world of the Zionist congress, his vision blinkered and ethnocentric. He
wept for Jewish suffering, preached Jewish pride and gloried in Jewish
might. If he was ready to talk peace with the Arabs, he would do it from
strength not weakness. Israel, he said when presenting his Cabinet to the
Knesset on 20 June, would not ask any nation to recognize its right to exist.

We were granted our right to exist by the God of our fathers, at the glimmer of
the dawn of human civilization nearly four thousand years ago. For that right,
which has been sanctified in Jewish blood from generation to generation, we
have paid a price unexampled in the annals of the nations. Certainly, this fact
does not diminish or enfeeble our right. On the contrary. Therefore, I re-
emphasize that we do not expect anyone to request, on our behalf, that our right
to exist in the land of our fathers be recognized. It is a different recognition
which is required between ourselves and our neighbours: recognition of sovereignty and of the common need for a life of peace and understanding. It is this
mutual recognition that we look forward to. For it we shall make every possible
effort.

In relations with the United States, Begin drew no distinction between
vision and policy. Israel, he contended, was an ally and an asset. America
needed Israel as much as Israel needed America. In the 1970 crisis over the
Rogers plan, Golda Meir and Abba Eban had derided Begin's 'naïveté', but
on issues that mattered to him the new Prime Minister was prepared to
court and resist American pressure. He was determined to fix the borders
of *Eretz Yisrael* once and for all. Whatever the realities of power, his bluff
was seldom called, his readiness to 'eat margarine' if necessary was not
tested. 'He is totally convinced that the Israeli public would go along with
him,' said one of his resident American affairs experts. 'He believes in the
power of persuasion, of words, in his own persuasive powers. I have

absolutely no doubt that if there were a showdown with the United States on an issue that to him is supreme, he would not bend.' During Begin's first visit to Washington in July 1977, President Jimmy Carter urged flexibility on the West Bank. Begin responded by unrolling a 'national security map', brought in anticipation, and explained the dangers of allowing Arab artillery to return to the pre-1967 borders. 'We were tertiated,' he told a perplexed President, meaning one in every three Jews had been killed in the Nazi Holocaust. Jewish men could not defend their women, he added, they had to deliver them to the slaughterer. 'I took a vow ...' he started to say, then broke down with emotion. When Carter warned Begin at the same meeting in the White House Cabinet room not to go through with the massive settlement programme he had promised for the occupied territories, the Prime Minister presented him with a prepared list of how many Salems, Jerusalems and other town with biblical names there were in the United States. 'What would you say,' he asked, 'if the governors of those states said no Jew could live in those towns?' Embassy officials accompanying Begin for the first time knew that could not be Israel's last word. They were alarmed by Carter's severity on the settlement issue. When they returned to Blair House, the elegant presidential guest-house across Pennsylvania Avenue from the White House, they asked the Prime Minister what he was going to do. Begin replied that he would build the settlements as planned. The Americans, he predicted, would turn cold for six months, then they would revert to normal.

The first Arab ruler Begin approached in his search for peace was the most accessible: King Hussein of Jordan. Israeli ministers had been meeting him secretly since before the 1967 war, when Hussein still ruled the West Bank and East Jerusalem. The dialogue persisted through the governments of Levi Eshkol, Golda Meir and Yitzhak Rabin. The record for face-to-face encounters was held by Yigal Allon, the late Foreign Minister, who met the King fourteen times. Another former Foreign Minister, Abba Eban, met him twelve times, while Rabin and his Defence Minister, Shimon Peres, met him eight times. Mrs Meir first met him in Paris before the Six-Day War, when she was not yet Prime Minister, and in Israel later when she was.[7] Naphtali Lavie adds that Dayan too had talked to the King 'several times' including some after his resignation as Defence Minister in 1974.[8] During the Rabin period all the meetings took place in Israel. 'Apart from the fact that no results came out of them,' one witness testifies, 'they were beautiful meetings, free, open and nice discussions between gentlemen.'

Soon after taking office, Begin hinted through intermediaries that he would like to join the Hussein club. The answer from Amman was a blunt no, which made him very angry. Nonetheless, he authorized Dayan to attend a clandestine meeting in London. It took place in a private house on the evening of 22 August, after the Israeli Foreign Minister had shaken off his Special Branch bodyguard by entering another house through the front door and ducking out into a waiting car through the back. Although the talks continued for a second day at Hussein's request, they were totally unproductive. The King said that he was washing his hands of the West Bank and the Palestinian problem. The Arab States had proclaimed the Palestine Liberation Organization the sole legitimate representative of the Palestinian people. If they didn't want him, they could run the affairs of the Palestinians without him. 'His attitude towards the subject of our discussion,' Dayan wrote, 'the attempt to find a suitable and agreed arrangement for the problem of the West Bank and the Gaza Strip, seemed to be one of indifference.' At the second meeting, Hussein clarified his position on a possible division of the West Bank between Israel and Jordan, a territorial compromise.

> He rejected it out of hand. A peace arrangement based on the division of the West Bank would mean that he, Hussein, would agree that part of it was to be joined to the State of Israel. I had to understand, he said, that he, as an Arab monarch, could not propose to the people of even a single Arab village that they cut themselves off from their brother Arabs and become Israelis. His agreement to such a plan would be regarded as treachery. He would be charged with selling Arab land to the Jews so that he could enlarge his own kingdom.... The sole solution in order to attain peace, he said, was for Israel to return to the pre-June 1967 borders.... On the question of sovereignty, we had to restore to Jordan all the territory we had captured in 1967.[9]

Dayan told his aides when he came back to Jerusalem that he was not surprised by Hussein's stand. Nor, it seems, was the Prime Minister. Begin, according to one of his confidants, never believed that any territorial compromise would induce Hussein to negotiate:

> He wanted to have his conscience clear, to get it out of his system, to test Hussein. Dayan didn't believe in it anyway. We knew Hussein's attitude from previous talks. Begin was clearing it from Dayan's agenda. If Hussein had said yes, nothing would have happened. But it wasn't even a gamble. We knew the answer in advance.

For all that, according to one well-placed source, Dayan did suggest before they parted that the King might meet Begin. Hussein replied that he saw no point in it. Begin's views were familiar enough. As far as is known, Dayan's encounter was the last the Jordanian monarch had with an Israeli minister. Begin was ready to search elsewhere.

18
Peace on our Terms

It was after eight on the evening of 9 November 1977. The Director-General of the Prime Minister's office, Eliahu Ben-Elissar, a former secret agent with a Ph.D. in history and a black Theodor Herzl beard, was reading in bed in his rented flat near the President's Jerusalem residence. It had been a long, exhausting day. Palestinian gunmen had broken the ceasefire across the Lebanese border, killing an Israeli civilian and wounding five others with Katyusha rockets. The air force had retaliated with a sixty-five-minute bombardment of Palestinian camps. The early-evening television news was dominated by claims and counter-claims of civilian casualties, and the Chief of Staff's assurance that Israel would honour the ceasefire if the other side did likewise. Begin had been briefed and consulted. There was nothing new on the TV bulletin. Ben-Elissar could relax. But not for long.

The bedside telephone rang. It was Anan Safadi, Middle East affairs editor of the *Jerusalem Post*. Safadi had been monitoring a live broadcast on Cairo radio of Anwar Sadat's opening address to the winter session of the Egyptian parliament, the People's Assembly. After announcing his readiness to go to a Geneva peace conference which the Americans were trying to revive, and castigating Israel for 'arguing over every word, every comma, every dash', Sadat dropped a bombshell. He was, he said, prepared to go to the end of the world to talk peace: 'Israel will be stunned to hear me tell you that I am ready to go to their home, to the Knesset itself, to argue with them, in order to prevent one Egyptian soldier from being wounded. Members of the People's Assembly, we have no time to waste.' The President's offer was greeted with enthusiastic chants of '*Allahu Akbar*' ('God is great') from the deputies, but other listeners either missed it in the general drone of the speech, or discounted it as a piece of Levantine hyperbole, like Sadat's threat four years before to sacrifice a million Egyptian soldiers to recover Arab land from the Zionist usurper. The Yom Kippur War had taught Anan Safadi that the President usually meant what he said. He was going to highlight the story, and he wanted Begin's reaction.

Ben-Elissar was incredulous, but the Israeli official had the good sense not to dismiss it out of hand.

> I asked him: 'Are you sure that this is what Sadat declared? I do not believe it.' In spite of all we knew in advance, I was surprised that Sadat was ready to come to Jerusalem. He said: 'Yes, this is what I heard with my own ears over Cairo radio.' I asked him: 'Are you sure that this is what you heard?' He told me he was absolutely sure. I asked if he had any agency cables, if he had it in writing. He said not yet. I said: 'Look, please check, and if it is true that this is what Sadat declared, you may write that he will be most welcome in Jerusalem.'[1]

The next morning the *Jerusalem Post* quoted 'a top aide of Prime Minister Menachem Begin' as saying Sadat 'would be more than welcome here and would be accorded a proper reception'. But the Israelis were still hesitating to treat the initiative seriously. The *Jerusalem Post* did not lead the front page with Safadi's story. Ben-Elissar did not disturb Begin's evening with the news, but waited until after seven in the morning. Only at eight a.m. did Israel radio broadcast a statement from the Prime Minister that Sadat would be welcomed with honour. The prospect still seemed unreal. With Sadat continuing to put the emphasis on Geneva and demanding an advance undertaking by Israel to withdraw from all occupied territories, Jerusalem was perplexed. There were no precedents. All previous meetings between Israeli and Arab leaders had been clandestine, from Golda Meir's earliest visit to King Abdullah in 1948 to Dayan's encounter with his grandson twenty-nine years later. Israel was conscious of Arab sensitivity, even employing military censorship to keep the meetings secret. But what do you do when the ruler of the biggest Arab state announces publicly that he is ready to come to Jerusalem and address the Knesset? Would a public invitation harm him among his own people? Like every one of his predecessors, Begin had said often enough that he would go anywhere, any time to talk peace. Nonetheless, Egypt was still formally at war with the Jewish State. How do you receive an enemy in a capital city which he does not recognize? The dilemma was magnified by the lack of clarity in Sadat's signal. What was he aiming at?

Despite the warm relationship he had already established with Jimmy Carter, Sadat had not consulted the Americans in advance of his announcement in the People's Assembly. According to the Secretary of State, Cyrus Vance, 'he merely let the President know the day before he made the announcement that he was thinking of going'.[2] Since he had earlier floated the idea of a summit conference in East Jerusalem, embracing the five permanent members of the United Nations Security Council and the Palestine Liberation Organization, as well as Israel and its immediate

neighbours, the message was not taken at face value. But once he had made
his statement, the United States became what its Tel Aviv ambassador,
Samuel Lewis, called 'a happy postman'. Messages passed back and forth
through diplomatic channels, through visiting congressmen, and most vividly through the media. In an English-language broadcast to the Egyptian
people, Begin coined an oath for the two nations: 'No more wars, no more
bloodshed, and no more threats.' Both Sadat and Begin were interviewed
by the star presenters of American television, Walter Cronkite and Barbara
Walters. It added to the carnival atmosphere, even if jaundiced diplomats
muttered that they were neither the only nor the prime means of communication between Jerusalem and Cairo. Cronkite's on CBS was the first joint
interview, by satellite from New York. Sadat said he must have a written
invitation. Begin agreed to send one. Sadat responded that he would be
ready then to go to Israel at 'the earliest possible time'. On 15 November,
Begin despatched a letter to Cairo by American courier:

> On behalf of the Government of Israel I have the honour to extend to you our
> cordial invitation to come to Jerusalem and to visit our country. Your Excel-
> lency's readiness to undertake such a visit, as expressed to the People's Assembly
> of Egypt, has been noted here with deep and positive interest, as has been your
> statement that you would wish to address the members of our parliament, the
> Knesset, and to meet with me.
> If, as I hope, you will accept our invitation, arrangements will be made for
> you to address the Knesset from its rostrum. You will also, should you so desire,
> be enabled to meet with our various parliamentary groups, those supporting the
> Government as well as those in opposition.... May I assure you, Mr President,
> that the parliament, the Government and the people of Israel will receive you
> with respect and cordiality.

Sadat's reply was equally positive. He told a fourteen-member delegation
from the American House of Representatives that he viewed the proposed
visit as 'a holy job', and that he would go as soon as possible.

> We must do the impossible to break the vicious circle in which Arabs and Israelis
> have been moving for thirty years. This is for the sake of future generations.
> Hence the holiness of the mission. If I do not try to break this vicious circle,
> God will bring me to account, and so will future generations.
> For me the Arab-Israeli conflict consists of seventy per cent psychological
> problems and thirty per cent substance. Let us overcome the psychological
> problems and go to the substance. For that I am going to the Knesset, and if
> need be I shall open a discussion with its 120 deputies to give them the real facts
> in the area here – the other point of view – so that they can decide for themselves.

The impending visit appealed to Begin's self-esteem and his flawed sense of history. The talks would prove to the doubters that his Government was 'on the right track'. Addressing the Herut central committee, he hinted that he would expect a return invitation to the Egyptian capital: 'In these matters there is reciprocity. One day, God willing, I shall visit Cairo, and I shall also see the Pyramids. After all, we had a hand in building them.' It took the Prime Minister eighteen months of fluctuating diplomacy to achieve his ambition – and almost as long before he was convinced that the Children of Israel had not built the Pyramids.

The Sadat initiative was not born in a vacuum. Two rulers from opposite ends of the international spectrum – a Communist president and an Arab king – assisted at the birth. In August, after returning from Washington, Begin had paid an official visit to Romania, the only Iron Curtain country which retained diplomatic relations with Israel after the 1967 war. He spent eight hours in conclave with its hard-line, but independent-minded, leader, Nicolae Ceausescu. Sadat followed Begin to Bucharest. He was anxious to hear Ceausescu's impressions of the new Israeli Prime Minister. Was he as fanatical as he sounded? 'Begin', Ceausescu assured him, 'wants a solution.' Sadat pressed the question: Was Begin honest, and was he a strong enough leader to deliver? The Romanian's answer was yes on both counts.[3] That was sufficient for Sadat, who was determined to break out of the cycle of Middle East wars, and had his own compelling reasons for cementing diplomatic and economic ties with the United States, Israel's traditional patron.

The Communist president had played his part. Now it was the turn of the Arab monarch. King Hassan of Morocco had long been the Arab head of state most receptive to the idea of dialogue with Israel. Yitzhak Rabin had visited him as Prime Minister, disguised in a Beatles wig and rising-young-executive spectacles. In September, after a preliminary session with a senior representative of the Mossad secret service, the King invited Moshe Dayan to the royal palace in Marrakesh. At the Foreign Minister's request, Hassan sent a message to Cairo suggesting a high-level Israeli-Egyptian rendezvous. Within four days of Dayan's return to Jerusalem, the word came back that the Egyptians were ready. They proposed a meeting either between Sadat and Begin, or between the Egyptian Deputy Premier, Hassan Tohami, and Dayan. Despite reservations held by Dayan, Begin was prepared to go straight to the summit, but then the Egyptians had second thoughts. Dayan-Tohami talks were arranged for Rabat on 16 September. Although they were supposed to be secret, the Americans were kept in the picture, apparently by Morocco. The Foreign Minister stopped in Europe on his way to the United States. He 'vanished' in Brussels and was whisked by road to Paris and by private jet to Morocco, having acquired a wig, moustache and sunglasses along the way. Mrs Rachel Dayan and the Foreign Minister's aides flew on to New York by a Sabena airliner, apologizing profusely to the pilot, Henry Levy, who had been rescued from a hijacked Sabena plane at Lod airport in 1972 when Dayan was Defence Minister and had been looking forward to repaying his hospitality.

Although all the courtesies were respected, the Rabat meeting was not a success. Tohami explained that Sadat agreed to open a dialogue with Israel; but only after Begin accepted the principle of total withdrawal from the occupied territories would Sadat meet the Prime Minister and shake his hand. Israeli withdrawal was the basic problem, involving as it did the questions of sovereignty, national honour, and Sadat's survival in office. Dayan was cool, but non-committal. He would have to report back to the Prime Minister. Predictably, when he did so, Begin refused to give any pledge of a comprehensive withdrawal.[4] Tohami, a strict Moslem with no affection for Israel, had stuck loyally to his brief. There would, he told Dayan, be no summit meeting until the last Israeli soldier had evacuated Arab soil. A second Dayan-Tohami round was planned once they had received fresh instructions from Jerusalem and Cairo. But Sadat had no patience for protracted secret diplomacy. He was irritated by detail, indifferent to protocol. His offer to go to Jerusalem was a typical broad, dramatic stroke, cutting through the mesh of historic suspicion, challenging by its boldness and its simplicity. But, whatever his expectations, it could not alone dispel the seventy per cent of psychology, and it barely touched the thirty per cent of substance.

For most Israelis, Sadat's visit was a fantasy come true. When he arrived at Ben-Gurion airport after the end of the Jewish sabbath on 19 November 1977, his hosts were still frolicking in the improbability and improvisation of it all. The conductor of the army band had transcribed the Egyptian national anthem from Cairo radio. A Jerusalem flagmaker ran up hundreds of red, white and black Egyptian banners. A printer put out a commemorative poster in Hebrew, Arabic and English, 'Shalom – Salaam – Peace'. Jerusalem's three luxury hotels competed for the privilege of decanting their paying guests and entertaining the Egyptians in their royal suites (inevitably, the King David won). An enterprising estate agent advertised a 'magnificent fourteen-room house, prestige neighbourhood, terms negotiable. Suitable for Egyptian embassy.' The appropriately-named Shalom stores offered a ten per cent discount on all purchases.

'A new era has begun,' a television commentator gasped into his microphone as the Egyptian President descended the steps of his Boeing 707, codesigned Egypt 01, at eight p.m. 'I'm seeing it, but I don't believe it,' echoed a radio reporter from the tarmac. Golda Meir was among the dignitaries in the receiving line. 'Madame,' Sadat told her, 'I have been waiting to meet you for a long time.' The eighty-year-old matriarch, who had prayed in October 1973 for the day when an Arab leader would wake up and grieve for his own young men fallen in battle, replied: 'And I've waited a long time to meet you.' 'Well, the time has arrived, and here I am.' The President paused, shook hands and launched into an animated conversation with Ariel Sharon, the general-turned-politician who had changed the course of the Yom Kippur War by striking back across the Suez Canal. The Chief of Staff, General Mordechai Gur, had warned the nation in a controversial newspaper interview that Sadat might be planning a surprise attack under cover of the visit; the whole thing might be a trick. When he was presented to him, Sadat smiled: 'I wasn't bluffing.' The two presidents, Katzir of Israel and Sadat of Egypt, stood impassively shoulder-to-shoulder with Menachem Begin as the band struck up the two national anthems to the accompaniment of a twenty-one-gun salute. The drive to Jerusalem was heralded by a flutter of eighteen white doves. A rapturous crowd of 20,000 Israelis welcomed the convoy at the gates of the capital with bread, salt and songs of peace. Bells pealed as the limousines approached the King David. Another good-natured throng broke into a chant of 'Sadat, Sadat'.

After the excitement of Sadat's arrival and his Sunday-morning tour of the Old City, including noon prayers in Al Aqsa mosque, the Knesset speeches were almost an anti-climax. Despite the expectations of a chamber packed with past and present MPs, diplomats and reporters, Sadat and Begin demonstrated to their worldwide audience that peace would not come by oratory alone. Neither leader produced anything unfamiliar enough or radical enough to provoke the other to change his stance. Sadat was eager for peace on Egyptian terms, Begin no less so on Israeli terms. Judged on performance and as an exercise in international public relations, Sadat won with surprising ease. He was challenging and buoyant. Israel was thrown on the defensive. Begin, never at his best when delivering a formal rather than a fighting speech, was tired and predictable. Not only did he offer no new ideas, but he found no new words for expressing the old ones.

In his fifty-five-minute Arabic address, Sadat spelled out more precisely than ever before his readiness to accept Israel as a fact of Middle Eastern life: 'We welcome you to live among us in peace and security.' To achieve peace with justice, he offered 'borders secure against aggression' and whatever form of international guarantees Israel might want. In return he recited the entire catalogue of Arab demands, with the notable exception of promoting the Palestine Liberation Organization as the Palestinians' only legitimate representative. Dabbing the sweat from his gleaming bald patch, Sadat insisted on complete Israeli withdrawal from 'Arab territories occupied by force, including Arab Jerusalem'. Land was not open to argument. He would not concede one inch, or even the principle of bargaining over it. Jerusalem should be a 'free and open city for all believers'. It should not be cut off from 'those who had made it their abode for centuries'. Above all the Egyptian President emphasized that he had not come to sign a separate Egyptian–Israeli peace agreement. Nor would he negotiate another partial arrangement which would only defer real solutions. For all his omission of the PLO, he identified the Palestinian problem as 'the core and essence of the conflict'. It would be a grave error, he stressed, to brush aside the Palestinian rights of statehood and return.

Begin resisted any temptation to negotiate at the rostrum. A Western ambassador, listening in the gallery, confided that the Americans had warned the Prime Minister against a slanging match. Begin proclaimed his wish for 'real peace, involving full reconciliation between the Jewish and Arab nations, without being bogged down in memories of the past'. Nevertheless, he subjected Sadat to a lesson in recent Jewish history, pointing the moral of the Holocaust and of the 1948 War of Independence, which he maintained was forced on a weak Israel by its powerful Arab neighbours. The 'generation of the annihilation', he said, had taken an oath of loyalty never to put the Jewish people in danger again. Sadat, the Prime Minister said, knew that their attitudes on borders differed, but that did not mean there could be no negotiation. He suggested that they negotiate about every point in contention, and that neither side set conditions in advance. 'We shall negotiate as equals. There are no victors and no vanquished.'

On Begin's initiative, the two leaders shook hands at the end of the Prime Minister's forty-minute Hebrew address. But both in the press gallery and on the floor of the house there was a sense of disappointment. Perhaps we should not have expected miracles. Instead the battle-lines of peace had been drawn. At a joint press conference the following day, Sadat ended his visit by placing the burden squarely on Begin's shoulders:

> May God guide the steps of Premier Begin and the Knesset, because there is great need for hard and drastic decisions. I have already taken my share in my decision to come here, and I shall be waiting for those decisions of Premier Begin and the Knesset.

This became a persistent Egyptian refrain. The President had made his great concession, going to Jerusalem, recognizing Israel, risking his neck in Egypt and the Arab world at large. Wasn't that what Israelis had always yearned for? Now it was time to reciprocate. It is hard to believe, however, that Sadat expected to conquer so simply, that his frustration did not contain an element of play-acting. He was not, after all, an innocent abroad. No less than Begin's, his record was that of a conspirator. Although he abhorred paperwork, he did not act on impulse. His initiatives – the October crossing as much as the flight to Jerusalem – were built on calculation. He was entitled to expect a generous Israeli response, a *quid pro quo* he could wave in the faces of his Arab critics. But after thirty years of war it was at best naïve to expect the walls to tumble at the first toot of the trumpet.

Like most Israelis, Begin remembered Sadat's chequered history: his pro-Nazi activity during the Second World War, his role in the Nasserite revolt against King Farouk, his launching of the Yom Kippur invasion. His choice of a tie with a swastika motif for the official banquet hardly helped anyone to forget. But Begin systematically erased his instinctive hostility towards the Egyptian leader, except when he felt that Sadat was playing dirty. Then, in private meetings with his staff, he allowed the old animus to show. 'Sadat', he would say, 'is a liar.' Begin tended to be contemptuous of Arabs in general, and in this mood he despised Sadat as another Arab. Overriding it all, however, was Begin's recognition that Sadat wanted peace and had taken risks to attain it. Yehiel Kadishai sums up the Prime Minister's attitude in the Hebrew saying 'respect and suspect'. On one occasion when one of his friends urged him to keep an eye on the wily Sadat, he answered: 'The Almighty gave us some brains too.'

Begin believed his own propaganda about Israel's vulnerability. He was determined not to take any steps that would expose the Jewish State to danger. Even if Begin did not share General Gur's deepest suspicions, he was not prepared to take Sadat's friendship on trust. The Egyptian leader had been an enemy too long. Despite the assiduously fostered stories that 'the chemistry is working', Begin needed practical proof of Sadat's good faith. He was also wary of running too far ahead of his Herut loyalists, who had so recently backed his campaign against the Labour Government's Sinai agreements. They needed to be reassured, they needed time to catch up. But above all Begin resolved not to be trapped into a comprehensive peace which would lead to the redivision of *Eretz Yisrael*. He wanted peace, but not at the price of everything he had fought for in the underground, on the hustings and in the Cabinet. Peace with Egypt was attractive for a variety of reasons. Egypt was the biggest and most powerful Arab state. Without Egypt, so the prevailing doctrine ran, the Arabs could not make war. Sinai, unlike the West Bank and Gaza, was expendable, so long as it could be kept free of Egyptian armour and military airfields, though Begin hoped some way might be found to retain the Jewish settlements. Despite Sadat's protestations to the contrary, and Dayan's pessimism, Israel negotiated on the working hypothesis that Egypt would be content with a separate peace, that what Sadat was after was the recovery of *his* lost territory, and American help in solving his horrendous economic problems. If he needed a fig-leaf to show that he had not abandoned the Palestinians, Begin would try and give him one.

It was in that spirit that Begin went to Ismailia at Christmas 1977, for his first visit to Egypt and his second summit with Sadat. If the Israelis expected as warm and spontaneous a welcome to the Suez Canal town as Sadat had received in Jerusalem, they were soon disabused. Emotions had been spiced on El-Al flight 447 from Ben-Gurion airport when a stewardess flung her arms around Begin's neck and burst into tears. Her husband had fallen on the Egyptian front in the 1973 war. But the atmosphere at the Abu Suweir military airfield was distinctly chilly. Sadat sent his deputy, Hosni Mubarak, to receive the Israeli party. There were no flags, no band, no anthems. On the drive to Ismailia, Ezer Weizman heard Dayan rasp to Begin: 'Look! Not a single Israeli flag, not even a placard to welcome us!' By contrast, Ismailia itself was resplendent with portraits and banners, flags and triumphal arches – all in praise of Egypt and its President. No Star of David, no Begin portraits, no florid welcome in Hebrew or English. This one-sided pattern was to repeat itself through the long months of negotiation, but Ismailia shocked the Israelis more than any other reception because it was the first at ministerial level. Ordinary Egyptians, taxi-drivers, waiters, shopkeepers, were genial enough, grasping Israeli hands, chorusing '*Salaam, shalom*'. But Egypt remained a controlled society. Public display was a matter for the authorities, and as one Egyptian editor put it, the authorities were seeking a 'secular peace', a reconciliation of the head rather than the soul. Sadat was still looking over his shoulder at the Arab and third worlds. He had been shaken by the failure of even the most 'moderate' among them, Jordan or Saudi Arabia, to rally to his standard after Jerusalem. According to Boutros Ghali, the Egyptian Minister of State for Foreign Affairs, this was reflected in Sadat's personal attitude towards Begin, despite the fact (so important to the Israeli Prime Minister with his Polish sense of propriety) that he soon put them on first-name terms.

The first contacts were never easy between Sadat and Begin. Good contact was only realized with Ezer Weizman. He was the middle man between Begin and Sadat. Up to the signature of the peace treaty [in March 1979], the chemistry between Begin and Sadat was not working. After the treaty was signed and Begin had delivered, Sadat began to trust Begin. But you can trust without sympathy. There was always a reserve.[5]

After a couple of false starts at a lower level, Begin tried at Ismailia to take the initiative for Israel. Sadat had won acclaim throughout the world, especially in the United States where the Carter Administration warmed to his apparent candour and sweeping attack, his charm and reasonableness. Israel had been made to look doctrinaire and mean-minded. Begin retaliated with what he hoped would prove a no-less-appealing Israeli peace plan. In Sinai it offered a phased Israeli withdrawal, balanced by demilitarization, but the Jewish settlements in the Rafah salient would stay and the Israeli army would remain responsible for their defence. In the West Bank and Gaza Strip, the Palestinian Arabs who had lived under Israeli rule since 1967 were to be granted 'administrative autonomy' under an elected council. Israel would keep control over security and public order, and Israeli citizens would be free to acquire land and settle in the territories. Clause 24 stated that 'Israel stands by its right and its claim of sovereignty' there, but since other claims existed Israel proposed that the question be left open. The twenty-sixth and final clause suggested a review of the entire package after five years, but in subsequent exchanges with the Americans and the Egyptians it emerged that Begin regarded autonomy as a permanent arrangement, not a transition to independence. That was the most the Palestinians could hope for.

Sadat rejected both halves of the Israeli plan. He insisted that no Israeli, civilian or soldier, could stay in Sinai. As for the West Bank and Gaza, the Egyptians demanded a total Israeli withdrawal, Palestinian self-determination, and no separate peace. In their private exchanges, Sadat told Begin: 'I cannot agree to surrender a single inch of Arab land. It is sacred.' Begin retorted: 'Mr President, I cannot give up a single inch of *Eretz Yisrael*. It is sacred.'

Dayan returned home consoled by the fact that neither national leader had broken off the talks, but convinced that the Egyptians were in earnest.

> I was deeply concerned about the price Egypt was determined to exact from us – total evacuation from Sinai; a commitment to withdraw completely from the West Bank and Golan; the rise of a Palestinian State. I sensed that there was deep feeling behind these words: they were not mere lip-service. And I suspected that Israel would indeed be faced by the grim alternative of having to make heavy concessions or achieving no peace treaty with Egypt.[6]

Begin had drafted his autonomy plan in elaborate secrecy. First, he dictated it in Hebrew, then rewrote it in English in his own hand. Since the Prime Minister's writing was notoriously illegible to all but the initiated few, Yehuda Avner, his English speedwriter, was mobilized to make a fair copy. Begin took this with him on a pilot trip to Washington and London, where he tried his ideas on President Carter and the British Prime Minister, James Callaghan. Both of them found the document a promising basis for negotiation, but were disconcerted to hear Begin translate these confidential opinions into endorsement. This was the first of several occasions when Carter felt that Begin had pulled a fast one on him. Only when he reached Washington did Begin allow his staff to have the plan typed by a secretary at the Israeli embassy, so anxious was he to avoid the slightest risk of a leak.

Ezer Weizman, Begin's Defence Minister, resented this cloak-and-dagger form of government, not least because he seems to have been left outside. But his criticism offers an insight into Begin's Prime Ministerial style:

> Begin does not work with a Cabinet; he operates by means of an office. Leaders of this type need no advisers; they make do with aides. He is incapable of taking into account views or proposals that do not fit in with his basic philosophy. The people in Begin's immediate vicinity do not submit different proposals or put forward a range of alternatives. This is partly the result of their past experience, which has taught them that such alternatives have no chance of being adopted; but mostly it is because Begin has chosen aides of a very specific human and political stamp. They think as he does. Having learned to guess what Begin wants, they try to outdo one another in proposing ideas that will be to the Prime Minister's liking and thus win his approval.[7]

Weizman, who quickly became the Cabinet's most demonstrative dove, recognized sooner than most that Begin conceived of autonomy as a way to perpetuate Israeli rule over the West Bank and Gaza, rather than as a first step towards a Palestinian State. That, the Defence Minister argued, was why he consulted nobody who might seek to deflect him from his course.

Although autonomy failed its first test at Ismailia, it remained the framework for all future negotiations between Israel and Egypt on the Palestinian issue. Sadat was uneasy with the entire concept, but neither he nor the Americans came up with an alternative that offered any chance of an agreed solution. Begin had succeeded in defining the terms of the argument.

For the first eight months of 1978 Israel's relations with Egypt and the United States went from bad to worse. Because of the chasm between the two Middle Eastern powers, America became a full and indispensable partner to the negotiations. Begin was cast as the bad guy, 'an obstacle to peace', but he would not budge from his basic stand. 'To my mind,' he told the Herut central committee in July, 'I am indeed an obstacle – an obstacle against capitulation, together with my colleagues in the Government, the Knesset, the faction and the movement.' The Israeli peace plan, he promised Herut critics as well as loyalists, would 'open up prospects for peace and security, and the settlement of *Eretz Yisrael*'.[8]

When Begin won the 1977 election, Washington was aware of his maximalist position on the territorial issue, but the State Department tended to underestimate the degree of his commitment to an *Eretz Yisrael* stretching from the Mediterranean to the Jordan. Harold Saunders, former Assistant Secretary of State for Near East Affairs, says they were advised by people who knew him that Begin could also be a pragmatic politician.

> We were persuaded that we could work with him, and that we would not necessarily have to expect to meet an ideological stone wall. We knew that his view was firm, we knew what it was, but we were told that on previous occasions in Israeli political life he had recognized the need to tack once in a while in the face of superior political winds. I guess we were not immediately aware of the differences [from the previous Government] or the difficulty in moving Begin.[9]

With the benefit of hindsight, William Quandt, the Carter National Security Council's Middle East expert, sees Begin's strength as his knowledge of what he wanted and what he was prepared to pay for it:

> Begin combined something you don't often find in politicians, a very clear sense of what he wanted to do, but a strict sense of what the political realities were and how you have to deal with them. He knew that he would have to manoeuvre, and sometimes he would have to delay, but he never lost sight of the objective. He always knew where he was heading, but he was quite capable of tactically adjusting here and there and taking the temperature. I was always struck by what a good politician he was, judging the lie of the land and what the political forces were that he had to contend with.[10]

One example of this manoeuvrability was his apparent openness on the West Bank during his talks with Carter in December, 1977, when he unveiled the autonomy plan. 'Begin sounded much more flexible than I had expected,' the President wrote in his memoirs, 'but I was to discover that his good words had multiple meanings, which my advisers and I did not understand at the time.'[11]

The Egyptians complained that Begin injected ideology into the negotiations. Boutros Ghali was perturbed by his knack of switching from the legalistic approach to the polemical:

> Begin negotiates like a lawyer, a mixture of a lawyer and a good parliamentarian. He can mix legal argumentation, demagogic argumentation, plus ideological argumentation, and move from one plane to another according to his own strategy. When he finds himself weak on the legal argument, he will jump to the demagogic or ideological approach. He was used to this kind of parliamentary debate, he is a good debater, and would use the same techniques in private as he used on the rostrum.

It is difficult to answer whether it was always controlled and calculated, whether it corresponded to real emotion or religious feeling. It was not the same with Ezer Weizman, nor with a religious man like Yosef Burg (Minister of the Interior and National Religious Party leader, who headed Israeli's autonomy negotiating team). We did not have the same feeling. Burg and Begin had the same mixture of religion and Zionism. Both are religious, but Begin prefers a more dramatic, a more theatrical approach.[12]

The Egyptians were slow to appreciate that Begin's ideology was not some exotic graft, but the very trunk of the tree. The ideology was the man. When he was asked by the veteran BBC correspondent Michael Elkins how he would like to be remembered by history, Begin answered: 'As the man who set the borders of *Eretz Yisrael* for all eternity.' That was not an ambition he discovered in his old age. From his adolescence in Poland, Begin had lived in the cultural and intellectual cloister of the Jabotinsky movement, which soon forfeited the founder's open-mindedness and fascination with ideas whatever their origins. He had no extraneous enthusiasm, like Dayan's passion for archaeology, no separate career, like Weizman's in the air force or Ya'acov Meridor's in business. Begin was a politician twenty-four hours a day. He could be convivial, but seldom relaxed. His gregariousness with outsiders was the gregariousness of his profession, watchful and calculating. The struggle was all.

With varying degrees of fluency, Begin knows nine languages (Hebrew, Yiddish, Polish, Russian, English, German, French, Spanish and Latin). In his youth he steeped himself in the European classics (he once sent President Sadat's wife a telegram when she misquoted *King Lear*), but he read little or nothing of modern literature later than Ibsen. In his opposition years, he liked to read history and biography, but gave up books almost completely when he became Prime Minister, though he read the Nixon and Kissinger memoirs in hospital. He scanned almost the entire Hebrew press, as well as half a dozen American and European newspapers. Before he took office, he went regularly twice a week to the cinema, especially to see Westerns, taking his seat conspiratorially just after the lights were dimmed and slipping out just before they went up again. He was addicted to the radio and television (*Dallas* was one of his favourite shows, after the nine o'clock news), but seldom if ever attended a concert, a theatre or an art gallery. Once when he joined in a sing-song, his daughter Hassia told him he was better at speeches. He lived frugally because anything richer or more exotic, in food or decor, was irrelevant. Begin was incurably a man of the desert generation.

*   *   *

TOP With President Ceausescu of Romania, Bucharest,
August 1977

ABOVE An emotional moment in the Bucharest synagogue

TOP Begin and President Ephraim Katzir (right) greet President Sadat of Egypt on his arrival in Israel, November 1977

ABOVE Eyeball to eyeball: Sadat and Begin at the banquet at the King David Hotel, 20 November 1977

TOP Playing chess with Zbigniew Brzezinski, watched by Simha Dinitz (second from left), Israeli Ambassador to the United States, and General Ephraim Poran, Begin's military secretary, Camp David, September 1978

ABOVE The Israeli delegation at Camp David, September 1978. Left to right: Moshe Dayan, Ezer Weizman, Simha Dinitz, General Avraham Tamir, Professor Aharon Barak (the Attorney-General), Meir Rosenne (head of the Foreign Ministry's legal department), Yehiel Kadishai (Begin's political secretary), Dan Pattir (Begin's spokesman), Begin and General Ephraim Poran.

Begin, Sadat and President Carter
celebrate the agreement reached at
Camp David, 17 September 1978

Helping his granddaughter blow out the
candles on her birthday cake, 1978

Artur Rubinstein congratulates Begin
on winning the Nobel Prize,
October 1978

At the pyramids, Giza, April 1979

TOP Entering 10 Downing Street with Margaret Thatcher, May 1979
ABOVE Mixing with the Egyptian crowd during a visit to Alexandria, July 1979

TOP With Aliza and their two daughters, Leah (left) and Hassia, October 1979
ABOVE Speaking at the press conference given after the bombing of the Iraqi nuclear reactor, 1981

RIGHT With Defence Minister Ariel
Sharon at Beaufort Castle,
June 1982

BELOW 'I can't go on' – Begin's
meeting with coalition
representatives after announcing his
resignation, 30 August 1983. Left to
right: Justice Minister Moshe
Nissim, Avraham Shapira of Agudat
Yisrael, Avraham Sharir (Minister
of Tourism of the Liberal Party),
Mordechai Zipori (Minister of
Communications), David Levy and
Rabbi Menachem Porush of Agudat
Yisrael.

From the earliest days of the Sadat initiative, the three principal Israeli actors – Begin, Dayan and Weizman – adopted separate, but complementary, roles. The Prime Minister set the objectives and the tone of the Israeli diplomacy. He took the decisions. Dayan was constantly searching and probing for accommodation, redefining the terms of the argument, coaxing his own leader into concessions, planting ideas. Weizman's contribution, no less significant in the period before the Camp David conference, was to keep the human contact alive. At the lowest points of the negotiation, Weizman was the Israeli the Egyptians could still talk to, the Israeli who convinced Sadat that peace was still attainable. Weizman was the first Israeli, apart from Begin, that the Egyptian President met alone during his Jerusalem visit. 'I like that Ezra,' he told the Prime Minister afterwards, even though it was months before he got Ezer's first name right.

Dayan and Weizman were determined not to let the chance of peace slip. Although the Defence Minister was a member of Herut and had managed its election campaign, both were outsiders. Their loyalty to the Prime Minister and to his ideals was not unlimited, which was at once an advantage and a disadvantage. It gave them scope for flexibility, but it alerted Begin to keep them on a tight rein. Dayan had the ear of the Americans, Weizman was at home with the Egyptians. Cyrus Vance, who brought the patience and ingenuity of a corporation lawyer to the State Department, was disturbed by Weizman's ebullience:

> Ezer is a very attractive, energetic, able man, but he tends to be too optimistic. He doesn't face reality sufficiently. That you could never accuse Dayan of. He would see all the pitfalls. Ezer would sometimes get carried away. Therefore I felt much more comfortable when I had thrashed something out with Dayan because you knew that he saw it in all its stark reality. I did not feel that was the case with Ezer. I have great affection for Ezer, and I'm sure he was a splendid Defence Minister, but he didn't have the kind of input in any way that Dayan did.[13]

At the National Security Council, William Quandt judged Weizman 'a little too impatient to deal with Begin's legalisms and the endless drafting and redrafting'. Weizman badly wanted an agreement, Quandt says, and he was prepared at any point to say, 'Let's sign and get out of here.'[14] But one American career diplomat, who is still handling Middle East questions and must therefore remain anonymous, is convinced that peace would not have been achieved without all three of the Israeli players:

> Weizman's contribution was to keep the Egyptians', particularly Sadat's, frustration with Begin's diplomacy, the style of Israeli diplomacy, from boiling over so much that it would destroy the process. Over and over again he succeeded

with crucial timing in keeping personal relations going between the Israeli leaders and the Egyptians, and giving them hope to keep on at it. Even when they had lost hope.

The Egyptians were seldom at ease with Dayan. According to his spokesman, Naphtali Lavie, there was a coldness from the moment Sadat stepped down from Egypt on that first November Saturday night.

> Sadat said to him: 'Don't worry, Moshe, it will be all right.' In the car driving to Jerusalem with Boutros Ghali, Dayan asked: 'Are you ready for a separate peace?' Ghali said: 'No.' Dayan told him he was misreading the Arab reaction. Ghali conveyed that to Sadat and to the Americans. Sadat interpreted it as meaning Dayan didn't trust him. A general who was Sadat's aide-de-camp said Sadat felt uncomfortable in Dayan's presence. He was perceived as the Israeli with whom you don't win. Sadat and Dayan were both shrewd men. They didn't trust each other very much. Dayan wouldn't join in the kind of artificial relationship that Weizman had with Sadat.[15]

Boutros Ghali says, however, that it was not so much Egyptian memories of the 1956 and 1967 wars, or Dayan's reputation for deviousness, that put them off. They were alienated by his 'mixture of shyness and arrogance'. Weizman played the mediator between Sadat and Dayan, as well as between Sadat and Begin, Ghali recalls.

> He would say: 'Dayan is depressed. How about giving him dinner, or a phone call?' He would say things like: 'I'm in a difficult position. Sadat has seen me four times. Dayan is shy, but he hasn't seen Sadat.' Begin had a great respect for Dayan, as a *sabra* and a general. He listened to Dayan, but not enough. I had very long conversations with Dayan. Very often he said: 'I can promise you nothing. If I were working with Ben-Gurion, I could give you an answer in two hours.' He left it implicit, he never drew an explicit comparison with Begin, but it was clear. The Israelis would joke about each other, but they were never disloyal. I did not feel that Dayan was going beyond his instructions. Dayan was the chief negotiator. He negotiated with imagination. He was precise as a negotiator. He never promised something he could not deliver. He wanted to pinpoint what he meant and what we meant.[16]

Dayan was not disloyal, but he recognized that Begin, perhaps alone in the Israeli team, was prepared to countenance failure. If Sadat set too high a price for peace, Begin would say no and live with the consequences. Dayan strove to stretch the limits of acceptability. One of his favourite techniques was to persuade others – Ezer Weizman or the Americans – to present his ideas as their own. Another, used in extreme circumstances, was to endorse a compromise formula in his personal capacity, making it clear to the Egyptians and the Americans that he was not committing the

Government, then to challenge Begin to repudiate his own Foreign Minister. Both stratagems worked when it mattered most, but Begin noted and remembered.

The only tangible outcome of the Ismailia summit was an agreement to establish two working committees, one political and one military, to conduct the detailed negotiations. The work of the political committee began disastrously in Jerusalem on 17 January. President Carter had visited Sadat in Aswan earlier in the month and enunciated a new American doctrine on the Palestinian question. 'There must be a resolution of the Palestinian problem in all its aspects,' he said. 'The problem must recognize the legitimate rights of the Palestinian people and enable the Palestinians *to participate in the determination of their own future.*' The formula was carefully crafted so as not to provoke an outright Israeli denunciation. The first reaction in Jerusalem was: 'We can live with it.' But Begin made it clear that Israel would not accept the Carter terminology as a cover for Palestinian self-determination: 'We don't beat about the bush. The term self-determination, as it is understood in international law and practice, means a Palestinian State, and we will not agree to such a mortal danger to Israel.'

The Jerusalem talks went wrong from the arrival of the Egyptian team at Ben-Gurion airport. Dayan welcomed his opposite number, Mohammed Ibrahim Kamel, with what he called 'the polite generalities customary on such occasions'. Instead of replying in kind, Kamel drew a sheet of paper from his pocket and read a hard-line reiteration of Egypt's demands: 'There can be no peace with the occupation of land, there can be no peace with the denial of the national rights of the Palestinian people, foremost among which is the right to self-determination.' Rather than perpetuate the row at the airport, Dayan waited until the following morning. In answer to a hostile question at a press conference, he said it would be better for the peace initiative to slip through their fingers than for Israel's security to be snatched from its hands. Israel would not negotiate with a pistol at its head. That was hard enough for the Egyptians to stomach, but Begin compounded the offence at a festive dinner that night. Although the Prime Minister and Kamel had agreed in a private exchange to stop the war of words, Begin delivered a political speech setting out the conditions that Israel could never accept: the redivision of Jerusalem, the establishment of a Palestinian State, and a return to the pre-1967 borders. Dayan wrote in his memoirs:

In his flow of eloquence Begin unwittingly offended Kamel by calling him 'young man', little realizing that to an Arab ear this term sounded derisive. When it was his turn to speak, Kamel, hurt and embarrassed, instead of reading his prepared address, simply said that the place for discussing the subjects raised by the Prime Minister was the committee and not there. He then sat down and did not even raise his glass to toast the President of Israel.[17]

Begin, Weizman commented afterwards, was 'absolutely convinced that he held the truth in his back pocket'. He could not resist giving Kamel a lesson in Jewish history, and a lecture on statesmanship.[18]

The next evening, Sadat surprised everyone, including his own delegation, by summoning Kamel home to Cairo. The Egyptians left in disarray. The Israelis and Americans did not know what had hit them. According to an official explanation broadcast by Cairo radio, Sadat acted 'when it became clear from statements made by Begin and Dayan that Israel's purpose is to secure partial solutions which cannot bring about a comprehensive, just and lasting peace'. On the way to Ben-Gurion airport, Kamel told Dayan that the President had been particularly offended by Begin's words. 'This was due not to what Begin had said in his speech, but to the fact that he had made such a speech, in direct breach of the agreement made only three hours before, which Kamel had reported to Sadat and [for which he had] received presidential approval.'[19]

Relations were soured still further by the strange episode of the dummy settlements in the Sinai desert. Ariel Sharon was Minister of Agriculture with a special responsibility for settlement policy. He was also a retired general who knew the peninsula better than anyone else in the Cabinet. He had fought over it in three wars and had ruled over it as chief of Southern Command. Begin consulted him on strategic as well as settlement questions. While the Prime Minister was in Washington in December 1977, Sharon telephoned and urged that Israel fill the gaps in its Sinai settlement line. In the light of Egypt's maximalist demands, he wanted to strengthen Israel's bargaining position. The experience of 1948 suggested that the location of settlements was a significant factor in where borders were drawn. The same might apply if Israel were negotiating to keep a strip of northern Sinai. Begin was impressed by the argument, and authorized Sharon to go ahead with the planning. The Agriculture Minister's idea was to construct phantom settlements – a water-tower, caravan and security trench – at key points without actually stationing more than a token force there. Ezer Weizman, who opposed the scheme when it was brought belatedly to the Cabinet, condemned it as 'a sad parody of the history of Jewish resettlement in Israel'. Nevertheless, it was approved overwhelmingly and work began. No announcement was made, but Israel radio picked up the story and broadcast it. The Egyptians and the Americans were furious at this sharp practice which they saw as an effort to pre-empt the negotiations. Sharon was left to bear the brunt of the criticism and the mockery the dummy settlements evoked. Begin did not disclose his part in authorizing Sharon to go ahead, and for once the notoriously leaky Cabinet kept its collective secrets. The affair soon faded, but it left an unhappy after-taste. Not for the last time, Begin had followed Sharon into a minefield. He deferred too quickly to military expertise, and paid a political penalty for it. Weizman's speculation that the dummy settlements cost Israel the chance of keeping the Sinai settlements and perhaps the military airfields is not convincing. Territory meant as much to Sadat as to Begin. He was determined to regain the whole of the peninsula down to the last inch. Israelis could come as tourists, but not as residents or garrison.

Despite this interlude, the main focus of the dispute remained the occupied Palestinian territories, the West Bank and Gaza Strip. The dialogue with the United States reached a new low in March 1978, when Begin again visited Washington. The Americans tried to use Security Council Resolution 242 as a crowbar to prise open Israel's resistance to any territorial compromise. Begin had, after all, acknowledged that his Government was bound by its predecessor's acceptance of the resolution. *Pacta sunt observanda*, he said, agreements are to be observed. And Resolution 242 spoke of withdrawal from occupied territory and the inadmissibility of its acquisition by war. Begin's lawyers were not daunted by such considerations. They argued that the resolution did not specify withdrawal from *each one* of the territories; that the 1967 war was a war of self-defence for Israel (and, therefore, border changes were admissible); and that Jordanian sovereignty over the West Bank had never been recognized by the international community. At a farewell meeting, Carter spelled out what he termed the six noes of Menachem Begin. 'Though Carter spoke in a dull monotone,' Dayan noted, 'there was fury in his cold blue eyes, and his glance was dagger-sharp. His portrayal of our position was basically correct, but it could not have been expressed in a more hostile form.'[20] Carter had concluded that 'Begin was becoming an insurmountable obstacle to further progress', and was trying to shock him and his supporters into recognizing the logic of their stand. If there were no movement on the Israeli side, there would be no peace. The six noes, as Carter recorded them in his diary on 22 March, were that Begin was

> not willing to withdraw politically or militarily from any part of the West Bank; not willing to stop the construction of new settlements or the expansion of existing settlements; not willing to withdraw the Israeli settlers from the Sinai,

or even leave them there under UN or Egyptian protection; not willing to acknowledge that UN Resolution 242 applies to the West Bank-Gaza area; not willing to grant the Palestinian Arabs real authority, or a voice in the determination of their own future to the extent that they can choose between the alternatives outlined above (affiliation with Israel or Jordan, or the continuation of an interim government of their own).

Six weeks later when Begin returned to Washington for the American celebration of Israel's independence anniversary, Carter wrote: 'My guess is that he will not take the necessary steps to bring peace to Israel – an opportunity that may never come again.'[21]

Begin tried to accentuate the positive (no mean endeavour), but it was left to Dayan to explore a way forward. His first attempt to strike a more flexible pose cut little ice. The Foreign Minister set out four principles of Israeli policy:

1 Resolution 242 was a basis for negotiations between Israel and all its Arab neighbours, Egypt, Jordan, Syria and Lebanon;
2 Israel's peace plan, including self-rule for Judea, Samaria and the Gaza Strip, was in harmony with the principles of Resolution 242;
3 If the Arab states put forward counter-proposals, Israel would discuss them on their merits;
4 Resolution 242 called for negotiations.

This new presentation was discounted as a public relations exercise. Sadat began setting deadlines (July, according to one version, October, according to another) and to flaunt the war option. Weizman stormed out of a Cabinet meeting announcing that he was ordering the army to prepare for battle, and on another occasion the Defence Minister ostentatiously tore up a peace poster. In reply to American questions, Begin stated on 18 June that Israel was willing, after five years of West Bank autonomy, to 'consider and agree upon *the nature of the future relations* between the parties'. This was a long way short of the American requirement that Israel be prepared to discuss sovereignty after a transitional period. The Egyptians dismissed the formula as another example of Begin's 'intransigence'. Dayan hardly improved matters by explaining that most Israeli ministers had refused to commit Israel to decide after five years on the permanent status of the territories 'because they regard administrative autonomy as the permanent framework'. Predictably, Israel rejected an Egyptian proposal to return the West Bank and Gaza to the Arabs for an interim period. Sadat tried in early July to go behind Begin's back by holding talks in Austria with Weizman and the Labour Opposition leader, Shimon Peres. The Prime Minister put a stop to that with the sharp retort: 'I am the address.' The Cabinet warned

Sadat that all future official contacts must be with Begin or his designated representative:

> The exclusive authority to negotiate with Egypt or with any other country which is in a state of war with Israel is given to the Government and its authorized representatives. The level of representation in the negotiating process will be reciprocal. The heads of state, or their authorized ministers, will head their delegations.

The first breach in the wall of mutual intransigence came out of an otherwise unproductive meeting of American, Israeli and Egyptian foreign ministers at Leeds Castle in Kent. This was one of the occasions when Dayan chanced his arm. He handed the Secretary of State, Cyrus Vance, a note expressing 'my personal opinion', and given on 'my personal responsibility only', in which he suggested that Israel would be prepared to discuss the key issue of sovereignty over the West Bank and Gaza after five years of autonomy. At the same time, he repeated that Israel would never withdraw to the pre-1967 lines, even with the security arrangements, but that it would 'consider' any concrete Arab proposal for peace based on territorial compromise. As Dayan must have expected, Begin was infuriated by both his idea and his insubordination. The Foreign Minister responded by offering Begin a choice between backing him or sacking him, tolerating him on his own terms or humiliating him.

> I told the Prime Minister that what I had said and written reflected, to the best of my understanding, the Government's position, but I would not take it amiss, nor would it be improper, if he or the Government revoked it. I would accept their verdict and inform Vance accordingly. At all events, I added, I did not think I could conduct negotiations without being permitted to put forward ideas and suggest proposals, while stressing that they represented my personal views to which my Government might not agree. This was a well-trodden subject on which Begin and I held firm and differing opinions. I was not prepared to behave otherwise, and Begin knew it. The practical option open to him if he insisted on my accepting his approach was to get himself another Foreign Minister.[22]

It was still too early in the Begin administration for the Prime Minister to take so drastic a step, though Dayan had gone far beyond the Government's position, and they both knew it. Begin still needed Dayan. To the Foreign Minister's astonishment, Begin proposed that the Cabinet endorse his memorandum to Vance and bring it to the Knesset for approval, which it won by sixty-four votes to thirty-two on 24 July. 'The memorandum which I had given to Vance at Leeds Castle', Dayan recorded with justifiable satisfaction, 'became an official document representing Israel's position.' Despite continued deadlock, the Dayan formula eased the way to President Carter's last fling, the desperate gamble of the Camp David summit. Begin had again allowed an ex-general to tease him beyond his better judgement, but this time in a more benign cause.

19
Concentration Camp *De Luxe*

'You must decide whether at this stage you are prepared to see this matter through to the very end,' the National Security Adviser, Zbigniew Brzezinski, wrote in a confidential memorandum to Jimmy Carter on 18 July 1978. 'It seems to me that if we go public and then do not prevail, our Middle East policy will be in shambles, and Sadat and others will be either repudiated or will turn in a radical direction. In other words, if we go public, *we must prevail*.'[1] In full awareness of the risks involved, the President convened a summit conference with the Israeli and Egyptian leaders at Camp David, his official retreat in the hills of Maryland seventy miles from Washington. It was better, he concluded, to try to work *through* Begin than *against* him.

The conference began on 5 September and ended thirteen days later with all three delegations in an advanced state of physical and mental exhaustion. The camp, padded and protected by a thick poultice of mature trees and shrubs, was built for Franklin D. Roosevelt during the Second World War. President Eisenhower changed its name from Shangri-la to Camp David after his grandson. Ezer Weizman found it claustrophobic and gloomy, despite the mischievous squirrels. Moshe Dayan was ill-at-ease amid the alien vegetation and golden-brown carpet of autumn leaves. The great appeal of the setting was that the press and its customers could be kept at bay. The three leaders and their respective teams were penned in a private world of cabins and trails, bowling-alleys and tennis-courts, swimming-pool, billiards hall and cinema. After Dayan had returned from a reconnaissance mission and reported on the fearsome security fence, Begin dubbed it a 'concentration camp *de luxe*'. As their sentence lengthened, he joked that he would have to send for the old Irgun escapologist, Ya'acov Meridor, to tunnel them out. The Israelis took it for granted that their cabins were bugged, but Brzezinski insists that they were not (his recommendation was overruled).

Camp David was a quintessentially American playground. Few, if any, of the Israelis or Egyptians played tennis or went bowling. Sadat and Dayan took separate walks every day. Weizman rode a bicycle for the first time since his childhood. The more junior Israelis played endless games of billiards and went to the movies. Begin played a mean game of chess with Brzezinski. By accident or design, he gave the National Security Adviser the impression that he had not played since the NKVD interrupted his game with Yisrael Eldad in Pavilnius thirty-eight years earlier, but Aliza blew his cover. 'Menachem', she purred, 'just loves to play chess.' The Polish-born professor found that Begin played 'a very good systematic, somewhat aggressive, but strategically very deliberate game'. The two conversed in English rather than the language of their childhood. Dayan, an occasional spectator, was struck by the competitiveness. 'The game', he wrote, 'proved less a form of peaceful relaxation than a battlefield confrontation, with each one trying desperately to defeat the other.' Like much else at Camp David, the result was misted in ambiguity. It is common ground that the first two games were split one-all. Brzezinski claims that he won the third and the series. But according to Yehiel Kadishai they played a fourth game which Begin won, making it two-two. Hamilton Jordan, Carter's chief staff aide, telephoned to congratulate the Prime Minister. If Brzezinski had won, he said, they wouldn't have been able to talk to him.

The Americans knew that the summit was a gamble, but they misjudged the odds. The White House set aside three days, with an option of another four if the conference were making good progress on the principles of peace. No one, Carter confessed afterwards, dreamed that they would be there through 'thirteen intense and discouraging days, with success in prospect only during the final hours'. The negotiations were unbalanced in more ways than one. Both Begin and Sadat arrived at Camp David determined to drive a hard bargain, but the Israeli leader had the advantage that he alone of the three summiteers could contemplate failure with equanimity. Many Israelis would be bitterly disappointed, among them senior members of his own delegation, but Begin would explain that he had done everything to win peace, short of sacrificing *Eretz Yisrael*. The Likud would close ranks, his Government would come through, and Israel would still have Sinai. On the other hand, Carter was not an impartial mediator. 'Sadat seemed to trust me too much,' he wrote, 'and Begin not enough.'[2] It was equally true that the American President trusted Sadat too much and suspected Begin. 'I would not even try to deny that I was pro-Sadat,' he admitted in an interview with *Time*. 'He was completely open, courageous, generous, far-sighted. He was willing to ignore details to reach an ultimate goal of peace that was beneficial to him and to Egypt.'[3] Carter was prepared to tolerate far more from the Egyptian leader than he was from the Israeli. This was partly because Sadat showed him some of his cards in advance, and partly because he succumbed to Sadat's charm. Sadat's demands were no less extreme than Begin's, but he left the haggling to his aides. It made it easier to sustain the pose of the reasonable and courageous man of peace. Begin, by contrast, was the most intransigent of the Israeli negotiators, scrutinizing every word and punctuation mark, beavering day and night. When Rosalynn Carter, the President's wife, suggested that all three leaders call on the world to join them in a prayer for success, Begin insisted on seeing the text. Begin represented the awkward squad, irritating and familiar. Sadat was a man of a different culture with its own pace and its own mint-tea values. Allowances had to be made. Sadat wanted Carter to float his ideas for him, Begin was constantly resisting anything of the kind. He could fight Sadat to the limit, but he refused to fight the Americans as well. Throughout the negotiations Begin beseeched Carter not to present Egyptian proposals as made-in-America.

Sadat took the offensive from Day Two. He submitted what Carter acknowledged to be an 'extremely harsh' plan for a comprehensive peace filled with 'all the unacceptable Arab rhetoric'. It called, among other things, for: Israeli withdrawal from all the occupied territories; removal of all Israeli settlements; abolition of the Israeli military government, and the transfer of its authority to the Arabs of the West Bank and Gaza Strip, with a five-year transitional period during which Jordan would supervise the West Bank and Egypt the Gaza Strip, 'in co-operation with freely elected representatives of the Palestinian people who shall exercise direct authority over the administration'. Six months before the end of the five-year transitional period, the Palestinians would 'exercise their fundamental right to self-determination' and be enabled to 'establish their national entity'. Israel would be required to withdraw from East Jerusalem to the 1949 armistice lines and Arab sovereignty and administration should be restored to the Arab sector. Finally, Sadat demanded that Israel pay 'full and prompt compensation for the damage which resulted from the operations of its armed forces against the civilian population and installations, as well as its exploitation of natural resources in occupied territories'.[4] The latter would include indemnity for the millions of barrels Israel had pumped from the Sinai oilfields since 1967. Begin chose not to kick over the traces at this first joint meeting. Both Middle Eastern leaders were on their best behaviour. Carter suspected that Begin was relieved at the harshness of the Sadat document, citing it for days to come as proof of the unreasonable attitude of the Egyptians.

On Day Three, having consulted his colleagues, he rejected it root and branch. 'This smacks of a victorious state dictating peace to the defeated,' he told Carter. 'This document is not a proper basis for negotiations.' Sadat wanted peace with an Israel that would not only be vulnerable but doomed. In what proved to be their last face-to-face round of the Camp David summit, Begin dissected the Sadat proposals clause by clause. 'Premier Begin,' Sadat retorted, 'you want land!' Egypt was offering Israel security, but not land. 'All restraint was now gone,' Carter recorded. 'Their faces were flushed, and the niceties of diplomatic language and protocol were stripped away. They had almost forgotten that I was there.'[5] Before they adjourned after three hours of concentrated argument, Sadat complained that the warm feelings he had developed during his visit to Jerusalem had been destroyed because 'minimum confidence does not exist any more since Premier Begin has acted in bad faith'. When the meeting resumed later in the day, the two leaders quickly talked themselves into a deadlock over the Sinai settlements. Sadat said that the Egyptian people would 'never accept an encroachment on their land or sovereignty'. Begin answered that there was no way he could sell a dismantling of the settlements to his Cabinet or to his people. To move the settlers would spell the downfall of his Government. At this Sadat stood up and threatened to walk out – of the meeting and of the summit. Carter blocked the way to the door, and urged them both not to break off the talks. Begin agreed immediately, Sadat stood fuming before he nodded his head, then stalked out without another word.

The Americans saw more clearly than ever that they would have to take the initiative. Sadat sulked in his cabin. His aides informed Brzezinski that the President was thinking of going home. Begin dug in over the two key questions of the Sinai settlements and the application of Resolution 242 to the West Bank and Gaza, but he dropped what Carter took to be a hint of flexibility when he told the American President: 'I will never personally *recommend* that the settlements in the Sinai be dismantled.' That was not the same as saying he would never *acquiesce* in their removal.[6] But Begin was adamant on the occupied Palestinian territories. At one point Carter rounded on the Prime Minister: 'What you want to do is make the West Bank part of Israel.' Begin replied that autonomy was one thing, Arab sovereignty another. The Israelis would not agree to sign any document which incorporated the Resolution 242 principle of the 'inadmissibility of the acquisition of territory by war'. Quoting the Psalm 'If I forget thee, O Jerusalem', Begin told Carter: 'Better my right hand should lose its cunning than I should sign such a document.' Despite growing fatigue, the Americans prepared their own draft agreement on Day Five. By Day Nine, they recognized that neither side would endorse it without drastic amendment. Begin produced a brief, uninformative communiqué with which he suggested they might all go home. Carter then took an unconventional step, which eventually, slowly and falteringly, led to agreement. He established a working party comprising himself, Cyrus Vance, the Israeli Attorney-General, Aharon Barak, and the waspish Egyptian Under-Secretary for Foreign Affairs, Osama el-Baz. It was unheard of for a head of state to negotiate over detail in this way with two technical experts, who then had to go back and sell the agreed clauses to their masters. But it worked.

Along with Dayan, Barak emerged as one of the heroes of the Israeli team. In 1978 he was a boyish, forty-one-year-old, bespectacled law professor who had already been nominated to the Supreme Court bench, but had stayed as Attorney-General for the duration of the peace talks. Although Barak had been appointed by the Labour Government, Begin developed an extraordinary respect for his talents as scholar and jurist. Barak, like Dayan and Weizman, was hungry for peace. He used all his skill and prestige to break down Begin's resistance. Vance, a fellow lawyer, was impressed by the quality of Barak's mind.

> He is a man of great sensitivity and judgement, invaluable at many difficult points in the negotiations. He had a marvellous gift of words, and he could always put himself in the other person's shoes, and then try to find a way of satisfying the other person's need without undercutting the vital interests of his country. Dayan and I would agree on a way of getting around a problem, and Barak would find the words to provide the road around the obstacle or to bridge it.[7]

William Quandt, the President's Middle East expert, found Barak to be the Israeli who had learned most successfully to work on Begin's wavelength.

> He worked patiently through the text and the language, playing an almost Talmudic game of changing a phrase, without really having his heart in it. He did not really believe it was worth fussing with all of these things, but he also realized it was very important to bring Begin along. He would do a lot of the drafting and redrafting and thinking of formulations that Begin might buy.[8]

Another American diplomat, who knew Begin and Barak well, suggests that Carter exploited Barak's interest in agreement and flexibility:

> The President got Barak to come up with ways to express concepts in legal language which were ambiguous, but which Barak could then justify to Begin in legal terms and convince Begin that there was a legitimate legal interpretation which would protect Begin's position, despite the ambiguity. There are a number of places in the text where it was Barak's ability to explain to Begin how this could be interpreted to mean x when on the surface you might think it meant y that gave Begin the rationalization to permit him to make these concessions, when he decided to make them rather than lose the agreement. Nobody else

could have done that. Meanwhile Dayan was arguing the diplomatic or the political reasons for accepting things, but Begin had to have a legal rationalization to satisfy himself and his own peculiar view of legal principles.[9]

The Attorney-General also contributed to the rapprochement with the Egyptians, though they were not as sure as the Americans of how influential he was. 'Barak succeeded in creating an atmosphere of legal confidence,' Boutros Ghali says, 'as Weizman had created an atmosphere of human confidence. We trusted Barak when he said: "I want this word in Article Four for such and such reason." '[10]

Nevertheless, Begin never yielded control of the Israeli negotiating strategy. He determined the issues on which to stick and those on which they could give. He decided when and how they should make their concessions. 'Begin', one American witness testifies, 'showed a masterly sense of timing. He knew when was the very last moment to compromise. He bought more for a small concession than a different kind of negotiator would get for giving up more.' The Prime Minister had all the patience in the world. Sometimes he seemed to be playing a game of attrition for its own sake, losing sight of the wood for the trees. Carter found him 'rigid and unimaginative'. His wife, Rosalynn, told Brzezinski that the President had called Begin 'a psycho', a term Carter was too honest to deny when taxed with it on Israel television during a private visit to Jerusalem in March 1983. But by the end of the thirteen-day ordeal of Camp David no one doubted that there was method in Begin's madness. Vance commends Begin as 'one of the finest poker-players' he has ever seen.

> He could exhibit a wounded heart in a very effective fashion: 'How could you possibly expect me to accept that kind of position?' He'd show all the anguish and disbelief. He would sit there without his face registering anything. He'd try and sit his opponent out. He was a feller who could outsit almost anybody else on the other side of the table if necessary. All the qualities of a very skilful negotiator or poker-player.
>
> Begin was very clear in his objectives, very precise in his thinking. He put in some demands that he was willing to sacrifice. I can think of a number of times when he said this is something on which we will never compromise, and later that same day, having pounded the table, he changed his mind. Fairly early I found that out, and so I never accepted his statements 'I will never yield on that point'. I came to the conclusion that it was part of his style, and he did not mean it.[11]

Begin held out on three issues: the Sinai settlements, the language of Resolution 242 ('acquisition of territory by war'), and finally Jerusalem. Despite progress made in Carter's working group and the parallel team of foreign ministers shepherded by Brzezinski, the summit again came close to collapse on Day Ten and Day Eleven. The Israelis presented a united front for keeping the settlements. The Egyptians refused to let them stay. Carter began to make plans to wind up the conference and minimize the damage. He set Sunday, 17 September, as the deadline. It would be better to acknowledge failure than to let the summit die a lingering death. Sadat and his aides packed their bags and asked the Americans to provide a helicopter. The Egyptian President had had an abrasive exchange with Dayan, but responded to a last-ditch personal appeal from Carter. Some of the more sceptical Americans felt that Sadat was play-acting. He didn't take much persuading. 'There was a part of Sadat that was an actor,' William Quandt notes, 'and he knew that Carter was quite susceptible to his kind of emotional appeal. He had done it before.'

Some of the pieces were falling into place. Weizman, whose main role so far had been to 'keep the embers glowing', conceded the Sinai airfields in return for a pledge by the American Defence Secretary, Harold Brown, to build replacements in the Negev. Barak and Osama el-Baz agreed to remove the 'inadmissibility of the acquisition of territory by war' from the main text and publish the entire resolution as an annex, with a note in the preamble that both parties agree to 'Resolution 242 in all its parts'. Begin swallowed the phrase 'the legitimate rights of the Palestinian people', which he had previously maintained would pose a mortal danger to Israel. 'Can a right be illegitimate?' he asked disingenuously after lecturing his colleagues on the Latin root of 'legitimate'.

But the dispute over the Sinai settlements could not be resolved without a *deus ex machina*. One appeared in the unholy and unlikely form of Ariel Sharon, Begin's favourite war hero and settlement chief. General Avraham Tamir, Weizman's head of military planning, suggested telephoning Sharon, briefing him on the Camp David crisis, and persuading him to urge Begin to evacuate the settlements. Weizman doubted whether Sharon, the moving spirit behind the settlement programme, would co-operate, but they had nothing to lose. He authorized Tamir to try his luck.

> A few hours later, a deeply moved Begin was telling the Israeli delegation that Arik Sharon had phoned him. To his surprise, Sharon was in favour of evacuating the settlements if they were the last remaining obstacle to a peace agreement. 'I see no military objection to their evacuation,' Sharon had told the Prime Minister.[12]

Begin was moved, but he was still inhibited about giving up the settlements. His argument for keeping them had been couched in security terms. The Rafah salient was a valuable buffer between Sinai, which would be restored to Egypt, and the 400,000 Palestinian refugees of the Gaza Strip, a fertile recruiting-ground for terrorists. But security was not his only concern. Like many Israelis of varied political persuasions, the Prime Minister was disturbed at the prospect of uprooting settlers. It went against the grain of the national ethos. He was reluctant to create a precedent for the West Bank and the Golan Heights. But above all, Begin feared that abandonment of the settlements would divide his own ranks, as indeed it soon did.

When he met Carter on Day Twelve, Begin was still playing hard to get. He suggested negotiating with Sadat on every other outstanding issue with the aim of achieving a peace treaty in three months. Then he would submit the settlement question to the Knesset. Carter told him that it was a forlorn hope. Sadat would never buy it. 'It was obviously very painful for Prime Minister Begin,' the President wrote. 'He was shouting words like "ultimatum", "excessive demands", and "political suicide".' In the end, however, Begin agreed to submit to the Knesset within two weeks the question: 'If agreement is reached on all other Sinai issues, will the settlers be withdrawn?' He rejected a request from Carter to maintain a neutral position in this debate, but promised a free vote.[13] Begin hoped to separate the two votes, one on the peace agreement and one on the settlements. He predicted an overwhelming parliamentary majority *for* the former and a smaller one *against* the latter. But he was outmanœuvred by the Labour Opposition, whose support he needed and which insisted on a single vote covering both the agreement and the evacuation. It is barely conceivable that a parliamentarian of Begin's experience expected to get away with the two-vote solution, or that it would have satisfied the Egyptians or the Americans. But the Labour intervention gave him an alibi. Menachem Begin had not traded away Jewish settlements, the Opposition had. It convinced no one who did not want to be convinced, but it salved Begin's conscience. Perhaps that was all it was meant to do.

Begin kept his word. The Rafah settlements, including the model town of Yamit, were evacuated at great financial and emotional cost on schedule in April 1982. An American demand for a freeze on Israeli settlement activity on the West Bank ended less amicably. Carter and Vance spent more than six hours on the Saturday night (Day Twelve) arguing their case with Begin, Dayan and Barak. The Arabs could hardly be expected to take the autonomy negotiations seriously if Jewish settlement continued unrestricted. The Israelis refused to sign such an undertaking with Sadat as part of the autonomy 'Framework for Peace'. They maintained that settlement on the West Bank was no business of Egypt's. In the end Begin agreed to write Carter a letter, which would be published among the conference documents. Five years later, the surviving participants were still arguing over just what the Prime Minister promised. Was it a long-term freeze, or one limited to three months? Was it pegged to the autonomy negotiations, or to negotiations for an Israeli–Egyptian peace treaty? Carter and Vance are convinced that Begin cheated them. Both sides have unimpeachable witnesses, but they tell diametrically opposed stories.

According to the President, it was agreed that 'no new Israeli settlements would be established after the signing of the Framework for Peace, and that the issue of additional settlements would be resolved by the parties during the negotiations'.[14] Vance, who took notes during the meeting, confirms Carter's interpretation:

> It was keyed, according to my notes, to the autonomy negotiations. We were not assuming that negotiations on the peace treaty and autonomy would end simultaneously and in a relatively short time. It was hoped that we could make more progress on the negotiations for autonomy than was actually the case, but we all recognized that it was going to be a very tough job. The roots of the problem were much deeper. We saw the negotiations as going on in parallel, but separately. They were not mutually dependent.[15]

Harold Saunders, the State Department's Middle East expert, was briefed immediately after the Saturday night meeting, notebook-to-notebook, by Vance. He puts the discussion in context:

> Carter and Vance went into the meeting knowing what they wanted, what their preferred outcome on the settlement freeze was, and what their fallback was. Their preferred option would have been a settlement freeze through the entire five-year transitional period (for the Palestinians). The fallback would have been a freeze during 'these negotiations', but referring to the autonomy talks, on the theory that during the autonomy talks the negotiators would have to deal with the question of a settlement freeze through the transitional period.
>
> In any case they were talking at that moment about a paragraph in that document which became the Framework for Peace, in other words the document which dealt primarily with the negotiations relating to the West Bank and Gaza. The sentence they were focusing on was a sentence in a paragraph that had to do with the negotiations relating to autonomy and then to the final status of the West Bank and Gaza.
>
> Prime Minister Begin said he could not agree in a document to be signed by President Sadat on a settlement freeze. That was a matter for the Israeli Government to decide. It was not a matter on which the Government of Egypt had any say. The solution to that problem was the same as the solution to similar problems on other issues – we would have a side letter. Vance explained this to me after the meeting, and asked me to draft a letter from Prime Minister Begin

to President Carter explaining the Prime Minister's position. So I took that sentence out of the text and I put it in a side letter.[16]

Barak took copious notes on the Israeli side. He is just as emphatic that the American version is mistaken:

> What was agreed was that the freeze on settlements would be through three months and that it was to do with the negotiations about the peace treaty with Egypt. There are two limitations here: a. it is within the framework of a peace treaty with Egypt; b. it's three months. It was not related at all to the autonomy negotiations.[17]

The Israelis also call in evidence a statement by Sadat while briefing American correspondents in Washington on 19 September, two days after the end of Camp David. 'We agreed', he said, 'to freeze the establishment of settlements for the next three months, which is the period during which the peace agreement is supposed to be concluded.'[18] The Americans argue, however, that Sadat was not present when the agreement was reached and was not a party to it. Nevertheless, what he understood from those who were bears out the Israeli version.

After Carter had talked in Washington of a five-year freeze, Dayan was asked for an explanation by reporters at Ben-Gurion Airport. He had returned immediately to Israel with Weizman, leaving Begin in the United States. The Foreign Minister's answer seems designed to blur rather than to clarify the issue.

> It is our assessment, and that of the Prime Minister, that the period of negotiation on the subject of Judea and Samaria need not go on for longer than two to three months. ... While the duration of the negotiations on the Israeli-Egyptian issue was determined at three months, the duration of the negotiations on the Palestinian question was not determined at all. But *let us assume* it will actually take about two or three months. During that negotiating period, after we had clarified things with Israel [from Camp David], it emerged that in fact there is no immediate question of the establishment of further settlements within two or three months, and perhaps beyond that period. And this even if there were no agreement and the question had not come up. ... As regards the five-year period, as far as I know, there is no clause on this in the agreement.[19]

Confusion worse confounded. But perhaps the last word should rest with Sol Linowitz, who served afterwards as head of the American autonomy negotiating team: 'I read all Carter's notes when I was appointed special ambassador to the Middle East. I was impressed by the fatigue under which they were operating, the possibilities of misunderstanding, especially over a complex question like the settlements.'[20]

It is hard to imagine that Begin would knowingly have conceded an open-ended settlement freeze on the West Bank, especially after he had given way in Sinai. It would have been against his own instincts, and against his interests as leader of a party already stretched on the rack by the Sadat initiative. It is quite conceivable that he and Dayan deliberately fudged the issue.

With the dawn of Day Thirteen, 17 September, Carter was convinced that a deal was in the bag. Camp David had produced two frameworks, one on an Israeli–Egyptian peace treaty, the other on Peace in the Middle East. It would take a lot more hard bargaining to fill in the frames, but the summit had done its job. The United States had prevailed, as Brzezinski had advised the President it must. But even Day Thirteen brought its last-minute snag. It had been agreed not to mention the highly sensitive issue of Jerusalem in the text itself. At one stage, when the Americans proposed that an Arab or Moslem flag fly over Al Aqsa mosque, which stands on the site of the Jewish Temple, Begin had warned them that the very idea gave him heart palpitations. By 17 September the Americans were talking of nothing more than an exchange of letters in which all three leaders – Carter, Begin and Sadat – reserved their familiar positions on the disputed city. The American draft adapted the language of statements made by successive ambassadors to the United Nations, refusing to recognize Israel's annexation of East Jerusalem after the Six-Day War. As soon as Begin heard about it, he announced that he would never sign any document if the United States wrote any such letter to Sadat. The entire agreement was suddenly back in the melting-pot. But Carter was not going to let go at this stage. He solved the problem by a mixture of drafting (he dropped all specific reference to the Israeli annexation and said simply that American policy was as spelled out by its UN ambassadors) and *schmaltz*. Begin had asked him to sign some photographs for his grandchildren. Carter instructed his secretary to find out their names, and inscribed each picture individually. When he took them to Begin's cabin, the Israeli leader was overwhelmed and told him about each grandchild in turn. Then he accepted the new draft letter like a lamb. What proud grandfather could do otherwise? Especially when he had won his point.

Camp David ended on a note of relief and reconciliation. Sadat paid a courtesy call on Begin, their first meeting in ten days. Then the two Middle East leaders paid court to Carter, embracing him enthusiastically before flying by helicopter to the White House. The President reflected that this was the first time he had been glad to leave Camp David for Washington. The cameras and correspondents at last came into their own. The two framework agreements were signed, and three weary statesmen answered questions as best they could. Israel and Egypt had made their first peace agreement.

Begin had driven as hard a bargain as he had always planned, but he had contributed his share of concessions. Israel had agreed to evacuate the entire Sinai peninsula, including the oilfields, the air bases and the settlements in return for a peace treaty. The Prime Minister was conscious, in private consultations with his staff as well as in public pronouncements, that Israel was giving up tangible assets and was receiving something intangible from Egypt. For that reason, he insisted on cast-iron built-in guarantees for Israel's southern border. Begin's reluctant sacrifice of the Sinai settlements cost him the support of some of his oldest and closest friends. Shmuel Katz, the Irgun Zvai Leumi publicist, deserted the ranks. So did Geula Cohen, late of the Stern Gang, whose passion for *Eretz Yisrael* matched that of Begin himself. Others, like the veteran Yohanan Bader, distanced themselves more discreetly from their leader.

Within days of Camp David, Begin was bragging to American Jewish audiences that he had agreed to nothing more for the Palestinians than he had offered at Ismailia in December 1977. This claim infuriated the Carter Administration, which recognized that he was trying to deter the Jordanians and other Arab 'moderates' from backing Sadat, and the West Bank and Gaza Palestinians from taking the role assigned to them. In fact Begin yielded far more at Camp David than at Ismailia. He agreed that negotiations must take place on the basis of Resolution 242 'in all its parts' for a resolution of 'the Palestinian problem in all its aspects'. Negotiations were to start after three years 'to determine the final status of the West Bank and Gaza and its relationship with its neighbours', and were to be concluded by the end of the five-year transitional period. He undertook to reach a solution that would 'recognize the legitimate rights of the Palestinian people and their just requirements'. Jordan was invited to join these negotiations, and was permitted to include Palestinians 'as mutually agreed' in its delegation. Israeli forces were to be withdrawn from the territories and limited units deployed in 'specified security locations'. Responsibility for security and public order was left open, but the Palestinians were offered the prospect of a 'strong local police force, which may include Jordanian citizens'.

Many of these points were declaratory and imprecise. They were not cheques that could be taken to the bank and cashed over the counter. Begin had written in all manner of ambiguities and safeguards unremarked by either the Americans or the Egyptians. For instance, the 'self-governing authority' which the Palestinians were to elect for themselves is mentioned six times in the Framework agreement. On only one of these occasions, the fourth, were the words 'administrative council' added in brackets at Israel's request. But that was enough for Begin to refer to it for ever after as the 'administrative council', something much more modest than the Americans and the Egyptians had in mind. William Quandt suspects that the Israeli delegation deliberately left the Palestinian question to the last day at Camp David to avoid specific commitments. The conscientious Barak suggested that they should spend as long over the West Bank as over Sinai, Quandt says, but everyone else wanted to get home.[21]

For all that, Camp David offered the Palestinians their best diplomatic opening since 1947. Everything was there to negotiate for, with the Americans and the Egyptians behind them. It was Menachem Begin's good fortune that they did not call his bluff – and that they allowed him to build his defences. The Americans' greatest mistake was not to link the West Bank and Gaza to an Israeli-Egyptian peace treaty, making the one contingent on the other. Brzezinski blames this failure on Carter's acquiescence in Begin's vaguer formulas. 'That came back to haunt us', he wrote, 'in the subsequent phases of the negotiations.'[22] The Israelis had their own priorities. 'The Sinai was considered by Begin as a *quid pro quo* for the Israeli presence in Judea and Samaria,' says Eliahu Ben-Elissar, who as director-general of the Prime Minister's office was commissioned to draft a tight-fisted Israeli strategy for the autonomy negotiations.[23] By the end of Begin's reign in September 1983, he could look back on Camp David with satisfaction. The peace with Egypt, however cold, was intact. So was Israel's grip on *Eretz Yisrael*.

The Egyptians were coaxed into accepting the Camp David package with the argument that everything would be different in five years' time. 'The spirit of Camp David', Boutros Ghali maintains, 'was a kind of armistice. The decisions would be taken by somebody other than Begin. Under the influence of Dayan and Weizman, we thought that Begin had accepted this to obtain peace.'[24] American doubts were lulled in a similar way. According to Vance, Begin told the Americans he would never preside over the transfer of one inch of Judea and Samaria to another sovereignty; the territories belonged to Israel. But he added: 'There may be others who come after me who may feel differently. By the end of the five-year period I won't be around.'[25] What the Prime Minister did not say was that he would do his damnedest in the meantime to ensure that there was not much left to transfer.

20
A Premature Prize-Giving

Instead of the three months blithely predicted in September, it took another six months of diplomatic attrition to translate Camp David into an Israeli-Egyptian peace treaty. Both sides tried to claw back some of the concessions they regretted having made at the Maryland retreat. Israel launched an emergency programme of 'thickening' existing West Bank settlements, though many of the extensions were separate settlements in all but name. An inter-departmental committee, chaired by the director-general of the Prime Minister's office, Eliahu Ben-Elissar, whittled down Israel's definition of autonomy so that the Palestinians would have even less to bargain for. State land and water resources, for example, were to stay under Israeli control. This would keep open an option for Jewish settlement, while reserving an Israeli veto on the expansion of Arab towns and villages. Such details had not been discussed at Camp David, where they were regarded as too tangled for a general framework. The Israelis were quick to fill the vacuum, especially after they had been put on their guard by the Americans' wooing King Hussein to join the peace process. The Carter Administration was disappointed that Sadat had neglected to stop over in Amman to do the job himself. It compensated by delivering written answers to Jordanian questions on the implications of Camp David, with a copy to Begin as an earnest of good faith. Some American diplomats regretted afterwards that their diplomacy had been quite so open, but Cyrus Vance and his Assistant Secretary, Harold Saunders, who brought the letters to the Middle East, could see no honourable alternative. There was nothing in the answers that Israel did not know already, but they made explicit American interpretations – on such issues as the status of Jerusalem – that Begin had fought to keep out of the Camp David documents. The Israeli Prime Minister responded by threatening to transfer his office to Arab East Jerusalem. Despite the American blandishments, Hussein and the elected West Bank leadership turned their backs on Camp David. They were too weak or too timid to take Sadat's risks. The Egyptian President tried to recoup his position by making a treaty conditional on progress for the Palestinians, but, having evaded that trap at Camp David, Begin was not going to walk into it now.

The Cabinet approved the Camp David agreements by eleven votes to two. Begin's most devoted lieutenant, Haim Landau, abstained. The package, including the evacuation of the Sinai settlements, was endorsed by the Knesset after a seventeen-hour debate that ended at three a.m. on 28 September. The vote was eighty-four to nineteen with seventeen abstentions. Of the eighty-four 'yes' votes, only forty-seven were cast by coalition MPs. The Likud Liberals voted for the motion, but Herut was split down the middle. Begin would not have won without the backing of the Labour Opposition. Two Herut members who were to hold key posts in the second Begin Cabinet – Yitzhak Shamir and Moshe Arens – withheld their support. Shamir, the future Foreign Minister and Begin's eventual successor, abstained. Arens, a future Defence Minister, voted against. Shamir was at the time Speaker of the Knesset (in Israel the Speaker remains a party politician and uses his vote), Arens was chairman of the Knesset foreign affairs and defence committee. Other Likud abstainers included the next Finance Minister, Yigal Hurvitz, and his successor, Yoram Aridor, as well as the former Irgun Zvai Leumi operations chief Eitan Livni. In Washington, President Carter noted in his diary that the vote was 'a remarkable demonstration of courage, political courage, on the part of Prime Minister Begin, who had to go against his own previous commitments over a lifetime and against his own closest friends and allies who sustained and protected him during his revolutionary days'.[1] The American leader was less happy with the consequences. The defections demonstrated how much strain Camp David had imposed on Herut loyalty to the old commander. Begin and his party managers resisted a demand to submit the agreements to the central committee before the Knesset, but the weight of dissent in his own ranks reinforced the Prime Minister's determination not to go one inch beyond what he had signed on 17 September. He applied a brake to the peace process and insisted on spreading responsibility for future decisions as widely as possible across the Cabinet.

Formally, however, the votes in the Cabinet and the Knesset cleared the way for negotiations to resume. The conventional wisdom was that ninety-eight per cent of the problems had been solved, leaving only two per cent to be disposed of before a peace treaty could be signed. Moshe Dayan and Ezer Weizman went to Washington for the Blair House conference, but soon found that both they and their Egyptian counterparts had no freedom of manœuvre. The Cabinet in Jerusalem intervened at every stage. After Camp David their colleagues trusted the Foreign and Defence Ministers less than ever. Each point had to be referred back to base. The most recalcitrant issues proved to be: a target date for establishing the autonomy regime in the West Bank and Gaza; linkage between the peace treaty and autonomy; Israel's continued access to Sinai oil; and Begin's insistence that the peace treaty take priority over Egypt's commitments to fight alongside its Arab brethren in any future war with the Jewish State.

In mid-November, one year after Sadat's pilgrimage to Jerusalem, Israel accepted an American first draft, but Egypt was still holding out. The 'last two per cent' carried the negotiations through the dismal winter of 1978-9. Cyrus Vance was despatched to the Middle East for a round of shuttle diplomacy. Dayan went to Brussels for talks with the Egyptian Prime Minister, Mustapha Khalil, then back to Camp David. Begin rejected an invitation to go to Washington for negotiations with Khalil. He would deal with Sadat or nobody. Despite his title, Khalil was not his opposite number. Eventually Begin was persuaded to visit Carter, with the prospect that Sadat would follow, while Dayan went on talking to the Egyptian Premier. Sub-clause by sub-clause, agreement drew closer. Begin provoked palpitations in the Finance Ministry when he pledged in one of his more expansive moments on American television that Israel would repay 'every last cent' of the $3 billion it was to receive from the United States for redeploying its forces from Sinai to the Negev. The Finance Ministry was counting on at least one third of the total taking the form of a grant rather than a loan. Gestures always meant more to Begin than figures.

Long before anybody could be confident of success, the Nobel committee announced that it was awarding the 1978 peace prize jointly to Menachem Begin and Anwar Sadat. The Norwegians at least were still betting on Camp David. The Israeli leader received the news on Friday evening, 26 October, but he did not respond publicly until the end of the sabbath when he was entertaining the pianist Artur Rubinstein to tea in his Jerusalem residence on the corner of Balfour and Smolenskin Streets. Begin and Sadat congratulated each other by telephone. The prize was the ultimate accolade of international recognition for the underground chieftain, but it came at an embarrassing time for Sadat, uncomfortably aware of his isolation in the Arab world and his vulnerability in Egypt.

Begin and Aliza flew to Oslo on 9 December with an entourage of relatives, friends, Israeli and American Jewish personalities. Sadat stayed at home, sending Said Marei, his special assistant, to accept the award on his behalf. The distinguished-looking Egyptian diplomat won the hearts of his Norwegian hosts when he stood at Oslo airport in a temperature of minus eighteen degrees centigrade and thanked them for their 'warm reception'. The Begins were lifted straight from the airport to the royal palace in a red-and-white helicopter, shadowed by two heavily-armed police choppers. The Norwegians were taking no chances. Peace prize winners normally stay in a hotel and receive their award in the hall of Oslo University. This year Begin and his wife stayed in the royal palace and the ceremony took place the next day in the fourteenth-century Akershus Castle – two of the most fortified buildings in the land. Said Marei stayed at the Grand Hotel.

The Begins were entertained to dinner by King Olav V, who put them up in his own wing of the palace, all gilt, purple and scarlet. Members of the royal family had read *White Nights* and were eager to hear about Begin's experiences in the Soviet labour-camp (it was safer, anyhow, than *The Revolt*). But the sparkle was taken out of the occasion by the death in Israel of Golda Meir, and by a sense that the award was a trifle premature. An iconoclastic Israeli columnist said that what the people of Israel wanted was not peace prizes, but peace. 'Where', he demanded, 'is the baby?' In the grim Norwegian fortress, with armed guards and police dogs deployed on the battlements, Begin's acceptance speech, only the fourth he had read from a script in thirty years of free-flowing oratory, surprised no one. Swords were beaten into ploughshares, the six million Holocaust victims were remembered, Jabotinsky and Garibaldi were given their due. Begin insisted that the prize had been earned by the people of Israel, not just by their Prime Minister – and put his money where his mouth was by donating the entire $85,000 cheque to an Israeli foundation that gives bursaries to student volunteers who coach backward children.

Outside in the frost-bitten street, thousands of young Norwegians marched five-deep in torchlight protest behind a dozen Arabs carrying Palestinian flags. Many of the Norwegians wore chequered *kefiyeh* head-dresses. They chanted: 'Begin is a terrorist! Support the PLO!' Sadat somehow escaped their wrath. The Foreign Ministry, with a show of Nordic neutrality, refused to let the demonstrators hold a protest rally in the traditional Nobel prize hall at the university, but included the march in its official calendar of the day's events.

Like the Camp David Summit, Jimmy Carter's visit to Jerusalem and Cairo in March 1979 was a desperate last fling. The President was banking his prestige on reaching an agreement. He was disturbed by Begin's and Sadat's mutual distrust and personal incompatibility. Begin had been at his most miserly when he went to Washington at the beginning of the month. At their first meeting in the Oval Office of the White House, Carter found the Israeli Prime Minister 'very strong, negative, apparently confident'. He warned him of the 'adverse consequences of failure, and the ultimate threat to Israel if Begin should permit his country to become isolated in the world because of intransigence and belligerent acts or statements'. The United States had gone as far as it could in putting forward compromise language, with what the President bemoaned as 'practically no constructive response from Israel'. Begin confided the next day that he had lost a night's sleep worrying about the President's strictures.[2] The outcome was an ingenious compromise on the priority of Egypt's obligations (to Israel and to the Arabs), which would mean one thing to Jerusalem and the opposite to Cairo. Begin's acquiescence was a tacit acknowledgment that although the issue itself was critical, it would not be decided by a piece of paper. If Egypt were ever forced to choose between peace and pan-Arab solidarity, it would not be influenced by a clause in a treaty. If it joined a war front, the treaty would be dead.

Carter flew to Cairo well aware that a non-productive trip would dramatize the failure, but he could see no better way forward. Sadat was forthcoming, offering to exchange ambassadors with Israel in return for territory, and hinting at an agreement to sell Israel oil via the Americans. The contrast was all the more marked when the President went on to Jerusalem. Begin informed Carter that he would not even initial an agreement without first submitting it to the Cabinet and the Knesset. The President asked him if he actually wanted a peace treaty. 'My impression', he wrote in his diary, 'was that everything he could do to obstruct it, he did with apparent relish.' Begin seemed to be blocking a treaty and the start of the autonomy talks. 'He was obsessed with keeping all the occupied territories except the Sinai, and seemed to care little for the plight of the Arabs living without basic rights under Israeli rule.'[3]

Begin was exceptionally tense, fatalistic, but determined not to be dictated to when Carter came to address a special meeting of the Cabinet the next morning. He stood rigidly to attention with his two aides waiting to welcome the guest at the door of his office building. One of them heard him singing tunelessly between clenched teeth '*Ani ma'amin*', the Jewish hymn of faith ('I believe') which thousands of Hitler's victims sang as they entered the gas chambers. Carter was going the same day to Yad Vashem, the Holocaust memorial on the flank of Mount Herzl. During the Cabinet session the President told Israeli ministers they would have to agree. Begin interrupted him: 'We shall agree to what we agree to agree.' According to one Israeli witness, Carter replied: 'I understand.' The meeting ended with Israel and the United States still deadlocked over two issues: guaranteed oil sales and Egypt's request to open a liaison office in Gaza, which it had ruled from 1948 to 1967.

The President's impatience showed through a speech he delivered that afternoon to the Knesset. 'The people of the two nations are ready now for peace,' he said. 'The leaders have not yet proven that we are also ready for peace enough to take a chance.' The point was made with tact, but no one in the chamber had any doubt which leader he had in mind. Begin's reply was constantly interrupted from the far left and the far right. Geula Cohen, his most vociferous nationalist critic, was evicted from the Knesset after refusing to let the Prime Minister go on. 'I shall continue my struggle,' she shouted from the door. The Americans were shocked by the commotion, though they affected to be impressed by the vitality of Israeli democracy. 'We'd seen the British parliament,' Cyrus Vance reflects, 'but this was worse than the British parliament. That was a very noisy day.'

Perceptive reporters noticed Moshe Dayan leave the floor of the house and go up to whisper to the Secretary of State in the distinguished visitors' gallery. He had come to apologize for the heckling, which might be interpreted as a discourtesy to the President. But his mission upstairs was also the beginning of a private initiative that led within twenty-four hours to agreement and a peace treaty. The Foreign Minister suggested a quiet talk later in the day. Vance agreed. In any case they were scheduled to meet at another encounter between the Cabinet and the Americans (this time without the President). Dayan asked some of his colleagues to stay behind once the Americans had left. The ministers agreed with him that Israel could not let the President go home with nothing to show for his journey. Dayan, according to his spokesman, Naphtali Lavie, did not want to antagonize Carter. Above all, he did not want him to feel it was Israel which had let him down. 'Also he saw in Carter's ideas some light, something that could be developed – a US commitment to guarantee oil supplies, and the status of Gaza. Dayan felt he could get an agreement. He asked Shmuel Tamir, the Justice Minister, to formulate a sentence that would bind the US on oil supplies.'[4]

When Dayan went to see Vance in his hotel room after that rump Cabinet meeting, they both knew that the real differences were not very important, but that it would be hard to put the pieces together again. Dayan, according to one of Begin's staff, was one of the few men who could convince the Prime Minister by force of argument to change his mind. But this time the Foreign Minister preferred stealth. 'I know he'd gotten some latitude from Begin,' Vance says, 'but I felt that he was probably pushing at the outer edges. I'm sure he had to sell his ideas to Begin afterwards.' On the Gaza issue, Dayan suggested that the Egyptians be persuaded to make no mention at this stage of a liaison office. They could always propose early elections in Gaza during the autonomy negotiations. He also emphasized that once Israel had started pulling back from Sinai and normal relations prevailed, any Egyptian would be able to travel to Gaza on an Israeli visa. Vance accepted this, provided Israel would meet Sadat halfway on oil sales. The Egyptians were touchy about rewarding Israel for Sinai with cut-price oil. Dayan recognized their problem. He and Vance then studied the implications of an American guarantee. Dayan insisted on a clause in the peace treaty stating that Israel was entitled to buy oil directly from Egypt. Otherwise Cairo would still be honouring the Arab boycott. Israel would be content with the right to purchase Egyptian oil at market prices, plus a twenty-year American guarantee to make good the deficit if supplies stopped. At the Foreign Minister's suggestion, Carter invited him and Begin to breakfast at the King David the next morning. The package was sealed over the orange juice. Rather than risk alarming Begin, Dayan let Vance take the lead in presenting their ideas. The Secretary of State recalls:

> We took it that morning as if we were taking the initiative. I think that's the way Moshe wanted it to be done. My guess is that he probably presented this to Begin as largely an American initiative. I left it to him to present it to Begin whatever way he wanted to present it. [5]

Dayan's sales strategy worked. At the farewell ceremony at Ben-Gurion airport, Begin murmured to Carter: 'You have succeeded.' The American and Egyptian Presidents met at Cairo airport, and Sadat readily agreed to exchange ambassadors early (a gesture of normal relations), to offer a pipeline from the oilfields to Israel, and to curb the anti-Begin (often anti-Semitic) propaganda in the Egyptian press. Sadat's advisers were uncertain about the package, but he cut them short with a characteristic: 'This is satisfactory with me.' Carter telephoned Begin there and then with the good news, and all three leaders were reunited for the signing ceremony at the White House on 26 March. Israel had won its first peace treaty. Menachem Begin might never have reached that point without the machinations of Dayan, Weizman and Barak, but he earned credit by taking the political risks and by defining which sacrifices he would make and which he would not. Despite the beaming photographs, he made few friends along the way. 'I almost never had a pleasant surprise in my dealings with him' was Carter's epitaph on an exasperating partnership. [6]

Sadat was more generous once Begin had proved himself by returning El Arish, the dusty capital of Sinai, to Egypt on 25 April. According to Boutros Ghali, Egypt's perennial 'Deputy Foreign Minister', it was then that Sadat started to trust him. Begin had delivered. He was duly rewarded during the 1981 election campaign when Sadat accepted an invitation to a summit meeting at Sharm el Sheikh that was pure show business. Ghali testifies:

Sadat was in favour of Begin's re-election. In calculating that a Begin victory would be better for Egypt, his priority was the Sinai withdrawal. He believed that he had begun a process with Mr A. Mr A had delivered the first time, and he would deliver the second time. He was being nice to Begin to ensure completion of the Sinai withdrawal.[7]

The last Israeli soldier and civilian left Egyptian soil on 25 April 1982, three years to the day after the return of El Arish. By then Sadat had been killed by Moslem fanatics and succeeded by his deputy, Hosni Mubarak. Menachem Begin was still Prime Minister of Israel, still ruling over the Palestinians of the West Bank and Gaza Strip. The autonomy negotiations ran into the sand. Israeli-Egyptian reconciliation was like a premature rosebud stunted by a late frost. The border remained open, but the traffic was all one way. Hardly any Egyptian tourists visited Israel. Commerce was negligible. Cultural exchanges petered out. But the peace treaty stood the test of the 1982 Lebanese war. After the Sabra and Shatilla massacre, Mubarak summoned home his ambassador for indefinite consultations. The embassy and the border were not closed, however, and Egypt rattled no sabres. The 'priority of obligations' held good. In November 1977 the people on the streets of Jerusalem had hoped for something more.

21
Divide and Rule

Menachem Begin was a creature of moods. The Government swung back and forth between despair and euphoria, paralysis and frenzied activity, with the Prime Minister's state of mind and body. The two years between the peace treaty with Egypt and the general election of 30 June 1981, saw the fluctuations at their wildest. Begin remained the dominant personality. The Cabinet could do nothing without him, but for much of the time it could do nothing with him either. The two most independent-minded ministers, Moshe Dayan and Ezer Weizman, resigned in October 1979 and May 1980 respectively. Begin no longer needed Dayan for his experience or for his prestige. He had not forgotten the Foreign Minister's indiscipline during the peace negotiations. Dayan soon recognized that he would be allowed no further scope for personal diplomacy. Weizman fretted and fumed, increasingly unhappy that Begin was putting the peace at risk by his tight-fisted approach to Palestinian autonomy. 'For the people of Israel,' the Defence Minister wrote in his resignation letter, 'there were days of richness and hopes during your term of office. The people believed in the Government and believed in peace. It was not the people who stopped believing in peace.' At the same time the failure of Simha Erlich's free-market economic policy became more and more apparent. The Finance Minister was replaced by Yigal Hurvitz. The myth that the Liberal businessmen knew how to take care of the economy was exploded. Hurvitz, who had drifted steadily right since breaking with the Labour movement in the wake of Ben-Gurion, had the courage to impose a necessary restraint on public spending. He became known as Mr *Ein-Li* ('I don't have'), but his efforts only provoked a string of Cabinet crises. Hurvitz lacked the muscle to force his colleagues to comply, and the Prime Minister was simply indifferent. Begin's sole preoccupations were the 'struggle for *Eretz Yisrael*', and the battle to hold his coalition and his party together.

In the second half of 1980, Begin descended into one of his periodic troughs of depression. He had by now suffered three heart attacks and a mild stroke. The effects were showing. Ministers complained of his lack of leadership. Visitors found him apathetic, remote and sentimental. He often did not know who they were or why they had come. A deputation from the Foreign Press Association, which went to lobby Begin in his role as acting Defence Minister after Weizman's resignation, left his office frustrated and pitying. Begin, they were convinced, was fading fast. Rumours in the Israeli press that he fell asleep during briefing sessions with the general staff are confirmed by military witnesses. As far as one can judge without being able to interview his doctors, reports that he was suffering from the side-effects of drugs prescribed for his heart condition seem to have been less accurate. Begin was on a regular course of anti-coagulants. When one of his aides asked the Prime Minister's personal physician, Dr Mervyn Gotsman, about their effect, the doctor told him that the drugs did not impair Begin's mental capacity. He was tired because he was sick. At most they might make him more drowsy. He was advised to cut his working day to four hours. Another member of Begin's staff testifies that even after the Prime Minister was felled by a heart attack, he continued to conduct essential affairs of state from his hospital bed.

> He was never so incapacitated that he had to give up. There was one occasion when he was in hospital after a minor stroke. The doctors told us that it was very unlikely that he would get back full vision in his left eye. He still dictated notes and letters. Two months later, in his room in the Prime Minister's office, his vision suddenly corrected itself. He said: 'I can see perfectly.' I have no evidence that he was under the effect of drugs. He is a man given to moods, which often goes hand-in-hand with an emotional being, which he is. I have never seen him in the course of a working day under an intensive drug regime. I have never seen him looking at his watch and taking drugs every couple of hours.[1]

During one Cabinet meeting, when the Prime Minister bounced back into a manic phase, Yosef Burg, the perpetual Minister of the Interior who was four years older than Begin, pased a note to a colleague: 'If that's what the pills do for you, I want some too.' On another occasion, however, when Begin was at his lowest ebb, he walked into the Knesset chamber and made straight for the Leader of the Opposition's seat, which had been his until 1977. An usher gently pointed out his error and led him to his proper place at the head of the Cabinet bench.[2]

Menachem Begin's administration was the first in Israeli parliamentary history to face early elections by choice. The decision was taken in January 1981, after Hurvitz had acknowledged defeat in trying to cut the education budget and taken his three-man Rafi faction into opposition. Two months earlier the Government's majority had fallen to three in a vote of confidence, and Begin preferred to go to the country rather than cling to office at the whim of splinter groups and floating opportunists. Despite Opposition protests, he did, however, set the election day as late as possible, 30 June. The Prime Minister came out of a special Cabinet meeting looking more buoyant than he had done for months, but the prospects for a second Begin administration appeared negligible. Opinion polls put Labour so far ahead that Shimon Peres looked as if he might end the campaign as the first Israeli party leader to win an outright majority. Begin had lost two finance ministers in thirteen months. In 1976 he had flayed Yitzhak Rabin's faltering Government for letting inflation reach 35 per cent and had promised to cut it by half. In 1980 consumer prices rose by 132.9 per cent, and the gap between the richest and the poorest was widening. Surveys indicated that only a third of the oriental Jews who voted for Begin in 1977 intended to support him this time. The defectors were dissatisfied with his Government's economic and social performance, though they still backed him on security, foreign policy and settlements.[3] What attracted less attention in January was that 37 per cent of the electorate had not yet made up their mind for whom to vote. A poll in the daily paper *Ha'aretz* suggested that although 55 per cent wanted an immediate change of government, 39.7 per cent did not think Labour would make a better job of the economy. Israelis were disenchanted with Begin, but they were not yet lining up behind Peres. The Likud and its leader had everything to fight for – and six months at their disposal.

The foundation of the Likud revival was laid not by Begin but by Hurvitz's successor, Yoram Aridor, a Herutnik of the post-1948 generation. Aridor was billed as Israel's first Finance Minister with a degree in economics, but that did not deter him from launching an unashamedly electioneering programme which pushed inflation higher than ever and the balance of payments deeper into the red. His professors must have taught him that inflation cannot be cured by encouraging consumers to go out and buy luxury goods, but he was enough of a machine politician to know that that was how to win votes. Tax cuts reduced the price of colour television sets by ten to fifteen per cent and that of new cars by ten to seventeen per cent, with similar reductions on domestic appliances and furniture. The Finance Ministry blatantly announced that purchase tax on sweet wine would be halved until 1 July, the day after polling day. Within a month the chambers of commerce reported that Israelis had ordered 8,000 new cars and 60,000 television sets (colour was just being introduced), all of them imported. Wholesalers chartered jumbo jets to meet the demand. Car sales alone went up four hundred per cent. Aridor's policy, Matti Golan wrote in *Ha'aretz*, was working.

People are beginning to ask themselves: 'Maybe, after all?' Economic experts explain to them that they'll pay dearly for Aridor's election economics – after the elections. They listen and shake their heads doubtfully. The average Israeli doesn't know much about economics, certainly not long-term economics. Today the prices are going down, and that's what's important. Labour doesn't know how to react. How can it come out against price reductions, but how can it not come out against unrestrained and irresponsible election economics?[4]

A Jerusalem window-shopper was overheard to say: 'Everybody knows we'll have to pay in the end, but we're buying all the same. There might not be another chance until the next election.' Aridor's bonanza soon began to show in the opinion polls. By mid-March the Likud was recovering lost votes, with Labour struggling to hold its ground. The gap in Labour's favour was still wide, but a trend had begun. The oriental voters were coming off the fence; Aridor had given them a pretext for returning to the fold. Labour strategists, fearful of peaking too soon, had allowed the Government to seize the initiative.

It was at this point in the campaign that Menachem Begin made the biggest comeback since Lazarus. In a radio interview marking Israel's thirty-third birthday, the Prime Minister boasted that he felt much better than at any time in the four years since he had come to power *because now I am in a fight*. The Likud won the 1977 election on Begin's name, but without the man himself. For the last two months of the 1981 election, the party fought on Begin's name and on Begin's terms. The Prime Minister took to the hustings, smiting his old enemies one after another hip and thigh – the Labour movement which had treated him and his followers with such contempt for twenty-nine years, the Germans who had massacred six million Jews, the Communists who had sent him to the Gulag, the British who had hanged his young fighters. His constituency in the city slums and scattered development towns responded with passion and frequently with violence. Begin was 'King of Israel', and dissent was high treason. 'You can tell me you wouldn't buy a used car from Peres,' a hostile Israeli columnist wrote, 'but I wouldn't hire Begin in his present state to babysit for me. He'd frighten the children.'[5]

The first open act of intimidation occurred at the Moroccan Jews' traditional *Mimouna* festival in a Jerusalem park at the end of the Passover holiday. Peres had come to extend Labour's greetings to the North African community, but young men jeered at the mention of his name and pelted him with oranges and tomatoes as soon as he mounted the podium. He was forced to leave without uttering a word. The violence spread through the country, with Begin ignoring all calls to control his followers. His rhetoric, taunting and intoxicating, fanned the flames. At a Labour rally in Petah

Tikva in mid-June, Peres was mobbed by 200 Likud supporters chanting 'Begin, Begin, King of Israel'. They rolled barrels of burning refuse into the middle of the crowd of 10,000 and smashed windows at the local Labour headquarters. Eighteen people were hurt and twenty-six arrested. During a similar confrontation in Jerusalem, an Israeli reporter was threatened with retribution if he named the ringleader of a gang that refused to let Peres speak. Violence and communal hatred became the central issues in the campaign. Labour exploited a photograph of a Likud supporter waving a knife at a Begin meeting, and reprinted pictures of the 1952 attack on the Knesset. Begin, the Polish Jew, divided the country between east and west as it had never been divided before. Prejudices were reinforced on both sides. For the western Jews, the orientals posed a primitive threat to Israeli democracy. For the orientals, the westerners were snobs fearful of losing their privileges, alien Europeans adrift on the tide of the Middle East. It was a clash of political cultures as much as of ethnic origins. Shlomo Hillel, an Iraqi-born Labour leader, accused the Prime Minister of pushing Israel towards fascism. 'There is an atmosphere of social incitement and nationalist incitement. Experience teaches us that when these two elements are combined it always leads to fascism. Begin is appealing to the lowest section of the population.'

In the same surge of ecstasy, the Prime Minister talked Israel to the brink of war with Syria and sent his air force to bomb an Iraqi nuclear reactor. He exulted in both episodes as proof that he alone knew how to deal with the Arabs. In April, the Lebanese Phalangist militia, armed and trained by Israel, took the offensive in Eastern Lebanon, threatening Syrian positions near the strategic town of Zahle. The Syrians responded with heavy shelling. Begin announced that Israel would not stand by in the face of such murderous deeds in a neighbouring country. His air force struck at Palestinian guerrilla bases in Southern Lebanon, and on 28 April shot down two Syrian helicopters. They were described at the time as 'assault helicopters', though Begin admitted two weeks later that they were transporting troops and weapons.[6] He justified Israeli intervention by invoking the Holocaust.

He asked the American ambassador, Samuel Lewis, whether he had read Arthur D. Morse's book, *While Six Million Died*, which catalogued the indifference of the free world to the destruction of European Jewry. The Prime Minister told the Knesset foreign affairs and defence committee that he himself had read it six times.

> Every time I read it, I am not ashamed that tears come to my eyes when I think how our people were left to themselves. The Germans murdered, but the world

left us on our own. I want to tell you, I said [to Lewis], that we are a Jewish
State, with our own experiences, and under no circumstances will we acquiesce
in the Syrian's attempt to transform the Christians in Lebanon in the 1980s
into the Jews in Europe of the 1940s. The Syrians along with the terrorists are
treating a civilian population exactly as the Nazis did. They care nothing about
men, women and children.[7]

Two Labour politicians, both former chiefs of staff, Yitzhak Rabin and
Haim Bar-Lev, interjected that what the Syrians were doing was nothing
like Nazism. The analogy did not fit. Begin insisted that even though the
Syrians had not built gas-chambers for the Lebanese Christians, their tanks
and artillery were doing the same job. It suited his purpose to ignore the
fact that the Phalangists were armed, and that they had provoked the
bombardment. He talked as if the Lebanese civil war had never happened.
The Syrians reacted to the downing of their helicopters by introducing
mobile SAM-6 anti-aircraft missiles into the Beqa'a, the first time they had
stationed them on Lebanese soil. Begin demanded their removal, arguing
that they threatened the Israeli air force's freedom of operation over
Lebanon.

To the dismay of the military professionals, Begin's tongue started to
run away with him. He told a wildly cheering audience at a Likud convention that unless the Syrians removed their missiles, Israel would send its air
force to destroy them. Security personnel were shocked. Hirsh Goodman,
the *Jerusalem Post* military correspondent, wrote. 'Why tell the Syrians that
Israel's response would come from the air? The Syrians had just completed
deploying an armoured brigade alongside their missiles on the Syrian-
Lebanese border – because they did not know whether a possible attack
would come from the ground, from the air or from both.'[8]

The next day, Begin compounded the offence by revealing in the Knesset
that the air force had been ordered to take out the SAM-6 batteries on 30
April, but that the mission had been cancelled because of heavy cloud
cover. Begin was both Prime Minister and acting Defence Minister; his
information was accurate and damaging. A former chief of air force intelligence, Brigadier-General Yeshayahu Bareket, said on Israel television that
in twenty-five years in the service he could not recall operational secrets
being revealed like this. Anyone in uniform doing what Begin had done
would have been charged with a serious violation of security. Another
officer was quoted as saying: 'The enemy has been given on a golden platter
what it would have had to spend years and millions collecting, and even
then it would not be sure of the veracity of the information.'[9] The case
against Begin was that by analysing the weather on the day in question, the
Syrians would know under what conditions the Israeli air force could

operate, and when it could not. The limitations of Israeli planes had been revealed, and dozens of other details could be deduced from that information. Similar material had indeed been heavily censored in the Israeli press. The reaction to Begin's indiscretions was not just counter-politicking. But the air force's performance against the Syrians one year later suggests that the damage was put right quickly enough.

Soon after three on the afternoon of Sunday, 7 June, a flight of sixteen advanced Israeli warplanes flew low and fast from the Etzion base, near Eilat, bombed the Iraqi nuclear reactor outside Baghdad, some six hundred miles away, and returned home without loss. It was one of those daring, precisely planned and executed raids for which the Israelis had been celebrated since the 1967 war and the Entebbe rescue. Iraq's chances of building an Arab nuclear bomb, with French and Italian help, were set back for years. The raid was no hastily-improvised election stunt. Begin's Cabinet had taken the decision in principle the previous October, and some of the best pilots in the Israeli air force had been training for it ever since.[10] Their route and tactics had been refined to minimize the risks of detection and interception as the F-16 Fighting Falcons and F-15 Eagles swooped across the Arabian desert. The F-16 multi-role fighters pinpointed the target with 2,000-pound bombs, while the F-15 air superiority fighters provided a protective umbrella. Begin publicized the operation a day later, the Jewish harvest festival of *Shavuot*, after the Jordanians had accused Israeli aircraft of aiding Iran in its war with Jordan's ally Iraq. Although there was no mention of the reactor, that was pretext enough for the Israeli Prime Minister to break the story. There might have been international advantages in concealing Israel's involvement, but there is reason to think Begin always intended to go public. The timing of the operation was influenced by the imminence of elections.

The Americans and other more-or-less friendly inquirers were told afterwards that Begin acted in June because he was by no means sure of winning the election, and he did not trust his Labour successors to do the job. That was one consideration. So was the Prime Minister's genuine anxiety about the Iraqi nuclear threat. Israel had no doubt that President Saddam Hussein intended to manufacture a bomb. But according to well-placed witnesses, Begin also wanted a coup of this kind for electoral purposes. A majority of the Government's expert advisers thought that the reactor would not go critical for three years, but a minority believed that it might do so in July 1981. The weight of opinion in the intelligence community in Washington was that it was about a year away. Begin was convinced, although again the experts differ, that to bomb the reactor after it had gone critical would cause thousands of radiation casualties in Baghdad. He was not prepared to accept responsibility for that. In any case the word of even one Israeli expert that the fatal day might be only a month away was enough for the Prime Minister. The military planners advised him that the risks of failure were very small. At worst the aircraft might have to turn back, or one or two might be shot down on the way home or by missiles over the Iraqi capital. The air force was confident that it could solve the problem of range (getting to Baghdad and back at low altitude without refuelling in the air). If the planners were right, the danger of an electoral backlash was negligible. The doubts of the director of military intelligence, General Yehoshua Saguy, who feared that the bombing would cause 'a deep rift and severe crisis between Israel and the United States', were discounted. So was his argument that it would take the Iraqis at least five years to build a bomb, thus giving Israel sufficent time to try non-military methods.[11] General Saguy was supported by a majority of the general staff, but they were outgunned by three outspoken advocates of an early strike: Begin; the Agriculture Minister, Ariel Sharon; and the rapacious Chief of Staff, General Rafael Eitan. To neutralize the effect of political reservations within the Cabinet, Begin transferred the decision on timing to a subcommittee of three – himself, Sharon and the Foreign Minister, Yitzhak Shamir – all hardliners.

As soon as he was informed of the Jordanian 'revelation', Begin instructed his spokesman, Uri Porat, to announce the success of the Israeli operation. Porat was new in the post, and the duty editor at Israel radio did not recognize his voice. He hesitated about broadcasting the story until the head of the radio's news division, Begin's nephew Emanuel Halperin, had checked with the Prime Minister that it was not a hoax. The story went out as a special bulletin at 3.30 p.m. At a press conference the next day, Begin swept aside international condemnation of the raid, insisting that Israel had acted out of 'supreme national self-defence'. He accused President Saddam Hussein of plotting to bring Israel to its knees, 'to destroy our existence, our future and our country'. With three bombs like that dropped on Hiroshima in 1945, he maintained, Iraq could destroy greater Tel Aviv, the hub of Israel's industrial, commercial, farming and cultural life. 'Six hundred thousand casualties we would suffer,' he said. 'Where is the country that would tolerate such a danger? There won't be another Holocaust in the history of the Jewish people. Never again. We shall defend our people against any enemy.' Arthur D. Morse's nightmare would not be repeated.

Begin was not always so precise with his figures. He met a Reuters news agency correspondent at a British embassy garden-party and told him that

Israeli bombs had destroyed a secret laboratory forty metres below ground. When sceptical eyebrows were raised, Begin repeated his claim. Asked why this had not been disclosed earlier, he replied archly: 'Why should I give you all at one time?' The Prime Minister's spokesman, Uri Porat, explained that the Iraqis were 'doing things they didn't want checked' in the underground chamber. The next day Begin himself telephoned the Reuters man, Patrick Massey, and apologized for misleading him. He now understood that the laboratory was *four* metres below ground. There were other embarrassments. The head of the Mossad security service, General Yitzhak Hofi, publicly urged the politicians to stop compromising Israel's contacts with foreign intelligence services by revealing secret information derived from them. He did not need to name the politicians he had in mind. The Foreign Ministry misquoted Saddam Hussein in a briefing paper distributed to the press and Israeli missions abroad. But at home there is no doubt that the reactor raid enhanced Begin's image as a leader who took courageous decisions and followed them through. Israelis shared his relief that the nuclear threat had been removed. Labour was left quibbling about the dates when the Iraqi installation would have gone critical, which meant little to the voting public.

The Likud overtook Labour in the opinion polls in late May, two weeks before the reactor raid. Support was growing for the Government across the board – on domestic as well as foreign and security policies. Sympathy was on the rise for Ariel Sharon's West Bank settlement drive, publicized as 'We are on the map' in television commercials and in bus tours of the territories conducted by the minister. The Baghdad operation increased the Likud lead, but Labour pulled back in the last few days of the campaign. The Opposition's concentration on electoral violence forced many middle-of-the-road voters to reassess their priorities. If their main purpose was to get the Likud out, they could not afford the luxury of voting for one of the smaller parties of the left and centre. Shimon Peres improved his rating with a creditable performance in a televised debate with Begin, and by bringing his rival, Yitzhak Rabin, into his leadership team. The outcome was the closest race in Israeli electoral history. At one point, as early results were being fed into the television computer, Peres claimed victory. But, as Begin recognized in 1977, what counts is the tally of votes cast. The tighter the finish, the more fickle the computer. The Likud won forty-eight seats to Labour's forty-seven. The margin of votes was only 10,000 in a poll of nearly two million. The smaller parties won only twenty-five seats between them. The ethnic divide was even more pronounced than in 1977. The electoral analyst Hanoch Smith concluded:

The Labour Alignment scored impressive gains in all the cities with majorities of European origin, the gains roughly equalling the previous size of the DMC vote. In contrast, the Likud vote remains, overall, unchanged.... Where the pattern changes is in the sizeable gains made by the Likud in cities and towns with Asian/African majorities, which suggest that the Likud increase in seats from forty-five to forty-eight is due to a further gain in Asian/African votes, especially in the development towns.[12]

Coalition-building was harder this time than in 1977, but Begin was ready once again to pay the price of the ultra-Orthodox Agudat Yisrael and of the less clamant National Religious Party and the new North African Tami. It became easier for *yeshiva* students and their teachers to avoid conscription and reserve service. More money was poured into their institutions from the public purse. The national airline, El Al, was forced to stop flying on Saturdays. For Begin the religious parties' support was worth every shekel. For the first time he had won an election by his own populist instincts and old-fashioned campaign skills. The ad-men had been kept in their place. He had achieved the impossible, and the victory was not going to elude him at the thirteenth hour.

22
A Choice of War

At eleven a.m. on Sunday, 6 June 1982, Israel launched a massive ground, sea and air assault on Palestinian strongholds in Southern Lebanon from the Mediterranean Sea to the foothills of Mount Hermon. Within hours, fighting was reported from the ancient ports of Tyre and Sidon. By next morning the Star of David was flying over Beaufort Castle, a Crusader fortress high above the Litani gorge, from which Yasser Arafat's *fedayeen* had cast a brooding shadow over the Galilee panhandle, repelling all previous attempts to dislodge them. Within a week Israeli tanks were at the gates of Beirut. A reprisal raid had escalated into a war that Menachem Begin defined as 'a war of choice'. For the first time Israel's leaders did not take cover behind the faded slogan of *ein breira*, 'there is no choice'. They had planned, waited, and taken their chance when it was offered. It was a war not so much of conquest as of vaulting ambition, a war that brought the Prime Minister a terrible retribution.

Israeli armour had last crossed the border in anger four years earlier in retaliation for the massacre of thirty-two civilians in a hijacked tour-bus on the coastal road between Tel Aviv and Haifa. The 1978 Litani Operation, a hasty, often disorderly sweep through Southern Lebanon, cleared a narrow zig-zag security-belt, which was bequeathed to Israel's protégé, Major Sa'ad Haddad. Until then, the Palestinian guerrillas had been within sight of Israeli villages and had made life intolerable for their Lebanese Christian and Shi'ite Moslem neighbours. This first incursion brought a measure of peace. Infiltrators had to run the gauntlet of a United Nations buffer force, Haddad's local militia and Israeli frontier patrols (some of them inside Lebanon), or take the risk of striking from the sea. But a static, mini-war of attrition that grew out of the Syrian missiles crisis in the summer of 1981 demonstrated that the Palestinians were still far too close for Israel's comfort.

Arafat's new Soviet 130 mm artillery pieces and mobile Katyusha launchers, capable of firing forty rockets at a time, could hit the border towns and villages whenever they wanted. During the 1981 election campaign, Begin had promised that 'no more Katyushas' would fall on Kiryat Shmona, a Galilee development town that had become a symbol of fear and disrupted lives. A month after his re-election, a new attack, heavier than ever, had driven half the population on an unplanned 'holiday' and confined the rest to bomb-shelters. Israelis became refugees in their own land. The army drew up plans for pushing the Palestinian guns out of range, but the idea was shelved when the American mediator, Philip Habib, contrived a welcome ceasefire.[1] The seeds of the 1982 invasion had been sown.

The appointment of Ariel Sharon as Defence Minister after the Likud's election victory – an appointment which Begin had long resisted because of Sharon's unruly reputation – ensured that the plans would not gather dust. Both the new minister and the Chief of Staff, Rafael Eitan, were convinced that they had a military answer to the problem of the Palestine Liberation Organization. Israel, they argued, could destroy Arafat's power base in Lebanon, the only country from which he could still operate independently against the Jewish State, and thus loosen his hold on the Arabs living under Israeli rule in the West Bank and Gaza Strip. At the same time a friendly government would be installed in Beirut under the Phalangist commander, Bashir Gemayel, who had been cultivated by Israel since the mid-1970s. The prospect appealed to Begin ideologically and temperamentally. Israel would be asserting its might against the latest enemy who sought to destroy it, the Jews would be taking their fate in their own hands. The Prime Minister had won the Nobel Peace Prize, but he had not forsworn Jabotinsky. He was neither saint nor pacifist.

It was Begin who first brought the invasion plan to the Cabinet as early as 20 December 1981, a week after Israel had annexed the Golan. The Syrians were in ferment, and the Prime Minister preferred to face them in Lebanon rather than on the heights. Ministers listened in astonishment as first Sharon then Eitan outlined the objectives of Operation Pine-Trees, which envisaged an Israeli penetration as far north as the Beirut–Damascus highway, the encirclement of Beirut, a possible link-up with the right-wing Christian Phalangists in the north and a landing at the port of Jounieh, about fifteen kilometres beyond the capital. Begin pressed for an early decision to go ahead, but so many ministers spoke against the plan that he withdrew it without calling a vote.[2]

At about the same time, Sharon twice spelled out his grand design to American officials. According to one of his listeners, 'he gave a pretty accurate personal version of what he would like to do about the Lebanon problem, carefully saying it was his view and the Cabinet did not accept it, then laying out in some considerable detail roughly what ultimately happened'. American diplomats claim that they immediately warned the Defence Minister against any such enterprise. Whenever Washington spotted signs of an Israeli military build-up in the north, it sent strong cautionary messages to Begin through the ambassador in Tel Aviv, Samuel Lewis. These messages helped to restrain Israel on four occasions in the first half of 1982 when Begin's Cabinet was tempted to go to war.

The Prime Minister was among a majority in the Cabinet who opposed a large-scale reprisal for a guerrilla raid on Mehola, a Jordan Valley settlement, at the end of January. He gave the thumbs down again in March when Sharon and Eitan pushed their luck by proposing an initiative in Lebanon to test Egyptian intentions before the final evacuation of Sinai, but he joined the hawks at the end of that month when an Israeli soldier was killed by a hand-grenade in Gaza. Begin and Sharon were, however, a minority of two and nothing was done. The Americans recognized that the pendulum was swinging towards action. Habib's ceasefire terms had never been published, but the Israelis contended that the truce covered all terrorist operations, at home or abroad, and not just those across the Lebanese border. This reading was disputed by the Palestinians and the United States, but it remained an article of faith for Begin and Sharon.

The Defence Minister again proposed what was dubbed his 'big plan' in early April after an Israeli diplomat had been assassinated in Paris. He did not conceal its true scope from the Cabinet, though he intended to start with air strikes on Palestinian bases. The operation was planned to last forty-eight hours, reaching Beirut and the Beirut–Damascus road. The army would stay in Lebanon for a week. But when Opposition leaders were briefed on the plan, Yitzhak Rabin estimated that Israel would have to hold the whole of Lebanon for up to six months. When the former Prime Minister asked Begin whether he was ready to accept that eventuality, he said no. The big plan was dropped in favour of aerial bombardment. Following various postponements, the air force was despatched on 20 April after an army lieutenant had been killed by a mine while patrolling in Southern Lebanon. The PLO did not react, but it did shell Galilee two weeks later in retaliation for a second wave of Israeli air strikes – the first Palestinian harassment on that front since the truce. Begin proposed a full-scale reprisal, even though the shelling had been on a token scale and deliberately off-target. The Cabinet was equally balanced for and against, and Begin agreed to postpone the operation. It was decided, however, that if a Jew were killed or wounded by terrorists anywhere in the world, Israel would act.

Begin and Sharon again briefed Opposition leaders on the Government's intentions. But the process of disinformation had begun. Rabin asked Sharon whether his plan included Sidon, about sixty kilometres north of the border. The Defence Minister gave three different answers, Rabin recalled a year later.

> It was clear that he did not want to tell the truth. He answered like this: 'I think so.' Then he said; 'I don't remember exactly.' Afterwards he said: 'I'll go and check.' And he left the room in the middle of the meeting to check whether Sidon was included in the plan or not. He came back and said; 'It's not included.' After that he left again, came back and said: 'Sidon is included.'
> I asked him about Beirut, but Arik gave the impression that Sidon was the limit. I asked if Beirut was included, and the answer was: 'No.' I was deceived, but I wasn't the only one. The Cabinet was deceived too, perhaps to gain its approval.[3]

On 20 May, Sharon went to Washington, where he had a *tête-à-tête* with the Secretary of State, Alexander Haig. Once more the Defence Minister outlined his plan for crushing the Palestinians, though he did not specify how far the Israeli thrust would go. American diplomats say that he did not mention Beirut. His main concern was that the Reagan Administration should not complain after the event that it had been surprised by Israel, as it had done over the raid on the Iraqi reactor. Haig, like Sharon a hard-line general turned politician, was not unsympathetic. He would be happy to see the PLO, which he detested as an instrument of the Kremlin, cut down to size. The Israelis interpreted his attitude as encouragment to go ahead. One senior official, who was against the Sharon plan, read with distress a cable on the Sharon-Haig meeting sent back to Jerusalem by Israel's ambassador, Moshe Arens. This official's reaction, long before the term became common currency, was: 'My God, they're giving us a green light.'

Haig has denied giving his blessing to an invasion of Lebanon, but his chief assistant, Woody Goldberg, concedes that the Secretary of State did say that no American official had the right to tell an ally how to defend itself. 'He also said that anyone who was surprised by the Israeli move into Lebanon just wasn't following the news. He also said that if Israel were to go in, they had to ensure that the reaction was proportionate to whatever provocation had caused it.'[4]

Other American officials acknowledge that once the war started, the military man in Haig saw the advantages to be gained. He wanted it finished soon, but successfully. 'Haig had no love for the PLO,' one diplomat testifies. 'He was sympathetic to the idea that the PLO should be run out of Lebanon, and he was opposed to premature ceasefires once the war began. There were no lines being drawn by us, but he certainly was never sympathetic to the idea of attacks on Beirut, or shelling of Beirut.' The Secretary of State's enthusiasm was again reflected on the diplomatic wires between Washington and Jerusalem. In one cable that was widely circulated among Israeli officials and military planners, Moshe Arens quoted Haig as saying: 'You are doing a great job in Lebanon that is important for everyone.'

Whatever the Secretary's intention, his 'no' sounded suspiciously like a 'yes' to Israeli ears. It is hard to disagree with Ze'ev Schiff, the dean of Israeli military correspondents, that even if there was no Israeli-American conspiracy, there was an implicit partnership. 'The Americans having received advance information about Israeli intentions – chose to look the other way, making ambiguous comments about Lebanon that the Israeli Government could interpret any way it liked.'[5] As one State Department veteran sums it up: 'If Haig didn't give a green light, he gave an amber light tinged with green.' It amounted to the same thing, and Alexander Haig paid the penalty when American public opinion turned against Israel.

In the early summer of 1982 Lebanon was a war waiting for a pretext. Just before midnight on Thursday, 3 June, the Palestine National Liberation Movement, an extremist splinter group led by Sabri al-Banna ('Abu Nidal'), provided one. Hassan Said, a twenty-three-year-old Palestinian from a village near the West Bank town of Nablus, shot the Israeli ambassador to London, Shlomo Argov, three times in the head and upper body with a Polish-made WZ-63 machine-pistol as he was leaving a dinner at the Dorchester Hotel. The hit team was commanded by Nawaf Rosan, a Jordanian-born 'merchant', who was later identified as a senior officer in Iraqi intelligence. The Iraqi embassy was believed to have supplied the weapon. When the first reports of the assassination attempt reached Jerusalem, Begin was asleep. Once the story was confirmed, his aides woke him and told him what had happened. At five o'clock the next morning, the Prime Minister talked by telephone to Norman Grant, a London surgeon, who reported that he had just finished operating on the ambassador. When Begin asked how he was, the doctor replied: 'I can't promise you anything. I cannot say if he will live, and if so how he will live.' Argov faced twelve to twenty-four critical hours. Slowly, the ambassador did recover, but he remained paralysed and bedridden. He lived badly.

Begin summoned the Cabinet to an emergency session at 8.30 a.m. He had already decided that Israel could not let this provocation pass. The ambassador, he said, was chosen as a target 'because he was a Jew, because he was an Israeli, because he was a symbol of the State of Israel'. The bullet that hit his head was aimed at the head of the State of Israel.[6] Sharon was abroad on a secret mission, but General Eitan knew what was expected of him. At the Prime Minister's invitation, he proposed to the Cabinet that the air force bomb nine Palestinian targets in Beirut and seven in Southern

Lebanon. Several ministers voiced misgivings about bombing the capital. They remembered the uproar similar strikes had caused a year earlier. The Chief of Staff promised that the targets would be picked with care to avoid civilian casualties. At Begin's suggestion, five were approved: three training bases in the South and two sites in Beirut, a sports stadium, which housed a large Palestinian arms depot, and another training facility. Ministers knew that they might be voting for the prelude to a war, but even the doves felt they could not gainsay Begin this time. One of them explained:

> We had said 'no' so many times, but now, in face of a world drama and in the face of the Prime Minister's agitated state of mind, we could not hold out. We also understood that it was inconceivable to disregard the assassination attempt and not react. We were not enthusiastic, but we realized that the snowball could no longer be halted.[7]

Later that day the Israeli planes pounded their targets. The Palestinians, as expected, retaliated in kind. This time they did not aim to miss. More than eight hundred shells and Katyushas rained on Northern Galilee. One rocket landed in Kiryat Shmona near the car of Ya'acov Meridor, the Minister for Economic Co-ordination, spattering it with shrapnel. Meridor telephoned the Prime Minister to relay local demands that he fulfil his promise of 'no more Katyushas'. Begin replied: 'You can tell them that it will be all right.' He urged him to say no more, but Meridor recognized that the scales were tilting towards a ground operation.

Sharon hurried back from Europe, and the Cabinet was called into session at nine o'clock on the Saturday evening. Eitan briefed ministers on a smaller version of Operation Pine-Trees, a three-pronged assault to drive back the Palestinian artillery. Under questioning from sceptical colleagues, Sharon said the operation was designed to secure peace for Galilee, not to conquer Beirut. Ministers understood him to be talking about a limit of approximately forty kilometres. This was confirmed by Begin, who assured them that if there were any need to go further the Cabinet would decide. It was agreed that every effort should be made to avoid confrontation with the Syrians, who had up to 30,000 men stationed in Northern and Eastern Lebanon, but it was part of the Sharon-Eitan plan to 'persuade' the Syrians to draw back, if only because they provided an umbrella for Palestinian cannons that could hit the Galilee pan-handle. Sharon predicted that Israeli troops would reach the forty kilometre line within twenty-four hours and that the operation would end in forty-eight hours. Ministers had given unanimous support to the air strikes at their Friday meeting, but three withheld their votes from the invasion. They were the Deputy Premier,

Simha Erlich; the Energy Minister, Yitzhak Berman, both Likud Liberals; and Yosef Burg of the National Religious Party.

Begin wound up the debate with an emotional speech. He had not, he said, submitted his proposal with a light heart. They were sending soldiers into battle. Everything would be done to prevent casualties, but combat meant losses, losses meant bereavement and orphans. The unacceptable alternative was Auschwitz. As the Prime Minister left his office to fly north to a forward command-post, his aides heard him murmur as if in prayer: 'May there be no casualties.' The echoes were to haunt him for months afterwards.

At Begin's suggestion, the operation was given the public relations codename Peace for Galilee. The communiqué issued after the invasion was under way said that the army had been instructed 'to place all the civilian population of the Galilee beyond the range of the terrorist fire from Lebanon'. There was no specific reference to forty kilometres. This was cited later by Sharon and Eitan when they were pilloried for thrusting further north. But ministers had no doubt that forty kilometres was what they were voting for. Begin said as much in a letter to President Reagan the same day, Sunday, 6 June: 'The army has been instructed to push back the terrorists to a distance of forty kilometres to the north so that all our civilians in the region of Galilee will be set free of the permanent threat to their lives.'

From the opening shot, Sharon and Eitan had no intention of limiting the operation to forty kilometres. Reserve officers reported that a senior commander briefed them on the first day that the aim was to cut the Beirut–Damascus highway and to establish a new regime in Lebanon. The Defence Minister declined to deny this allegation when questioned by an opposition Shinui party MP, Mordechai Wirshubski.[8] As early as 25 June Sharon defined the war aims on Israel television as: the elimination of the PLO, the removal of the Syrian army, and a peace agreement with Lebanon. Nothing about the Galilee border. On 1 August, in an address to high-school graduates about to join the army, he said:

> We went to war against terrorism, and to remove the obstacle threatening and preventing a reconciliation betwen us and the Arabs of *Eretz Yisrael*. We went to war so that we may live together in peace, Jew and Arab, in Nazareth and Beersheba, in Judea and Samaria, so that peace may reign between us, in due course, on both banks of the Jordan.[9]

The Chief of Staff was less tactful. In early July he told officers and men in a front-line unit that the fighting had created a 'once-in-a-generation opportunity to change conditions in our favour in the struggle over *Eretz Yisrael*. Destroying and uprooting the terrorists' bases in Lebanon, he said, would weaken Palestinian opposition to the Jewish presence in *Eretz Yisrael*.[10] In an interview with Dov Goldstein of *Ma'ariv*, Sharon acknowledged that the Cabinet had approved the more modest of his two plans, but said he 'knew there was a possibility' that in the end the more extensive version would be implemented. In a parallel interview with the same journalist, Eitan admitted that the war was not meant merely to secure a forty kilometre strip north of the border.

> The Cabinet instructed the IDF to push the terrorists back from the northern border and to destroy the terrorists, their headquarters and facilities in Lebanon. Three things were not mentioned in the Cabinet's instructions: forty kilometres, Beirut and the Beirut-Damascus highway. When I presented the general war plan to the Cabinet, I presented the whole plan, including the encirclement of Beirut and severance of the Beirut-Damascus highway. The Cabinet approved this plan, but the Cabinet determined in its directives to the army that movement from one stage of the war to the next would be subject to the political echelon. Every stage of the war, every movement from stage to stage, was carried out with the approval of the political echelon.[11]

That was not how it appeared to the Cabinet. From the third day of the war, with the initial objectives clearly achieved, Sharon's critics suspected that they were being deliberately misled. They were not convinced by the Prime Minister's repeated assurance that in this war, as distinct from previous ones, nothing would 'roll' without approval. Mordechai Zipori, the Herut Minister of Communications, joined the original doubters. He was a military professional, having attained the rank of brigadier-general, and an old rival of Sharon's, having served in the first Begin Government as Deputy Defence Minister. When Eitan repeated his claim a year later that the Cabinet had authorized the army from the start to exceed the forty kilometre limit, Zipori accused him of lying. At a Cabinet meeting on 11 September 1983, Zipori quoted from the minutes of the last pre-war Cabinet to disprove the Chief of Staff's contention. He recalled that on that Saturday night, Eitan had shown ministers the forty kilometre line on a map and had sought approval for a limited operation, saying it would take two days to complete. According to Zipori, both Sharon and Begin had spoken in similar terms. Sharon, by then a Minister Without Portfolio, was present at the September 1983 meeting. He did not dispute Zipori's version, which is confirmed by the Cabinet Secretary, Dan Meridor. 'The Defence Minister and the Chief of Staff presented a plan for fighting and pushing the terrorists away to a line of about forty kilometres (artillery range) from our northern border,' Meridor says. 'This is the plan and this is the range that was approved by the Cabinet that Saturday night.'[12]

In an Israel television interview shortly before his death from heart failure in June 1983, Simha Erlich said: 'There were interpretations of Cabinet decisions between the decision formulated at the Cabinet table and the actions at the front. Sometimes they were acceptable, tolerable irregularities. But there were also irregularities that were unacceptable and intolerable.' Sharon, he charged, had always wanted to deviate from the forty kilometre decision.

Sharon exploited his colleagues' shortage of military expertise. A favourite device was to seek approval for a small, tactical advance, then come back when that had been achieved and explain that a few more kilometres were essential to secure what had just been gained, to 'improve positions'. On one occasion Yitzhak Berman, the most persistent of the Defence Minister's critics, asked him: 'What area shall we be asked to approve the day after tomorrow in order to protect the unit you will station at the site you will capture tomorrow following our approval today?' Sharon grinned sheepishly like a man caught with his hand in the till. 'Mr Berman,' he replied, 'you have an excellent sense of humour.' Berman complained that minor operations were never undertaken without previous approval, but that was not the case with bigger ones.

> The fog fell very often over major operations. For instance, [Christian] East Beirut. We suddenly learned that there were Israeli troops in East Beirut, as if it were common knowledge, which it wasn't. There was never a Government decision about entering East Beirut. Nothing rolled on minor steps, but it did on major ones.[13]

The penetration of East Beirut, which was visible to anyone who visited the Lebanese capital, was one of the more blatant cases. On 13 June, at the end of the first week of the war, ministers quizzed Sharon on what Israeli troops were doing in East Beirut, at the international airport and around Ba'abda, a suburb which houses the presidential palace and Defence Ministry. They received two answers: Israeli troops were not *in* Beirut. Ba'abda and the airport were outside city limits. Where they had entered Beirut itself, they had done so in response to Palestinian ceasefire violations. The IDF had to silence sources of danger to Israeli troops. *Ma'ariv* reported:

> Ministers would get telephone calls at home from soldiers and officers, including senior officers, telling of fictitious ceasefire violations by the enemy and fire initiated by the IDF, even as Israel radio was saying that the other side had opened fire first. There were also complaints about situations in the field which

were totally different from what was reported on the radio. Through his military
secretary, Lieutenant-Colonel Azriel Nevo, Begin also heard reports about
Israeli violations of the ceasefire and IDF provocations.

When the Prime Minister and other ministers asked for an explanation, they
were told that the IDF did not always react in the place where it had come under
fire. Sometimes, for various reasons, it would respond in a different sector. The
soldier who was ordered to open fire there might not be wholly aware that it was
actually the enemy who had fired first elsewhere. While not all the ministers
accepted this explanation, they were helpless in the face of allegations that it was
the enemy who was violating the ceasefire.[14]

Telephone calls on the scale politicians and Israeli journalists were
receiving, often from strangers, were without precedent in wartime. They
reflected the nation's uneasiness at fighting a war of choice, and they
deepened the Cabinet's sense of being led by the nose. 'For the first time in
Israel's unfortunately rich history of conflict', wrote Hirsh Goodman, who
had fought in the paratroops in two major wars, 'there was an almost total
breakdown of trust between those giving the orders and those being asked
to put their own lives and the lives of their men on the line.'[15] Beirut was
only one example. Cutting the Beirut-Damascus highway was another.
Begin had gone to Washington for consultations with the Reagan Administration. Erlich was acting Prime Minister. On 22 June the IDF began
attacking Syrian and Palestinian positions near Bahamdoun east of Beirut.
Erlich heard of it for the first time on his car radio on the way from Tel
Aviv to Jerusalem. As soon as he reached the Knesset, where ministers and
Opposition leaders were demanding information, Erlich tried to contact
Sharon. Eventually, the Chief of Staff called back in his place. Erlich asked
what was happening on the Beirut-Damascus road. Eitan replied that the
radio reports were inaccurate. The army had only returned enemy fire. He
added that there had been no movement of Israeli forces. Two days later
the road was cut, and the operation was approved retroactively. Erlich
believed what he was told and passed on Eitan's reassurance to his colleagues. He recognized soon enough that he had been misled. 'I was given
information', he said in his June 1983 television interview, 'which was
proved afterwards to be inaccurate.'

Ministers were again outflanked over the decision to do battle with the
Syrians and Palestinians in Eastern Lebanon. Sharon even overrode his
Chief of Staff, who was worried about the high casualties Israel could
expect to take. Clashes were provoked by the IDF, and the Defence Minister
then went to the Cabinet for permission to take out the SAM-6 missiles still
stationed in the Beqa'a. The troops, he urged, could not be left without air
cover. Sharon pressed for a quick decision so that the air force could strike

before dark. The Cabinet had little choice but to agree. In the face of an American ceasefire ultimatum, Sharon ordered further unauthorized advances on the ground.

Despite persistent complaints by Sharon and Eitan that they were treated as scapegoats by a Cabinet which had to accept its share of responsibility for everything that was done in Lebanon, there is ample evidence that ministers were denied the chance to exercise control over the war. But what about the Prime Minister? Begin himself said wrily: 'I know about all the moves, sometimes before they are executed, sometimes afterwards.'[16] He favoured the grandiose aims of the Sharon-Eitan plan. On occasion he was more hawkish than the Cabinet. Towards the end of July, for instance, the Prime Minister strongly supported an operation to slice off the Palestinian camps and neighbourhoods of south-western Beirut, an area containing 6,000 buildings and tens of thousands of people, civilians as well as fighters. The Chief of Staff proposed a heavy artillery and aerial bombardment to soften up the enemy and reduce Israeli casualties, which he estimated at anything from twenty to eighty (Colonel Eli Geva, an armoured brigade commander who asked to be relieved of his post rather than attack West Beirut, advised Begin that there could easily be 250 Israeli dead). Several ministers were disturbed at the prospect of fighting in densely populated areas, and of the international repercussions. The operation was approved by a majority of one, nine to eight, but Begin held back authorization because of the narrow margin. There were times when the Prime Minister defended Sharon from his critics, which suggests that he did not entirely disapprove of what the Defence Minister was up to. 'It is better,' he once said of Sharon, 'to ride a racehorse you can rein in than an old nag you can't get to gallop.' But there were well-attested (and embarrassing) cases where Begin seems not to have known what was going on. In a Knesset speech on 8 June, two days after the start of the war, the Prime Minister said:

> We want only one thing: that no one harm our settlements in the Galilee any more, that our citizens in the Galilee settlements will not have to choke in shelters day and night, that they will not have to live under the threat of sudden death from the missile called a Katyusha. That is what we want. We do not want any clash with the Syrian army. *If we achieve the forty kilometre line from our northern border, the job is done, all the fighting will cease.*

In fact the Cabinet had already given Sharon permission to execute a flanking operation to the north and east of the Syrian garrison in the Beqa'a, thus crossing the forty kilometre line, and the armoured corps was soon authorized to improve its positions, thus risking a clash. Even if Begin did not appreciate what was happening in the field, the Labour Opposition, which included three former chiefs of staff (Rabin, Bar-Lev and Gur) did. It gave Sharon a grilling when the Defence Minister briefed the Knesset foreign affairs and defence committee later the same day. Begin assured Peres and Rabin, who were sent to intercede with him, that no decision had been taken to engage the Syrians in combat.

On the weekend of 6-7 August, with Beirut under siege and the United States trying desperately to negotiate a Palestinian evacuation from the capital, Sharon ordered a large-scale mobilization of reserves without informing the Prime Minister and without seeking Cabinet authorization. It looked as if the Defence Minister was planning a pre-emptive advance into Moslem West Beirut. Begin heard of the mobilization in an agitated midnight telephone call from Yosef Burg, whose son Avraham, a reserve officer, became a leading anti-war campaigner. 'I did not approve any mobilization,' a surprised Begin told the Interior Minister. Questioned about it the next day, Sharon argued that since it had been agreed that an operation might be imminent in Beirut, it was 'self-evident' that he must call up reservists. The Prime Minister was not so easily mollified. 'What does self-evident mean?' he asked. 'You cannot take a step like that without approval. So many people know about the mobilization – and the Prime Minister knows nothing!' Sharon accepted the reprimand and apologized.

Begin censured his Defence Minister more openly at a Cabinet meeting on 12 August, the day after the heaviest and most horrendous Israeli bombing of Beirut. Wave after wave of planes attacked populated areas for eleven hours without pause. A senior air force officer claimed afterwards that most of the explosions were sonic booms, but that was not how it looked to people on the ground or to television viewers the world over. President Reagan was one of the latter. He telephoned Begin twice and demanded that Israel 'stop this holocaust'. Begin retorted that the President did not know what the word meant. But Sharon came under heavy fire in the Cabinet from David Levy, the Herut Deputy Premier, and Burg, who feared that the bombing would block an evacuation agreement at the last minute, and that Israel would be blamed. Begin agreed with them that the bombings no longer served any useful purpose, and that Israel would be ostracized by the United States. How would Israel look to the world, Begin asked, if Philip Habib were recalled from his ceasefire mission? When Sharon tried to argue back, accusing Begin of yielding to American pressure, the Prime Minister angrily asserted his authority. The Cabinet endorsed his recommendation that there should be no more initiatives 'to protect Israeli soldiers' without Cabinet approval. There was to be no bombardment from land, sea or air without the Prime Minister's knowledge and authorization. Although some ministers saw this as a vote of no confidence in Sharon, the Prime Minister did not disown him. At the next Cabinet meeting three days later, Begin proposed that a line be drawn across the past. They had to stand together and get on with the job. 'Fortunate is the country', he said later, 'in which Ariel Sharon is Defence Minister.'

Begin was briefed regularly by Sharon, sometimes five or six times a day. But as the forty-eight-hour campaign dragged on through June, July, August and into September, doubts were raised about his staying-power. He paid only one visit to the troops in Lebanon, on the second day when he went to congratulate the crack infantry unit that captured Beaufort Castle. He tried to take a week's holiday in the northern seaside resort of Nahariya, but that was interrupted by visits from Bashir Gemayel and the American Defence Secretary, Caspar Weinberger. How much did Sharon and Eitan tell him, and how much did they conceal? How hard did they try to find the Prime Minister at moments of crisis? The assassination of Bashir Gemayel and the subsequent massacre of Palestinians in the Sabra and Shatilla refugee camps – the turning-point of the entire Israeli enterprise – supplied a devastating answer.

Gemayel, by then President-elect of Lebanon, was killed on the night of 14 September when a time-bomb demolished party offices in East Beirut. Begin was fully consulted by Sharon and Eitan, who briefed him on rumours and counter-rumours about Gemayel's fate as rescuers dug amid the rubble. At about eleven p.m., when his death was confirmed, the Prime Minister advised Sharon that the IDF should immediately seize the main crossing-point between East and West Beirut to prevent chaos and bloodshed, to keep the two mutually hostile populations apart. That, at least, is what the Prime Minister told the Kahan Commission set up to investigate the Sabra and Shatilla massacre. The army put a different gloss on the decision taken in this emergency by Begin and Sharon. In Lebanon's anguish, the military spokesman announced the following day, it would be immoral for Israel not to assist in keeping the peace.

> The tragic assassination of President-elect Bashir Gemayel indicates a desire on the part of certain elements to return by violence to the previous state of anarchy. Under such anarchy, anti-Israel terrorism flourished. Israel will not let this happen again. . . . Present Israeli troop movements ensure that calm will prevail and anarchy will be forestalled.

Begin and the Foreign Ministry emphasized that Israel had acted during the night to keep the peace. Sharon and the IDF seized on the Gemayel assassination as an occasion to comb out any Palestinian guerrillas and their

Left-wing Lebanese allies who had stayed behind in West Beirut after the PLO's evacuation at the end of August. Armoured personnel carriers went *through* the strategic crossing-points into the old Moslem and Palestinian stamping-ground, where they encountered spirited if small-scale resistance. On Thursday, 16 September, Phalangist militiamen entered the two refugee camps ostensibly to hunt down fugitive guerrillas. Their entry was co-ordinated with the Israeli army, which assisted them with flares and covering fire. It was like putting a fox in the chicken-coop. As anyone with the slightest knowledge of Lebanon's recent gory history could have predicted, the Phalangists forgot about the terrorists and slaughtered any and every Palestinian they could find, men, women and children. Begin acknowledged under cross-examination by the Kahan Commission that he knew nothing of the decision to deploy the Phalangists until it was reported to an emergency Cabinet meeting on the night of the sixteenth. He had been neither consulted nor informed. Sharon again sought retroactive authorization, claiming later that the deployment was covered by a decision of 15 June, three months earlier, that the Lebanese army and the Phalangists rather than the IDF would take West Beirut. Only David Levy raised any objection, and even he saw no point in forcing a vote against a *fait accompli*.

The Phalangists entered the camps on the Thursday, but it was not until the Saturday, 18 September, that the world learned what they had done. The suspicions of local Israeli commanders were aroused on the Friday. They ordered the Phalangists to cease their operation, but did not compel them to leave the camps before the Saturday morning. Yet by his own testimony, nobody bothered to inform the Prime Minister. Saturday was the Jewish New Year, but a messenger could easily have been sent into the synagogue. Instead Begin learned of the massacre from his old standby the BBC World Service at five o'clock on the Saturday afternoon. He was not told after the event, and he was not advised of the risks beforehand. Asked by Aharon Barak, now a Supreme Court judge and member of the inquiry commission, whether the security services ought to have warned him, Begin could only reply: 'What they should tell me is a matter which is basically left to their initiative.'

Begin's manner in the witness-box was uncharacteristically disorganized. Unlike the commission, the Prime Minister had not done his homework. He was surprised when Chief Justice Yitzhak Kahan confronted him with transcripts of Cabinet meetings and of conversations with President Reagan's special envoy, Morris Draper, yet his staff knew that the commission had received these documents. Begin could not remember things that he and others had said, including a statement by General Eitan that the

Phalangists were 'sharpening their knives' for revenge after Bashir Gemayel's murder. Although he was testifying less than two months after the
massacre, he did not always understand what was being asked of him. The
impression was of a Prime Minister losing his grip. 'The picture being
drawn', Amnon Dankner commented in *Ha'aretz*, 'is that of a Prime
Minister who does not go into details, somewhat detached, relying on the
Defence Minister and Chief of Staff, but not urging them to keep him
posted.'[17]

The breakdown was one of organization as much as communication.
Brigadier-General Ephraim Poran resigned as Begin's military secretary in
1981. At Sharon's suggestion, he was replaced by a more junior officer,
Lieutenant-Colonel Azriel Nevo. Sharon himself dispensed with a senior
military aide when he became Defence Minister, explaining that he did not
need an intermediary between himself and the general staff. Similarly, he
would be Begin's main link with the army. Nevo was a capable career
soldier, but he had neither the age nor the rank to serve as the Prime
Minister's eyes and ears in the way that his predecessor had done. Poran,
a veteran of the 1948 War of Independence, knew the commanders as
comrades and equals. He did not need to go through channels when he
wanted information. He could go directly to the man on the spot. Those
who knew him were convinced that while he might not have been able to
prevent the massacre, he would have ensured that the Prime Minister did
not have to learn about it from the BBC.

The international hue and cry provoked by Sabra and Shatilla threw Begin
on the defensive and exposed, not for the first time, his selective compassion.
Whether it was the King David, Deir Yassin, or the Beirut camps, the loss
of non-Jewish lives evoked no remorse. Someone else was always at fault.
'*Goyim* kill *goyim*,' he said when the Cabinet met in emergency session on
Sunday, 19 September, 'and they blame the Jew.' A Cabinet communiqué
which bore the Prime Minister's fingerprints accused the world of levellings
'a blood libel at the Jewish State and its Government, against the Israel
Defence Forces'. Characteristically, Begin adopted attack as the best form
of defence. Israeli troops were not stationed in the camps at the time of the
massacre, which had been carried out by 'a Lebanese unit', the communiqué
contended. Israeli troops had put an end to the slaughter and forced the
Lebanese to leave. Without the intervention of the IDF there would have
been much greater loss of life.

All the direct or implicit accusations that the IDF bears any blame whatsoever
for this human tragedy are entirely baseless and without foundation. The

Government of Israel rejects them with the contempt which they deserve.... Despite the internal incitement, we call upon the people of Israel to unite around its democratically elected Government in its struggle for security and peace for Israel and all its citizens. No one will preach to us ethics and respect for human life, values on which we have educated, and will continue to educate, generations of Israeli fighters.

As the Kahan Report was to show, the moral issues were not that simple. The Cabinet communiqué was an advocate's case founded on limited information. It included the merest token expression of 'grief and regret' for the death of hundreds of Palestinians. Begin declined to make any personal statement of regret, just as he had dismissed Eli Geva's concern for civilian casualties when the colonel's tanks were poised before West Beirut. After Geva had explained to the Prime Minister that he saw children through his binoculars when he looked into the city, Begin replied: 'Did you receive an order to kill children?' Geva said no. 'Then what are you complaining about?' Begin demanded.[18] The Prime Minister's silence on the refugee camp massacre so outraged President Yitzhak Navon that he took the unprecedented step of going on television to deliver the nation's condolences to the bereaved families, some of whom, he noted, were Israeli Arabs or Palestinians living under Israeli rule in the West Bank and Gaza.

Under intense pressure from the Israeli media and public opinion (the 'internal incitement' referred to in the Cabinet communiqué), Begin was forced to establish an independent inquiry into Israel's complicity in the massacre. He tried at first to limit its powers to summon persons and papers, but was outmanœuvred by the legal establishment, buttressed by a protest rally of up to 400,000 Israelis in a Tel Aviv square. The Kahan Commission – two judges and a retired general – was granted full judicial status. Its patient, searching and for the most part public investigation produced a definitive account of what happened in Sabra and Shatilla – and what need not have happened. Although it absolved Israel of direct responsibility, it held Israel indirectly responsible.

> The decision on the entry of the Phalangists into the refugee camps was taken without consideration of the danger – which the makers and executors of the decision were obligated to foresee as probable – that the Phalangists would commit massacres and pogroms against the inhabitants of the camps, and without an examination of the means for preventing this danger.
>
> Similarly, it is clear from the course of events that when the reports began to arrive about the actions of the Phalangists in the camps, no proper heed was taken of these reports, the correct conclusions were not drawn from them, and no energetic and immediate actions were taken to restrain the Phalangists and put a stop to their actions.

The commission blamed Sharon for disregarding the dangers of a massacre, and for failing to take steps to prevent bloodshed. It recommended in circuitous language that was to cause trouble for the Prime Minister that Sharon either resign from the Defence Ministry, or be dismissed. General Eitan was severely censured, and the commission hinted that if the Chief of Staff had not been close to retirement it would have recommended dismissing him. The director of military intelligence, Major-General Yehoshua Saguy, and the divisional commander in Beirut, Brigadier-General Amos Yaron, were penalized for 'shortcomings and omissions'.

The Kahan Report recommended no action against Begin, but blamed him for ignoring the dangers of a massacre when the Phalangists were sent into the camps, and for failing to take an interest in what happened afterwards.

> It may be assumed that a manifestation of interest by him in this matter, after he had learned of the Phalangists' entry, would have increased the alertness of the Defence Minister and Chief of Staff to the need to take appropriate measures to meet the expected danger. The Prime Minister's lack of involvement in the entire matter casts on him a certain degree of responsibility.

The Foreign Minister, Yitzhak Shamir, was criticized for not doing enough to check a report he received from his colleague, Mordechai Zipori, and to call the Defence Minister's attention to rumours that the Phalangists were slaughtering non-combatants.[19]

With his ingrained sense of legal propriety, Begin knew from the moment he appointed the Kahan Commission that he would have to implement its recommendations, however severe they might be. Its findings would be morally binding, even if they were not legally binding. He was extremely reluctant, however, to dismiss Sharon if the Defence Minister refused to go quietly. After all, so far as the Prime Minister was concerned, Israel had been cleared of direct responsibility. Its soldiers had not killed the Sabra and Shatilla refugees. Sharon deserved a better fate than to end his military and political career in disgrace because of a massacre perpetrated by Lebanese Christians. Besides, Begin had no doubt that those baying for Sharon's blood were after his too. When Sharon called on Begin the morning the report was published, the Prime Minister asked him what was to be done. Sharon replied that Begin could either accept it or reject it. The Defence Minister would not resign, but Begin could dismiss him. The Prime Minister answered: 'I will not *ask* you to resign.' The inference was clear. If Sharon 'drew personal conclusions', in the report's words, Begin would not stand in his way. But Sharon was not going to make it easy. He would not voluntarily accept the 'mark of Cain'. Begin concluded that if Sharon stood his ground, his only choice was to go to the President, resign on behalf of the entire Government, and seek early elections. The people, he believed, were still with him. A majority rejected the Kahan Report as too harsh. At a stroke, he would have done the decent thing and won an improved mandate from the country. That was his fallback position, but he was prepared to let the Cabinet simmer for a while before implementing it.

The Cabinet met three times in as many days, debating the report and its consequences for a total of eleven hours. The third meeting, which lasted for five hours on the evening of 10 February, ended with a terse announcement that 'the Cabinet decided to accept the recommendations of the commission'. The voting was sixteen to one. Ariel Sharon was the odd man out. The Minister of Justice, Moshe Nissim, told reporters: 'Every paragraph must be implemented. If a paragraph is not carried out, the Cabinet will find a way to implement it.' The decision amounted to an ultimatum. Either Sharon jumped, or he would be pushed. The Cabinet Secretary, Dan Meridor, emphasized that nobody was playing with words. Another senior official said he hoped never to have to sit through so difficult a debate again. Sharon left the Prime Minister's office defiant, but uncommunicative. The next morning he bowed to the inevitable, telephoned Begin and submitted his resignation. Truculent to the last, he wrote that he would 'honour the Cabinet's decision to remove him from the post of Defence Minister', but was not resigning from the Cabinet. After the Attorney-General, Yitzhak Zamir, a non-political appointee, had ruled that it was enough for Sharon to leave the Defence Ministry, it was agreed that he stay in the Cabinet as a Minister Without Portfolio. A week later he was reappointed to the ministerial defence committee. Begin was severely criticized by the opposition for honouring the letter rather than the spirit of the Kahan Report, but the commission had been deliberately imprecise in its recommendation and Begin had every right to argue that he had fulfilled his obligations.

The decisive Cabinet meeting of 10 February was attended by tragedy. A peace march against the Government from the centre of Jerusalem to the Prime Minister's office was assailed by Begin supporters with a venom unrivalled since the electoral violence of 1981. The marchers were threatened, abused and spat upon. As pro- and anti-Government demonstrators were starting to disperse midway through the Cabinet meeting, a grenade was thrown into the crowd, killing Emil Grunzweig, a reserve combat officer and peace activist, and wounding half a dozen others, including Avraham Burg, the son of the Interior Minister.

At the end of the Cabinet meeting, Begin was escorted to his room by his personal staff. According to one of them, he was in a highly emotional state about the killing. 'How could something like this happen?' he kept asking. But he refused to go outside and make a statement to the waiting television cameras. It seemed as if he did not want to be associated with the wretchedness of the murder, and perhaps that he did not want to speak out against his own supporters, just as he had hesitated to condemn intimidation during the election campaign. Begin pleaded that he had not shaved all day and could not appear in front of the cameras with an eleven o'clock shadow. It was a thin excuse for inaction. The Prime Minister's son, Binyamin, who had been waiting to take him home, urged him to say something. Begin then agreed that he would talk to the radio, but not to television. In the end his son and staff persuaded him that that was not enough. 'I have never seen him so distressed,' one of his aides confided afterwards. A grey, drawn Prime Minister finally addressed the cameras, condemning 'this horrible tragedy' and appealing to citizens of Israel of all political persuasions to maintain calm and eschew violence. He acknowledged that a difficult debate was dividing the nation, but declared emotionally: 'God forbid that we should embark on the road of violence.' It was a little late for that.

23
'I Cannot Go On'

The slow decline of body and spirit that culminated in Menachem Begin's resignation in September, 1983, started almost two years earlier on the evening of 26 November 1981. The Prime Minister was reading official papers that had been sent to his residence on the corner of Balfour and Smolenskin Streets in the well-heeled Talbiyeh district of Jerusalem. Having perused the last diplomatic cable, he went to wash his hands before joining his wife and daughter Leah for supper. Between the basin and the towel-rail Begin tripped over his own feet and fell heavily on the hard tiles of the bathroom floor. The events of that Thursday evening are chronicled, wince by wince, in an extraordinarily graphic open letter[1] he sent a week later to the *Ha'aretz* columnist Yoel Marcus, who had written an article criticizing Israel's leaders and their medical advisers for concealing the truth about their ailments from the public. Begin wrote:

> I remained on the floor trying to get up. I could not. I sighed from the pain. I tried to call out for my wife to come and help me, but she did not hear my calls because the radio I had with me was on very loud. By coincidence, she also came to wash her hands. She opened the door and found me lying on the floor. She asked: 'What happened to you?' I answered: 'I fell.' She said: 'So get up.' I replied: 'I cannot.' She said: 'Wait, I'll get Leah.' Leah came. She asked: 'Daddy, what happened?' I said: 'I fell, and I cannot get up. Let me lie a little, then I'll try to get up.' My wife and daughter consulted with one another and agreed that they should pick me up and put me in the nearby bed. I heard their conversation and told them: 'No, don't do that. You don't have the strength. You will have to move me, and moving causes terrible pains. I think I have broken something. Call two of the security guards, and I'll tell them what to do with me.'
>
> After a little while two of our fine boys came. I asked them to do the following: put their hands underneath me, without moving [my limbs], and in that position carry me to the bed and put me on it. ... The two security guards approached me and did exactly as I had asked them. Thanks to them, I was in my bed, on my right side. The pain was considerable but bearable.

Three senior doctors from Hadassah Hospital, including Begin's personal physician Mervyn Gotsman, were summoned to his bedside. They called an ambulance to take him to the hospital in Ein Karem on the western edge of the city, where an X-ray confirmed that he had a fractured left femur. The sooner they could operate the better. In the operating theatre, Begin was told that he would be awake throughout with only a local anaesthetic.

> The pains were bad, but they did not increase. I watched the surgeons' preparations, how they put on robe upon robe, how they were assisted in tying the different knots. All those present in the room wore masks over their faces, among them Professor Gotsman and a security man. The anaesthesia started. Professor [Florella] Magora administered several injections in the vicinity of my spine. The left side of my body was gradually becoming numb. The moment came when it felt completely frozen, as if it were a block of ice. I felt nothing, then the pains also disappeared and I felt much better. Professor [Myer] Makin ordered a curtain to be placed between the upper half of my body and the area where the operation was about to be performed. They explained that this was required so that germs being exhaled with my breath would not reach the area of the operation. I accepted that explanation, but I thought that they might not want me to see all that they were doing. And indeed I saw nothing.
>
> The operation began. I did not feel it begin. I felt nothing. I spoke with Professor Gotsman, who was by my side, and he talked to me. I was in no pain. Suddenly I heard the pounding of a hammer on a nail. The pounding increased. I felt nothing. I did not count, but I think I distinguished nine or ten intermittent hammer-blows. After a while they told me that the operation would soon be over and that everything had gone well. A little while later, they said it was done. They removed the curtain, and I saw Professor Makin's slightly blood-stained gloves. He removed them, came to me and said: 'Everything's fine.' I was put on a stretcher and taken back to Professor Gotsman's intensive care ward. ... That night the pains did not return, but on Friday, probably as the local anaesthetic faded, the pains began. They were very bad, but because they allowed me to stay in bed and not move for two days, they were bearable.

The neck of the femur, the bone joining the thigh and pelvis, was repaired and Begin was discharged from hospital eighteen days later. But he remained in excruciating pain and discomfort for months afterwards. When the French President François Mitterrand paid a state visit in March 1982, Begin addressed the Knesset from a wheelchair (Israeli political reporters had taken to calling him Ironside after the irascible television detective). As late as the end of May, he excused himself from briefing the Knesset foreign affairs and defence committee because his 'broken leg' was still hurting him. He told his staff that he had never known such agony in his life. The Prime Minister abandoned his desk, which he found uncomfortable, and conducted his working day from a sofa and coffee-table. Long after it was strictly necessary, he continued walking with a stick. The fall had shaken his self-confidence and had reminded him that he was growing old. He confessed that he was afraid of falling again.

Begin exploited his injury as a prop and a joke. 'I broke my leg,' he would tell rapturous American Jewish audiences when the Reagan Administration was threatening to put pressure on Israel, 'but my knee is not bent.' Nonetheless, it made him aware of being an invalid as his heart condition had seldom done. 'Do you feel like a sick man?' he once asked a fellow heart-sufferer. Although Begin never travelled without the faithful Dr Gotsman, he did not feel particularly vulnerable. During his visit to Cairo in 1979 he stomped around the Pyramids in suit and tie in temperatures well over forty degrees centigrade. With his broken leg, however, he began to look frail. He needed assistance.

Almost from the start of his premiership, Begin had shown the classic symptoms of manic depression. For months at a time, in 1978 and again in 1980, he was plunged deep in gloom and inertia. Then he would bound back, stimulated perhaps by a fight, an insult, an opportunity to make history. In the twenty-two months after he fell in his Jerusalem bathroom, Begin had his ups as well as his downs, but gradually the impulse to action weakened, the manic phases became fewer and less sustained. The resilience that had seen him through the Gulag and the underground, the disdain of permanent opposition, the trials of office, began to sag. The long-term trend was remorselessly downhill.

None of this was apparent when Begin was discharged from Hadassah Hospital on 14 December. He came out with a bang as if to demonstrate that it was too early to write him off. The Prime Minister's 'long Monday' was carried through with all the despatch of a guerrilla operation: secrecy, surprise and speed of execution. It began at 7.15 a.m. with Begin still in his hospital robe. He telephoned Ariel Sharon and asked what his plans were for the day. The Defence Minister, a little peeved at being called at that hour, replied that he was going to Yamit in Northern Sinai. Begin suggested that he forget about Yamit and come to Jerusalem. The Foreign Minister, Yitzhak Shamir, was also summoned. 'What's it all about?' they asked. 'When you get here I'll tell you,' Begin answered. These two most senior Herut colleagues were the first to know, but even they had not guessed that the Prime Minister intended to celebrate his release by annexing the Golan Heights, captured from Syria in the 1967 war. The Cabinet was then called into emergency session at noon in Balfour Street. Begin was home and busy.

The press knew something was afoot, but what? The Cabinet meeting broke up before lunch and it was announced that there would be a statement in the Knesset that afternoon. Was Begin more sick than we imagined? Was he going to resign? Or was it some military operation, a blow perhaps at the half-forgotten Syrian missiles in Eastern Lebanon? The whole affair demonstrated Begin's ascendancy and taste for conspiracy. The Prime Minister decided and steamrolled. The Cabinet, whatever its misgivings, was swept along. The Knesset was dragooned into giving the bill 'extending Israeli law, jurisdiction and administration' to the Heights three readings and a committee stage before midnight. International lawyers might argue about the correct terminology, but to the world at large the 1,675 square kms with their 13,000 Druze and 6,600 Jewish settlers, in four hill villages and thirty-one settlements respectively, had been annexed. The Prime Minister set a dramatic seal on the initiative by going to the Knesset in a wheelchair, presenting the legislation from his place at the Cabinet table, and following through with a raucous running battle with dissenting MPs.

Annexation had been foreshadowed in the coalition guidelines for the tenth Knesset, but why did Begin choose this day and these means? His aides say that his first priority was to spike the guns of Geula Cohen and the new Tehiya party, which won three seats in the 1981 elections and was sniping at the Likud from the Right. Mrs Cohen, who defected from Herut after Camp David, had tried once to force the pace on the Golan and was threatening to do so again. Begin, ever slow to forgive desertions, was determined to deny her the satisfaction. The tail would not wag the dog. There was too his theatrical sense of occasion, the urge to command the spotlight. But circumstances had conspired to make this an ideal time for the annexation. The world was preoccupied with a crisis in Poland. Syria was playing into Israel's hands with increasingly intransigent statements about the 'treachery' of making peace with Israel. President Hafez Assad had said only the previous day that he would never recognize the Jewish State, 'even if the Palestinians will deign to do so'. David Kimche, the director-general of the Foreign Ministry, justified the Begin coup to the international press corps as an act of self-protection. 'If we cannot neutralize the Golan Heights by a peace treaty,' he said, 'this is how we have to do it.' Begin taunted the parliamentary opposition with charges of a ghetto mentality. 'The phenomenon, recurring throughout Jewish history from generation to generation, is that of self-accusation. The Jew is to blame. If a pogrom is launched against him, the Jew is to blame. If they spill his blood, the Jew is to blame. Now the Knesset members say: Syria will not negotiate with you, the Jewish Government is to blame.' The Prime Minister was making sure that the Syrians – and thus their Palestinian protégés – stayed in the rejectionist camp, from which they would pose no danger to Israeli rule over the West Bank and Gaza Strip. He was also striking before the April deadline for Israel's final withdrawal from Sinai so as to minimize the Egyptian reaction. Cairo, he gambled, would do nothing to jeopardize the recovery of its lost territory, and by April the Golan would be a dead issue.

Begin was right about the Egyptians, but he underestimated the vehemence of the American reaction. Washington was angry not only because Israel had annexed occupied Syrian territory, but because it had done so without prior notification, let alone consultation. That was no way for an ally to behave. The Reagan Administration responded by suspending a memorandum of strategic understanding which Sharon had recently negotiated and by withholding financial benefits promised to Israel. There were doubts in the United States and in Israel about the practical value of the memorandum, but Begin and Sharon set great store by it. The suspension was a blow to their prestige. The Prime Minister's reply could only be verbal. Israel had nothing of substance to deny the United States. But within those limits, Begin let fly as though Israel were the super power and America the beleaguered client. The suspension struck at his cherished doctrine of a balanced alliance, at his pride in Jewish independence. Begin had always treated words as weapons. The sermon he preached to the unfortunate American ambassador, Samuel Lewis, must rank among the most vitriolic assaults ever directed by a junior partner at a rich and mighty patron.

The Prime Minister summoned Lewis to Balfour Street. The ambassador found him still in pain from his broken leg, holding himself rigid throughout what turned into a fifty-five-minute monologue. As though to show that his wrath was not directed at Lewis, he went out of his way to exchange pleasantries about their respective health and families before getting down to business. Then, as if turning on a light, Begin said: 'Now, Mr Ambassador, I have a statement I want to make.' It was, he explained, a personal message which he wanted transmitted immediately to the President and the Secretary of State. Lewis noticed a sheaf of papers beside Begin, but the Prime Minister never once referred to them.

Begin recalled that this was the third time in six months that the Administration had 'punished' Israel. The first occasion was after the destruction of the Iraqi reactor, the second when Israel bombed Beirut in the summer of 1981.

A week ago the Knesset adopted the Golan law, and again you declare that you are 'punishing' Israel. What kind of talk is that, 'punishing' Israel? Are we a vassal state? A banana republic? Are we fourteen-year-old boys, that if they don't behave they have their knuckles smacked? I will tell you of whom this Government is composed. It is composed of men who fought, risked their lives

and suffered. You cannot and will not frighten us with 'punishments and threats'.
... The people of Israel have lived for 3,700 years without a memorandum of understanding with America and will continue to live without it for another 3,700 years.

Begin accused the Administration of breaking the President's word by imposing 'pecuniary sanctions'. What did they want to do? Hit Israel in the pocket?

In 1946 there lived in this very house a British general whose name was Barker. Today I live in this house. When we fought against him you called us terrorists and we continued the fight. After we blew up his headquarters in the sequestered part of the King David, Barker said: 'You can punish that race only by hitting at its pocket', and he issued an order to his British troops that all the Jewish coffee-shops be out of bounds. To hit us in our pockets? That is the philosophy of Barker.

The Prime Minister defended the right of American Jews and their friends in the Congress to speak up for Israel without being intimidated by anti-Semitic propaganda or being accused of unpatriotically preferring Begin to Reagan.

Nobody will frighten the great and free Jewish community in the United States. They will stand by us, this is the land of their forefathers. They have the right and duty to support it. There are those who say that the law adopted by the Knesset has to be rescinded. The word 'rescind' is a concept from the time of the Inquisition. Our forefathers went to the stake rather than rescind their faith. We are not going to the stake. Thank God, we have enough strength to defend our independence and defend our rights. ... Please tell the Secretary of State that the Golan law shall remain in force. There is no force in the world that can bring about its abrogation.

As for the charge of embarrassing the United States, Begin maintained that Israel had acted in secret precisely so as not to embarrass the President. 'We did not want you to say no, and then apply the law to the Golan Heights.' That was little consolation to Samuel Lewis, who was surprised to see the entire Israeli Cabinet gathered in an ante-room, ready to hear the same monologue all over again in Hebrew. The ambassador was even more surprised when he heard a verbatim account on the car radio before he had time to get back to Tel Aviv and send the 'personal message' to the White House. It was, he felt, a gross violation of diplomatic propriety between two friendly countries. He told Begin as much when the opportunity presented itself. The Prime Minister had no regrets, even when the Israeli press pointed out that General Barker had actually lived in the house next door.

*   *   *

The confrontation over the Golan annexation marked a low point in Israeli–American relations. James Reston was believed by Israelis in Washington to be reflecting the President's thinking when he wrote in his *New York Times* column that senior American officials 'feel Mr Begin is a certified disaster for Israel and the rest of the world', and hinted that they were waiting for the Israeli people to do something about it. Of forty-one major American newspapers that commented on the Golan affair, only two showed much understanding for the Israeli case.[2] On the way home from a Middle East tour in February 1982, the Defence Secretary, Caspar Weinberger, was asked whether there was a concerted effort to redirect the United States away from Israel and towards the Arabs. He replied: 'Yes. In military policy the US is not going to be hostage to Israel.' Weinberger, who was suspect in Begin's eyes as a Christian who had to live down his Jewish name, also disclosed to correspondents that the Administration was planning to cultivate support in Congress for the sale of mobile Hawk air-defence missiles and advanced F-16 fighters to Jordan. Israel immediately mobilized its friends to fight the Jordanian deal, which it argued would change the strategic balance. But Washington did not force the crisis to a head. Reagan was reluctant to give Israel a pretext for reneging on the Sinai evacuation, due to be completed by 25 April. In a series of letters and statements, the President reaffirmed his commitment to maintaining Israel's qualitative edge over the Arab armies and his refusal to talk to the Palestine Liberation Organization unless it acknowledged Israel's right to exist within secure and recognized borders.

Begin's conviction that the Americans will always come back in the end seemed to have been proved right again. But the tension took its toll, contributing its share to the Prime Minister's cumulative exhaustion. So did the Sinai withdrawal, which he had accepted with the gravest misgivings and which went against all his instincts. Jews had settled in the peninsula because successive governments had said Israel needed them there. Three months after taking office, Begin had been admitted as an honorary member to Neot Sinai, a settlement between El Arish and Yamit founded by graduates of his Herut youth organization, and had promised to retire there in due course and write his memoirs. Rather than provoke a 'war of the Jews', he agreed to pay the 3,000 settlers inflated compensation in return for their voluntary evacuation. He also ordered the army to go to extreme lengths to avoid a violent showdown with a few hundred fanatics, most of whom had never lived in Sinai, who squatted there as the deadline drew near. In the end the evacuation of all eighteen settlements was completed on time after token clashes, but a precedent had been created and Begin knew it. No Arab ruler would contemplate peace without demanding his Yamit.

Six weeks after the Sinai withdrawal, Israel was at war in Lebanon. Begin believed in its aims, but he wanted it over quickly and cheaply. As the IDF sank deeper into the mire, with the casualty toll increasing week by week for more than twelve months, the Prime Minister became more and more depressed. Every death seemed a personal indictment. Whenever his military secretary, Azriel Nevo, brought him the news of another victim, his staff saw the distress on his face. 'It piled sadness on sadness on sadness,' says Yehiel Kadishai. Begin's private secretary, Yona Klimovitzky, said after his resignation that he felt betrayed by certain people he had trusted. 'He'd been given to understand that we would go into Lebanon, and then get out quickly.[3] The 'certain people' presumably were his Defence Minister and Chief of Staff. Israelis noticed that Begin attended none of the military funerals and never visited the wounded in hospital. It was, it seems, too much of an ordeal. On 15 September, the day he sent his resignation letter to President Chaim Herzog, the IDF buried its five hundred and eighteenth fallen soldier of the Lebanese war, a forty-nine-year-old reserve corporal hit by a bazooka in an ambush near Tyre.

The massacre in the Beirut refugee camps added to his burden. He was hurt by the huge demonstrations, the press campaign and the imputations of murder. Begin, his ministers and his generals were 'on trial' for almost six months. From November nine public figures, including Begin, Sharon and Shamir, were under notice that they might have to share the blame. The Kahan Commission advised them that they were at risk and gave them an opportunity to defend themselves. Its report, published in February, assigned only limited responsibility to the Prime Minister, sins of omission rather than commission. But Begin, with his jurist's mind and sense of honour, can hardly have been oblivious to the stain. The crisis over Sharon's resignation forced him to assert his authority, but he did so with a heavy heart. At the same time, in the autumn of 1982, he was fending off the Reagan Plan for drawing Jordan into the peace process. Begin rejected the plan, which was sprung on Israel without consultation, as another threat to the unity of *Eretz Yisrael*. He need not have worried. King Hussein would not act without the PLO's blessing, and the Palestinians yet again exercised their veto.

All this was acted out against the backcloth of Aliza Begin's deteriorating health and eventual death on 13 November 1982. The Prime Minister's wife had suffered for years from chronic asthma. In her last months, she had great difficulty breathing. According to a friend of the family, only thirty per cent of the normal oxygen supply was reaching her lungs. The doctors could do little to help beyond keeping her on a life-support system.

Begin would visit her daily in Hadassah Hospital, sometimes twice a day, and telephone whenever he could. A few weeks before her death, the Jewish-American oil magnate and art collector Armand Hammer, who had used his Kremlin connections to help Begin in the campaign for Soviet Jewry, sent two specialists to examine her. They recommended treatment which for a while made her breathing easier. She felt well enough to urge the Prime Minister to accept an invitation to Washington for his first meeting in five months with President Reagan. On the way he was to address a fund-raising dinner in Los Angeles. The news of Aliza's death was telephoned to Begin's hotel suite there by his son Binyamin. Yehiel Kadishai took the message, but wanted Dr Gotsman to be present when he broke it to the Prime Minister. It was Saturday afternoon in California and the physician had gone to synagogue for the *minha* and *ma'ariv* services. Begin's political secretary reached him by radio-beeper. By the time Gotsman made his way back to the hotel, Begin was dressed in tuxedo and black tie for the dinner. Hart Hasten, a veteran American Herutnik, and his wife were also present, as was Begin's daughter Leah, an El Al ground hostess who had accompanied him on the trip. Leah burst into tears when she and her father were told. Arrangements were made for them to fly home immediately in the Prime Minister's specially fitted Israel air force Boeing 707. 'The fact that he was not at his wife's side in the last hours of her life caused him great pain,' Kadishai testifies. Begin hardly emerged from his small, curtained sleeping-cabin throughout the sixteen-hour flight from Los Angeles to Tel Aviv. He stayed on board when they stopped for refuelling in New York. For most of the time he was alone with his grief.

Back in Balfour Street, Begin mourned the 'bride of one's youth' for the traditional seven days and went for a month without shaving. His staff and friends are convinced that Aliza's death, after forty-three years of marriage, was the final straw in breaking his will to rule. Begin, one of them argues, had been through difficult times before, taking life-and-death decisions, but he had never despaired, never lost his capacity to lead.

> After Aliza's death, he became a lonely person. He is not a talkative man, even if he can be a spellbinder with words. He speaks *to* people rather than *with* them. As a dominant personality, he never shifted responsibility to others. The only person he could talk with and share his responsibilities and problems with was his wife. They were very, very close. After she died, he would come home and there was nobody to talk to. He was in a war, people were dying, and he had nobody to share it with.

Begin's son Binyamin tried to fill the gap. He was close to the Prime Minister personally and politically, and was often spotted in his office when critical decisions were being taken. But Binyamin could not take his mother's place. He had a wife and six children, a job as a geologist. He hated being in the public eye. 'Benny did his best,' says one of his friends, 'but it was not the same.' From the end of 1982, barely a month after Aliza's death, Begin started losing weight and strength. He was not eating properly. At his favourite table in the Knesset dining-room, he made do with a meagre plate of vegetables. He stopped ordering chicken and soup, which had been his staple fare. It began to show. His clothes hung loosely on his bony frame. His face and neck became hollow and scrawny. When one of his aides urged him to eat, he answered: 'I don't have the appetite any more.'

Despite the visible decline, senior officials insisted in public and in private that he was receiving no special treatment, either medical or psychological. But the melancholia was deepening. 'He was sobered,' one of his closest aides testifies. 'He was dealing more with the macro than the micro. He was not reading papers as intensively as he used to. His meetings were more paced. He had aged.' An American diplomat who knew Begin well felt that he no longer enjoyed being Prime Minister of Israel. It had become a chore, and an onerous chore at that. He took part in negotiations, he understood what was being discussed, but he left much more of the Israeli presentation to his colleagues. The dominance had gone. His contributions had lost their creative spark. He was no longer looking for new formulas, ways around problems. On lesser occasions his mind seemed to wander. The Peace Now movement mounted a four-month vigil outside the Prime Minister's residence, with a scoreboard of the dead hounding him whenever he left or returned. A Likud MP, Meir Cohen, retaliated with a hunger strike. Begin came out to ask him to call it off, but walked like an automaton to the wrong demonstration. A security man took him by the shoulders and pointed him the right way. When he received a group of young American Christian friends of Israel, their leader asked if the Prime Minister had any message for them to take home. He replied with his standard exhortation to diaspora Jews: 'Learn Hebrew and come and live in Israel.'

Although loyal spokesmen claimed to the last that Begin was still running the show, his hold was slackening. He was embarrassed by an invitation to visit President Reagan at the end of July, though earlier in the year he had been angling desperately for it. From the moment that Samuel Lewis delivered the President's message, Begin was looking for a way out. 'I'm not capable of standing before the public,' he told his staff. The ambassador asked for an immediate answer because the White House wanted to announce the visit the next day, Friday, but Begin played for time. 'Please tell the President I shall reply at the beginning of next week,' he said. With the assistance of Yehuda Avner, who handled his English correspondence, Begin accepted the invitation the next week, but built in an escape clause. He would be happy to come to Washington, 'subject to my being able to leave the country on that day'. The visit was three weeks away, and the letter won him two weeks' grace. It made little difference. Begin still could not face the world. Various diplomatic letters were drafted, but the Prime Minister decided that the only way was to telephone Reagan and plead 'personal reasons' for a postponement. To the Israelis' relief, the White House issued a tactful announcement using those words without further explanation. The Prime Minister's office seized on it as if it were an agreed joint communiqué. 'Personal reasons' suited Jerusalem as well as Washington.

At home Begin hardly ever appeared on the platform or the television screen. He gave no interviews. The economy was in disarray, ministers were wrangling over budget cuts, medical services were slowly paralysed by a 117-day doctors' strike, there was still no way out of Lebanon. For most of the time, Begin stood aloof. Yet no one else assumed his authority. His old crony and Deputy Premier Simha Erlich died in June, and the Prime Minister seemed more adrift than ever. It was left to Aharon Uzan, of the small, rebellious Tami party, to break the conspiracy of silence. Uzan, the Minister of Social Welfare, a farmer from Tunisia, said that the Cabinet was 'like a ship without a captain'. The budget debate, for example, had been conducted in unbelievable chaos.

> Three out of the nine hours they sat thinking how to decide instead of deciding. At the end they didn't know what had been decided. All of the ministers, including the Finance Minister, stood in line at the Cabinet secretariat to look at the minutes in order to know what they had decided.[4]

In retrospect there was an inevitability about Begin's retirement. The truth could not be hidden for ever, and he was increasingly aware of his own incapacity. He had said often enough that he would retire at seventy, and had just celebrated three score years and ten. Yet his announcement, towards the end of an otherwise routine Cabinet meeting on 28 August 1983, that he intended to resign surprised all but a handful of confidants. Even they knew nothing of his plans until just before the Cabinet assembled. As so often, in the underground and in government, Begin took his own counsel and made his own decision. Only then did he inform his son Binyamin, his political secretary, Yehiel Kadishai, the Cabinet Secretary, Dan Meridor, and his old Irgun comrade Ya'acov Meridor. The announcement to the Cabinet was a necessary constitutional preliminary to going to the President. 'I feel I cannot carry on shouldering my responsibilities, with things as they are, the way I would like to and the way I ought to,' Begin explained to colleagues who came to his room after the Cabinet broke up. He agreed, however, to listen to representatives of all the coalition parties, who were alarmed at the electoral consequences and hoped to persuade him to think again. For two days they appealed in the name of God and Jabotinsky, while hundreds of Likud voters paraded outside his house chanting: 'Begin, King of Israel!' But it was to no avail. This was not the Begin of 1966, scaring his followers into line with a threat of resignation. 'Ya'acov, it won't help you,' he told Meridor. 'I cannot go on,' he said with a finality that silenced the supplicants.

As a last service to his party, Begin agreed to wait until a successor had been chosen and was sure of parliamentary support before notifying President Herzog. It was a political manœuvre that detracted from the dignity of his departure, especially when he delayed even longer than necessary, but it was an act of loyalty that a Ben-Gurion or Golda Meir would have understood. The Likud-Labour balance was so fine that the slightest miscalculation might have let in the Opposition.

The final curtain in the drama of Menachem Begin's public life fell on an empty stage. The Prime Minister drew into his shell, eating little, no longer shaving, seeing only his family and closest aides. He stayed away from Cabinet meetings and did not attend services for the Jewish New Year. He had no farewell message for the nation, played no part in the Herut central committee's choice of Yitzhak Shamir as its new leader, sent no congratulations. At noon on Thursday, 15 September, Begin despatched Dan Meridor to the President's house with his formal resignation. A spokesman explained that he did not want to appear in public because a rash prevented him from shaving. It was acknowledged later that he had been using ointment for this condition for thirty-five years. Once again, Begin simply could not face the world. Seven weeks later a memorial service was held at the Mount of Olives cemetery on the first anniversary of Aliza's death. Begin, still living like a recluse in the Prime Minister's residence, did not attend.

24
The House that Menachem Built

Menachem Begin governed Israel for six years and three months, which made him the longest-serving Prime Minister after the founding father David Ben-Gurion. He revealed himself as a complex, but not a mysterious, man, a paradox but not a puzzle: an unrepentant terrorist who won the Nobel Peace Prize, then launched another war. A democrat and an autocrat. A courtly rabble-rouser, Polish gentleman and Levantine cult hero. A man of honour with whom it was wise to read the small print. A conspirator who found it hard to keep a secret.

Israelis called him their first ideological Prime Minister. He was certainly the most single-minded. His overriding priority was to secure the whole of the ancient homeland west of the Jordan for the Jewish people. By the time he retired even his opponents acknowledged that it would take a leader no less dedicated and no less commanding to restore the partition lines. In May 1977, when Begin promised 'many Eilon Morehs', there were twenty-three Jewish settlements on the West Bank and one in the Gaza Strip. In September 1983 there were 112 on the West Bank and five in Gaza. The Jewish population living beyond the old 'green line' had grown from 3,000 to 40,000 (including the new towns of Ma'aleh Adumim and Emanuel).[1] The pattern of settlement had changed, too. Under the Labour Government, the emphasis was on the Jordan valley, on peopling the strategic frontier. Settlements were deliberately kept away from the hill country of Judea and Samaria, where most of the Arab population was concentrated. Labour wanted to preserve the option of territorial compromise. Begin's Likud set the engine in reverse, drawing resources away from the eastern fringe and scattering settlements among the Arab towns and villages. At first only the ideologues volunteered for these outposts, but gradually ordinary families swallowed the Government bait and moved to the West Bank because housing was cheaper there. The settlements were near enough to Jerusalem and Tel Aviv to serve as commuter suburbs. After years of unremitting hostility, even the United States recognized that the settlers were there to stay. On 2 August 1983 Charles Lichtenstein, the deputy US representative at the United Nations, told the Security Council:

We don't believe that it is at all practical, or even appropriate, to call for dismantling of the existing settlements. The future of the settlements is one of the key issues which will need to be addressed in the negotiations. Nor can we accept continuing argument as to whether the settlements are 'illegal', an argument which unfortunately has dominated discussions in the United Nations on this question to the detriment of the basic issue, namely how to bring about a just and peaceful resolution of the conflict over the occupied territories.

In other words, facts had been created, and the Reagan Administration was too realistic to wish them away. At the same time, Palestinian autonomy as envisaged at Camp David was a dead letter. Five years after the Begin-Sadat agreement, there was not only no self-governing council, there were no negotiations. Slice by slice the occupied Palestinians were losing their rights, month by month the status of the Jewish settlers was consolidated and legitimized. Yet Egypt did not abrogate the peace treaty. It was a cold peace on both sides, but it allowed Begin to wage war in Lebanon without worrying unduly about his southern flank, and it allowed him to go on winning his 'struggle for *Eretz Yisrael*'.

On the Prime Minister's seventieth birthday, the London *Times*, never numbered among his admirers, commented:

All in all, Mr Begin at seventy has cause for satisfaction. His policies have provoked strains in Israeli society and on its economy. *But he holds the strategic initiative now against his neighbours, and they know it.* That is an unusual situation for Israel, an unwelcome one for the Arabs, and an uncomfortable one for all onlookers who tend to be sucked into the affair.[2]

The world was acknowledging that under the Likud the Israeli armed forces had erased the stigma of October 1973. For good or ill, Israel was back as the regional super power. The strike on the Iraqi reactor and the humbling of the PLO in Beirut and of the Syrians in Eastern Lebanon had restored Israel's deterrent. Within days of the *Times* leader, however, hawkish claims that Begin 'retrieved and reasserted Israelis' self-confidence and their conviction that they can, at least partly, determine historical circumstances',[3] were back in question. The renewal of the Lebanese civil war after Israeli troops had withdrawn from the Shouf mountains was the last nail in the coffin of Ariel Sharon's grand design. The Israeli-Maronite axis had collapsed. Syria was still Lebanon's big brother, the Palestinian guerrillas were filtering back, and Arab diplomacy was President Amin Gemayel's last hope. The previous summer the Phalangists had asked too much of Israel. They were eager to massacre Palestinians, but not to fight the PLO. There was a limit, however, to the sacrifice Israel could contemplate on their behalf, a sacrifice in lives and in reputation. As a result the Syrians and the Palestinians were not evicted from Eastern and Northern Lebanon. Amin Gemayel, who replaced the murdered Bashir, had little of his brother's taste for the Zionist connection. An agreement just short of a peace treaty was hammered out between Jerusalem and Beirut in early 1983, but it was never ratified by the Lebanese and it soon lapsed. There was a whiff of nemesis in a visit Sharon paid to his old Christian allies in August. He reported on his return to Tel Aviv:

> I met with central figures, and I told them again and again that in spite of the fact that Israel did not go to war so as to create a new situation in Lebanon, or to enable them to rule in Lebanon, still, they have an opportunity, which I think won't come again, to have an independent state of their own. This opportunity is gradually disappearing. I think its days are numbered. With its own hands, Lebanon has lost an opportunity to exist as an independent country.

The Lebanese were no longer listening. In Israel other, duller men were making policy. The first concern of Sharon's successor, Moshe Arens, was to cut Israel's losses, literally and figuratively, while salvaging the original modest aims of Operation Peace for Galilee. When Begin stepped down, it looked as if the only way Israel could ensure that no more Katyushas fell on Kiryat Shmona would be to keep a permanent garrison along the Awali river.

During his six years of office, Begin redrew the map of Palestine, but he did not solve the problem of the Palestinians. The *Eretz Yisrael* he bequeathed to Yitzhak Shamir was a bi-national state in the making, a land of three-and-a-half million Jews and two million Arabs. The Palestinians were *in* the expanded homeland, but not *of* it. Israel's Zionist aspirations were not theirs. Nor, for the most part, were its democracy, its citizens' army or its institutions, which were themselves endangered by the habit of occupation. The Arabs were subdued by Jabotinsky's 'iron wall', but they were not resigned to Israeli domination. There were too many of them – in the occupied territories and in Israel proper – to be absorbed as an ethnic minority, and their high birth-rate put demography on their side. Begin's autonomy plan was a tacit acknowledgement of the problem, but he made no determined effort to implement it. The Lebanese war failed to destroy the PLO as a political factor in the equation, just as it failed to foster an independent local leadership ready to make peace on anything like Israel's conditions.

The occupied territories became the arena for a confrontation of extremes, Arab terror versus Jewish terror, with the odds heavily loaded against the Arabs. Men and women who had defied successive Labour and Likud governments were now sitting in the Cabinet and on the coalition benches. The aberrant became the norm. Jewish vigilantes, armed with IDF weapons, enforced their own version of an eye for an eye. When a Jew was killed in Hebron, for instance, they went on the rampage and burned the Arab market. The security services complained of political interference when they tried to bring them to book. The thugs were 'good Jewish boys' doing the nation's dirty work, and there was always an MP or a rabbi on the line to remind the police of it. Under General Eitan, the army on the West Bank became an instrument of Gush Emunim, and its cohesion was put at risk. The settlers were given ever more assistance and support by the army, Yoram Peri wrote in *Between Battles and Ballots*, a study of the military in politics.

> Illegal settlers were not only spared court proceedings, but even, in some cases, housed in IDF camps. Acts of provocation and sabotage by settlers against the Arab population of the territories were overlooked by the army. On the other hand, the settlers were helped by the IDF to set up their own self-defence units, they were supplied with weapons and allowed to do their own policing in the territories. . . .
>
> From the moment the Chief of Staff took one side in the public debate – bringing the IDF with him – the army lost the advantage of high esteem in the eyes of the entire community. It no longer reflected the whole of society, and though it came to be admired by one political camp, the other side regarded it as a political adversary. The next stage – of certain groups being altogether alienated from the army – thus became inevitable.[4]

Begin's 'war of choice' in Lebanon accelerated the process. A brigade commander asked to be relieved of his post, reservists went to prison rather than serve north of the border, parents demonstrated against the exploitation of their soldier sons. The cultural divide grew wider, with dissenters condemned as PLO collaborators and thus rendered fair game for violence and even for murder.

Like all Israel's Prime Ministers before him, Begin was preoccupied with security and foreign affairs. But his reign suffered from his autocratic style of leadership. Ben-Gurion entrusted financial and internal affairs to Levi Eshkol. Golda Meir had Pinhas Sapir and his little black book. Begin appointed no domestic overlord. He delegated responsibility, but not power. He would tolerate no rival focus of authority. Yet he had neither time nor inclination to direct the home front himself. Project Renewal, for example, an imaginative scheme for rehabilitating slums and development towns through Israeli-diaspora partnership, was the Prime Minister's brainchild. But once he had launched it in the flush of the 1977 election victory, he left it to an uncertain future in the hands of subordinates. Elsewhere he fell hostage by default to Yoram Aridor's adventurist economic policies.

By the time Begin retired, inflation was entrenched at around 130 per cent a year, the shekel was falling by one per cent every two days against the United States dollar, industrial production was stagnant, farmers were facing bankruptcy, imports were outpacing exports to an alarming degree, the stock exchange bubble had burst. Israel's foreign debt increased by $550 million to a total of $21.5 billion in the first half of 1983. Central bank officials were warning the Government of a crisis if the trend continued. Despite Begin's defiance of two presidents, Israel was more beholden – and so more vulnerable to pressure – than ever to its American benefactor.

The Israel Menachem Begin created in his own image was more narrowly Jewish, more aggressive and more isolated. Social and religious tensions were closer to the surface. But as the Kahan Commission demonstrated, government was still accountable to the people, democracy and the rule of law were alive and kicking. The press was not silenced by appeals to patriotism. In the autumn of 1983, the disengagement from the problems of Lebanon showed Israelis soberly aware of their limitations as well as their strengths. That was not the legacy the sixth Prime Minister had meant to leave his people, but it was one worth cherishing.

Notes

Chapter One: Born unto Zion

1 *Encyclopaedia Judaica*, Jerusalem, Keter, 1972, volume 4, pp. 1359-63.
2 Menachem Begin, transcript of interview for Israel Television series on the history of Zionism, *The Pillar of Fire* (*Amud Ha'esh*).
3 Rachel Halperin, interview with author.
4 R. Halperin, interview.
5 R. Halperin, interview.
6 R. Halperin, interview.
7 M. Begin, *The Pillar of Fire*, interview.
8 Quoted in Aharon Dolav: 'White Nights and Tempestuous Days', *Ma'ariv*, 10 June 1977.
9 R. Halperin, interview.
10 R. Halperin, interview.
11 R. Halperin, interview.
12 Amihai Yisraeli: *Ma'ariv L'noar* (*Ma'ariv* youth magazine), 4 February 1969.
13 David Jutan, interview with author.
14 M. Begin, *The Pillar of Fire*, interview.
15 R. Halperin, interview.
16 Interview with Eric Breindel, *Rolling Stone* (US), 3 November 1977.
17 R. Halperin, interview.

Chapter Two: At the Feet of the Master

1 Quoted in Aharon Dolav: 'White Nights and Tempestuous Days', *Ma'ariv*, 10 June 1977.
2 Rachel Halperin, interview with author.
3 A. Dolav, *op. cit.*
4 A. Dolav, *op. cit.*
5 Menachem Begin, transcript of interview for Israel Television series on history of Zionism, *The Pillar of Fire*.
6 Harold Beeley, letter to author.

7 See Shlomo Avineri: *The Making of Modern Zionism*, London, Weidenfeld & Nicolson, 1981.
8 *Homo Homini Lupus*, 1910, reprinted in his collected writings, *Ktavim*, Jerusalem (in Hebrew), 1947.
9 Quoted in S. Avineri, *op cit.*
10 *On the Iron Wall*, published in Russian in 1923, reprinted in *Ktavim*.
11 M. Begin, *The Pillar of Fire*, interview.
12 Joseph Schechtman, *Rebel and Statesman*, the first volume of a two-volume biography, New York, Thomas Yoseloff, 1956, page 424, quoted by Walter Laqueur in *A History of Zionism*. 'Marranism' was a reference to the Spanish Jews who pretended to adopt Christianity as a means of surviving the Inquisition, while preserving their Judaism under cover.
13 See Shabtai Teveth, *The Murder of Arlosoroff*, Tel Aviv, Schocken, 1982 (in Hebrew).
14 *Jerusalem Post*, 15 March 1982.
15 *Jerusalem Post*, 15 March 1982, and a signed article by M. Begin in the same paper on 19 March 1982: 'Anatomy of Incitement'.
16 Quoted in Haviv Cana'an: 'The Early Years', *Ha'aretz* weekend magazine, 17 June 1977.
17 David Jutan, interview with author.
18 Yisrael Eldad, interview with author.
19 Quoted in Cana'an article, see note 16.
20 Quoted in Joseph Schechtman, *Fighter and Prophet*, volume two of *The Jabotinsky Story*, New York, Yoseloff, 1961. The exchange is not mentioned in the official summary of the conference, lodged in the Jabotinsky archive in Tel

Aviv. Dr Yohanan Bader, a veteran
Polish Revisionist and Knesset
colleague of Begin's, gave the present
author a slightly different version, in
which Begin addressed Jabotinsky as
'our father', adding, 'you can forgive
Ben-Gurion, but we your children will
never forgive'.

21 See official summary of the Betar
congress in the Jabotinsky archives, Tel
Aviv.

22 Yohanan Bader, interview with author.

Chapter Three: Flight and Arrest

1 Yisrael Eldad, interview with author.
2 Y. Eldad, interview.
3 David Jutan, interview with author.
4 Yehuda Bauer, 'Lopsided
Understanding', *Jerusalem Post*, 3
March 1982.
5 Z. Mankowitz, 'Beirut is not Berlin',
Jerusalem Post, 4 August 1982.
6 Y. Eldad, interview.
7 Y. Eldad, interview. Eldad could not
resist adding: 'That is Begin, very
patriotic and very theatrical.'
8 Menachem Begin, *White Nights*, New
York, Harper and Row, 1977 (3rd ed.),
page 13.
9 Quoted by William E. Farrell, *New
York Times* Magazine, 17 July 1977.
10 Y. Eldad, interview.
11 D. Jutan, interview.

Chapter Four: Descent into the Gulag

1 Menachem Begin's two books of
memoirs, *White Nights* and *The Revolt*
(Steimatsky, Jerusalem, 1951), are the
main sources for this chapter and the
quotations in it. His description of
conditions in the prison and the slave
labour camp was confirmed by Dr
Miron Sheskin, a veteran Polish
Revisionist, who shared them with him
and lived in Jerusalem until his death in
August 1983.
2 M. Sheskin, interview with author.
3 In the end, Begin did not send his wife
a conditional divorce.

4 M. Sheskin, interview.
5 *Ze'ev* is Hebrew for Wolf.

Chapter Five: Eastwards to the Underground

1 Miron Sheskin, interview with author.
2 Yohanan Bader, interview with author.
3 Menachem Begin, *White Nights*, page
217.
4 M. Sheskin, interview.
5 Y. Bader, interview.
6 M. Begin, *The Revolt*, page 24.
7 Yisrael Eldad, interview with author.
8 Eitan Livni, interview with author.
9 E. Livni interview, conducted at a time
when Livni was a Likud member of
Knesset and Meridor a minister in
Begin's Cabinet. Meridor had recently
demonstrated his lack of realism by
backing a dubious invention that was
supposed to solve Israel's energy
problems.
10 D. Jutan, interview with author.
11 Marek Kahan, interview with author.
12 E. Livni, interview.
13 David Niv, interview with author.

Chapter Six: The End of the Truce

1 Menachem Begin, *The Revolt*, pages
42-3.
2 Natan Yellin-Mor, *Lohamei Herut
Yisrael* (*The Fighters for the Freedom of
Israel: People, Ideas, Deeds*), Jerusalem,
Shikmona, 1975 (in Hebrew), pages
178-81.
3 Moshe Sneh, report in *History of the
Haganah*, volume three, 'From
Resistance to War', Tel Aviv, Am
Oved, 1973 (in Hebrew), part three,
pages 1887-93.
4 M. Begin, *The Revolt*, page 52.
5 M. Sneh, report.
6 M. Sneh, report.
7 M. Sneh, report.
8 War office papers quoted in Bruce
Hoffman, *The Failure of British
Military Strategy Within Palestine,
1939-47*, Tel Aviv, Bar-Ilan University
Press, 1983, page 14.
9 Eitan Livni, interview.
10 M. Begin, interview with Nicholas

Bethell, March 1976. This interview together with other research papers for Bethell's *The Palestine Triangle*, London, André Deutsch, 1979, is in the Israeli State archive in Jerusalem.

11 E. Livni, interview.

12 *History of the Haganah*, volume three, pages 531-43.

13 N. Yellin-Mor, *Lohamei Herut Yisrael*, page 180.

14 M. Sneh, report.

15 M. Sneh, report. See also *The Revolt*, which focuses on Churchill's hint to Weizmann.

16 Quoted in *History of the Haganah*.

17 Quoted in *History of the Haganah*.

18 Quoted in *History of the Haganah*.

19 J. Bowyer Bell, *Terror out of Zion*, New York, St Martin's Press, 1977; Dublin, The Academy Press, 1979, page 133. This figure was also cited by Richard Crossman, then a Labour MP, in the House of Commons, on 31 July 1946, and by Shlomo Lev-Ami in *By Struggle and Revolt*, Tel Aviv, Israel Defence Ministry (in Hebrew).

20 Quoted in Shlomo Nakdimon, *Altalena*, Jerusalem, Edanim, 1978, page 30.

21 Meir Pa'il, interview with author.

22 M. Begin, *The Revolt*, page 112.

23 M. Begin, *The Revolt*, page 229.

24 Interview with Israel Television for *The Pillar of Fire*.

25 Evelyn Barker, interview with Nicholas Bethell (see note 10).

26 *Palestine Post*, 27 September 1945, repeated on 18 March 1947. At that time, £2,000 was worth about $8,000.

27 M. Begin, *Bamahteret* (In the Underground), Volume 1, Tel Aviv, Hadar, 1978, pages 221-3 (in Hebrew).

28 Ya'acov Amrami, interview with author.

29 Quoted in *History of the Haganah*.

30 Symposium first published in *Ma'ariv* on 4, 15, 24 and 29 April 1966. Reproduced in Ya'acov Shavit, *The Hunting Season*, Tel Aviv, Hadar, 1976, pages 193-225 (in Hebrew).

31 Yisrael Galili, interview with author.

Chapter Seven: A Tragedy of Errors

1 Harold Beeley, letter to the author. This chapter also draws on transcripts of Beeley's interviews with Nicholas Bethell (see note 10, chapter 6) and for the Israel television series *The Pillar of Fire*. For Bevin's earlier attitude to Zionism see Alan Bullock, *Ernest Bevin: Foreign Secretary*, London, Heinemann, 1983, page 165.

2 Michael Bar-Zohar, *Ben-Gurion: a Biography*, London, Weidenfeld & Nicolson, 1978, page 129.

3 M. Begin, *Ma'ariv* symposium (see note 30, chapter 6).

4 Yisrael Galili, interview with author.

5 M. Begin, *The Revolt*, page 185. Shmuel Katz, *Days of Fire*, London, W.H. Allen, 1968, page 87.

6 Y. Galili, interview.

7 M. Begin, *The Revolt*, page 217.

8 Y. Galili, interview.

9 See also Susan Hattis-Rolef, book review in *Jerusalem Post* magazine, 25 September 1981.

10 N. Bethel, *The Palestine Triangle*, page 251.

11 Quoted in Thurston Clarke, *By Blood and Fire*, London, Hutchinson, 1981, page 116.

12 Y. Galili, interview.

13 Jabotinsky archives.

14 Ya'acov Amrami, interview with author.

15 Adina Hai-Nisan, interview with author.

16 Naim Nisan, interview with author.

17 See T. Clarke, *By Blood and Fire*, page 234 and note on page 325.

18 Yitzhak Avinoam, interview with author.

19 Lady Shaw, letter to the author.

20 S. Katz, *Days of Fire*, page 94.

Chapter Eight: A Rope for a Rope

1 M. Begin, *The Revolt*, page 260.

2 Y. Amrami, interview with author.

3 This account draws on J. Bowyer Bell's *Terror out of Zion*, Nicholas Bethell's *The Palestine Triangle*, and Dan Kurzman's *Genesis 1948* (London,

Vallentine, Mitchell, 1972), as well as *The Revolt*. Paglin went on to build the oven in which the Nazi war criminal Adolf Eichmann was cremated. In 1977, Menachem Begin appointed him adviser on counter-terrorism. He died in a road accident in February 1978.

4 Y. Amrami, interview.

Chapter Nine: Out of the Wasps' Nest

1 Quoted in Michael J. Cohen, *Palestine and the Great Powers*, Princeton University Press, 1982, pages 269-76 which gives a detailed account from British documents of the decision to get out. Cohen's book is the main source of papers quoted in this chapter.

2 Elizabeth Monroe, *Mr Bevin's 'Arab Policy'*, Oxford, St Antony's Papers, No. 11, 1961, page 34.

3 Foreign Office Report quoted in Alan Bullock, *Ernest Bevin: Foreign Secretary*, page 450.

4 Harold Beeley, letter to the author.

5 Carter Davidson's Associated Press report can be seen in the *Jerusalem Post* archives. The meeting is also described at length in *The Revolt* and in a blow-by-blow account prepared by Ralph Bunche for the United Nations.

6 Nicholas Bethell, *The Palestine Triangle*, page 358. The total of British dead is taken from *The Times* of London, 14 May 1948.

7 *Palestine and the Great Powers*, page 249.

8 Abba Eban, *An Autobiography*, London, Weidenfeld & Nicolson, 1978, pages 79-80.

9 For an insider's account of the Revisionist role in illegal immigration see William R. Pearl, *The Four-Front War*, New York, Crown, 1979.

10 Joseph B. Schechtman, *Fighter and Prophet*, volume 2 of *The Jabotinsky Story*, 1961, page 232.

11 Edward Luttwak and Dan Horowitz, *The Israeli Army*, London, Allen Lane, 1975, pages 23-7.

Chapter Ten: As in Deir Yassin . . .

1 Jabotinsky archives, Tel Aviv, quoted by Yisrael Segal in 'The Deir Yassin File', published in the Jerusalem magazine *Koteret Rashit*, 19 January 1983.

2 Muhammad Arif Sammour, interview with author.

3 Yehuda Lapidot, interview with author.

4 Testimony in Jabotinsky archives. This material was unknown outside the ranks of those immediately involved until it was brought to light by the Israeli journalist Yisrael Segal (see note 1 above).

5 Jabotinsky archives testimony.

6 Y. Lapidot, interview.

7 Meir Pa'il, interview with author.

8 Y. Lapidot, interview. This contradicts a different Irgun version that the villagers were to be told to flee to Ein Karem, another Arab village further west.

9 Y. Lapidot, interview.

10 Full text translated from *David Shaltiel, Jerusalem 1948*, Tel Aviv, Ministry of Defence, 1981, pages 139-43 (in Hebrew). The letter is also quoted in *The Revolt*.

11 *David Shaltiel, Jerusalem 1948*, incorporating testimony Shaltiel gave to the history branch of the Israel Defence Forces in 1960.

12 Y. Lapidot, interview.

13 Jabotinsky archives testimony.

14 Yair Tsaban, interview with author.

15 Meir Pa'il, interview with author. His report was written on the Friday night. Galili confirms receiving it and the photographs taken by Pa'il's cameraman. It was, he says, full of 'horrors'. There is what seems to be an oblique reference to this document in the Shaltiel book, which cites a report of 'great cruelty' and a loss of control by the commanders.

16 M.A. Sammour, interview.

17 Yehoshua Arieli, interview with author.

18 Larry Collins and Dominique Lapierre, *O Jerusalem!*, New York, Simon &

Schuster, 1972, pages 303-14 (Pocket Book edition).

19 Jacques de Reynier, *A Jerusalem un Drapeau Flottait sur la Ligne de Feu*, Neuchâtel, Editions de la Baconnière, 1950, pages 69-74 (Deir Yassin material reprinted in English in *From Haven to Conquest*, Beirut, Institute for Palestinian Studies, 1971, pages 761-6).

20 Y. Tsaban, interview.

21 M.A. Sammour, interview.

22 Quoted in *David Shaltiel, Jerusalem 1948*.

23 Y. Lapidot, interview.

24 M.A. Sammour, interview.

25 Y. Arieli, interview.

Chapter Eleven: Mutiny on the Altalena

1 See Uri Brenner, *Altalena*, Tel Aviv, Kibbutz Hameuhad Publishing House, 1978, and Shlomo Nakdimon, *Altalena*, Jerusalem, Edanim, 1978 (both in Hebrew).

2 Shmuel Katz, *Days of Fire*, page 238.

3 Knesset debate, 7 January 1959.

4 S. Katz, *Days of Fire*, page 235.

5 Edited transcript in Jabotinsky archives, Tel Aviv.

6 Hillel Kook, interview with author. In America, Kook was known by his alias, Peter Bergson.

7 Quoted in U. Brenner, *Altalena*, page 342.

8 Michael Bar-Zohar, *Ben-Gurion*, page 171.

9 M. Bar-Zohar, pages 171-2, the main source for this account of the Cabinet deliberations and Ben-Gurion's orders. See also Ben-Gurion's reconstruction in the Knesset, 7 January 1959.

10 Quoted in U. Brenner, *Altalena*, page 134.

11 Quoted in S. Nakdimon, *Altalena*, page 198.

12 Quoted in S. Nakdimon, *Altalena*, page 199.

13 M. Bar-Zohar, pages 172-3.

14 H. Kook, interview.

15 Quoted in U. Brenner, *Altalena*, page 208.

16 Quoted in S. Nakdimon, *Altalena*, page 253.

17 Quoted in M. Bar-Zohar, *Ben-Gurion*, page 174.

18 Dan Kurzman, *Genesis 1948*, London, Vallentine, Mitchell, 1972, page 483.

19 First mentioned in an article 'Dissent, Saison, Altalena', M. Begin, published in *Ma'ariv* on 6 August 1971. Ben-Gurion's denial appeared in the same paper on 27 August 1971.

20 Interview with Yeshayahu Ben-Porat, *Yediot Aharonot*, 6 October 1978.

21 Yisrael Galili, interview with author.

Chapter Twelve: Chosen to Oppose

1 Yohanan Bader, *The Knesset and I*, Jerusalem, Edanim, 1979, page 57 (in Hebrew). Ya'acov Meridor and Haim Landau were to have resigned with Begin, but Bader persuaded them all to wait until Begin's return.

2 Herut press conference, 19 September 1948. An English text of Begin's statement, as issued to the press, is in the *Jerusalem Post* archives.

3 Knesset debate, 7 January 1959.

4 Knesset debate, 8 March 1949.

5 Knesset debate, 4 April 1949.

6 Knesset debates, 5 December 1949, and 2 January 1950.

7 Knesset debate, 9 November 1949.

8 Knesset debate, 5 May, 1950.

9 Michael Bar-Zohar, *Ben-Gurion*, page 195.

10 Terence Prittie, *Adenauer, a Study in Fortitude*, London, Tom Stacey, 1972, page 204.

11 Knesset debate, 7 January 1952. Quoted in M. Bar-Zohar, *Ben Gurion*.

12 Yehoshua Ophir, *Sefer Ha'oved Haleumi*, volume 2, Tel Aviv, National Labour Federation, 1983, page 111 (in Hebrew).

13 Quoted in Prittie, *Adenauer*, page 206.

14 See for instance letter quoted in Eitan Haber, *Menachem Begin*, page 385.

15 Knesset debate, 28 May 1962.

Chapter Thirteen: Out of the Wilderness

1 Although the writer of this letter left Herut after the Camp David peace agreement with Egypt in 1978, he asked that his identity remain confidential.
2 Yohanan Bader, *The Knesset and I*, page 186.
3 Quoted in Yehoshua Ophir, *Sefer Ha'oved Haleumi*, the history of the National Labour Federation, volume 2, page 416. These two books, together with daily reports in the *Jerusalem Post*, are the main sources of this account.
4 *Jerusalem Post*, 8 July 1966.
5 Yitzhak Rabin, *The Rabin Memoirs*, Boston, Little, Brown, 1979, page 75.
6 Moshe Dayan, *The Story of My Life*, London, Weidenfeld & Nicolson, 1976, page 270.

Chapter Fourteen: Apprenticeship of Power

1 Yehiel Kadishai, interview with author. Kadishai is the prime source for this account of Begin's role in the decision to take the Old City. See also Michael Brecher, *Decisions in Crisis - Israel 1967 and 1973*, Berkeley, University of California Press, 1980, pages 259-73: and 'June 1967: the Way we Were', *Jerusalem Post* weekend magazine, 4 June 1982.
2 Interview in *Jerusalem Post*, 4 June 1982.
3 Interview in *Yediot Aharonot*, 7 August 1970.
4 Abba Eban, *An Autobiography*, page 454.
5 *Yediot Aharonot* interview, 7 August 1970.
6 Interview in *Jerusalem Post*, 4 June 1982.
7 Eitan Haber, *Menachem Begin*, pages 412-13.
8 The full text is published in Meron Medzini (ed.), *Israel's Foreign Relations: Selected Documents*, Jerusalem, Ministry of Foreign Affairs, 1976, volume 2, pages 875-9. Other official Israeli and American statements quoted in this section are taken from the same volume.
9 A. Eban, *An Autobiography*, page 467.
10 Golda Meir, *My Life*, London, Weidenfeld & Nicolson, 1975, pages 322-3.
11 Arieh Dulzin, interview with author.
12 Ezer Weizman, *On Eagles' Wings*, London, Weidenfeld & Nicolson, 1976, page 284.

Chapter Fifteen: Unity or Bust

1 *Sunday Express*, 9 January 1972. Its sister paper, the *Daily Express*, had published a full-page picture of the hanging in 1947.
2 Quoted in the *Jerusalem Post*, 17 September 1973.
3 *Ma'ariv*, 26 September 1973.
4 Golda Meir, *My Life*, pages 378-9.

Chapter Sixteen: A Summer Earthquake

1 Knesset debate, 13 November 1973.
2 *Jerusalem Post*, 'Ezer's battle plan', 28 January 1977.
3 Alex Ansky, *The Selling of the Likud*, quoted in *Ma'ariv* weekly magazine, 15 May 1981.
4 Eliahu Ben-Elissar, interview with author. Ben-Elissar was appointed director-general of the Prime Minister's office in June 1977, and later served as Israel's first ambassador to Cairo and chairman of the Knesset foreign affairs and defence committee.
5 Hassia Milo (*née* Begin), interview with author.
6 Yehiel Kadishai, interview with author.
7 Ze'ev Chafets, interview with author. Chafets was appointed director of the Government Press Office under the Likud administration, but took extended leave in protest at Begin's initial refusal to appoint an inquiry commission into the Sabra and Shatilla massacre in September 1982.
8 See Hanoch Smith, *Ma'ariv*, 22 May 1977. His analysis of the results was expanded in a study for the American Jewish Committee.

9 Knesset debate, 12 December 1964.
10 Amos Oz, *Davar*, 26 December 1982.

**Chapter Seventeen: A Terrifying
    Credibility**

1 Arieh Dulzin, interview with author.
2 Moshe Dayan, *Breakthrough*, London,
   Weidenfeld & Nicolson, 1981. Dayan's
   account is taken from the opening
   chapter, pages 1–6.
3 Knesset debate, 19 May 1982.
4 Yehiel Kadishai, interview with author.
5 Naphtali Lavie, interview with author.
   Lavie stayed at the Foreign Ministry
   under Dayan's successor, Yitzhak
   Shamir, until his appointment as
   Israel's Consul-General in New York.
6 *Davar*, 20 May 1977.
7 Moshe Zak, 'All the meetings with
   Hussein', *Ma'ariv*, 31 March 1980. See
   also the *Guardian*, 18 April 1980.
8 N. Lavie, interview.
9 M. Dayan, *Breakthrough*, pages 35–7.
   Unattributed material in this and
   subsequent sections of the present book
   derives from the author's off-the-record
   conversations with Israeli and other
   witnesses.

**Chapter Eighteen: Peace on our
    Terms**

1 Eliahu Ben-Elissar, interview with
   author.
2 Cyrus Vance, *Hard Choices*, New York,
   Simon and Schuster, 1983, page 194.
3 Anwar Sadat, *In Search of Identity*,
   London, Fontana, 1978, pages 363–4.
4 This account is based on Moshe
   Dayan's *Breakthrough*, pages 38–54.
5 Boutros Ghali, interview with author.
6 M. Dayan, *Breakthrough*, page 104.
7 Ezer Weizman, *The Battle for Peace*,
   New York, Bantam, 1981, pages 118–
   19.
8 Quoted in *Israel's Foreign Relations:
   Selected Documents*, volume five, page
   466.
9 Harold Saunders, interview with
   author.
10 William Quandt, interview with author
   and Charles Weiss.

11 Jimmy Carter, *Keeping Faith*, New
   York, Bantam, 1982, page 300.
12 B. Ghali, interview.
13 Cyrus Vance, interview with author.
14 W. Quandt, interview.
15 Naphtali Lavie, interview with author.
16 B. Ghali, interview.
17 M. Dayan, *Breakthrough*, page 113.
18 E. Weizman, *The Battle for Peace*, page
   193.
19 M. Dayan, *Breakthrough*, page 114.
20 M. Dayan, *Breakthrough*, page 126.
21 J. Carter, *Keeping Faith*, pages 312–13.
22 M. Dayan, *Breakthrough*, pages 146–8.

**Chapter Nineteen: Concentration
    Camp *De Lux***

1 Zbigniew Brzezinski, *Power and
   Principle*, London, Weidenfeld &
   Nicolson, 1983, page 250.
2 Jimmy Carter, *Keeping Faith*, page 322.
3 *Time* magazine, 11 October 1982.
4 Quoted in Moshe Dayan, *Breakthrough*,
   pages 161–2.
5 J. Carter, *Keeping Faith*, pages 350–5.
6 J. Carter, *Keeping Faith*, page 365.
7 Cyrus Vance, interview with author.
8 William Quandt, interview with author.
9 This official, still handling Middle East
   affairs at the time of writing, spoke to
   the author off the record.
10 Boutros Ghali, interview with author.
11 C. Vance, interview with author.
12 Ezer Weizman, *The Battle for Peace*,
   page 370.
13 J. Carter, *Keeping Faith*, page 396.
14 J. Carter, *Keeping Faith*, page 397.
15 C. Vance, interview.
16 Harold Saunders, interview with
   author.
17 Aharon Barak, interview with author.
18 Distributed by the American State
   Department monitoring service, FBIS,
   quoting Cairo radio and the Middle
   East News Agency.
19 Text of press conference in *Israel's
   Foreign Relations: Selected Documents*,
   volume five, pages 535–40.
20 Sol Linowitz, interview with author.
21 W. Quandt, interview.

22 Z. Brzezinski, *Power and Principle*, page 273.
23 Eliahu Ben-Elissar, interview with author.
24 B. Ghali, interview.
25 C. Vance, interview.

Chapter Twenty: A Premature Prize-Giving

1 Jimmy Carter, *Keeping Faith*, page 407.
2 J. Carter, *Keeping Faith*, pages 414-19.
3 J. Carter, *Keeping Faith*, page 421.
4 Naphtali Lavie, interview with author.
5 Cyrus Vance, interview with author.
6 *Time* magazine, 11 October 1982.
7 Boutros Ghali, interview with author.

Chapter Twenty-One: Divide and Rule

1 The two officials quoted here were professional rather than political appointees. Neither was ready to speak on the record.
2 *Davar*, 22 December 1979.
3 Hanoch Smith, quoted in the *Guardian*, 20 January 1981.
4 *Ha'aretz*, 8 March 1981.
5 Amnon Dankner, *Ha'aretz*, 8 May 1981.
6 See Asher Wallfish, 'Playing Begin's Record', *Jerusalem Post*, 19 August 1983 - a devastating reconstruction of the 1981 Lebanese crisis.
7 A transcript of the normally secret committee hearing was first published by Dan Margalit in *Ha'aretz* on 13 May 1981, after Begin had denied making the comparison.
8 Hirsh Goodman, 'Shocking Revelations', *Jerusalem Post*, 15 May 1981.
9 Quoted in the *Jerusalem Post*, 12 and 13 May 1981.
10 See Amos Perlmutter, Michael Handel and Uri Bar-Yosef, *Two Minutes Over Baghdad*, London, Vallentine, Mitchell, 1982.
11 General Saguy made public his dissenting advice on Israel television on 17 August 1983, after he had retired from the service. The interview was reported by *Ha'aretz* the following day.
12 Hanoch Smith, *The Israeli Elections: Significant Trends Behind the Figures*, report prepared for the American Jewish Committee.

Chapter Twenty-Two: A Choice of War

1 See interview with the Chief of Staff, Lieutenant-General Rafael Eitan, *Ma'ariv*, 2 July 1982.
2 See Avraham Tisosh's and Avi Bettelheim's excellent reconstruction of the decision-making process in a special supplement of *Ma'ariv* published on 3 June 1983, to mark the first anniversary of the war.
3 Yitzhak Rabin, in the monthly magazine, *Monitin*, July 1983.
4 Woody Goldberg, interview with author.
5 Ze'ev Schiff, 'The Green Light', *Foreign Policy*, Washington, Spring, 1983, no. 50, pages 73-85.
6 Quoted in Shlomo Nakdimon: 'How the Government Decided to Go to War', *Yediot Aharonot*, 3 June 1983.
7 Quoted in *Ma'ariv* supplement, 3 June 1983.
8 *Jerusalem Post*, 19 October 1982.
9 Summary distributed by Israel Government Press Office.
10 *Jerusalem Post*, 7 July 1982.
11 *Ma'ariv*, 17 September 1982
12 Dan Meridor, interview with author. Zipori's account was reported in the *Jerusalem Post*, 12 September 1983.
13 Yitzhak Berman, interview with author.
14 *Ma'ariv* supplement, 3 June 1983.
15 Hirsh Goodman, '365 Days and 72 Hours', *Jerusalem Post* magazine, 10 June 1983.
16 Quoted in Erlich's television interview and in *Ma'ariv* reconstruction.
17 *Ha'aretz*, 9 November 1982.
18 The exchange was reported by the Prime Minister in the Knesset on 28 July 1982, and was carried in the Israeli press on the following day.
19 *Final Report of the Commission of Inquiry into the Events at the Refugee*

Camps in Beirut, Jerusalem, 8 February 1983 (in Hebrew and authorized English translation).

Chapter Twenty-Three: 'I Cannot Go On'

1 Published in *Ha'aretz*, 4 December 1981. The letter dictated from Begin's bed to Yehiel Kadishai, ran to seven foolscap pages when translated into English by the Government Press Office.
2 Quoted by Wolf Blitzer, 'Message behind the massage', *Jerusalem Post*, 1 January 1982. The Reston column appeared in the *New York Times* on 23 December 1981.
3 Quoted in *Jerusalem Post*, 23 September 1983.

4 Quoted by Yoel Marcus, 'The decline of Begin', *Ha'aretz*, 29 August 1983.

Chapter Twenty-Four: The House that Menachem Built

1 Jewish Agency figures.
2 *The Times*, first leader, 23 July 1983. This was Begin's birthday according to the Jewish calendar. Italics added by author.
3 Mordecai Nisan, 'The Begin legacy', *Jerusalem Post*, 11 September 1983.
4 Yoram Peri, *Between Battles and Ballots*, Cambridge University Press, 1983, pages 268-72. Peri was writing before the Lebanese war, which took the process a stage further.

Select Bibliography

Shlomo Avineri, *The Making of Modern Zionism: the Intellectual Origins of the Jewish State*, London, 1981.

Michael Bar-Zohar, *Ben-Gurion*, London, 1978.

Yehuda Bauer, *From Diplomacy to Resistance*, New York, 1973.

Menachem Begin, *The Revolt*, London, 1951.
> *White Nights*, London, 1978.
> *Bamahteret* (In the Underground) four volumes in Hebrew, Tel Aviv, 1977.

J. Bowyer Bell, *Terror out of Zion*, New York, 1977.

Nicholas Bethell, *The Palestine Triangle*, London, 1979.

Uri Brenner, *Altalena*, in Hebrew, Tel Aviv, 1978.

Zbigniew Brzezinski, *Power and Principle*, New York, 1983.

Alan Bullock, *The Life and Times of Ernest Bevin*, three volumes, London 1960–83.

Jimmy Carter, *Keeping Faith*, New York, 1982.

Dan Caspi, Abraham Diskin and Emanuel Gutmann (eds), *The Roots of Begin's Success: The 1981 Israeli Elections*, London, 1983.

Thurston Clarke, *By Blood and Fire: the Attack on the King David Hotel*, London, 1981.

Michael J. Cohen, *Palestine, Retreat from the Mandate*, London, 1978.
> *Palestine and the Great Powers*, Princeton, 1982.

Larry Collins and Dominique Lapierre, *O Jerusalem!*, New York, 1972.

Moshe Dayan, *The Story of My Life*, London, 1976.
> *Breakthrough*, London, 1981.

Abba Eban, *An Autobiography*, London, 1978.

Yisrael Eldad, *The Jewish Revolution*, New York, 1971.

Harold Fisch, *The Zionist Revolution*, London, 1978.

Martin Gilbert, *The Arab-Israeli Conflict: its History in Maps*, London, 1974.
> *Exile and Return*, London, 1978.

Eitan Haber, *Menachem Begin*, New York, 1978.

Gertrude Hirschler and Lester Eckman, *From Freedom Fighter to Statesman: Menachem Begin*, New York, 1979.

Rael Jean Isaac, *Israel Divided: Ideological Politics in the Jewish State*, Baltimore, 1976.
> *Party and Politics of Israel*, New York, 1981.

Vladimir Ze'ev Jabotinsky, *Ktavim* (Writings), eighteen volumes in Hebrew, Tel Aviv, 1958.

Shmuel Katz, *Days of Fire*, London, 1968.
> *The Hollow Peace*, Tel Aviv, 1981.

Walter Laqueur, *A History of Zionism*, London, 1972.

Edward Luttwak and Dan Horowitz, *The Israeli Army*, London, 1975.

Meron Medzini (ed.), *Israel's Foreign Relations: Selected Documents 1947–79*, five volumes, Jerusalem, 1976–81.

Golda Meir, *My Life*, London, 1975.

Elizabeth Monroe, *Britain's Moment in the Middle East*, London, 1963.

Shlomo Nakdimon, *Altalena*, in Hebrew, Jerusalem, 1978.

David Niv, *History of the Irgun Zvai Leumi*, six volumes in Hebrew, Tel Aviv, 1980.

Amos Oz, *In the Land of Israel*, London, 1983.

Yoram Peri, *Between Battles and Ballots*, Cambridge, 1983.

Amos Perlmutter, Michael Handel and Uri Bar-Joseph, *Two Minutes Over Baghdad*, London, 1982.

Terence Prittie, *Eshkol of Israel*, London, 1969.

Yitzhak Rabin, *The Rabin Memoirs*, Boston, 1979.

Howard M. Sachar, *A History of Israel*, New York, 1981.

Anwar Sadat, *In Search of Identity*, London, 1978.

Nadav Safran, *Israel, the Embattled Ally*, Harvard, 1978.

Joseph B. Schechtman, *The Vladimir Jabotinsky Story*, two volumes, New York, 1956 and 1961.

Christopher Sykes, *Cross Roads to Israel*, London, 1965.

Eli Tavin and Yonah Alexander (eds), *Psychological Warfare and Propaganda: Irgun Documentation*, Wilmington, 1982.

Shabtai Teveth, *The Murder of Arlosoroff*, in Hebrew, Tel Aviv, 1982.

Cyrus Vance, *Hard Choices*, New York, 1983.

David Vital, *The Origins of Zionism*, Oxford, 1975.

   Zionism: The Formative Years, Oxford, 1982.

Ezer Weizman, *On Eagles' Wings*, London, 1976.

   The Battle for Peace, New York, 1981.

Chaim Weizmann, *Trial and Error*, New York, 1949.

Natan Yellin-Mor, *Fighters for the Freedom of Israel*, in Hebrew, Jerusalem, 1975.

Index